OUR FATHER CARES

OUR FATHER CARES

Devotional Readings
for 1992
by
Ellen G. White

Review and Herald® Publishing Association
Hagerstown, MD 21740

This book was
Cover by Bill Kirstein
Typeset: 10 pt. Century Light Condensed

Bible texts credited to ASV are from the American Standard Version. Thomas Nelson, Publishers, 1901.

Texts credited to NIV are from the *Holy Bible, New International Version.* Copyright © 1973, 1978, International Bible Society. Used by permission of Zondervan Bible Publishers.

Texts credited to NKJV are from The New King James Version. Copyright © 1979, 1980, 1982, Thomas Nelson, Inc., Publishers.

Bible texts credited to RSV are from the Revised Standard Version of the Bible, copyrighted 1946, 1952 © 1971, 1973.

Texts credited to RV are from the Revised Version, Oxford University Press, 1911.

Printed in U.S.A

Library of Congress Cataloging in Publication Data

White, Ellen Gould Harmon, 1827-1915.
  Our Father cares: devotional readings for 1992 / by Ellen G. White.
    p.   cm.
  Includes indexes.
  1. Devotional calendars—Seventh-day Adventists.   I. Title.
  BV4811.W487 1991
  242'.2—dc20   90-23503
                                                                                    CIP

96 95 94 93 92 91   10 9 8 7 6 5 4 3 2 1

ISBN 0-8280-0622-9

TO THE READER

This is the sixteenth "Morning-Watch"-type book compiled from the writings of Ellen G. White. The first in this long series, *Radiant Religion*, was published in 1946 for use the following year. It was followed three years later by *With God at Dawn*. The materials for these two early devotional works were drawn entirely from Ellen G. White books already in print.

Beginning with *My Life Today*, published in 1952, recourse has been made consistently to the wealth of previously unpublished materials in the Ellen G. White Manuscript and Letter file. Titles published, with the year of publication, are as follows:

- *Radiant Religion*, 1946
- *With God at Dawn*, 1949
- *My Life Today*, 1952
- *Sons and Daughters of God*, 1955
- *The Faith I Live By*, 1958
- *Our High Calling*, 1961
- *That I May Know Him*, 1964
- *In Heavenly Places*, 1967
- *Conflict and Courage*, 1970
- *God's Amazing Grace*, 1973
- *Maranatha*, 1976
- *This Day With God*, 1979
- *The Upward Look*, 1982
- *Reflecting Christ*, 1985
- *Lift Him Up*, 1988

The records of the Review and Herald Publishing Association reveal a steadily increasing sale of these books over the years. In the 1950s *My Life Today* sold 24,000 copies, while *Sons and Daughters of God* had a sale of 33,000. In the 1960s both *That I May Know Him* and *In Heavenly Places* had sales exceeding 63,000 copies. These figures have escalated to sales of more than 90,000 for several of the more recent devotional books. Many of these books have also enjoyed a large sale in Spanish, Portuguese, Korean, and other non-English languages.

A sampling of opinion among church members reveals that the rich materials published in the earlier devotionals are largely unknown to many Adventists today. This present book has been published to remedy this situation. It consists of selections from 12 of the books named above—one book a month for the 12 months of 1992. The source for each reading can be located by referring to the source index at the back of this volume. Refer to the books listed there for primary sources.

Ellen White states that "Christ's favorite theme was the paternal character and abundant love of God" *(Testimonies,* vol. 6, p. 55). This also seems to be Ellen White's favorite theme. For that reason the compilers have chosen the title OUR FATHER CARES. The title has a double significance. Not only have readings been selected on the topic of God's great love and care for us, but they also reflect the fact that God cares so much for us that He is interested in every aspect of our daily lives. He cares about our health, our homes, our study of His Word, our victory over sin, our preparation for His second coming. He also longs for us to be with Him in His kingdom, which is soon to be established on earth. How much He cares!

We invite you to read each day's devotional with both aspects of God's concern in mind, trusting that as you meditate on each passage you will come to appreciate more than ever how much God loves and cares for you.

—The Trustees of the Ellen G. White Estate

THE AUTHOR*

Ellen Gould (Harmon) White, cofounder of the Seventh-day Adventist Church, writer, lecturer, and counselor, and one upon whom Seventh-day Adventists believe the gift of prophecy was bestowed, was born in Gorham, Maine, November 26, 1827, one of eight children of Robert and Eunice Harmon.

During her 70 years of active service to the church, she found time to write voluminously. She is credited with having written 100,000 manuscript pages. This remarkable legacy to the church could alone have occupied Ellen White's entire life, had she dedicated her time to little else but writing.

However, her service for the church embraces much more than writing. Her diaries tell of her public work, her travels, her personal labor, hostessing, contacts with neighbors, as well as of her being a mother and housewife. God blessed her abundantly in these activities. Her ambitions and concerns, her satisfactions and joys, her sorrows—her whole life— were for the advancement of the cause she loved.

Ellen G. White is reputed to be the most translated woman author and the most translated author in American history. For example, her little book *Steps to Christ* is available in more than 100 languages.

After a full life dedicated to the service of God and others, she died on July 16, 1915, confidently trusting in Him whom she had believed.

---

* This page and the biographical notes on the following pages have been reproduced from *The Upward Look,* pages 7-13.

BIOGRAPHICAL NOTES

Ellen G. White, 1827-1915

The Early Years, 1827-1860

Born on a late fall day in a farmhouse near Gorham, Maine, Ellen Harmon spent her childhood and youth in nearby Portland. She married James White in 1846, and the struggling young couple lived in a variety of New England locations as they sought to encourage and instruct fellow Advent believers by their preaching, visiting, and publishing. After 11 irregular issues of *The Present Truth,* they launched the *Second Advent Review and Sabbath Herald** in Paris, Maine, in 1850. Thereafter they followed a steadily westward course—to Saratoga Springs, New York, and then Rochester, New York, in the early 1850s, and finally, in 1855, to Battle Creek, Michigan, where they resided for the next 20 years.

1827, November 26	Born at Gorham, Maine.
1836 (c.)	Broken nose and concussion at Portland, Maine.
1840, March	First heard William Miller present the Advent message.
1842, June 26	Baptized and accepted into Methodist Church.
1844, October 22	Disappointed when Christ did not come.
1844, December	First vision.
1845, Spring	Trip to eastern Maine to visit believers; met James White.
1846, August 30	Married James White.
1846, Autumn	Accepted Seventh-day Sabbath.
1847-1848	Set up housekeeping at Topsham, Maine.
1847, August 26	Birth of first son, Henry Nichols.
1848, April 20-24	Attended first conference of Sabbathkeeping Adventists at Rocky Hill, Connecticut.
1848, November 18	Vision to begin publishing work—"Streams of Light."
1849, July	First of 11 numbers of *The Present Truth,* published as a result of the vision of November 1848.
1849, July 28	Birth of James Edson, second son.
1849-1852	Moved from place to place with her publisher-husband.
1851, July	First book published, *A Sketch of Experience and Views*.
1852-1855	In Rochester, New York, where husband published *Review and Herald* and *Youth's Instructor*.
1854, August 29	Third son, William Clarence, born.
1855, November	Moved with the publishing plant to Battle Creek, Michigan.

1855, December	"Testimony for the Church," number 1, a 16-page pamphlet, published.
1856, Spring	Moved into their own cottage on Wood Street.
1858, March 14	"Great Controversy" vision at Lovett's Grove, Ohio.
1860, September 20	Fourth son, John Herbert, born.
1860, December 14	Death of John Herbert at 3 months.

Years of Church Development, 1860-1868

The 1860s saw Ellen White and her husband in the forefront of the struggle to organize the Seventh-day Adventist Church into a stable institution. The decade was also crucial in that it encompassed the beginnings of Adventist health emphasis. Responding to Mrs. White's appeal, the church as a body began to see the importance of healthful living in the Christian life. In response to her "Christmas vision" of 1865, our first health institution, the Western Health Reform Institute, was opened in 1866. The institute later grew into the Battle Creek Sanitarium.

1860, October 1	Name Seventh-day Adventist chosen.
1861, October 5/6	Michigan Conference organized.
1863, May	Organization of General Conference of Seventh-day Adventists.
1863, June 6	Health reform vision at Otsego, Michigan.
1863, December 8	Death of eldest son, Henry Nichols, at Topsham, Maine.
1864, Summer	Publication of *Spiritual Gifts,* volume 4, with 30-page article on health.
1864, August-September	Visit to James C. Jackson's medical institution, Our Home on the Hillside, Dansville, New York, en route to Boston, Massachusetts.
1865	Publication of six pamphlets, *Health: or How to Live.*
1865, August 16	James White stricken with paralysis.
1865, December 25	Vision calling for a medical institution.
1865, December	Mrs. White takes James White to northern Michigan as an aid to his recovery.
1866, September 5	Opening of Western Health Reform Institute, forerunner of Battle Creek Sanitarium.
1867	Purchased a farm at Greenville, Michigan, and built a home and engaged in farming and writing.

The Camp Meeting Years, 1868-1881

Residing at Greenville and Battle Creek, Michigan, respectively, until late 1872, and then dividing her time between Michigan and California, Ellen White spent her winters writing and publishing. During the summer she attended camp meetings, some years as many as 28! *Testimonies,* numbers 14-30, now found in *Testimonies,* volumes 2-4, were published during these years.

1868, September 1-7	Attended first SDA camp meeting, held in Brother Root's maple grove at Wright, Michigan.
1870, July 28	Second son, James Edson, married on his twenty-first birthday.
1870	*The Spirit of Prophecy,* volume 1, published; forerunner of *Patriarchs and Prophets.*
1872, July-September	In Rocky Mountains resting and writing en route to California.
1873-1874	Divided time between Battle Creek and California, attended camp meetings, and spent some months in 1873 in Colorado resting and writing.
1874, April 1	Comprehensive vision of the advance of the cause in California, Oregon, and overseas.
1874, June	With James White in Oakland, California, as he founded the Pacific Press Publishing Association and the *Signs of the Times.*
1875, January 3	At Battle Creek for dedication of Battle Creek College. Vision of publishing houses in other countries.
1876, February 11	William Clarence, third son and manager of the Pacific Press, married at the age of 21.
1876, August	Spoke to 20,000 at Groveland, Massachusetts, camp meeting.
1877	*The Spirit of Prophecy,* volume 2, published; forerunner of *The Desire of Ages.*
1877, July 1	Spoke to 5,000 at Battle Creek on temperance.
1878	*The Spirit of Prophecy,* volume 3, published; forerunner of last part of *The Desire of Ages,* and *The Acts of the Apostles.*
1878, November	Spent the winter in Texas.
1879, April	Left Texas to engage in the summer camp meeting work.
1881, August 1	With husband in Battle Creek when he was taken ill.
1881, August 6	Death of James White.
1881, August 13	Spoke for 10 minutes at James White's funeral at Battle Creek.

The 1880s, 1881-1891

Following James White's death in August, 1881, Ellen White resided in California, at times in Healdsburg and at times in Oakland. She labored there, writing and speaking, until she left for Europe in August 1885, in response to the call of the General Conference. During the two years in Europe she resided in Basel, Switzerland, except for three extended visits to the Scandinavian countries, England, and Italy. Returning to the United States in August 1887, she soon made her way west to her Healdsburg home. She attended the 1888 General Conference session at Minneapolis in October and November; following the conference, while residing in Battle Creek, she worked among the churches in the Midwest and the East. After a year in the East she returned to California, but was called back to attend the General Conference session at Battle Creek in October 1889. She remained in the vicinity of Battle Creek until she left for Australia in September 1891.

1881, November	Attended the California camp meeting at Sacramento and participated in planning for a college in the West, which opened in 1882 at Healdsburg.
1882	*Early Writings* published, incorporating three of her early books.
1884	Last recorded public vision, at Portland, Oregon, camp meeting.
1884	*The Spirit of Prophecy,* volume 4, published; forerunner of *The Great Controversy.*
1885, Summer	Left California for trip to Europe.
1888	*The Great Controversy* published.
1888, October-November	Attended Minneapolis General Conference session.
1889	*Testimonies,* volume 5, published, embodying *Testimonies,* numbers 31-33—746 pages.
1890	*Patriarchs and Prophets* published.
1891, November 12	Sailed to Australia via Honolulu.

The Australian Years, 1891-1900

Responding to the call of the General Conference to visit Australia to aid in establishing an educational work, Ellen White arrived in Sydney, December 8, 1891. She accepted the invitation somewhat reluctantly, for she had wanted to get on with her writing of a larger book on the life of Christ. Soon after her arrival she was stricken with inflammatory rheumatism, which confined her to her bed for some eight months. Although suffering intensely, she persisted in writing. In early 1893 she went to new Zealand, where she worked until the end of the year. Returning to Australia in late December, she attended the first Australian camp meeting. At this camp meeting, plans for a rural school were developed that resulted in the establishment of what became Avondale College at Cooranbong, 90 miles north of Sydney. Ellen White purchased land nearby and built her Sunnyside home late in 1895. Here she resided, giving her attention to her writing and traveling among the churches until she returned to the United States in August 1900.

1892, June	Spoke at opening of Australian Bible School in two rented buildings in Melbourne.
1892	*Steps to Christ* and *Gospel Worker* published.
1894, January	Joined in planning for a permanent school in Australia.
1894, May 23	Visited the Cooranbong site.
1895, December	Moved to her Sunnyside home at Cooranbong, where much of *The Desire of Ages* was written.
1896	*Thoughts From the Mount of Blessing* published.
1898	*The Desire of Ages* published.
1899-1900	Encouraged the establishment of Sydney Sanitarium.
1900	*Christ's Object Lessons* published.
1900, August	Left Australia and returned to United States.

The Elmshaven Years, 1900-1915

When Ellen White settled at Elmshaven, her new home near St. Helena in northern California, she hoped to give most of her time to writing her books. She was 72 and still had a number of volumes that she wished to complete. She little realized how much traveling, counseling, and speaking she would also be called upon to do. The crisis created by the controversies in Battle Creek would also make heavy demands on her time and strength. Even so, by writing early in the morning, she was able to produce nine books during her Elmshaven years.

1900, October	Settled at Elmshaven.
1901, April	Attended the General Conference session at Battle Creek.
1902, February 18	Battle Creek Sanitarium fire.
1902, December 30	Review and Herald fire.
1903, October	Met the pantheism crisis.
1904, April-September	Journeyed east to assist in the beginning of the work in Washington, D.C., to visit her son Edson in Nashville, and to attend important meetings.
1904, November-December	Involved in securing and establishing Paradise Valley Sanitarium.
1905, May	Attended General Conference session in Washington, D.C.
1905	*The Ministry of Healing* published.
1905, June-December	Involved in securing and starting Loma Linda Sanitarium.
1906-1908	Busy at Elmshaven with literary work.

1909, April-September	At the age of 81 traveled to Washington, D.C., to attend the General Conference session. This was her last trip east.
1910, January	Took a prominent part in the establishment of the College of Medical Evangelists at Loma Linda.
1910	Gave attention to finishing *The Acts of the Apostles* and the reissuance of *The Great Controversy,* a work extending into 1911.
1911-1915	With advancing age, made only a few trips to southern California. At Elmshaven engaged in her book work, finishing *Prophets and Kings* and *Counsels to Parents and Teachers.*
1915, February 13	Fell in her Elmshaven home and broke her hip.
1915, July 16	Closed her fruitful life at the age of 87. Her last words were "I know in whom I have believed." *Testimonies,* volumes 6-9, were also published in the Elmshaven years.

---

* Now known as the *Adventist Review*, it is one of the oldest continuously published religious journals in the United States.

OUR FATHER CARES

WE ARE CALLED
THE SONS OF GOD

Behold, what manner of love the Father hath bestowed upon us, that we should be called the sons of God: therefore the world knoweth us not; because it knew him not. **1 John 3:1.**

As John thought of the love of Christ, he was led to exclaim, "Behold, what manner of love the Father hath bestowed upon us, that we should be called the sons of God."

People think it a privilege to see a royal personage, and thousands go great distances to see one. How much greater privilege it is to be sons and daughters of the Most High. What greater privilege could be conferred on us than to be given entrance into the royal family?

In order to become the sons and daughters of God, we must separate from the world. "Come out from among them, and be ye separate," the Lord says, "and I will be a Father unto you, and ye shall be my sons and daughters." . . .

There is a heaven before us, a crown of life to win. But to the overcomer only is the reward given. He who gains heaven must be clothed with the robe of righteousness. "Every man that hath this hope in him purifieth himself, even as he is pure." In the character of Christ there was no discord of any kind. And this must be our experience. Our lives must be controlled by the principles that controlled His life.

Through the perfection of the sacrifice given for the guilty race, those who believe in Christ, coming unto Him, may be saved from eternal ruin. . . .

Let no one be so deluded by the enemy as to think that it is a condescension for any man, however talented or learned or honored, to accept Christ. Every human being should look to heaven with reverence and gratitude, and exclaim with amazement, "Behold, what manner of love the Father hath bestowed upon us, that we should be called the sons of God."

WE ARE PURIFIED
AS CHRIST IS PURE

And every man that hath this hope in him purifieth himself, even as he is pure. **1 John 3:3.**

Christ would elevate and refine man's mind, purifying it from all dross, that he may appreciate the love that is without a parallel.

Through repentance, faith, and good works he may perfect a righteous character, and claim, through the merits of Christ, the privileges of the sons of God. The principles of divine truth, received and cherished in the heart, will carry us to a height of moral excellence that we had not deemed it possible for us to reach. . . . "And every man that hath this hope in him purifieth himself, even as he is pure."

Holiness of heart and purity of life were the great subjects of the teachings of Christ. In His sermon on the mount, after specifying what must be done in order to be blessed, and what must not be done, He says, "Be ye therefore perfect, even as your Father which is in heaven is perfect." Perfection, holiness,—nothing short of this would give them success in carrying out the principles He had given them. Without this holiness, the human heart is selfish, sinful, and vicious. Holiness will lead its possessor to be fruitful, and abound in all good works. He will never become weary in well-doing; neither look for promotion in this world; but he will look forward to be promoted by the Majesty of heaven when He shall exalt His sanctified and holy ones to His throne. . . . Holiness of heart will produce right actions.

As God is pure in His sphere, so man is to be pure in his. And he will be pure if Christ is formed within, the hope of glory; for he will imitate Christ's life and reflect His character.

The princely dignity of the Christian character will shine forth as the sun, and the beams of light from the face of Christ will be reflected upon those who have purified themselves even as He is pure.

Purity of heart will lead to purity of life.

January 3   Sons and Daughters of God

POWER IS GIVEN US TO BECOME THE SONS OF GOD

But as many as received him, to them gave he power to become the sons of God, even to them that believe on his name. John 1:12.

Divine sonship is not something that we gain of ourselves. Only to those who receive Christ as their Saviour is given the power to become sons and daughters of God. The sinner cannot, by any power of his own, rid himself of sin. For the accomplishment of this result, he must look to a higher Power. John exclaimed, "Behold the Lamb of God, which taketh away the sin of the world." Christ alone has power to cleanse the heart. He who is seeking for forgiveness and acceptance can say only,—

"Nothing in my hand I bring;
Simply to Thy cross I cling."

But the promise of sonship is made to *all* who "believe on his name." Every one who comes to Jesus in faith will receive pardon.

The religion of Christ transforms the heart. It makes the worldly-minded man heavenly-minded. Under its influence the selfish man becomes unselfish, because this is the character of Christ. The dishonest, scheming man becomes upright, so that it is second nature to him to do to others as he would have others do to him. The profligate is changed from impurity to purity. He forms correct habits; for the gospel of Christ has become to him a savor of life unto life.

God was to be manifest in Christ, "reconciling the world unto himself." Man had become so degraded by sin that it was impossible for him, in himself, to come into harmony with Him whose nature is purity and goodness. But Christ, after having redeemed man from the condemnation of the law, could impart divine power, to unite with human effort. Thus by repentance toward God and faith in Christ, the fallen children of Adam might once become "sons of God."

When a soul receives Christ, he receives power to live the life of Christ.

Sons and Daughters of God   January 4

GOD IS NEAR
TO ALL THAT CALL UPON HIM

The Lord is nigh unto all them that call upon him, to all that call upon him in truth. **Ps. 145:18.**

God is pleased when we keep our faces turned toward the Sun of Righteousness. . . . When we are in trouble and pressed down with anxieties, the Lord is near, and He bids us cast all our care upon Him, because He cares for us. . . .

He comes to all His children in their affliction. In time of danger He is their refuge. In sorrow, He offers them joy and consolation. Shall we turn from the Redeemer, the fountain of living water, to hew out for ourselves broken cisterns, which can hold no water? When danger approaches, shall we seek for help from those as weak as ourselves, or shall we flee to Him who is mighty to save? His arms are open wide, and He utters the gracious invitation, "Come unto me, all ye that labour and are heavy laden, and I will give you rest." . . .

It is not the manifestation of His great and awful majesty and unparalleled power that will leave us without excuse if we refuse Him our love and obedience. It is the love, the compassion, the patience, the

17

long-suffering that He has shown which will witness against those who do not offer Him the willing service of their lives. Those who turn to God with heart and soul and mind will find in Him peaceful security. . . .

He knows just what we need, just what we can bear, and He will give us grace to endure every trial and test that He brings upon us. My constant prayer is for a greater nearness to God.

Every provision has been made to meet the needs of our spiritual and our moral nature. . . . Light and immortality are brought to light through the Lord Jesus Christ. Jesus has said that He has set before us an open door, and no man can shut it. The open door is before us, and through the grace of Christ, beams of merciful light stream forth from the gates ajar.

BELIEF IN CHRIST
MEANS EVERLASTING LIFE

He that believeth on the Son hath everlasting life. **John 3:36.**

When the soul surrenders itself to Christ, a new power takes possession of the new heart. A change is wrought which man can never accomplish for himself. It is a supernatural work, bringing a supernatural element into human nature. The soul that is yielded to Christ becomes His own fortress, which He holds in a revolted world, and He intends that no authority shall be known in it but His own. A soul thus kept in possession by the heavenly agencies is impregnable to the assaults of Satan.

Christ is ready to impart all heavenly influences. He knows every temptation that comes to man, and the capabilities of every human agent. He weighs his strength. He sees the present and the future, and presents before the mind the obligations that should be met, and urges that common, earthly things shall not be permitted to be so absorbing that eternal things shall be lost out of reckoning.

The gifts of His grace through Christ are free to all. There is no election but one's own by which any may perish. God has set forth in His Word the conditions upon which every soul will be elected to eternal life—obedience to His commandments, through faith in Christ. God has elected a character in harmony with His law, and any one who shall reach the standard of His requirement, will have an entrance into the kingdom of glory. Christ Himself said, "He that believeth on the Son hath everlasting life."

What an exalted position to be identified with one in whom is all perfection centered, who is indeed the Majesty of heaven, but who loved us, although fallen, so much that language cannot express it! He for our sakes laid aside His royal robe, stepped down from the throne of heaven, and condescended to clothe His divinity with humility, and became like one of us except in sin, that His life and character should be a pattern for all to copy, that they might have the precious gift of eternal life.

THE SPIRIT BRINGS WISDOM AND UNDERSTANDING

And the spirit of the Lord shall rest upon him, the spirit of wisdom and understanding, the spirit of counsel and might, the spirit of knowledge and of the fear of the Lord. **Isa. 11:2.**

As the Holy Spirit opens to you the truth, you will treasure up the most precious experiences, and will long to speak to others of the comforting things that have been revealed to you. When brought into association with them, you will communicate some fresh thought in regard to the character or the work of Christ. You will have some fresh revelation of His pitying love to impart to those who love Him and to those who love Him not.

"Give, and it shall be given unto you;" for the word of God is "a fountain of gardens, a well of living waters, and streams from Lebanon." The heart that has once tasted the love of Christ, cries out continually for a deeper draught, and as you impart, you will receive in richer and more abundant measure. Every revelation of God to the soul increases the capacity to know and to love. The continual cry of the heart is, "More of Thee," and ever the Spirit's answer is, "Much more." For our God delights to do "exceeding abundantly above all that we ask or think." To Jesus, who emptied Himself for the salvation of lost humanity, the Holy Spirit was given without measure. So it will be given to every follower of Christ when the whole heart is surrendered for His indwelling. Our Lord Himself has given the command, "Be filled with the Spirit," and this command is also a promise of its fulfillment. It was the good pleasure of the Father that in Christ should "all the fullness dwell;" and "in him ye are made full."

God has poured out His love unstintedly, as the showers that refresh the earth. He says: "Let the skies pour down righteousness; let the earth open, and let them bring forth salvation, and let righteousness spring up together." . . . "Of his fulness have we received, and grace for grace."

19

ANGELS MINISTER TO THE HEIRS OF SALVATION

Are they not all ministering spirits, sent forth to minister for them who shall be heirs of salvation? Heb. 1:14.

God has angels whose whole work is to draw those who shall be heirs of salvation. . . . The angels' work is to keep back the powers of Satan.

The work of these heavenly beings is to prepare the inhabitants of this world to become children of God, pure, holy, undefiled. But men, though professing to be followers of Christ, do not place themselves in a position where they can understand this ministry, and thus the work of the heavenly messengers is made hard. The angels, who do always behold the face of the Father in heaven, would prefer to remain close by the side of God, in the pure and holy atmosphere of heaven; but a work must be done in bringing this heavenly atmosphere to the souls who are tempted and tried, that Satan may not disqualify them for the place the Lord would have them fill in the heavenly courts. Principalities and powers in heavenly places combine with these angels in their ministration for those who shall be heirs of salvation.

Angels, who will do for you what you cannot do for yourselves, are waiting for your cooperation. They are waiting for you to respond to the drawing of Christ. Draw nigh to God and to one another. By desire, by silent prayer, by resistance of satanic agencies, put your will on the side of God's will. While you have one desire to resist the devil, and sincerely pray, Deliver me from temptation, you will have strength for your day. It is the work of the heavenly angels to come close to the tried, the tempted, the suffering ones. They labor long and untiringly to save the souls for whom Christ has died. And when souls appreciate their advantages, appreciate the heavenly assistance sent them, respond to the Holy Spirit's working in their behalf; when they put their will on the side of Christ's will, angels bear the tidings heavenward. . . . And there is rejoicing among the heavenly host.

WE RECEIVE A FAITH THAT WORKS BY LOVE

For in Jesus Christ neither circumcision availeth any thing, nor uncircumcision; but faith which worketh by love. Gal. 5:6.

When you present your petitions to the Lord, it should be in humility, without boasting of superior attainments, but with real soul hunger for the blessing of God. Christ always knows what is cherished in the heart. We must come in faith that the Lord will hear and answer our prayers; for "whatsoever is not of faith is sin." Genuine faith is the faith that works by love, and purifies the soul. A living faith will be a working faith. Should we go into the garden and find that there was no sap in the plants, no freshness in the leaves, no bursting buds or blooming flowers, no signs of life in stalk or branches, we would say, "The plants are dead. Uproot them from the garden; for they are a deformity to the beds." So it is with those who profess Christianity, and have no spirituality. If there are no signs of religious vigor, if there is no doing of the commandments of the Lord, it is evident that there is no abiding in Christ, the living vine.

Faith and love are the essential, powerful, working elements of Christian character. Those who possess them are one with Christ, and are carrying forward His mission. . . . We are to sit at Christ's feet as continual learners, and to work with His gifts of faith and love. We shall then wear Christ's yoke, and lift His burdens, and Christ will recognize us as one with Him; in heaven it will be said, "Ye are labourers together with God." Will our youth remember that without faith it is impossible to please God? and it must be faith that works by love and purifies the soul.

We cannot overestimate the value of simple faith and unquestioning obedience. It is by following in the path of obedience in simple faith that the character obtains perfection.

DEPENDENCE UPON GOD

For without me ye can do nothing. **John 15:5, last part.**

The first lesson to be taught . . . is the lesson of dependence upon God. . . . As a flower of the field has its root in the soil; as it must receive air, dew, showers, and sunshine, so must we receive from God that which ministers to the life of the soul.

The presence of God is guaranteed to the Christian. This Rock of faith is the living presence of God. The weakest may depend upon it. Those who think themselves the strongest may become the weakest unless they depend on Christ as their efficiency, their worthiness. This is the Rock upon which we may build successfully. God is near in Christ's atoning sacrifice, in His intercession, His loving, tender ruling power over the church. Seated by the eternal throne, He watches them with intense interest. As long as the members of the church shall through faith draw sap and nourishment from Jesus Christ, and not from man's opinions and devisings, and methods; if having a conviction of the nearness of God in Christ, they put their entire trust in Him, they will have a vital connection with Christ as the branch has connection with the parent stock. The church is established not on theories of men, on long-drawn-out plans and forms. It depends upon Christ their righteousness. It is built on faith in Christ, "and the gates of hell shall not prevail against it." . . .

The strength of every soul is in God and not in man. Quietness and confidence is to be the strength of all who give their hearts to God. Christ has not a casual interest in us but an interest stronger than a mother for her child. . . . Our Saviour has purchased us by human suffering and sorrow, by insult, reproach, abuse, mockery, rejection and death. He is watching over you, trembling child of God. He will make you secure under His protection. . . . Our weakness in human nature will not bar our access to the heavenly Father, for He [Christ] died to make intercession for us.

THE RENEWED HEART
LOVES AS CHRIST LOVED

A new commandment I give unto you, That ye love one another; as I have loved you, that ye also love one another. **John 13:34.**

Jesus says, "Love one another as I have loved you." Love is not simply an impulse, a transitory emotion, dependent upon circumstances; it is a living principle, a permanent power. The soul is fed by the streams of pure love that flow from the heart of Christ, as a well-spring that never fails. O, how is the heart quickened, how are its motives ennobled, its affections deepened, by this communion! Under the education and disci-pline of the Holy Spirit, the children of God love one another, truly, sincerely, unaffectedly, — "without partiality, and without hypocrisy." And this because the heart is in love with Jesus. Our affection for one another springs from our common relation to God. We are one family, we love one another as He loved us. When compared with this true, sanctified, disciplined affection, the shallow courtesy of the world, the meaningless expression of effusive friendship, are as chaff to the wheat.

To love as Christ loved means to manifest unselfishness at all times and in all places, by kind words and pleasant looks. . . . Genuine love is a precious attribute of heavenly origin, which increases its fragrance in proportion as it is dispensed to others. . . .

Christ's love is deep and earnest, flowing like an irrepressible stream to all who will accept it. There is no selfishness in His love. If this heaven-born love is an abiding principle in the heart, it will make itself known, not only to those we hold most dear in sacred relationship, but to

22

all with whom we come in contact. It will lead us to bestow little acts of attention, to make concessions, to perform deeds of kindness, to speak tender, true, encouraging words. It will lead us to sympathize with those whose hearts hunger for sympathy.

WE ARE TO TAKE TIME TO THINK ABOUT GOD

Be still, and know that I am God; I will be exalted among the heathen, I will be exalted in the earth. Ps. 46:10.

Christians should . . . cultivate a love for meditation, and cherish a spirit of devotion. Many seem to begrudge moments spent in meditation, and the searching of the Scriptures, and prayer, as though the time thus occupied was lost. I wish you could all view these things in the light God would have you; for you would then make the kingdom of Heaven of the first importance. To keep your heart in Heaven, will give vigor to all your graces, and put life into all your duties. To discipline the mind to dwell upon heavenly things, will put life and earnestness into all our endeavors.

Let every one who desires to be a partaker of the divine nature appreciate the fact that he must escape the corruption that is in the world through lust. There must be a constant, earnest struggling of the soul against the evil imaginings of the mind. There must be a steadfast resistance of temptation to sin in thought or act. The soul must be kept from every stain, through faith in Him who is able to keep you from falling. We should meditate upon the Scriptures, thinking soberly and candidly upon the things that pertain to our eternal salvation. The infinite mercy and love of Jesus, the sacrifice made in our behalf, call for most serious and solemn reflection. We should dwell upon the character of our dear Redeemer and Intercessor. We should seek to comprehend the meaning of the plan of salvation. We should meditate upon the mission of Him who came to save His people from their sins. By constantly contemplating heavenly themes, our faith and love will grow stronger. Our prayers will be more and more acceptable to God, because they will be more and more mixed with faith and love. They will be more intelligent and fervent.

When the mind is thus filled . . . the believer in Christ will be able to bring forth good things from the treasure of the heart.

LET US COME BOLDLY
TO THE THRONE OF GRACE

Let us therefore come boldly unto the throne of grace, that we may obtain mercy, and find grace to help in time of need. **Heb. 4:16.**

Jesus knows the needs of His children, and He loves to listen to their prayers. Let the children shut out the world and everything that would attract the thoughts from God, and let them feel that they are alone with God, that His eye looks into the inmost heart, and reads the desire of the soul, and that they may talk with God. In humble faith you may claim His promises, and feel that although you have nothing in yourself whereby you may claim the favor of God, because of the merits and righteousness of Christ, you may come boldly to the throne of grace, and find help in time of need. There is nothing that can make the soul so strong to resist the temptations of Satan in the great conflict of life, as to seek God in humility, laying before Him your soul in all its helplessness, expecting that He will be your helper and your defender.

With the trusting faith of a little child, we are to come to our heavenly Father, telling Him of all our needs. He is always ready to pardon and help. The supply of divine wisdom is inexhaustible, and the Lord encourages us to draw largely from it. The longing that we should have for spiritual blessings is described in the words, "As the hart panteth after the water brooks, so panteth my soul after thee, O God," We need a deeper soul-hunger for the rich gifts that heaven has to bestow.

We are to hunger and thirst after righteousness.

O that we might have a consuming desire to know God by an experimental knowledge, to come into the audience chamber of the Most High, reaching up the hand of faith, and casting our helpless souls upon the One mighty to save. His loving kindness is better than life.

He desires to bestow on the children of men the riches of an eternal inheritance. His kingdom is an everlasting kingdom.

REJOICE IN THE
RICH TREASURES OF GRACE

And thou shalt rejoice in every good thing which the Lord thy God hath given unto thee, and unto thine house, thou, and the Levite, and the stranger that is among you. **Deut. 26:11.**

Thanksgiving and praise should be expressed to God for temporal blessings and for whatever comforts He bestows upon us. God would have every family that He is preparing to inhabit the eternal mansions above, give glory to Him for the rich treasures of His grace. Were children, in the home life, educated and trained to be grateful to the Giver of all good things, we would see an element of heavenly grace manifest in our families. Cheerfulness would be seen in the home life, and coming from such homes, the youth would bring a spirit of respect and reverence with them into the schoolroom, and into the church. There would be an attendance in the sanctuary where God meets with His people, a reverence for all the ordinances of His worship, and grateful praise and thanksgiving would be offered for all the gifts of His providence. . . .

Every temporal blessing would be received with gratitude, and every spiritual blessing become doubly precious because the perception of each member of the household had become sanctified by the Word of truth. The Lord Jesus is very near to those who thus appreciate His gracious gifts, tracing all their good things back to the benevolent, loving, care-taking God, and recognizing Him as the great Fountain of all comfort and consolation, the inexhaustible Source of grace.

If we would give more expression to our faith, rejoice more in the blessings that we know we have, —the great mercy and love of God, —we should have more faith and greater joy. No tongue can express, no finite mind can conceive, the blessing that results from appreciating the goodness and love of God. Even on earth we may have joy as a wellspring, never failing, because fed by the streams that flow from the throne of God.

WE HAVE RECEIVED OF GOD'S FULNESS

And of his fulness have all we received, and grace for grace. **John 1:16.**

Christ sought to save the world, not by conformity to it, but by revealing to the world the transforming power of the grace of God to mold and fashion the human character after the likeness of the character of Christ.

Satan has represented God as selfish and oppressive, as claiming all, and giving nothing, as requiring the service of His creatures for His own glory, and making no sacrifice for their good. But the gift of Christ reveals the Father's heart. . . . It declares that while God's hatred of sin is as strong as death, His love for the sinner is stronger than death. Having undertaken our redemption, He will spare nothing, however dear, which is necessary to the completion of His work. No truth essential to our salvation is withheld, no miracle of mercy is neglected, no divine agency is left unemployed. Favor is heaped upon favor, gift upon gift. The whole treasury of heaven is open to those He seeks to save. Having collected the riches of the universe, and laid open the resources of infinite power, He gives them all into the hands of Christ, and says, All these are for man. Use these gifts to convince him that there is no love greater than Mine in earth or heaven. His greatest happiness will be found in loving Me.

The Father appreciates every soul whom His Son has purchased by the gift of His life. Every provision has been made for us to receive divine power, which will enable us to overcome temptations. Through obedience to all God's requirements the soul is preserved unto eternal life.

God has a heaven full of blessings that He wants to bestow on those who are earnestly seeking for that help which the Lord alone can give.

WE ARE CHANGED
FROM GLORY TO GLORY

But we all, with open face beholding as in a glass the glory of the Lord, are changed into the same image from glory to glory even as by the Spirit of the Lord. **2 Cor. 3:18.**

When enlightened by the Spirit of God, the believer beholds the perfection of Jesus, and beholding this perfection, he rejoices with joy unspeakable. In self he sees sin and helplessness; in the Redeemer sinlessness and infinite power. The sacrifice that Christ made in order that He might impart to us His righteousness—this is a theme upon which we may dwell with deeper and still deeper enthusiasm. Self is nothing; Jesus is everything. . . .

The transforming power of grace can make me a partaker of the divine nature. On Christ the glory of God has shone, and by looking upon Christ, contemplating His self-sacrifice, remembering that in Him dwells all the fulness of the Godhead bodily, the believer is drawn closer and closer to the Source of power. . . .

How essential that we have the enlightenment of the Spirit of God; for thus only can we see the glory of Christ, and by beholding become changed from character to character in and through faith in Christ. . . . He has grace and pardon for every soul. As by faith we look to Jesus, our faith pierces the shadow, and we adore God for His wondrous love in giving us Jesus the Comforter. . . .

The sinner may become a child of God, an heir of heaven. He may rise from the dust, and stand forth arrayed in garments of light. . . . At every step of advance, he sees new beauties in Christ, and becomes more like Him in character.

The love that was manifested toward him in the death of Christ, awakens a response of thankful love, and in answer to sincere prayer, the believer is brought from grace to grace, from glory to glory, until by beholding Christ, he is changed into the same image.

LOVE FOR OTHERS

Be ye therefore followers of God, as dear children; and walk in love, as Christ also hath loved us, and hath given himself for us an offering and a sacrifice to God for a sweetsmelling savour. **Eph. 5:1, 2.**

You are to follow God as dear children, to be obedient to all His requirements, walking in love as Christ also hath loved us. . . . Love was the element in which Christ moved and walked and worked. He came to embrace the world in the arms of His love. . . .

We are to follow the example set by Christ, and make Him our pattern, until we shall have the same love for others as He has manifested for us. He seeks to impress us with this profound lesson of love. . . . If your hearts have been given to selfishness, let Christ imbue you with His love. He desires that we shall love Him fully, and encourages, yes, even commands, that we shall love others as He has given us an example. He has made love the badge of our discipleship. . . . This is the measurement to which you are to reach, — "Love one another; as I have loved you." What height, what depth and breadth of love! This love is not simply to embrace a few favorites, it is to reach to the lowliest and humblest of God's creatures. Jesus says, "Inasmuch as ye have done it unto one of the least of these my brethren, ye have done it unto me." . . .

The love and sympathy which Jesus would have us give to others does not savor of sentimentalism, which is a snare to the soul; it is a love that is of heavenly extraction, which Jesus exemplifies by both precept and example. But instead of manifesting this love, how often we are alienated and estranged one from another. . . . The result is estrangement from God, a dwarfed experience, a blighting of Christian growth. . . .

The love of Jesus is an active principle, uniting heart with heart in bonds of Christian fellowship. Every one who enters heaven will on earth have been perfected in love; for in heaven the Redeemer and the redeemed will be objects of our interest.

WE ARE TO OVERCOME
AS CHRIST OVERCAME

These things I have spoken unto you, that in me ye might have peace. In the world ye shall have tribulation: but be of good cheer; I have overcome the world. **John 16:33.**

Satan made stronger attacks upon Christ than he will ever make upon us. There was much at stake with him, whether Christ of himself should be conqueror. If Christ resisted his most powerful temptations, and Satan did not succeed in leading Him to sin, he knew that he must lose his power, and finally be punished with everlasting destruction. Therefore Satan worked with mighty power to lead Christ to do a wrong action, for then he would gain advantage over Him. . . . You can never be tempted in so determined and cruel a manner as was our Saviour. Satan was upon His path every moment.

Will man take hold of divine power, and with determination and perseverance resist Satan, as Christ has given him example in His conflict with the foe in the wilderness of temptation? God cannot save man against his will from the power of Satan's artifices. Man must work with his human power, aided by the divine power of Christ, to resist and to conquer at any cost to himself. In short, man must overcome as Christ overcame. And then, through the victory that it is his privilege to gain by the all-powerful name of Jesus, he may become an heir of God and joint-heir with Jesus Christ. This could not be the case if Christ alone did all the overcoming. Man must do *his* part; he must be victor on his own account, through the strength and grace that Christ gives him. Man must be a co-worker with Christ in the labor of overcoming, and then he will be partaker with Christ in His glory.

The Saviour overcame to show man how he may overcome. All the temptations of Satan, Christ met with the Word of God. By trusting in God's promises, He received power to obey God's commandments, and the tempter could gain no advantage.

JESUS IS A FRIEND
THAT IS CLOSER THAN A BROTHER

There is a friend that sticketh closer than a brother. **Prov. 18:24.**

Disappointments you will have, but ever bear in mind that Jesus, the living, risen Saviour, is your Redeemer, your Restorer. He loves you, and it is better to share His love than to sit with princes and be separated from Him. . . .

Come daily to Jesus, who loves you. Open your heart to Him freely. In Him there is no disappointment. You will never find a better counselor, a safer guide, a more sure defense.

Through all your trials . . . you have had a never-failing Friend, who has said, "I am with you alway, even unto the end of the world."

But how often is the Lord neglected for the society of others, and for things of no value! . . . We dare not let His name languish on our lips, and His love and memory die out of our hearts. "Well," says the cold, formal professor, "this is making Christ too much like a human being;" but the Word of God warrants us to have these very ideas. It is the want of these practical, definite views of Christ, that hinders so many from having a genuine experience in the knowledge of our Lord and Saviour Jesus Christ. This is the reason that many are fearing and doubting and mourning. Their ideas of Christ and the plan of salvation are vague, dreary, and confused. . . . If ever there was a time when men needed the presence of Christ at their right hand, it is now, so that when the enemy shall come in like a flood, the Spirit of the Lord shall lift up a standard against him.

Communion with Christ—how unspeakably precious! Such communion it is our privilege to enjoy, if we will seek it.

The everlasting assurance shall be yours that you have a Friend that sticketh closer than a brother.

CAREFUL HABITS
ENSURE GOOD HEALTH

I will restore health unto thee, and I will heal thee of thy wounds, saith the Lord. **Jer. 30:17.**

The mind does not wear out nor break down so often on account of diligent employment and hard study, as on account of eating improper food at improper times, and of careless inattention to the laws of health. . . . Irregular hours for eating and sleeping sap the brain forces. The apostle Paul declares that he who would be successful in reaching a high standard of godliness must be temperate in all things. Eating, drinking, and dressing all have a direct bearing upon our spiritual advancement.

Health is a blessing which few appreciate. . . . Many eat at all hours, regardless of the laws of health. Then gloom covers the mind. How can men be honored with divine enlightenment when they are so reckless in their habits, so inattentive to the light which God has given in regard to these things. . . . Life is a holy trust, which God alone can enable us to keep, and to use to His glory. But He who formed the wonderful structure of the body will take special care to keep it in order if men do not work at cross-purposes with Him.

Health, life, and happiness are the result of obedience to physical laws governing our bodies. If our will and way are in accordance with God's will and way; if we do the pleasure of our Creator, He will keep the human organism in good condition, and restore the moral, mental, and physical powers, in order that He may work through us to His glory. . . . If we cooperate with Him in this work, health and happiness, peace and usefulness, are the sure result.

He did not die for us in order that we might become slaves to evil habits, but that we might become the sons and daughters of God, serving Him with every power of the being.

My dear young friends, advance step by step, until all your habits shall be in harmony with the laws of life and health.

DIVINE WISDOM

For wisdom is better than rubies; and all the things that may be desired are not to be compared to it. **Prov. 8:11.**

If Adam and Eve had never touched the forbidden tree, the Lord would have imparted to them knowledge,—knowledge upon which rested no curse of sin, knowledge that would have brought them everlasting joy. The only knowledge they gained by their disobedience was a knowledge of sin and its results. . . .

Age after age, the curiosity of men has led them to seek for the tree of knowledge; and often they think they are plucking fruit most essential, when, like Solomon's research, they find it altogether vanity and nothingness in comparison with that science of true holiness which will open to them the gates of the city of God. The human ambition has been seeking for that kind of knowledge that will bring to them glory and self-exaltation and supremacy. Thus Adam and Eve were worked upon by Satan until God's restraint was snapped asunder, and their education under the teacher of lies began in order that they might have the knowledge which God had refused them.

True wisdom is a treasure as lasting as eternity. Many of the world's so-called wise men are wise only in their own estimation. Content with the acquisition of worldly wisdom, they never enter the garden of God, to become acquainted with the treasures of knowledge contained in His holy Word. Supposing themselves to be wise, they are ignorant concerning the wisdom which all must have who gain eternal life. . . . The unlearned man, if he knows God and Jesus Christ, has a more enduring wisdom than has the most learned man who despises the instruction of God.

Divine wisdom is to be a lamp to your feet. . . . Everything that can be shaken will be shaken; but rooted and grounded in the truth, you will abide with those things that cannot be shaken.

STUDY THE SCRIPTURES

For whatsoever things were written aforetime were written for our learning, that we through patience and comfort of the scriptures might have hope. **Rom. 15:4.**

This Holy Book has withstood the assaults of Satan, who has united with evil men to make everything of divine character shrouded in clouds and darkness. But the Lord has preserved this Holy Book by His own miraculous power in its present shape, — a chart or guidebook to the human family to show them the way to heaven. . . . This Word . . . is the guidebook to the inhabitants of a fallen world, bequeathed to them, that by studying and obeying the directions, not one soul would lose its way.

There never was a time when it was so important that followers of Christ should study the Bible as now. Deceptive influences are upon all sides, and it is essential that you counsel with Jesus, your best friend. . . . David declares, "Thy word have I hid in my heart, that I might not sin against thee." How many are betrayed into sin, because they have not, through prayerful study of the Word of God, realized the sinfulness of sin, and found out how they may steadfastly resist it. When temptation comes upon them, they seem to be off guard, and ignorant of the devices of the enemy. We are living in perilous times, and as we draw near the close of earth's history, there will be no safety for those who do not become familiar with the Word of God. . . . Everything that can be shaken, will be shaken. . . . The children of God have reached the most critical part of their pilgrimage; for the nets and pitfalls of the enemy are on every side. And yet with the guidance of the Lord, with that which is plainly revealed in His Word, we may walk securely and not stumble. . . . A voice from heaven is addressing us in its pages.

Obedience to God's Word is our only safeguard against the evils that are sweeping the world to destruction.

WALK IN HIS WAY

The way of the Lord is strength to the upright: but destruction shall be to the workers of iniquity. **Prov. 10:29.**

If from the beginning we had walked in the counsel of God, thousands more would have been converted to the present truth. But many have made crooked paths for their feet. My brethren, make straight paths, lest the lame be turned out of the way. Let no one follow a crooked path that some one else has made, for thus you would not only go astray yourself, but would make this crooked path plainer for some one else to follow. Determine that as for yourself, you will walk in the path of obedience. Know for a certainty that you are standing under the broad shield of Omnipotence. Realize that the characteristics of Jehovah must be revealed in your life, and that in you a work must be accomplished that will mold your character after the divine similitude. Yield yourself to the guidance of Him who is the Head over all.

We are doing our work for the judgment. Let us be learners of Jesus. We need His guidance every moment. At every step we should inquire, "Is this the way of the Lord?" not, "Is this the way of the man who is over me?" We are to be concerned only as to whether we are walking in the way of the Lord.

God will honor and uphold every true-hearted, earnest soul who is seeking to walk before Him in the perfection of Christ's grace. He will never leave nor forsake one humble, trembling soul. Shall we believe that He will work in our hearts? that if we allow Him to do so, He will make us pure and holy, by His rich grace qualifying us to be laborers together with Him? Can we with keen, sanctified perception appreciate the strength of His promises, and appropriate them, not because we are worthy, but because by living faith we claim the righteousness of Christ?

There is nothing so great and powerful as God's love for those who are His children.

January 23

ALL MEN ARE DRAWN TO THE UPLIFTED SAVIOUR

And I, if I be lifted up from the earth, will draw all men unto me. **John 12:32.**

Never before was there such a general knowledge of Jesus as when He hung upon the cross. He was lifted up from the earth, to draw all to Him.

Into the hearts of many who beheld that crucifixion scene, and who heard Christ's words, was the light of truth to shine. With John they would proclaim, "Behold the Lamb of God, which taketh away the sin of the world." There were those who never rested until, searching the scriptures and comparing passage with passage, they saw the meaning of Christ's mission. They saw that free forgiveness was provided by Him whose tender mercy embraced the whole world. They read the prophecies regarding Christ, and the promises so free and full, pointing to a fountain opened for Judah and Jerusalem.

The sacrifice of Christ as an atonement for sin is the great truth around which all other truths cluster. In order to be rightly understood and appreciated, every truth in the Word of God, from Genesis to Revelation, must be studied in the light which streams from the cross of Calvary, and in connection with the wondrous, central truth of the Saviour's atonement. Those who study the redeemer's wonderful sacrifice grow in grace and knowledge.

I present before you the great, grand monument of mercy and regeneration, salvation and redemption,—the Son of God uplifted on the cross of Calvary. This is to be the theme of every discourse.

Jesus is inviting and drawing by His Holy Spirit the hearts of young and old to Himself. . . . When Christ crucified is preached, the power of the gospel is demonstrated by the influence it exerts over the believer. In place of remaining dead in trespasses and sins, he is awakened.

Lift up the Man of Calvary higher and still higher; there is power in the exaltation of the cross of Christ.

RECONCILED TO GOD
BY CHRIST'S DEATH

For if, when we were enemies, we were reconciled to God by the death of his Son, much more, being reconciled, we shall be saved by his life. Rom. 5:10.

The cross is invested with a power that language cannot express. Christ's sacrifice in behalf of the human race puts to shame our meager efforts and methods to meet and uplift humanity, to help sinful men and women to find Jesus.

The work of the sons and daughters of God must be of a different character than has yet been manifested by a large number. If they love Jesus, they will have enlarged ideas of the love that has been expressed for fallen man, which required the provision of so expensive an offering to save the human race. Our Saviour asks the cooperation of every son and daughter of Adam who has become a son or daughter of God. . . . Our Saviour declares that He brought from heaven as a donation eternal life. He was to be lifted up upon the cross of Calvary to draw all men unto Him. How then shall we treat the purchased inheritance of Christ? Tenderness, appreciation, kindness, sympathy, and love should be shown to them. Then we may work to help and bless one another. In this work we have more than human brotherhood. We have the exalted companionship of heavenly angels. They cooperate with us in the work of enlightening high and low.

Having engaged in the work, the amazing work of our redemption, Christ determined in council with His Father to spare nothing, however costly, to withhold nothing however highly it might be estimated, that would rescue the poor sinner. He would give all heaven to this work of salvation, of restoring the moral image of God in man. . . . To be a child of God is to be one with Christ in God, and to put forth our hands in earnest, self-sacrificing love to strengthen and bless the souls that are perishing in their sins.

TRUE MISSIONARY EFFORT BEGINS IN THE HOME

And they were both righteous before God, walking in all the commandments and ordinances of the Lord blameless. **Luke 1:6.**

In forming a relationship with Christ, the renewed man is but coming back to his appointed relationship with God. . . . His first duty is to his children and his nearest relatives. Nothing can excuse him from neglecting the inner circle for the larger circle outside. In the day of final reckoning fathers and mothers . . . will be asked what they did and said to secure the salvation of the souls they took upon themselves the responsibility of bringing into the world. Did they neglect their lambs, leaving them to the care of strangers? . . . A great good done for others will not cancel the debt you owe to God to care for your children. The spiritual welfare of your family comes first.

In rightly training and molding the minds of her children, mothers are entrusted with the greatest mission ever given to mortals.

Whenever you take up the duty that lies nearest you, then God will bless you, and hear your prayers. There are too many doing outside missionary work, while their own households are left destitute of any such efforts,—going to ruin through neglect. . . . The first missionary work is to see that love, light, and joy come into the home circle. Let us not be looking for some great temperance or missionary work to do until we have first done the duties at home. Every morning we should think, What kind act can I do today? What tender word can I speak? Kind words at home are blessed sunshine. The husband needs them, the wife needs them, the children need them. . . . It ought to be the desire of every heart to make as much heaven below as possible.

A soul saved in your own family circle or in your own neighborhood, by your patient, painstaking labor, will bring as much honor to the name of Christ, and will shine as brightly in your crown as if you had found that soul in China or India.

WE ARE TO DO GOOD
TO OUR NEIGHBORS

Withhold not good from them to whom it is due, when it is in the power of thine hand to do it. **Prov. 3:27.**

So ready, so eager is the Saviour's heart to welcome us as members of the family of God, that in the very first words we are to use in approaching God, He places the assurance of our divine relationship, — "Our Father." . . . In calling God our Father, we recognize all His children as our brethren. We are all a part of the great web of humanity, all members of one family. In our petitions we are to include our neighbors as well as ourselves. No one prays aright who seeks a blessing for himself alone.

We are bound to the Lord by the strongest ties, and the manifestation of our Father's love should call forth the most filial affection and the most ardent gratitude. The laws of God have their foundation in the most immutable rectitude, and are so framed that they will promote the happiness of those who keep them.

In the lesson of faith that Christ taught on the mount, are revealed the principles of true religion. Religion brings man into personal relation with God, but not exclusively; for the principles of heaven are to be lived out, that they may help and bless humanity. A true child of God will love Him with all his heart, and his neighbor as himself. He will have an interest for his fellow-men. True religion is the work of grace upon the heart, that causes the life to flow out in good works, like a fountain fed from living streams. Religion does not consist merely in meditation and prayer. The Christian's light is displayed in good works, and is thus recognized by others. Religion is not to be divorced from the business life. It is to pervade and sanctify its engagements and enterprises. If a man is truly connected with God and heaven, the spirit that dwells in heaven will influence all his words and actions. He will glorify God in his works, and will lead others to honor Him.

BEING UNITED
AS CHILDREN OF GOD

For ye are all the children of God by faith in Christ Jesus. **Gal. 3:26.**

We seldom find two persons exactly alike. Among human beings as well as among the things of the natural world, there is diversity. Unity in diversity among God's children—the manifestation of love and forbearance in spite of difference of disposition—this is the testimony that God sent His Son into the world to save sinners.

The unity that exists between Christ and His disciples does not destroy the personality of either. In mind, in purpose, in character, they are one, but not in person. By partaking of the Spirit of God, conforming to the law of God, man becomes a partaker of the divine nature. Christ brings His disciples into a living union with Himself and with the Father. Through the working of the Holy Spirit upon the human mind, man is made complete in Christ Jesus. Unity with Christ establishes a bond of unity with one another. This unity is the most convincing proof to the world of the majesty and virtue of Christ, and of His power to take away sin.

The powers of darkness stand a poor chance against believers who love one another as Christ has loved them, who refuse to create alienation and strife, who stand together, who are kind, courteous, and tender-hearted, cherishing the faith that works by love and purifies the soul. We must have the Spirit of Christ, or we are none of His.

In unity there is strength; in division there is weakness.

The closer our union with Christ, the closer will be our union with one another. Variance and disaffection, selfishness and conceit, are striving for supremacy. These are the fruits of a divided heart, open to the suggestions of the enemy of souls. Satan exults when he can sow seeds of dissension.

In unity there is a life, a power, that can be obtained in no other way.

GLAD IN THE LORD

My meditation of him shall be sweet: I will be glad in the Lord. **Ps. 104:34.**

Rest yourself wholly in the hands of Jesus. Contemplate His great love, and while you meditate upon His self-denial, His infinite sacrifice made in our behalf in order that we should believe in Him, your heart will be filled with holy joy, calm peace, and indescribable love. As we talk of Jesus, as we call upon Him in prayer, our confidence that He is our personal, loving Saviour will strengthen, and His character will appear more and more lovely. . . . We may enjoy rich feasts of love, and as we fully believe that we are His by adoption, we may have a foretaste of heaven. Wait upon the Lord in faith. The Lord draws out the soul in prayer, and gives us to feel His precious love. We have a nearness to Him, and can hold sweet communion with Him. We obtain distinct views of His tenderness and compassion, and our hearts are broken and melted with contemplation of the love that is given to us. We feel indeed an abiding Christ in the soul. . . . Our peace is like a river, wave after wave of glory rolls into the heart, and indeed we sup with Jesus and He with us. We have a realizing sense of the love of God, and we rest in His love. No language can describe it, it is beyond knowledge. We are one with Christ, our life is hid with Christ in God. We have the assurance that when He who is our life shall appear, then shall we also appear with Him in glory. With strong confidence, we can call God our Father. Whether we live or die, we are the Lord's. His Spirit makes us like Jesus Christ in temper, and disposition, and we represent Christ to others. When Christ is abiding in the soul the fact cannot be hid; for He is like a well of water springing up into everlasting life. We can but represent the likeness of Christ in our character, and our words, our deportment, produces in others a deep, abiding, increasing love for Jesus, and we make manifest . . . that we are conformed to the image of Jesus Christ.

STORE THE MIND
WITH DIVINE TRUTH

Whereby are given unto us exceeding great and precious promises: that by these ye might be partakers of the divine nature, having escaped the corruption that is in the world through lust. 2 Peter 1:4.

It is the duty of every child of God to store his mind with divine truth; and the more he does this, the more strength and clearness of mind he will have to fathom the deep things of God. And he will be more and more earnest and vigorous, as the principles of truth are carried out in his daily life.

That which will bless humanity is spiritual life. He who is in harmony with God, will constantly depend upon Him for strength. "Be ye therefore perfect, even as your Father which is in heaven is perfect." It should be our life work to be constantly reaching forward to the perfection of Christian character, ever striving for conformity to the will of God. The efforts begun here will continue through eternity. The advancement made here will be ours when we enter upon the future life.

Those who are partakers of Christ's meekness, purity, and love, will be joyful in God, and will shed light and gladness upon all around them. The thought that Christ died to obtain for us the gift of everlasting life, is enough to call forth from our hearts the most sincere and fervent gratitude, and from our lips the most enthusiastic praise. God's promises are rich, and full, and free. Whoever will, in the strength of Christ, comply with the conditions, may claim these promises, with all their wealth of blessing, as his own. And being thus abundantly supplied from the treasure-house of God, he may, in the journey of life, "walk worthy of the Lord unto all pleasing;" by a godly example blessing his fellow-men, and honoring his Creator. While our Saviour would guard His followers from self-confidence by the reminder, "Without me, ye can do nothing," He has coupled with it for our encouragement the gracious assurance, "He that abideth in me . . . bringeth forth much fruit."

TREES PLANTED
BY RIVERS OF WATER

He shall be like a tree planted by the rivers of water, that bringeth forth his fruit in his season; his leaf also shall not wither; and whatsoever he doeth shall prosper. **Ps. 1:3.**

Dangers beset every path, and he who comes off conqueror will indeed have a triumphant song to sing in the city of God. Some have strong traits of character that will need to be constantly repressed. If kept under the control of the Spirit of God, these traits will be a blessing; but if not, they will prove a curse. If those who are now riding upon the wave of popularity do not become giddy, it will be a miracle of mercy. If they lean to their own wisdom, as so many thus situated have done, their wisdom will prove to be foolishness. But while they shall give themselves unselfishly to the work of God, never swerving in the least from principle, the Lord will throw about them the everlasting arm and will prove to them a mighty helper. . . .

This is a dangerous age for any man who has talents which can be of value in the work of God; for Satan is constantly plying his temptations upon such a person, ever trying to fill him with pride and ambition; and when God would use him, it is too often the case that he becomes independent and selfsufficient, and feels capable of standing alone. . . .

Prayer and effort, effort and prayer, will be the business of your life. You must pray as though the efficiency and praise were all due to God, and labor as though duty were all your own. If you want power you may have it; it is waiting your draft upon it. Only believe in God, take Him at His word, act by faith, and blessings will come. . . . Those who have a humble, trusting, contrite heart, God accepts, and hears their prayer; and when God helps, all obstacles will be overcome. . . . The blessing of heaven, obtained by daily supplication, will be as the bread of life to the soul and will cause them to increase in moral and spiritual strength, like a tree planted by the river of waters.

WE SHALL
INHERIT ALL THINGS

He that overcometh shall inherit all things; and I will be his God, and he shall be my son (daughter). **Rev. 21:7.**

In order to inherit all things, we must resist and overcome sin.

We may have joy in the Lord if we will keep His commandments. If we indeed have our citizenship above, and a title to an immortal inheritance, an eternal substance, we have that faith which works by love and purifies the soul. . . . We are members of the heavenly family, children of the heavenly King, heirs of God, and joint heirs with Christ. At His coming we shall have the crown of life that fadeth not away.

The Monarch of heaven would have you possess and enjoy all that can ennoble, expand, and exalt your being and fit you to dwell with Him forever, your existence measuring with the life of God. What a prospect is the life which is to come! What charms it possesses! How broad and deep and measureless is the love of God manifested to man!

The privileges granted to the children of God are without limit, —to be connected with Jesus Christ, who, throughout the universe of heaven and worlds that have not fallen, is adored by every heart, and His praises sung by every tongue; to be children of God, to bear His name, to become a member of the royal family; to be ranged under the banner of Prince Immanuel, the King of kings and Lord of lords.

The Son of God was the heir of all things, and the dominion and glory of the kingdoms of this world were promised to Him. . . . Even as Christ was in the world, so are His followers. They are the sons of God, and joint heirs with Christ; and the kingdom and dominion belong to them.

In place of the world, He will give you, for a life of obedience, the kingdom under the whole heavens. He will give you an eternal weight of glory and a life that is as enduring as eternity.

I GIVE
MY HEART

My son, give me thine heart, and let thine eyes observe my ways.
Prov. 23:26.

The Lord says to every one of you, "My son, give Me thine heart."
He sees your disorders. He knows that your soul is diseased with sin, and
He desires to say to you, "Thy sins are forgiven." The Great Physician has
a remedy for every ill. He understands your case. Whatever may have been
your errors, He knows how to deal with them. Will you not trust yourself
to Him?

The blessing of God will rest upon every soul that makes a full
consecration to Him. When we seek for God with all the heart, we shall
find Him. God is in earnest with us, and He wants us to make thorough
work for eternity. He has poured out all heaven in one gift, and there is no
reason why we should doubt His love. Look to Calvary. . . .

God asks you to give Him your heart. Your powers, your talents, your
affections, should all be surrendered to Him, that He may work in you to
will and to do of His good pleasure, and fit you for eternal life.

When Christ dwells in the heart, the soul will be so filled with His
love, with the joy of communion with Him, that it will cleave to Him; and
in the contemplation of Him, self will be forgotten. Love to Christ will be
the spring of action. Those who feel the constraining love of God, do not
ask how little may be given to meet the requirements of God; they do not
ask for the lowest standard, but aim at perfect conformity to the will of
their Redeemer. With earnest desire they yield all, and manifest an interest
proportionate to the value of the object which they seek.

It is the submissive, teachable spirit that God wants. That which gives
to prayer its excellence is the fact that it is breathed from a loving, obedient
heart.

PRAY IN THE MORNING

*My voice shalt thou hear in the morning, O Lord; in the morning will
I direct my prayer unto thee, and will look up.* **Ps. 5:3.**

The very first outbreathing of the soul in the morning should be for the
presence of Jesus. "Without Me," He says, "ye can do nothing." It is
Jesus that we need; His light, His life, His spirit, must be ours continually.
We need Him every hour. And we should pray in the morning that as the

sun illuminates the landscape, and fills the world with light, so the Sun of Righteousness may shine into the chambers of mind and heart, and make us all light in the Lord. We cannot do without His presence one moment. The enemy knows when we undertake to do without our Lord, and he is there, ready to fill our minds with his evil suggestions that we may fall from our steadfastness; but it is the desire of the Lord that from moment to moment we should abide in Him, and thus be complete in Him. . . .

God designs that every one of us shall be perfect in Him, so that we may represent to the world the perfection of His character. He wants us to be set free from sin, that we may not disappoint Heaven, that we may not grieve our divine Redeemer. He does not desire us to profess Christianity, and yet not avail ourselves of that grace which is able to make us perfect, that we may be found wanting in nothing.

Prayer and faith will do what no power on earth can accomplish. We are seldom, in all respects, placed in the same position twice. We continually have new scenes and new trials to pass through, where past experience cannot be a sufficient guide. We must have the continual light that comes from God. Christ is ever sending messages to those who listen for His voice.

* * * * *

It is a part of God's plan to grant us, in answer to the prayer of faith, that which He would not bestow did we not thus ask.

My Life Today

THE BIBLE
BEGETS NEW LIFE

Being born again . . . by the word of God, which liveth and abideth for ever. **1 Peter 1:23.**

In the Bible the will of God is revealed. The truths of the Word of God are the utterances of the Most High. He who makes these truths a part of his life becomes in every sense a new creature. He is not given new mental powers, but the darkness that through ignorance and sin has clouded the understanding is removed. The words, "A new heart also will I give you," mean, "A new mind will I give you." A change of heart is always attended by a clear conviction of Christian duty, an understanding of truth. He who gives the Scriptures close, prayerful attention will gain clear comprehension and sound judgment, as if in turning to God he had reached a higher plane of intelligence.

The Bible contains the principles that lie at the foundation of all true greatness, all true prosperity, whether for the individual or for the nation.

The nation that gives free room for the circulation of the Scriptures opens the way for the minds of the people to develop and expand. The reading of the Scriptures causes light to shine into the darkness. As the Word of God is searched, life-giving truths are found. In the lives of those who heed its teachings there will be an undercurrent of happiness that will bless all with whom they are brought in contact.

Thousands have drawn water from these wells of life, yet there is no diminishing of the supply. Thousands have set the Lord before them, and by beholding have been changed into the same image. Their spirit burns within them as they speak of His character, telling what Christ is to them and what they are to Christ. . . . Thousands more may engage in the work of searching out the mysteries of salvation. . . . Each fresh search will reveal something more deeply interesting than has yet been unfolded.

THE SPIRIT TO GLORIFY CHRIST IN ME

He shall glorify me: for he shall receive of mine, and shall shew it unto you. **John 16:14.**

In these words Christ declares the crowning work of the Holy Spirit. The Spirit glorifies Christ by making Him the object of supreme regard, and the Saviour becomes the delight, the rejoicing, of the human agent in whose heart is wrought this transformation. . . .

Repentance toward God and faith in Jesus Christ are the fruits of the renewing power of the grace of the Spirit. Repentance represents the process by which the soul seeks to reflect the image of Christ to the world.

Christ gives them the breath of His own Spirit, the life of His own life. The Holy Spirit puts forth its highest energies to work in heart and mind. The grace of God enlarges and multiplies their faculties, and every perfection of the divine nature comes to their assistance in the work of saving souls. Through cooperation with Christ they are complete in Him, and in their human weakness they are enabled to do the deeds of Omnipotence.

It should be the work of the Christian's life to put on Christ and to bring himself to a more perfect likeness of Christ. The sons and daughters of God are to advance in their resemblance to Christ, our pattern. Daily they are to behold His glory and contemplate His incomparable excellence.

O that the baptism of the Holy Spirit might come upon you, that you might be imbued with the Spirit of God! Then day by day you will become more and more conformed to the image of Christ, and in every action of your life the question would be, "Will it glorify my Master?" By patient continuance in well-doing you would seek for glory and honor, and would receive the gift of immortality.

THE WHOLE EARTH
WILL BE LIGHTENED

And after these things I saw another angel come down from heaven, having great power; and the earth was lightened with his glory. **Rev. 18:1.**

The end of all things is at hand. God is moving upon every mind that is open to receive the impressions of His Holy Spirit. He is sending out messengers that they may give the warning in every locality. God is testing the devotion of His churches and their willingness to render obedience to the Spirit's guidance. Knowledge is to be increased. The messengers of Heaven are to be seen running to and fro, seeking in every possible way to warn the people of the coming judgments and presenting the glad tidings of salvation through our Lord Jesus Christ. The standard of righteousness is to be exalted. The Spirit of God is moving upon men's hearts, and those who respond to its influence will become lights in the world. Everywhere they are seen going forth to communicate to others the light they have received as they did after the descent of the Holy Spirit on the day of Pentecost. And as they let their light shine, they receive more and more of the Spirit's power. The earth is lighted with the glory of God.

This message will close with power and strength far exceeding the midnight cry. Servants of God, endowed with power from on high, with their faces lighted up, and shining with holy consecration, went forth to proclaim the message from heaven.

Many were praising God. The sick were healed, and other miracles were wrought. A spirit of intercession was seen, even as was manifested before the great Day of Pentecost. Hundreds and thousands were seen visiting families and opening before them the Word of God. Hearts were convicted by the power of the Holy Spirit, and a spirit of genuine conversion was manifest. On every side doors were thrown open to the proclamation of the truth. The world seemed to be lightened with the heavenly influence.

PRINCIPLE NOT TO BE
SACRIFICED FOR PEACE

Peace I leave with you, my peace I give unto you: not as the world giveth, give I unto you. Let not your heart be troubled, neither let it be afraid. **John 14:27.**

There always have been and always will be two classes on the earth to the end of time—the believers in Jesus, and those who reject Him. Sinners, however wicked, abominable, and corrupt, by faith in Him will be purified, made clean, through the doing of His word. . . . Those who reject Christ and refuse to believe the truth will be filled with bitterness against those who accept Jesus as a personal Saviour. But those who receive Christ are melted and subdued by the manifestation of His love and His humiliation, suffering, and death in their behalf. . . .

The peace that Christ gave to His disciples, and for which we pray, is the peace that is born of truth, a peace that is not to be quenched because of division. Without may be wars and fightings, jealousies, envies, hatred, strife; but the peace of Christ is not that which the world giveth or taketh away. It could endure amid the hunting of spies and the fiercest opposition of His enemies. . . . Christ did not for an instant seek to purchase peace by a betrayal of sacred trusts. Peace could not be made by a compromise of principles. . . . It is a grave mistake on the part of those who are children of God to seek to bridge the gulf that separates the children of light from the children of darkness by yielding principle, by compromising the truth. It would be surrendering the peace of Christ in order to make peace or fraternize with the world. The sacrifice is too costly to be made by the children of God to make peace with the world by giving up the principles of truth. . . . Then let the followers of Christ settle it in their minds that they will never compromise truth, never yield one iota of principle for the favor of the world. Let them hold to the peace of Christ.

I WILL LOVE
AS CHRIST LOVED

By this shall all men know that ye are my disciples, if ye have love one to another. **John 13:35.**

If we would be true lights in the world, we must manifest the loving, compassionate spirit of Christ. To love as Christ loved means that we must practice self-control. It means that we must show unselfishness at all times and in all places. It means that we must scatter round us kind words and pleasant looks. These cost the giver nothing, but they leave behind a precious fragrance. Their influence for good cannot be estimated. Not only to the receiver, but to the giver, they are a blessing; for they react upon him. Genuine love is a precious attribute of heavenly origin, which increases in fragrance in proportion as it is dispensed to others. . . .

God desires His children to remember that in order to glorify Him, they must bestow their affection on those who need it most. None with whom we come in contact are to be neglected. No selfishness in look, word, or deed is to be manifested to our fellow beings, whatever their position, whether they be high or low, rich or poor. The love that gives kind words to only a few, while others are treated with coldness and indifference, is not love, but selfishness. It will not in any way work for the good of souls or the glory of God. We are not to confine our love to one or two objects.

Those who gather the sunshine of Christ's righteousness, and refuse to let it shine into the lives of others, will soon lose the sweet, bright rays of heavenly grace, selfishly reserved to be lavished upon a few. . . . Self should not be allowed to gather to itself a select few, giving nothing to those who need help the most. Our love is not to be sealed up for special ones. Break the bottle, and the fragrance will fill the house.

My Life Today February 8

I WILL SING
UNTO THE LORD

Whoso offereth praise glorifieth me: and to him that ordereth his conversation aright will I shew the salvation of God. **Ps. 50:23.**

Come to Jesus just as you are, sinful, weak, and needy, and He will give you the water of life. You want a faith that reaches through the hellish shadow that Satan casts athwart your pathway. He is busily inventing amusements and fashions which will so take up men's minds that they shall not be able to spare any time for meditation. Teach your children to glorify God, not to please themselves. They are His children—His by creation and by redemption. Teach them to shun the amusements and follies of this degenerate age. Keep their minds clean and pure in the sight of God. . . . Praise God. Let your conversation, your music, your songs all praise Him who has done so much for us. Praise God here, and then you will be fitted to join the heavenly choir when you enter the city of God. Then you can cast your glittering crowns at the feet of Jesus, take up your golden harps, and fill all heaven with melody. We shall praise Him with an immortal tongue.

As our Redeemer leads us to the threshold of the Infinite, flushed with the glory of God, we may catch the themes of praise and thanksgiving from the heavenly choir round about the throne; and as the echo of the angels' song is awakened in our earthly homes, hearts will be drawn closer to the heavenly singers. Heaven's communion begins on earth. We learn here the keynote of its praise.

Praise the Lord; talk of His goodness; tell of His power. Sweeten the atmosphere that surrounds your soul. . . . Praise, with heart and soul and voice, Him who is the health of your countenance, your Saviour, and your God.

GROWTH IN GRACE
BEGINS AT HOME

The Lord will give grace and glory: no good thing will he withhold from them that walk uprightly. **Ps. 84:11.**

There are many who do not grow in grace because they fail of cultivating home religion.

The members of the family are to show that they are in constant possession of a power received from Christ. They are to improve in every habit and practice, thus showing that they keep constantly before them what it means to be a Christian.

Those who are Christians in the home will be Christians in the church and in the world.

Grace can thrive only in the heart that is being constantly prepared for the precious seeds of truth. The thorns of sin will grow in any soil; they need no cultivation; but grace must be carefully cultivated. The briers and thorns are always ready to spring up, and the work of purification must advance continually.

That which will make the character lovely in the home is that which will make it lovely in the heavenly mansions. If you are . . . to be the light of the world, that light is to shine in your home. Here you are to exemplify the Christian graces, to be lovable, patient, kind, yet firm. . . . You need to seek constantly the highest culture of mind and soul. . . . As a humble child of God, learn in the school of Christ; seek constantly to improve your powers, that you may do the most perfect, thorough work at home, by both precept and example. . . . Let the light of heavenly grace irradiate your character, that there may be sunlight in the home.

The measure of your Christianity is gauged by the character of your home life. The grace of Christ enables its possessors to make the home a happy place, full of peace and rest.

GOD MULTIPLIES MY TALENTS

Well done, thou good and faithful servant: thou hast been faithful over a few things, I will make thee ruler over many things: enter thou into the joy of thy lord. Matt. 25:21.

God has given us talents to use for Him. To one He gives five talents, to another two, and to another one. Let not him who has but one talent think to hide it from God. The Lord knows where it is hidden. He knows that it is doing nothing for Him. When the Lord comes, He will ask His servants, What have you done with the talents I entrusted to you? And as he who received five and he who received two tell Him that by trading they have doubled their talents, He will say to them, "Well done, good and faithful servant. Thou hast been faithful over a few things, I will make thee ruler over many things. . . . Enter thou into the joy of thy Lord." Thus He will say also to him who has improved the one talent lent him. . . .

To him who has but one talent I would say, Do you know that one talent, rightly used and improved, will bring the Lord one hundred talents? How? you ask. Use your gift in the conversion of one man of intellect, who sees what God is to him, and what he should be to God. Let him place himself on the side of the Lord, and as he imparts the light to others, he will be the means of bringing many souls to the Saviour. Through the right use of one talent one hundred souls may receive the truth. It is not to those who have the greatest number of talents to whom the "Well done" is spoken, but to those who in sincerity and faithfulness have used their gifts for the Master. . . .

There is a great work to be done in our world, and we are accountable for every ray of light that shines upon our pathway. Impart that light, and you will receive more light to impart. Great blessing will come to those who use their talents aright.

47

PRESERVE
THE BODY TEMPLE

Know ye not that ye are the temple of God, and that the Spirit of God dwelleth in you? **1 Cor. 3:16.**

God has given you a habitation to care for and preserve in the best condition for His service and glory. Your bodies are not your own. . . . "Know ye not that ye are the temple of God, and that the Spirit of God dwelleth in you?"

Health is a blessing of which few appreciate the value. . . . Life is a holy trust, which God alone can enable us to keep, and to use to His glory. But He who formed the wonderful structure of the body will take special care to keep it in order if men do not work at crosspurposes with Him. Every talent entrusted to us He will help us to improve and use in accordance to the will of the Giver.

Youth is the time to establish good habits, to correct wrong ones already contracted, to gain and to hold the power of self-control, and to lay the plan, and accustom one's self to the practice of ordering all the acts of life with reference to the will of God.

The sacred temple of the body must be kept pure and uncontaminated, that God's Holy Spirit may dwell therein. We need to guard faithfully the Lord's property, for any abuse of our powers shortens the time that our lives could be used for the glory of God. Bear in mind that we must consecrate all—soul, body, and spirit—to God. All is His purchased possession, and must be used intelligently, to the end that we may preserve the talent of life. By properly using our powers to their fullest extent in the most useful employment, by keeping every organ in health, by so preserving every organ that mind, sinew, and muscle shall work harmoniously, we may do the most precious service for God.

When we do all we can on our part to have health, then may we expect that the blessed results will follow, and we can ask God in faith to bless our efforts for the preservation of health.

A MERRY HEART
IS GOOD MEDICINE

A merry (rejoicing) heart doeth good like a medicine. **Prov. 17:22.**

The relation that exists between the mind and the body is very intimate. When one is affected the other sympathizes. The condition of the mind affects the health to a far greater degree than many realize. Many of the diseases from which men suffer are the result of mental depression. Grief, anxiety, discontent, remorse, guilt, distrust, all tend to break down the life forces and to invite decay and death.

Disease is sometimes produced, and is often greatly aggravated, by the imagination. Many are lifelong invalids who might be well if they only thought so. . . .

Courage, hope, faith, sympathy, love, promote health and prolong life. A contented mind, a cheerful spirit, is health to the body and strength to the soul.

Gratitude, rejoicing, benevolence, trust in God's love and care—these are health's greatest safeguard.

The power of the will and the importance of self-control, both in the preservation and in the recovery of health, the depressing and even ruinous effect of anger, discontent, selfishness, or impurity, and, on the other hand, the marvelous life-giving power to be found in cheerfulness, unselfishness, gratitude, should also be shown.

There is a physiological truth—truth that we need to consider—in the scripture, "A merry [rejoicing] heart doeth good like a medicine."

The true principles of Christianity open before all a source of inestimable happiness.

We should encourage a cheerful, hopeful, peaceful frame of mind; for our health depends upon our so doing.

My Life Today   February 13

THANKSGIVING AND PRAISE

Enter into his gates with thanksgiving, and into his courts with praise: be thankful unto him, and bless his name. Ps. 100:4.

If we will consecrate heart and mind to the service of God, doing the work He has for us to do and walking in the footsteps of Jesus, our hearts will become sacred harps, every chord of which will send forth praise and thanksgiving to the Lamb sent by God to take away the sins of the world. . . .

Christ would have our thoughts center upon Him. . . . Look away from self to Jesus Christ, the life of every blessing, every grace, the life of all that is precious and valuable to the children of God. . . .

The Lord Jesus is our strength and happiness, the great storehouse from which, on every occasion, men may draw strength. As we study Him, talk of Him, become more and more able to behold Him—as we avail ourselves of His grace and receive the blessings He proffers us, we have

49

something with which to help others. Filled with gratitude, we communicate to others the blessings that have been freely given us. Thus receiving and imparting, we grow in grace; and a rich current of praise and gratitude constantly flows from our lips; the sweet spirit of Jesus kindles thanksgiving in our hearts, and our souls are uplifted with a sense of security. The unfailing, inexhaustible righteousness of Christ becomes our righteousness by faith.

Let the fresh blessings of each new day awaken praise in our hearts for these tokens of His loving care.

When you open your eyes in the morning, thank God that He has kept you through the night. Thank Him for His peace in your heart. Morning, noon, and night let gratitude as a sweet perfume ascend to heaven. . . .

The angels of God, thousands upon thousands, . . . guard us against evil and press back the powers of darkness that are seeking our destruction. Have we not reason to be thankful every moment, thankful even when there are apparent difficulties in our pathway?

LOVE HEALS MANY WOUNDS

Beloved, let us love one another: for love is of God; and every one that loveth is born of God, and knoweth God. 1 John 4:7.

From the Christian standpoint, love is power. Intellectual and spiritual strength are involved in this principle. Pure love has special efficacy to do good, and can do nothing but good. It prevents discord and misery and brings the truest happiness. Wealth is often an influence to corrupt and destroy; force is strong to do hurt; but truth and goodness are the properties of pure love.

A man at peace with God and his fellow men cannot be made miserable. Envy will not be in his heart; evil surmising will find no room there; hatred cannot exist. The heart in harmony with God is lifted above the annoyances and trials of this life.

That which Satan plants in the heart—envy, jealousy, evil surmising, evil speaking, impatience, prejudice, selfishness, covetousness, and vanity—must be uprooted. If these evil things are allowed to remain in the soul, they will bear fruit by which many shall be defiled. Oh, how many cultivate the poisonous plants, that kill out the precious fruits of love and defile the soul.

Only the love that flows from the heart of Christ can heal. Only He in whom that love flows, even as the sap in the tree or the blood in the body, can restore the wounded soul.

Love's agencies have wonderful power, for they are divine. The soft answer that "turneth away wrath," the love that "suffereth long, and is kind," the charity that "covereth a multitude of sins"—would we learn the lesson, with what power for healing would our lives be gifted! How life would be transformed, and the earth become a very likeness and foretaste of heaven!

HOW PLEASANT
ARE WORDS FITLY SPOKEN

A word fitly spoken is like apples of gold in pictures of silver. **Prov. 25:11.**

When at a feast, Christ controlled the conversation, and gave many precious lessons. Those present listened to Him; for had He not healed their sick, comforted their sorrowing, and taken their children in His arms? Publicans and sinners were drawn to Him; and when He spoke, their attention was riveted on Him.

Christ taught His disciples how to conduct themselves when in the company of others. He instructed them in regard to the duties and regulations of true social life, which are the same as the laws of the kingdom of God. He taught the disciples, by example, that when attending any public gathering, they need not want for something to say. His conversation when at a feast differed most decidedly from that which had been listened to at feasts in the past. Every word he uttered was a savor of life unto life. He spoke with clearness and simplicity. His words were as apples of gold in pictures of silver.

Communion with Christ—how unspeakably precious! Such communion it is our privilege to enjoy. . . . When the early disciples heard the words of Christ, they felt their need of Him. They sought, they found, they followed Him. They were with Him in the house, at the table, in the closet, in the field. They were with Him as pupils with a teacher, daily receiving from His lips lessons of holy truth. They looked to Him as servants to their master. . . . They served Him cheerfully, gladly.

Great importance is attached to our associations. We may form many that are pleasant and helpful, but none are so precious as that by which finite man is brought into connection with the infinite God. When thus united, the words of Christ abide in us. . . . The result will be a purified heart, a circumspect life, and a faultless character. But it is only by acquaintance and association with Christ that we can become like Him, the one faultless example.

51

JESUS AND HIS FRIENDS
AT BETHANY

Jesus loved Martha, and her sister, and Lazarus. **John 11:5.**

There was one home that He loved to visit—the home of Lazarus, and Mary, and Martha; for in the atmosphere of faith and love His spirit had rest.

Among the most steadfast of Christ's disciples was Lazarus of Bethany. From their first meeting his faith in Christ had been strong; his love for Him was deep, and he was greatly beloved by the Saviour. It was for Lazarus that the greatest of Christ's miracles was performed. The Saviour blessed all who sought His help; He loves all the human family; but to some He is bound by peculiarly tender associations. His heart was knit by a strong bond of affection to the family at Bethany, and for one of them His most wonderful work was wrought.

At the home of Lazarus, Jesus had often found rest. The Saviour had no home of His own; He was dependent on the hospitality of His friends and disciples; and often, when weary, thirsting for human fellowship, He had been glad to escape to this peaceful household, away from the suspicion and jealousy of the angry Pharisees. Here He found a sincere welcome, a pure, holy friendship. Here He could speak with simplicity and perfect freedom, knowing that His words would be understood and treasured.

Our Saviour appreciated a quiet home and interested listeners. He longed for human tenderness, courtesy, and affection. Those who received the heavenly instruction He was always ready to impart were greatly blessed. . . . The multitudes were slow of hearing, and in the home at Bethany Christ found rest from the weary conflict of public life. Here He opened to an appreciative audience the volume of Providence. In these private interviews He unfolded to His hearers that which He did not attempt to tell to the mixed multitude. He needed not to speak to His friends in parables.

GIVE OTHERS
THE WATER OF LIFE

Whosoever drinketh of the water that I shall give him shall never thirst; but the water that I shall give him shall be in him a well of water springing up into everlasting life. **John 4:14.**

In His talk with the Samaritan woman, instead of disparaging Jacob's well, Christ presented something better. . . . He turned the conversation to the treasure He had to bestow, offering the woman something better than she possessed, even living water, the joy and hope of the gospel.

How much interest Christ manifested in this one woman! How earnest and eloquent were His words! When the woman heard them, she left her waterpot and went into the city, saying to those she met, "Come, see a man, which told me all things that ever I did: is not this the Christ?" We read that many of the Samaritans of that city believed on Him. And who can estimate the influence that these words have exerted for the saving of souls in the years that have passed since then!

Jesus came in personal contact with men. He did not stand aloof and apart from those who needed His help. He entered the homes of men, comforted the mourner, healed the sick, aroused the careless, and went about doing good. And if we follow in the footsteps of Jesus, we must do as He did. We must give men the same kind of help that He did.

The Lord desires that His word of grace shall be brought home to every soul. To a great degree this must be accomplished by personal labor. This was Christ's method. His work was largely made up of personal interviews. He had a faithful regard for the one-soul audience. Through that one soul the message was often extended to thousands. . . . There are multitudes who will never be reached by the gospel unless it is carried to them.

REMEMBER ESPECIALLY NEEDY CHURCH MEMBERS

As we have therefore opportunity, let us do good unto all men, especially unto them who are of the household of faith. Gal. 6:10.

In a special sense Christ has laid upon His church the duty of caring for the needy among its own members. He suffers His poor to be in the borders of every church. They are always to be among us, and He places upon the members of the church a personal responsibility to care for them. As the members of a true family care for one another, ministering to the sick, supporting the weak, teaching the ignorant, training the inexperienced, so is the "household of faith" to care for its needy and helpless ones.

It is the duty of each church to make careful, judicious arrangements for the care of its poor and sick.

Any neglect on the part of those who claim to be followers of Christ, a failure to relieve the necessities of a brother or a sister who is bearing the yoke of poverty and oppression, is registered in the books of heaven as shown to Christ in the person of His saints. What a reckoning the Lord will have with many, very many, who present the words of Christ to others but fail to manifest tender sympathy and regard for a brother in the faith who is less fortunate and successful than themselves.

A true Christian is the poor man's friend. He deals with his perplexed and unfortunate brother as one would deal with a delicate, tender, sensitive plant. God wants His workers to move among the sick and suffering as messengers of His love and mercy. He is looking upon us, to see how we are treating one another, whether we are Christlike in our dealing with all, high or low, rich or poor, free or bond.

There is no question in regard to the Lord's poor. They are to be helped in every case where it will be for their benefit.

WHAT GOD LOVES MOST
IS A BEAUTIFUL CHARACTER

Let the beauty of the Lord our God be upon us. **Ps. 90:17.**

God is a lover of the beautiful, but that which He most loves is a beautiful character. . . . It is beauty of character that shall not perish, but last through the ceaseless ages of eternity.

The great Master-Artist has taken thought for the lilies, making them so beautiful that they outshine the glory of Solomon. How much more does He care for man, who is the image and glory of God. He longs to see His children reveal a character after His similitude. As the sunbeam imparts to the flowers their varied and delicate tints, so does God impart to the soul the beauty of His own character.

All who choose Christ's kingdom of love and righteousness and peace, making its interest paramount to all other, are linked to the world above, and every blessing needed for this life is theirs. In the book of God's providence, the volume of life, we are each given a page. That page contains every particular of our history; even the hairs of the head are numbered. God's children are never absent from His mind.

Worldly display, however imposing, is of no value in God's sight. Above the seen and temporal He values the unseen and eternal. The former is of worth only as it expresses the latter. The choicest productions of art possess no beauty that can compare with the beauty of character, which is the fruit of the Holy Spirit's working in the soul.

Christ came to the earth and stood before the children of men with the hoarded love of eternity, and this is the treasure that, through our connection with Him, we are to receive, to reveal, and to impart. . . .

We are to be distinguished from the world because God has placed His seal upon us, because He manifests in us His own character of love.

PARTAKERS THROUGH GOD'S PROMISES

Whereby are given unto us exceeding great and precious promises: that by these ye might be partakers of the divine nature, having escaped the corruption that is in the world through lust. **1 Peter 1:4.**

Every promise that is in God's book holds out to us the encouragement that we may be partakers of the divine nature. This is the possibility—to rely upon God, to believe His Word, to work His works, and this we can do when we lay hold of the divinity of Christ. This possibility is worth more to us than all the riches in the world. There is nothing on earth that can compare with it. As we lay hold of the power thus placed within our reach, we receive a hope so strong that we can rely wholly upon God's promise; and laying hold of the possibilities there are in Christ, we become the sons and daughters of God. . . .

He who truly believes in Christ is made partaker of the divine nature, and has power that he can appropriate under every temptation. He will not fall under temptation or be left to defeat. In time of trial he will claim the promises, and by these escape the corruptions that are in the world through lust. . . .

To make us partakers of the divine nature, heaven gave its most costly treasure. The Son of God laid aside His royal robe and kingly crown and came to our earth as a little child. He pledged Himself to live from infancy to manhood a perfect life. He engaged to stand in a fallen world as the representative of the Father. And He would die in behalf of a lost race. What a work was this! . . . I hardly know how to present these points; they are so wonderful, wonderful. . . .

By His life of sacrifice and death of shame He has made it possible for us to take hold of His divinity, and to escape the corruption that is in the world through lust. . . . If you are partakers of the divine nature, you will day by day be obtaining a fitting for that life that measures with the life of God. Day by day you will purify your trust in Jesus and follow His example and grow into His likeness until you shall stand before Him perfected.

REVERENCE FOR
THE HOUSE OF GOD

Ye shall keep my sabbaths, and reverence my sanctuary: I am the Lord. **Lev. 19:30.**

God is high and holy; and to the humble, believing soul, His house on earth, the place where His people meet for worship, is as the gate of heaven. The song of praise, the words spoken by Christ's ministers, are God's appointed agencies to prepare a people for the church above, for that loftier worship.

When the worshipers enter the place of meeting, they should do so with decorum, passing quietly to their seats. . . . Common talking, whispering, and laughing should not be permitted in the house of worship, either before or after the service. Ardent, active piety should characterize the worshipers.

If some have to wait a few minutes before the meeting begins, let them maintain a true spirit of devotion by silent meditation, keeping the heart uplifted to God in prayer that the service may be of special benefit to their own hearts and lead to the conviction and conversion of other souls. They should remember that heavenly messengers are in the house. We all lose much sweet communion with God by our restlessness, by not encouraging moments of reflection and prayer. . . .

Elevate the standard of Christianity in the minds of your children; help them to weave Jesus into their experience; teach them to have the highest reverence for the house of God and to understand that when they enter the Lord's house it should be with hearts that are softened and subdued by such thoughts as these: "God is here; this is His house. I must have pure thoughts and holiest motives. . . . This is the place where God meets with and blesses His people." . . .

Parents should not only teach, but command, their children to enter the sanctuary with sobriety and reverence.

Practice reverence until it becomes a part of yourself.

GOD CARES FOR ME

Fear thou not; for I am with thee: be not dismayed; for I am thy God: I will strengthen thee; yea, I will help thee; yea, I will uphold thee with the right hand of my righteousness. **Isa. 41:10.**

The Lord is in active communication with every part of His vast dominions. He is represented as bending toward the earth and its inhabitants. He is listening to every word that is uttered. He hears every groan; He listens to every prayer; He observes the movements of every one. . . .

God has always had a care for His people. . . . Christ taught His disciples that the amount of divine attention given to any object is proportionate to the rank assigned to it in the creation of God. He called their attention to the birds of the air. Not a sparrow, He said, falls to the ground without the notice of our heavenly Father. And if the little sparrow is regarded by Him, surely the souls of those for whom Christ has died are precious in His sight. The value of man, the estimate God places upon Him, is revealed in the cross of Calvary.

God's mercy and love for the fallen race have not ceased to accumulate, nor lost their earthward direction.

It is true that disappointments will come; tribulation we must expect; but we are to commit everything, great and small, to God. He does not become perplexed by the multiplicity of our grievances, nor overpowered by the weight of our burdens. His watchcare extends to every household, and encircles every individual; He is concerned in all our business and our sorrows. He marks every tear; He is touched with the feeling of our infirmities. All the afflictions and trials that befall us here are permitted, to work out His purposes of love toward us—"that we might be partakers of His holiness," and thus become participants in that fullness of joy which is found in His presence.

CHRIST MY ELDER BROTHER

Wherefore in all things it behoved him to be made like unto his brethren, that he might be a merciful and faithful high priest in things pertaining to God, to make reconciliation for the sins of the people. **Heb. 2:17.**

The Elder Brother of our race is by the eternal throne. He looks upon every soul who is turning his face toward Him as the Saviour. He knows by experience what are the weaknesses of humanity, what are our wants, and where lies the strength of our temptations. . . . He is watching over you, trembling child of God. Are you tempted? He will deliver. Are you weak? He will strengthen. Are you ignorant? He will enlighten. Are you wounded? He will heal. The Lord "telleth the number of the stars"; and yet "He healeth the broken in heart, and bindeth up their wounds."

Whatever your anxieties and trials, spread out your case before the Lord. Your spirit will be braced for endurance. The way will be open for you to disentangle yourself from embarrassment and difficulty. The weaker and more helpless you know yourself to be, the stronger will you become in His strength. The heavier your burdens, the more blessed the rest in casting them upon your Burden Bearer.

Circumstances may separate friends; the restless waters of the wide sea may roll between us and them. But no circumstances, no distance, can separate us from the Saviour. Wherever we may be, He is at our right hand, to support, maintain, uphold, and cheer. Greater than the love of a mother for her child is Christ's love for His redeemed. It is our privilege to rest in His love; to say, "I will trust Him; for He gave His life for me."

Human love may change, but Christ's love knows no change. When we cry to Him for help, His hand is stretched out to save.

He desires us to realize that He has returned to heaven as our Elder Brother and that the measureless power given Him has been placed at our disposal.

ANGELS ARE PREPARING ME FOR ETERNITY

Behold, I send an Angel before thee, to keep thee in the way, and to bring thee into the place which I have prepared. Ex. 23:20.

All heaven is engaged in the work of preparing a people to stand in the day of the Lord's preparation. The connection of heaven with earth seems very close. . . .

The heavenly intelligences are waiting with almost impatient earnestness to make Him known to the human agents, that they may be laborers together with these heavenly angels in presenting Jesus—the world's Redeemer, full of grace and truth. . . .

The first tear of penitence for sins creates joy among the heavenly angels in the courts of heaven. The heavenly messengers are ready to be on the wing to minister to the soul who is seeking Jesus. . . .

Grand and glorious things hath God prepared for those who love Him. Angels are looking forward with earnest expectation to the final triumph of the people of God, when seraphim and cherubim and the "ten thousand times ten thousand, and thousands of thousands" shall swell the anthems of the blessed and celebrate the triumphs of the mediatorial achievements in the recovery of man.

Jesus counted the cost of the salvation of every son and daughter of Adam. He provided abundant means that, if they would but comply with the conditions, none need perish, but might have everlasting life. . . . Every heavenly intelligence works as His agent to win man to God.

The angels of glory find their joy in . . . giving love and tireless watchcare to souls that are fallen and unholy. Heavenly beings woo the hearts of men; they bring to this dark world light from the courts above; by gentle and patient ministry they move upon the human spirit, to bring the lost into a fellowship with Christ which is even closer than they themselves can know.

IN CHRIST
THERE IS STRENGTH

Let him take hold of my strength, that he may make peace with me; and he shall make peace with me. **Isa. 27:5.**

The enemy cannot overcome the humble learner of Christ, the one who walks prayerfully before the Lord. Christ interposes Himself as a shelter, a retreat, from the assaults of the wicked one. The promise is given, "When the enemy shall come in like a flood, the Spirit of the Lord shall lift up a standard against him." . . .

Satan was permitted to tempt the too-confident Peter, as he had been permitted to tempt Job; but when that work was done he had to retire. Had Satan been suffered to have his way, there would have been no hope for Peter. He would have made complete shipwreck of faith. But the enemy dare not go one hairbreadth beyond his appointed sphere. There is no power in the whole satanic force that can disable the soul that trusts, in simple confidence, in the wisdom that comes from God.

Christ is our tower of strength, and Satan can have no power over the soul that walks with God in humility of mind. The promise, "Let him take hold of My strength, that he may make peace with Me; and he shall make peace with Me." In Christ there is perfect and complete help for every tempted soul. Dangers beset every path, but the whole universe of heaven is standing on guard, that none may be tempted above that which he is able to bear. Some have strong traits of character, that will need to be constantly repressed. If kept under the control of the Spirit of God, these traits will be a blessing; but if not, they will prove a curse. . . . If we will give ourselves unselfishly to the work, never swerving in the least from principle, the Lord will throw about us the everlasting arms, and will prove a mighty helper. If we will look to Jesus as the One in whom we may trust, He will never fail us in any emergency.

THE WILL
IS THE DECIDING POWER

Be not conformed to this world: but be ye transformed by the renewing of your mind, that ye may prove what is that good, and acceptable, and perfect, will of God. **Rom. 12:2.**

There is nothing that can keep you away from God but a rebellious will.

The will is the governing power in the nature of man. If the will is set right, all the rest of the being will come under its sway. The will is not the taste or the inclination, but it is the choice, the deciding power, the kingly power, which works in the children of men unto obedience to God or to disobedience.

You will be in constant peril until you understand the true force of the will. You may believe and promise all things, but your promises and your faith are of no account until you put your will on the right side. If you will fight the fight of faith with your will power, there is no doubt that you will conquer.

Your part is to put your will on the side of Christ. When you yield your will to His, He immediately takes possession of you, and works in you to will and to do of His good pleasure. Your nature is brought under the control of His Spirit. Even your thoughts are subject to Him. If you cannot control your impulses, your emotions, as you may desire, you can control the will, and thus an entire change will be wrought in your life. When you yield up your will to Christ, your life is hid with Christ in God. It is allied to the power which is above all principalities and powers. You have a strength from God that holds you fast to His strength; and a new life, even the life of faith, is possible to you.

You can never be successful in elevating yourself, unless your will is on the side of Christ, cooperating with the Spirit of God. Do not feel that you cannot; but say, "I can, I will." And God has pledged His Holy Spirit to help you in every decided effort.

February 27

MAKE YOUR CALLING
AND ELECTION SURE

Wherefore the rather, brethren, give diligence to make your calling and election sure: for if ye do these things, ye shall never fall: for so an entrance shall be ministered unto you abundantly into the everlasting kingdom of our Lord and Saviour Jesus Christ. **2 Peter 1:10, 11.**

Here a life insurance policy is offered us which insures for us eternal life in the kingdom of God. I ask you to study these words of the apostle Peter. There is understanding and intelligence in every sentence. By taking hold upon the Lifegiver, who gave His life for us, we receive eternal life.

We are each deciding our eternal destiny, and it rests wholly with us whether we shall gain eternal life. Will we live the lessons given in the Word of God, Christ's great lesson book? It is the grandest, and yet the most simply arranged and easily understood book ever prepared for giving an education in proper behaviour, in speech, in manners, in affection. It is the only book that will prepare human beings for the life that measures with the life of God. And those who make this Word their daily study are the only ones who are worthy of receiving a diploma entitling them to educate and train the children for entrance into the higher school, to be crowned as victorious overcomers.

Christ Jesus is the only judge of the fitness of human agents to receive eternal life. The gates of the holy city will open to those who have been humble, meek, lowly followers of His, having learned their lessons from Him, and received from Him their life insurance policy, forming characters after the divine similitude.

When the ransomed are redeemed from the earth, the city of God will be opened to you. . . . Then the harp will be placed in your hand, and your voice will be raised in songs of praise to God and to the Lamb, by whose great sacrifice you are made partakers of His nature and given an immortal inheritance in the kingdom of God.

CHRIST PRESENTS ME
WITH A CROWN AND HARP

Henceforth there is laid up for me a crown of righteousness, which the Lord, the righteous judge, shall give me at that day: and not to me only, but unto all them also that love his appearing. **2 Tim. 4:8.**

Before entering the city of God the Saviour bestows upon His followers the emblems of victory and invests them with the insignia of their royal state. The glittering ranks are drawn up in the form of a hollow square about their King, whose form rises in majesty high above saint and angel, whose countenance beams upon them full of benignant love. Throughout the unnumbered host of the redeemed every glance is fixed upon Him, every eye beholds His glory whose "visage was so marred more than any man, and His form more than the sons of men." Upon the heads of the overcomers Jesus with His own right hand places the crown of glory. For each there is a crown, bearing his own "new name," and the inscription, "Holiness to the Lord." In every hand are placed the victor's palm and the shining harp. Then, as the commanding angels strike the note, every hand sweeps the harp strings with skillful touch, awaking sweet music in rich, melodious strains. Rapture unutterable thrills every heart, and each voice is raised in grateful praise: "Unto Him that loved us, and washed us from our sins in His own blood, and hath made us kings and priests unto God and His Father; to Him be glory and dominion for ever and ever."

Oh, what joy unspeakable, to see Him whom we loved—to see Him in His glory who so loved us that He gave Himself for us—to behold those hands once pierced for our redemption stretched out to us in blessing and welcome!

Those who . . . place themselves in God's hands . . . will see the King in His beauty. They will behold His matchless charms, and touching their golden harps, they will fill all heaven with rich music and with songs to the Lamb.

PRIVILEGE OF
OPEN COMMUNION WITH GOD

I saw no temple therein: for the Lord God Almighty and the Lamb are the temple of it. **Rev. 21:22.**

The people of God are privileged to hold open communion with the Father and the Son. "Now we see through a glass, darkly." We behold the image of God reflected, as in a mirror, in the works of nature and in His dealings with men; but then we shall see Him face to face, without a dimming veil between. We shall stand in His presence and behold the glory of His countenance.

We may address Him by the endearing name, "Our Father," which is a sign of our affection for Him and a pledge of His tender regard and relationship to us. And the Son of God, beholding the heirs of grace, "is not ashamed to call them brethren." They have even a more sacred relationship to God than have the angels who have never fallen.

All the paternal love which has come down from generation to generation through the channel of human hearts, all the springs of tenderness which have opened in the souls of men, are but as a tiny rill to the boundless ocean when compared with the infinite, exhaustless love of God.

Heaven is a ceaseless approaching to God through Christ. The longer we are in the heaven of bliss, the more and still more of glory will be opened to us; and the more we know of God, the more intense will be our happiness.

And what is the happiness of heaven but to see God? What greater joy could come to the sinner saved by the grace of Christ than to look upon the face of God and know Him as Father?

How much comfort it gives to behold Him here by the eye of faith, that we may by beholding be made like Him, but what will it be to behold Him as He is, without one dimming veil between?

A TABLE SET BEFORE ME

Whoso eateth my flesh, and drinketh my blood, hath eternal life; and I will raise him up at the last day. For my flesh is meat indeed, and my blood is drink indeed. **John 6:54, 55.**

Eternal life is the receiving of the living elements in the Scriptures, the doing of the will of God. This is what is meant by eating the flesh and drinking the blood of the Son of God. It is the privilege of all to partake of the bread of heaven by studying the Word, and thus gain spiritual sinew and muscle.

Each one must appropriate the blessing to his own soul, or he will not be fed. . . . You know you would not be nourished by seeing a well-spread table, and by others eating. We would starve if we did not partake of physical nourishment, and we shall lose our spiritual strength and vitality if we do not feed on spiritual bread. . . .

The table has been spread, and Christ invites you to the feast. Shall we stand back, refusing His bounties, and declaring, "He does not mean this for me"? We used to sing a hymn that described a feast where a happy household gathered to partake of the bounties of the board at a kind father's invitation. While the happy children gathered at the table, there stood a hungry beggar child at the threshold. She was invited to come in; but sadly she turned away, exclaiming, "I have no father there." Will you take this position as Jesus invites you in? Oh! if you have a Father in the courts above, I entreat you to reveal the fact. He wants to make you a partaker of His rich bounties and blessings. All who come with the confiding love of a little child will find a Father there.

Come to the water of life, and drink. Do not stay away and complain of thirst. The water of life is free to all.

Those who eat and digest this Word, making it a part of every action and of every attribute of character, grow strong in the strength of God. It gives immortal vigor to the soul, perfecting the experience, and bringing joys that will abide forever.

PREPARING FOR
THE HOLY DAY

Remember the sabbath day, to keep it holy. **Ex. 20:8.**

At the very beginning of the fourth commandment the Lord said, "Remember." He knew that amid the multitude of cares and perplexities man would be tempted to excuse himself from meeting the full requirement of the law, or would forget its sacred importance. Therefore He said: "Remember the sabbath day, to keep it holy."

All through the week we are to have the Sabbath in mind and be making preparation to keep it according to the commandment. . . .

When the Sabbath is thus remembered, the temporal will not be allowed to encroach upon the spiritual. No duty pertaining to the six working days will be left for the Sabbath. During the week our energies will not be so exhausted in temporal labor that on the day when the Lord rested and was refreshed we shall be too weary to engage in His service. . . .

On Friday let the preparation for the Sabbath be completed. See that all the clothing is in readiness and that all the cooking is done. . . . The Sabbath is not to be given to the repairing of garments, to the cooking of food, to pleasure seeking, or to any other worldly employment. Before the setting of the sun let all secular work be laid aside and all secular papers be put out of sight. Parents, explain your work and its purpose to your children, and let them share in your preparation to keep the Sabbath according to the commandment.

There is another work that should receive attention on the preparation day. On this day all differences between brethren, whether in the family or in the church, should be put away. Let all bitterness and wrath and malice be expelled from the soul. In a humble spirit, "confess your faults one to another, and pray one for another."

Before the setting of the sun let the members of the family assemble to read God's Word, to sing and pray.

We should jealously guard the edges of the Sabbath. Remember that every moment is consecrated, holy time.

GOD'S GIFT
TO THE HUMAN RACE

For God so loved the world, that he gave his only begotten Son, that whosoever believeth in him should not perish, but have everlasting life. **John 3:16.**

The heart of God yearns over His earthly children with a love stronger than death. In giving up His Son, He has poured out to us all heaven in one gift.

Through that gift there comes to us day by day the unfailing flow of Jehovah's goodness. Every flower, with its delicate tints and sweet fragrance, is given for our enjoyment through that one Gift. The sun and moon were made by Him; there is not a star that beautifies the heavens which He did not make. There is not an article of food upon our tables that He has not provided for our sustenance. The superscription of Christ is upon it all. Everything is supplied to man through the one unspeakable Gift, the only-begotten son of God. He was nailed to the cross that all these bounties might flow to God's workmanship.

In taking our nature, the Saviour has bound Himself to humanity by a tie that is never to be broken. Through the eternal ages He is linked with us. "God so loved the world, that he gave his only begotten Son." He gave Him not only to bear our sins, and to die as our sacrifice; He gave Him to the fallen race. To assure us of His immutable counsel of peace, God gave His only-begotten Son to become one of the human family, forever to retain His human nature. This is the pledge that God will fulfill His word. "Unto *us* a child is born, unto *us* a son is given: and the government shall be upon his shoulder." Isa. 9:6. God has adopted human nature in the person of His Son, and has carried the same into the highest heaven. . . . Heaven is enshrined in humanity, and humanity is enfolded in the bosom of Infinite Love.

Christ bowed down in unparalleled humility, that in His exaltation to the throne of God, He might also exalt those who believe in Him, to a seat with Him upon His throne.

THE CREATOR INCARNATE

And without controversy great is the mystery of godliness: God was manifest in the flesh, justified in the Spirit, seen of angels, preached

unto the Gentiles, believed on in the world, received up into glory. 1 Tim. 3:16.

The incarnation of Christ is the mystery of all mysteries.

Christ was one with the Father, yet . . . He was willing to step down from the exaltation of one who was equal with God.

That He might accomplish His purpose of love for the fallen race, He became bone of our bone and flesh of our flesh.

How wide is the contrast between the divinity of Christ and the helpless infant in Bethlehem's manger! How can we span the distance between the mighty God and a helpless child? And yet the Creator of worlds, He in whom was the fullness of the Godhead bodily, was manifest in the helpless babe in the manger. Far higher than any of the angels, equal with the Father in dignity and glory, and yet wearing the garb of humanity! Divinity and humanity were mysteriously combined, and man and God became one.

It would have been an almost infinite humiliation for the Son of God to take man's nature, even when Adam stood in his innocence in Eden. But Jesus accepted humanity when the race had been weakened by four thousand years of sin. Like every child of Adam He accepted the results of the working of the great law of heredity. What these results were is shown in the history of His earthly ancestors. He came with such a heredity to share our sorrows and temptations, and to give us the example of a sinless life.

Those who claim that it was not possible for Christ to sin, cannot believe that He really took upon Himself human nature. But was not Christ actually tempted, not only by Satan in the wilderness, but all through His life, from childhood to manhood?

Our Saviour took humanity, with all its liabilities. He took the nature of man, with the possibility of yielding to temptation. We have nothing to bear which He has not endured.

THE SAVING PROVIDENCES OF GOD

And we know that all things work together for good to them that love God, to them who are the called according to his purpose. **Rom. 8:28.**

The fact that we are called upon to endure trial shows that the Lord Jesus sees in us something precious which He desires to develop. If He saw in us nothing whereby He might glorify His name, He would not spend time in refining us. He does not cast worthless stones into His furnace. It is valuable ore that He refines.

God never leads His children otherwise than they would choose to be led, if they could see the end from the beginning and discern the glory of the purpose which they are fulfilling as co-workers with Him.

All that has perplexed us in the providences of God will in the world to come be made plain. The things hard to be understood will then find explanation. The mysteries of grace will unfold before us. Where our finite minds discovered only confusion and broken promises, we shall see the most perfect and beautiful harmony. We shall know that infinite love ordered the experiences that seemed most trying.

He who is imbued with the Spirit of Christ abides in Christ. The blow that is aimed at him falls upon the Saviour, who surrounds him with His presence. Whatever comes to him comes from Christ. He has no need to resist evil, for Christ is his defense. Nothing can touch him except by our Lord's permission, and "all things" that are permitted "work together for good to them that love God."

Our heavenly Father has a thousand ways to provide for us of which we know nothing. Those who accept the one principle of making the service of God supreme, will find perplexities vanish and a plain path before their feet.

As a little child, trust to the guidance of Him who will "keep the feet of his saints. 1 Sam. 2:9.

As we commit our ways to Him, He will direct our steps.

A SAVIOUR
FROM ETERNITY

Blessed be the God and Father of our Lord Jesus Christ, who hath blessed us with all spiritual blessings in heavenly places in Christ: according as he hath chosen us in him before the foundation of the world, that we should be holy and without blame before him in love. **Eph. 1:3, 4.**

Since the Fall the Lord has wrought out His will in the plan of redemption, a plan by which He is seeking to restore man to his original perfection. Christ's death on the cross has made it possible for God to receive and pardon every repentant soul.

As the divine Sufferer hung upon the cross, angels gathered about Him, and as they looked upon Him, and heard His cry, they asked, with intense emotion, "Will not the Lord Jehovah save Him?" . . . Then were the words spoken: "The Lord hath sworn, and He will not repent. Father and Son are pledged to fulfill the terms of the everlasting covenant. God so loved the world, that He gave His only-begotten Son, that whosoever believeth in Him should not perish, but have everlasting life." Christ was not alone in making His great sacrifice. It was the fulfillment of the covenant made between Him and His Father before the foundation of the world was laid. With clasped hands they had entered into the solemn pledge that Christ would become the surety for the human race if they were overcome by Satan's sophistry.

The salvation of the human race has ever been the object of the councils of heaven. The covenant of mercy was made before the foundation of the world. It has existed from all eternity, and is called the everlasting covenant. So surely as there never was a time when God was not, so surely there never was a moment when it was not the delight of the eternal mind to manifest His grace to humanity.

The more we consider this subject, the greater depths we find, and yet there are depths that we do not reach as we study the Redeemer's glory. It is the glory of the Prince of life, and the mightiest powers of man cannot reach it. The angels themselves desire to look into this mysterious and wonderful theme, the redemption of the human race.

DOES FAITH
CANCEL OBEDIENCE?

Do we then make void the law through faith? God forbid: yea, we establish the law. **Rom. 3:31.**

Faith is not an opiate, but a stimulant. Looking to Calvary will not quiet your soul into nonperformance of duty, but will create faith that will work, purifying the soul from all selfishness.

The faith in Christ which saves the soul is not what it is represented to be my many. "Believe, believe," is their cry; "only believe in Christ, and you will be saved. It is all you have to do." While true faith trusts wholly in Christ for salvation, it will lead to perfect conformity to the law of God.

There are two errors against which the children of God—particularly those who have just come to trust in His grace—especially need to guard. The first . . . is that of looking to their own works, trusting to anything they can do, to bring themselves into harmony with God. He who is trying to become holy by his own works in keeping the law, is attempting an impossibility. . . . It is the grace of Christ alone, through faith, that can make us holy.

The opposite and no less dangerous error is that belief in Christ releases men from keeping the law of God; that since by faith alone we become partakers of the grace of Christ, our works have nothing to do with our redemption.

But notice here that obedience is not a mere outward compliance, but the service of love. The law of God is an expression of His very nature; it is an embodiment of the great principle of love, and hence is the foundation of His government in heaven and earth. . . . Instead of releasing man from obedience, it is faith, and faith only, that makes us partakers of the grace of Christ, which enables us to render obedience.

As Jesus was in human nature, so God means His followers to be. In His strength we are to live the life of purity and nobility which the Saviour lived.

THE SAVING POWER
OF JESUS

And he said unto me, My grace is sufficient for thee: for my strength is made perfect in weakness. Most gladly therefore will I rather glory in my infirmities, that the power of Christ may rest upon me. 2 Cor. 12:9.

Our precious Saviour has invited us to join ourselves to Him and unite our weakness with His strength, our ignorance with His wisdom, our unworthiness with His merit.

Rigid precision in obeying the law would entitle no man to enter the kingdom of heaven.

There must be a new birth, a new mind through the operation of the Spirit of God, which purifies the life and ennobles the character. This connection with God fits man for the glorious kingdom of heaven. No human invention can ever find a remedy for the sinning soul.

There must be a power working from within, a new life from above, before men can be changed from sin to holiness. That power is Christ. His grace alone can quicken the lifeless faculties of the soul, and attract it to God, to holiness. . . . The idea that it is necessary only to develop the good that exists in man by nature, is a fatal deception. "The natural man receiveth not the things of the Spirit of God: for they are foolishness unto him: neither can he know them, because they are spiritually discerned." 1 Cor. 2:14. . . . Of Christ it is written, "In him was life; and the life was the light of men"—the only "name under heaven given among men, whereby we must be saved." John 1:4; Acts 4:12. . . .

Paul the apostle . . . longed for the purity, the righteousness, to which in himself he was powerless to attain, and he cried out, "O wretched man that I am! who shall deliver me from this body of death?" Rom. 7:24, margin. Such is the cry that has gone up from burdened hearts in all lands and in all ages. To all, there is but one answer, "Behold the Lamb of God, which taketh away the sin of the world." John 1:29.

PEACE
THROUGH THE CROSS

There is therefore now no condemnation to them which are in Christ Jesus, who walk not after the flesh, but after the Spirit. **Rom. 8:1.**

If sinners can be led to give one earnest look at the cross, if they can obtain a full view of the crucified Saviour, they will realize the depth of God's compassion and the sinfulness of sin.

As your conscience has been quickened by the Holy Spirit, you have seen something of the evil of sin, of its power, its guilt, its woe; and you look upon it with abhorrence. . . . You long to be forgiven, to be cleansed, to be set free. Harmony with God, likeness to Him—what can you do to obtain it?

It is peace that you need—Heaven's forgiveness and peace and love in the soul. Money cannot buy it, intellect cannot procure it, wisdom cannot attain to it; you can never hope, by your own efforts, to secure it. But God offers it to you as a gift, "without money and without price." Isa. 55:1. . . .

Go to Him, and ask that He will wash away your sins, and give you a new heart. Then believe that He does this *because He has promised.* . . . It is our privilege to go to Jesus and be cleansed, and to stand before the law without shame or remorse.

When at the foot of the cross the sinner looks up to the One who died to save him, he may rejoice with fullness of joy; for his sins are pardoned. Kneeling in faith at the cross, he has reached the highest place to which man can attain.

Thank God for the gift of His dear Son, and pray that He may not have died for you in vain. The Spirit invites you today. Come with your whole heart to Jesus, and you may claim His blessing.

As you read the promises, remember they are the expression of unutterable love and pity. . . . Yes, only believe that God is your helper. He wants to restore His moral image in man. As you draw near to Him with confession and repentance, He will draw near to you with mercy and forgiveness.

FILLED WITH
HIS RIGHTEOUSNESS

Blessed are they which do hunger and thirst after righteousness: for they shall be filled. Matt. 5:6.

Righteousness is holiness, likeness to God, and "God is love." 1 John 4:16. It is conformity to the law of God, for "all thy commandments are righteousness" (Ps. 119:172), and "love is the fulfilling of the law" (Rom. 13:10). Righteousness is love, and love is the light and the life of God. The righteousness of God is embodied in Christ. We receive righteousness by receiving Him.

Not by painful struggles or wearisome toil, not by gift or sacrifice, is righteousness obtained; but it is freely given to every soul who hungers and thirsts to receive it. "Ho, every one that thirsteth, come ye to the waters, and he that hath no money; come ye, buy, and eat; . . . without money and without price." Isa. 55:1. "Their righteousness is of me, saith the Lord," and, "This is his name whereby he shall be called, The Lord our righteousness." Isa. 54:17; Jer. 23:6.

No human agent can supply that which will satisfy the hunger and thirst of the soul. But Jesus says, . . . "I am the bread of life: he that cometh to me shall never hunger; and he that believeth on me shall never thirst." John 6:35. . . .

The more we know of God, the higher will be our ideal of character and the more earnest our longing to reflect His likeness. A divine element combines with the human when the soul reaches out after God and the longing heart can say, "My soul, wait thou only upon God; for my expectation is from him." Ps. 62:5. . . .

The continual cry of the heart is, "More of Thee," and ever the Spirit's answer is, "Much more." Rom. 5:9, 10. . . . It was the good pleasure of the Father that in Christ should "all the fulness dwell," and "in him ye are made full." Col. 1:19, RV; 2:10, RV

Christ is the great depository of justifying righteousness and sanctifying grace.

All may come to Him, and receive of His fullness.

THE JUST
SHALL LIVE BY FAITH

As ye have therefore received Christ Jesus the Lord, so walk ye in him. **Col. 2:6.**

Our growth in grace, our joy, our usefulness—all depend upon our union with Christ. It is by communion with Him, daily, hourly—by abiding in Him—that we are to grow in grace. He is not only the author, but the finisher of our faith. It is Christ first and last and always. He is to be with us, not only at the beginning and the end of our course, but at every step of the way. . . .

Do you ask, "How am I to abide in Christ?" In the same way as you received Him at first. "As ye have therefore received Christ Jesus the Lord, so walk ye in him." Col. 2:6. "The just shall live by faith." Heb. 10:38. You gave yourself to God, to be His wholly, to serve and obey Him, and you took Christ as your Saviour. You could not yourself atone for your sins or change your heart; but having given yourself to God, you believe that He for Christ's sake did all this for you. By *faith* you became Christ's, and by faith you are to grow up in Him—by giving and taking. You are to *give* all—your heart, your will, your service—give yourself to Him to obey all His requirements; and you must *take* all—Christ, the fullness of all blessing, to abide in your heart, to be your strength, your righteousness, your everlasting helper—to give you power to obey.

Consecrate yourself to God in the morning; make this your very first work. Let your prayer be, "Take me, O Lord, as wholly Thine. I lay all my plans at Thy feet. Use me today in Thy service. Abide with me, and let all my work be wrought in Thee." This is a daily matter. Each morning consecrate yourself to God for that day. Surrender all your plans to Him, to be carried out or given up as His providence shall indicate. Thus day by day you may be giving your life into the hands of God, and thus your life will be molded more and more after the life of Christ.

SINCERE CONFESSION
ESSENTIAL

If we confess our sins, he is faithful and just to forgive us our sins, and to cleanse us from all unrighteousness. **1 John 1:9.**

The apostle says, "Confess your faults one to another, and pray one for another, that ye may be healed.'' James 5:16. Confess your sins to God, who only can forgive them, and your faults to one another. If you have given offense to your friend or neighbor, you are to acknowledge your wrong, and it is his duty freely to forgive you. Then you are to seek the forgiveness of God, because the brother you have wounded is the property of God, and in injuring him you have sinned against his Creator. . . .

True confession is always of a specific character, and acknowledges particular sins. They may be of such a nature as to be brought before God only; they may be wrongs that should be confessed to individuals who have suffered injury through them; or they may be of a public character, and should then be as publicly confessed. But all confession should be definite and to the point, acknowledging the very sins of which you are guilty.

Many, many confessions should never be spoken in the hearing of mortals; for the result is that which the limited judgment of finite beings does not anticipate. . . . God will be better glorified if we confess the secret, inbred corruption of the heart to Jesus alone than if we open its recesses to finite, erring man, who cannot judge righteously unless his heart is constantly imbued with the Spirit of God. . . . Do not pour into human ears the story which God alone should hear.

The confession that is the outpouring of the inmost soul finds its way to the God of infinite pity.

Your sins may be as mountains before you; but if you humble your heart, and confess your sins, trusting in the merits of a crucified and risen Saviour, He will forgive, and will cleanse you from all unrighteousness. . . . Desire the fullness of the grace of Christ. Let your heart be filled with an intense longing for His righteousness.

A CHANGE
OF HEART NEEDED

Jesus answered and said unto him, Verily, verily, I say unto thee, Except a man be born again, he cannot see the kingdom of God. **John 3:3.**

Nicodemus held a high position of trust in the Jewish nation. . . . With others, he had been stirred by the teaching of Jesus. . . . The lessons that had fallen from the Saviour's lips had greatly impressed him, and he desired to learn more of these wonderful truths. . . .

Nicodemus had come to the Lord thinking to enter into a discussion with Him, but Jesus laid bare the foundation principles of truth. He said to Nicodemus, It is not theoretical knowledge you need so much as spiritual regeneration. You need not to have your curiosity satisfied, but to have a new heart. You must receive a new life from above before you can appreciate heavenly things.

The change of heart represented by the new birth can be brought about only by the effectual working of the Holy Spirit. . . . Pride and self-love resist the Spirit of God; every natural inclination of the soul opposes the change from self-importance and pride to the meekness and lowliness of Christ. But if we would travel in the pathway to eternal life, we must not listen to the whispering of self. In humility and contrition we must beseech our heavenly Father, "Create in me a clean heart, O God; and renew a right spirit within me." Ps. 51:10. As we receive divine light, and cooperate with the heavenly intelligences, we are "born again," freed from the defilement of sin by the power of Christ.

The mighty power of the Holy Spirit works an entire transformation in the character of the human agent, making him a new creature in Christ Jesus. . . . The words and actions express the love of the Saviour. There is no striving for the highest place. Self is renounced. The name of Jesus is written on all that is said and done.

Is not this, the renewal of man, the greatest miracle that can be performed? What cannot the human agent do who by faith takes hold of the divine power?

HOLINESS OF LIFE

Follow peace with all men, and holiness, without which no man shall see the Lord. **Heb. 12:14.**

No one who claims holiness is really holy. Those who are registered as holy in the books of heaven are not aware of the fact, and are the last ones to boast of their own goodness.

It is not a conclusive evidence that a man is a Christian because he manifests spiritual ecstasy under extraordinary circumstances. Holiness is not rapture: it is an entire surrender of the will to God; it is living by every word that proceeds from the mouth of God; it is doing the will of our heavenly Father; it is trusting God in trial, in darkness as well as in the light; it is walking by faith and not by sight; it is relying on God with unquestioning confidence, and resting in His love.

No one can be omnipotent, but all can cleanse themselves from filthiness of the flesh and spirit, perfecting holiness in the fear of the Lord. God requires every soul to be pure and holy. We have hereditary tendencies to wrong. This is a part of self that no one need carry about. It is a weakness of humanity to pet selfishness, because it is a natural trait of character. But unless all selfishness is put away, unless self is crucified, we can never be holy as God is holy. There is in humanity a tendency to suspicious imagining, which circumstances quicken into lively growth. If this trait is indulged, it spoils the character and ruins the soul.

God requires moral perfection in all. Those who have been given light and opportunities should, as God's stewards, aim for perfection, and never, never lower the standard of righteousness to accommodate inherited and cultivated tendencies to wrong. Christ took upon Him our human nature, and lived our life, to show us that we may be like Him. . . . We ought to be holy even as God is holy; and when we comprehend the full significance of this statement, and set our heart to do the work of God, to be holy as He is holy, we shall approach the standard set for each individual in Christ Jesus.

THE ARROW OF DEATH

O that they were wise, that they understood this, that they would consider their latter end! **Deut. 32:29.**

The Lord "doth not afflict willingly nor grieve the children of men." Lam. 3:33. "Like as a father pitieth his children, so the Lord pitieth them that fear him. For he knoweth our frame; he remembereth that we are dust." Ps. 103:13, 14. He knows our heart, for He reads every secret of the soul. . . . He knows the end from the beginning. Many will be laid away to sleep before the fiery ordeal of the time of trouble shall come upon our world. . . .

If Jesus, the world's Redeemer, prayed, "O my Father, if it be possible, let this cup pass from me," and added, "nevertheless not as I will, but as thou wilt" (Matt. 26:39), how very appropriate it is for finite mortals to make the same surrender to the wisdom and will of God.

We have but a brief lifetime here, and we know not how soon the arrow of death may strike our hearts. We know not how soon we may be called to give up the world and all its interests. Eternity stretches before us. The curtain is about to be lifted. But a few short years, and for everyone now numbered with the living the mandate will go forth: "He that is unjust, let him be unjust still: . . . and he that is righteous, let him be righteous still: and he that is holy, let him be holy still." Rev. 22:11.

Are we prepared? Have we become acquainted with God, the Governor of heaven, the Lawgiver, and with Jesus Christ whom He sent into the world as His representative? When our lifework is ended, shall we be able to say, as did Christ our example:

"I have glorified thee on the earth: I have finished the work which thou gavest me to do. . . . I have manifested thy name"? John 17:4-6.

The angels of God are seeking to attract us from ourselves and from earthly things. Let them not labor in vain.

SORROW WITH HOPE

But I would not have you to be ignorant, brethren, concerning them which are asleep, that ye sorrow not, even as others which have no hope. 1 Thess. 4:13.

To the afflicted ones I would say, be of good comfort in the hope of the resurrection morning. The waters of which you have been drinking are as bitter to your taste as were the waters of Marah to the children of Israel in the wilderness, but Jesus can make them so sweet with His love. . . .

God has provided a balm for every wound. There is a balm in Gilead, there is a Physician there. Will you not now as never before study the Scriptures? Seek the Lord for wisdom in every emergency. In every trial plead with Jesus to show you a way out of your troubles, then your eyes will be opened to behold the remedy and to apply to your case the healing promises that have been recorded in His Word. In this way the enemy will find no place to lead you into mourning and unbelief, but instead you will have faith and hope and courage in the Lord. The Holy Spirit will give you clear discernment that you may see and appropriate every blessing that will act as an antidote to grief, as a branch of healing to every draught of bitterness that is placed to your lips. Every draught of bitterness will be mingled with the love of Jesus, and in place of complaining of the bitterness, you will realize that Jesus' love and grace are so mingled with sorrow that it has been turned into subdued, holy, sanctified joy.

When Henry White, our eldest son, lay dying, he said, "A bed of pain is a precious place when we have the presence of Jesus." When we are obliged to drink of the bitter waters, turn away from the bitter to the precious and the bright. In trial grace can give the human soul assurance, and when we stand at the deathbed and see how the Christian can bear suffering and go through the valley of death, we gather strength . . . and we fail not, neither are we discouraged in leading souls to Jesus.

UTTERMOST SALVATION
FOR GOD'S CHILDREN

But this man, because he continueth ever, hath an unchangeable priesthood. Wherefore he is able also to save them to the uttermost that come unto God by him, seeing he ever liveth to make intercession for them. **Heb. 7:24, 25.**

Every provision has been made for our infirmities, every encouragement offered us to come to Christ.

Christ offered up His broken body to purchase back God's heritage, to give man another trial. . . . By His spotless life, His obedience, His death on the cross of Calvary, Christ interceded for the lost race. And now, not as a mere petitioner does the Captain of our salvation intercede for us, but as a Conqueror claiming His victory. His offering is complete, and as our Intercessor He executes His self-appointed work, holding before God the censer containing His own spotless merits and the prayers, confessions, and thanksgiving of His people. Perfumed with the fragrance of His righteousness, these ascend to God as a sweet savor. The offering is wholly acceptable, and pardon covers all transgression.

Christ has pledged Himself to be our substitute and surety, and He neglects no one. He who could not see human beings exposed to eternal ruin without pouring out His soul unto death in their behalf, will look with pity and compassion upon every soul who realizes that he cannot save himself.

He will look upon no trembling suppliant without raising him up. He who through His own atonement provided for man an infinite fund of moral power, will not fail to employ this power in our behalf. We may take our sins and sorrows to His feet; for He loves us. His every look and word invites our confidence. He will shape and mold our characters according to His own will.

In the whole satanic force there is not power to overcome one soul who in simple trust casts himself on Christ. "He giveth power to the faint; and to them that have no might he increaseth strength." Isa. 40:29.

THE BLOTTING OUT
OF SINS

He that overcometh, the same shall be clothed in white raiment; and I will not blot out his name out of the book of life, but I will confess his name before my Father, and before his angels. **Rev. 3:5.**

As the books of record are opened in the judgment, the lives of all who have believed on Jesus come in review before God. Beginning with those who first lived upon the earth, our Advocate presents the cases of each successive generation, and closes with the living. Every name is mentioned, every case closely investigated. Names are accepted, names rejected. When any have sins remaining upon the books of record, unrepented of and unforgiven, their names will be blotted out of the book of life, and the record of their good deeds will be erased from the book of God's remembrance. . . .

All who have truly repented of sin, and by faith claimed the blood of Christ as their atoning sacrifice, have had pardon entered against their names in the books of heaven; as they have become partakers of the righteousness of Christ, and their characters are found to be in harmony with the law of God, their sins will be blotted out, and they themselves will be accounted worthy of eternal life. . . .

The divine Intercessor presents the plea that all who have overcome through faith in His blood be forgiven their transgressions, that they be restored to their Eden home, and crowned as joint heirs with Himself to the "first dominion." . . .

While Jesus is pleading for the subjects of His grace, Satan accuses them before God as transgressors. . . .

Jesus does not excuse their sins, but shows their penitence and faith, and, claiming for them forgiveness, He lifts His wounded hands before the Father and the holy angels, saying, "I know them by name." . . . Their names stand enrolled in the book of life, and concerning them it is written, "They shall walk with me in white: for they are worthy." Rev. 3:4.

Christians may daily cultivate faith by contemplating the One who has undertaken their cause, their "merciful and faithful high priest."

SCHEMES OF SATAN

Be sober, be vigilant; because your adversary the devil, as a roaring lion, walketh about, seeking whom he may devour. **1 Peter 5:8.**

It is unsafe to trust to feelings or impressions; these are unreliable guides. God's law is the only correct standard of holiness. It is by this law that character is to be judged. If an inquirer after salvation were to ask, "What must I do to inherit eternal life?" the modern teachers of sanctification would answer, "Only believe that Jesus saves you." But when Christ was asked this question He said, "What is written in the law? how readest thou?" And when the questioner replied, "Thou shalt love the

Lord thy God with all they heart, . . . and thy neighbour as thyself," Jesus said, "Thou hast answered right: this do, and thou shalt live." Luke 10:26-28.

No value is attached to a mere profession of faith in Christ; only the love which is shown by works is counted genuine. Yet it is love alone which in the sight of Heaven makes any act of value. . . .

The hidden selfishness of men stands revealed in the books of heaven. . . . Sad is the record which angels bear to heaven. Intelligent beings, professed followers of Christ, are absorbed in the acquirement of worldly possessions or the enjoyment of earthly pleasures. Money, time, and strength are sacrificed for display and self-indulgence; but few are the moments devoted to prayer, to the searching of the Scriptures, to humiliation of soul and confession of sin.

Satan invents unnumbered schemes to occupy our minds, that they may not dwell upon the very work with which we ought to be best acquainted. The archdeceiver hates the great truths that bring to view an atoning sacrifice and an all-powerful Mediator. He knows that with him everything depends on his diverting minds from Jesus and His truth.

Those who would share the benefits of the Saviour's mediation should permit nothing to interfere with their duty to perfect holiness in the fear of God.

DEPOSITS IN
THE BANK OF HEAVEN

Pure religion and undefiled before God and the Father is this, To visit the fatherless and widows in their affliction, and to keep himself unspotted from the world. **James 1:27.**

The tender sympathies of our Saviour were aroused for fallen and suffering humanity. If you would be His followers, you must cultivate compassion and sympathy. . . . The widow, the orphan, the sick, and the dying will always need help. Here is an opportunity to proclaim the gospel—to hold up Jesus, the hope and consolation of all men. When the suffering body has been relieved, . . . the heart is opened, and you can pour in the heavenly balm.

A company of believers may be poor, uneducated, and unknown; yet in Christ they may do a work in the home, the neighborhood, the church, and even in "the regions beyond," whose results will be as far-reaching as eternity. It is because this work is neglected that so many young disciples never advance beyond the mere alphabet of Christian experience. The light which was glowing in their own hearts when Jesus spoke to them, "Thy sins be forgiven thee,'' they might have kept alive by helping those in need. The restless energy that is so often a source of danger to the young might be directed into channels through which it would flow out in streams of blessing.

The hours so often spent in amusement that refreshes neither body nor soul should be spent in . . . seeking to help someone who is in need.

Every opportunity to help a brother in need, or to aid the cause of God in the spread of the truth, is a pearl that you can send beforehand, and deposit in the bank of heaven for safe-keeping.

Love, courtesy, self-sacrifice—these are never lost. When God's chosen ones are changed from mortality to immortality, their words and deeds of goodness will be made manifest, and will be preserved through the eternal ages. . . . Through the merits of Christ's imputed righteousness, the fragrance of such words and deeds is forever preserved.

WHAT KIND
OF INHERITANCE?

And Manoah said, Now let thy words come to pass. How shall we order the child, and how shall we do unto him? **Judges 13:12.**

The words spoken to the wife of Manoah contain a truth that the mothers of today would do well to study.

The child will be affected for good or for evil by the habits of the mother. She must herself be controlled by principle, and must practice temperance and self-denial, if she would seek the welfare of her child.

If before the birth of her child she is unstable, if she is selfish, peevish, and exacting, the disposition of her child will bear the marks of her wrong course. . . . But if she unswervingly adheres to the right, if she is kind, gentle, and unselfish, she will give her child these traits of character.

And fathers as well as mothers are involved in this responsibility. Both parents transmit their own characteristics, mental and physical, their dispositions and appetites, to their children. . . . The inquiry of every father and mother should be, ''What shall we do unto the child that shall be born unto us?'' The effect of prenatal influences has been by many lightly regarded; but the instruction sent from heaven to those Hebrew parents . . . shows how the matter is looked upon by our Creator.

The mother who is a fit teacher for her children must, before their birth, form habits of self-denial and self-control; for she transmits to them her own qualities, her own strong or weak traits of character. The enemy of souls understands this matter much better than do many parents. He will bring temptations upon the mother, knowing that if she does not resist him, he can through her affect her child. The mother's only hope is in God. She may flee to Him for grace and strength. She will not seek help in vain. He will enable her to transmit to her offspring qualities that will help them to gain success in this life and to win eternal life.

DAY OF DAYS

And hallow my sabbaths; and they shall be a sign between me and you, that ye may know that I am the Lord your God. **Eze. 20:20.**

The Sabbath should be made so interesting to our families that its weekly return will be hailed with joy.

The Sabbath school and the meeting for worship occupy only a part of the Sabbath. The portion remaining to the family may be made the most sacred and precious season of all the Sabbath hours.

In the minds of the children the very thought of the Sabbath should be bound up with the beauty of natural things. . . . Happy the father and mother who can teach their children God's written word with illustrations from the open pages of the book of nature; who can gather under the green trees, in the fresh, pure air, to study the Word and to sing the praise of the Father above.

In pleasant weather let parents walk with their children in the fields and groves. Amid the beautiful things of nature tell them the reason for the institution of the Sabbath. Describe to them God's great work of creation. Tell them that when the earth came from His hand, it was holy and beautiful. Every flower, every shrub, every tree, answered the purpose of its Creator. . . . Show that it was sin which marred God's perfect work; that thorns and thistles, sorrow and pain and death, are all the result of disobedience to God. Bid them see how the earth, though marred with the curse of sin, still reveals God's goodness.

If we can cultivate within us a beauty of soul corresponding to the beauty of nature around us, there will be a blending of the divine and human agencies.

As the sun goes down, let the voice of prayer and the hymn of praise mark the close of the sacred hours and invite God's presence through the cares of the week of labor.

Thus parents can make the Sabbath, as it should be, the most joyful day of the week. They can lead their children to regard it as a delight, the day of days, the holy of the Lord, honorable.

A WELCOME TO
THE HEAVENLY HOME

Open ye the gates, that the righteous nation which keepeth the truth may enter in. **Isa. 26:2.**

The life on earth is the beginning of the life in heaven.

We are children of the heavenly King, members of the royal family, heirs of God, and joint heirs with Christ. The mansions Jesus has gone to prepare are to receive only those who are true, who are pure, who love and obey His words. . . . If we would enjoy eternal bliss, we must cultivate religion in the home. . . . Peace, harmony, affection, and happiness should be perseveringly cherished every day, until these precious things abide in the hearts of those who compose the family.

That which will make the character lovely in the home is that which will make it lovely in the heavenly mansions.

If we manifest the character of Christ here, keeping all the command-ments of God, we shall be cheered and blessed with glimpses of the pleasant home in the mansions Jesus has gone to prepare.

Let all that is beautiful in our earthly home remind us of the crystal river and green fields, the waving trees and the living fountains, the shining city and the white-robed singers, of our heavenly home—that world of beauty which no artist can picture, no mortal tongue describe.

There the loves and sympathies that God has planted in the soul will find truest and sweetest exercise. The pure communion with holy beings, the harmonious social life with the blessed angels and with the faithful ones of all ages, the sacred fellowship that binds together "the whole family in heaven and earth"—all are among the experiences of the hereafter. . . . With unutterable delight we shall enter into the joy and the wisdom of unfallen beings.

It is the privilege of parents to take their children with them to the gates of the city of God, saying, "I have tried to instruct my children to love the Lord, to do His will, and to glorify Him." To such the gate will be thrown open, and parents and children will enter in.

March 24

WHO SHALL RECEIVE
GOD'S SEAL?

And I saw another angel ascending from the east, having the seal of the living God: and he cried with a loud voice to the four angels, to whom it was given to hurt the earth and the sea, saying, Hurt not the earth, neither the sea, nor the trees, till we have sealed the servants of our God in their foreheads. **Rev. 7:2, 3.**

The seal of the living God will be placed upon those only who bear a likeness to Christ in character.

As wax takes the impression of the seal, so the soul is to take the impression of the Spirit of God and retain the image of Christ.

It is obedience to the principles of the commandments of God, that molds the character after the divine similitude.

The seal of God's law is found in the fourth commandment. This only, of all the ten, brings to view both the name and the title of the Lawgiver. It declares Him to be the Creator of the heavens and the earth, and thus shows His claim to reverence and worship above all others. Aside from this precept, there is nothing in the Decalogue to show by whose authority the law is given.

The Israelites placed over their doors a signature of blood, to show that they were God's property. So the children of God in this age will bear the signature God has appointed. They will place themselves in harmony with God's holy law. A mark is placed upon every one of God's people just as verily as a mark was placed over the doors of the Hebrew dwellings, to preserve the people from the general ruin. God declares, "I gave them my sabbaths, to be a sign between me and them, that they might know that I am the Lord that sanctify them." Eze. 20:12.

Just as soon as the people of God are sealed in their foreheads—it is not any seal or mark that can be seen, but a settling into the truth, both intellectually and spiritually, so they cannot be moved—just as soon as God's people are sealed and prepared for the shaking, it will come. Indeed, it has begun already; the judgments of God are now upon the land, . . . that we may know what is coming.

JESUS' EXAMPLE
IN HUMILITY

If I then, your Lord and Master, have washed your feet; ye also ought to wash one another's feet. For I have given you an example, that ye should do as I have done to you. **John 13:14, 15.**

There is in man a disposition to esteem himself more highly than his brother, to work for self, to seek the highest place; and often this results in evil surmisings and bitterness of spirit. The ordinance preceding the Lord's Supper is to clear away these misunderstandings, to bring man out of his selfishness, down from his stilts of self-exaltation, to the humility of heart that will lead him to serve his brother.

The ordinance of feet washing most forcibly illustrates the necessity of true humility. While the disciples were contending for the highest place, in the promised kingdom, Christ girded Himself, and performed the office of a servant by washing the feet of those who called Him Lord.

Reconciliation one with another is the work for which the ordinance of feet washing was instituted. . . . Whenever it is celebrated, Christ is present by His Holy Spirit. It is this Spirit that brings conviction to hearts.

As Christ celebrated this ordinance with His disciples, conviction came to the hearts of all save Judas. So we shall be convicted as Christ speaks to our hearts. The fountains of the soul will be broken up. The mind will be energized, and, springing into activity and life, will break down every barrier that has caused disunion and alienation. Sins that have been committed will appear with more distinctness than ever before; for the Holy Spirit will bring them to our remembrance.

Having washed the disciples' feet, He [Jesus] said, ''I have given you an example, that ye should do as I have done to you.'' . . . Christ was here instituting a religious service. By the act of our Lord this humiliating ceremony was made a consecrated ordinance. It was to be observed by the disciples, that they might ever keep in mind His lessons of humility and service.

BUILDERS, NOT DESTROYERS

And they that shall be of thee shall build the old waste places: thou shalt raise up the foundations of many generations; and thou shalt be called, The repairer of the breach, The restorer of paths to dwell in. **Isa. 58:12.**

Has God no living church? He has a church, but it is the church militant, not the church triumphant. We are sorry that there are defective members. . . . While the Lord brings into the church those who are truly converted, Satan at the same time brings persons who are not converted into its fellowship. While Christ is sowing the good seed, Satan is sowing the tares. There are two opposing influences continually exerted on the members of the church. One influence is working for the purification of the church, and the other for the corrupting of the people of God. . . .

Although there are evils existing in the church, and will be until the end of the world, the church in these last days is to be the light of the world that is polluted and demoralized by sin. . . .

There is but one church in the world who are at the present time standing in the breach, and making up the hedge, building up the old waste places; and for any man to call the attention of the world and other churches to this church, denouncing her as Babylon, is to do a work in harmony with him who is the accuser of the brethren. . . . The whole world is filled with hatred of those who proclaim the binding claims of the law of God, and the church who are loyal to Jehovah must engage in no ordinary conflict. . . . Those who have any realization of what this warfare means, will not turn their weapons against the church militant, but with all their powers will wrestle with the people of God against the confederacy of evil.

Those who start up to proclaim a message on their own individual responsibility, who, while claiming to be taught and led of God, still make it their special work to tear down that which God has been for years building up, are not doing the will of God. Be it known that these men are on the side of the great deceiver. Believe them not.

The Faith I Live By   March 27

TEARS AND CONFLICT

Serving the Lord with all humility of mind, and with many tears, and temptations, which befell me by the lying in wait of the Jews. **Acts. 20:19.**

From the days of Adam to our own time, our great enemy has been exercising his power to oppress and destroy. He is now preparing for his last campaign against the church.

The better to disguise his real character and purposes, he has caused himself to be so represented as to excite no stronger emotion than ridicule or contempt. He is well pleased to be painted as a ludicrous or loathsome object, misshapen, half animal and half human.

If Satan was so cunning at first, what must he be now, after gaining an experience of many thousands of years? Yet God and holy angels, and all those who abide in obedience to all the Lord's will, are wiser than he.

All who are actively engaged in the cause of God, seeking to unveil the deceptions of the evil one and to present Christ before the people, will be able to join in the testimony of Paul, in which he speaks of serving the Lord with all humility of mind, with many tears and temptations. . . .

The tempter has no power to control the will or to force the soul to sin. He may distress, but he cannot contaminate. He can cause agony, but not defilement.

Satan cannot read our thoughts, but he can see our actions, hear our words; and from his long knowledge of the human family, he can shape his temptations to take advantage of our weak points of character. And how often do we let him into the secret of how he may obtain the victory over us. Oh, that we might control our words and actions!

Satan assailed Christ with his fiercest and most subtle temptations; but he was repulsed in every conflict. Those battles were fought in our behalf; those victories make it possible for us to conquer. Christ will give strength to all who seek it.

SAFETY ONLY
IN OBEDIENCE

For the eyes of the Lord are over the righteous, and his ears are open unto their prayers: but the face of the Lord is against them that do evil. **1 Peter 3:12.**

No man is safe for a day or an hour without prayer. Especially should we entreat the Lord for wisdom to understand His Word. Here are revealed the wiles of the tempter, and the means by which he may be successfully resisted. Satan is an expert in quoting Scripture, placing his own interpretation upon passages, by which he hopes to cause us to stumble. We should study the Bible with humility of heart, never losing sight of our dependence upon God. While we must constantly guard against the devices of Satan, we should pray in faith continually, "Lead us not into temptation."

When Balaam, allured by the promise of rich rewards, practiced enchantments against Israel, and by sacrifices to the Lord sought to invoke a curse upon His people, the Spirit of God forbade the evil which he longed to pronounce, and Balaam was forced to exclaim: "How shall I curse, whom God hath not cursed?" Num. 23:8. . . .

The people of Israel were at this time loyal to God; and so long as they continued in obedience to His law, no power in earth or hell could prevail against them. But the curse which Balaam had not been permitted to pronounce against God's people, he finally succeeded in bringing upon them by seducing them into sin. When they transgressed God's commandments, then they separated themselves from Him, and they were left to feel the power of the destroyer.

Satan is well aware that the weakest soul who abides in Christ is more than a match for the hosts of darkness. . . . Only in humble reliance upon God, and obedience to all His commandments, can we be secure.

Let none deceive themselves with the belief that God will pardon and bless them while they are trampling upon one of His requirements. The willful commission of a known sin silences the witnessing voice of the Spirit, and separates the soul from God.

A CROWN
FOR EVERY SAINT

Blessed is the man that endureth temptation: for when he is tried, he shall receive the crown of life, which the Lord hath promised to them that love him. **James 1:12.**

I saw a very great number of angels bring from the city glorious crowns—a crown for every saint, with his name written thereon. As Jesus called for the crowns, angels presented them to Him, and with His own right hand the lovely Jesus placed the crowns on the heads of the saints. In the same manner the angels brought the harps, and Jesus presented them also to the saints. The commanding angels first struck the note, and then every voice was raised in grateful, happy praise, and every hand skillfully swept over the strings of the harp, sending forth melodious music in rich and perfect strains. . . .

Within the city there was everything to feast the eye. Rich glory they beheld everywhere. Then Jesus looked upon His redeemed saints; their countenances were radiant with glory; and as He fixed His loving eyes upon them, He said, with His rich, musical voice, "I behold the travail of My soul, and am satisfied. This rich glory is yours to enjoy eternally. Your sorrows are ended. There shall be no more death, neither sorrow nor crying, neither shall there by any more pain." . . .

I then saw Jesus leading His people to the tree of life. . . . Upon the tree of life was most beautiful fruit, of which the saints could partake freely, in the city was a most glorious throne, from which proceeded a pure river of water of life, clear as crystal. On each side of this river was the tree of life, and on the banks of the river were other beautiful trees bearing fruit. . . .

Language is altogether too feeble to attempt a description of heaven. As the scene rises before me, I am lost in amazement. Carried away with the surpassing splendor and excellent glory, I lay down the pen, and exclaim, "Oh, what love! what wondrous love!" The most exalted language fails to describe the glory of heaven or the matchless depths of a Saviour's love.

THE ETERNAL WEIGHT
OF GLORY

For our light affliction, which is but for a moment, worketh for us a far more exceeding and eternal weight of glory. **2 Cor. 4:17.**

I was pointed to the glory of heaven, to the treasure laid up for the faithful. Everything was lovely and glorious. The angels would sing a lovely song, then they would cease singing and take their crowns from their heads and cast them glittering at the feet of the lovely Jesus, and with melodious voices cry, "Glory, Alleluia!" I joined with them in their songs of praise and honor to the Lamb, and every time I opened my mouth to praise Him, I felt an unutterable sense of the glory that surrounded me. It was a far more, an exceeding and eternal weight of glory. Said the angel, "The little remnant who love God and keep His commandments and are faithful to the end will enjoy this glory and ever be in the presence of Jesus and sing with the holy angels."

Then my eyes were taken from the glory, and I was pointed to the remnant on the earth. The angel said to them, ". . . Get ready, get ready, get ready. Ye must have a greater preparation than ye now have, for the day of the Lord cometh, cruel both with wrath and fierce anger, to lay the land desolate and to destroy the sinners thereof out of it. Sacrifice all to God. Lay all upon His altar—self, property, and all, a living sacrifice. It will take all to enter glory. Lay up for yourselves treasure in heaven, where no thief can approach or rust corrupt. Ye must be partakers of Christ's sufferings here if ye would be partakers with Him of His glory hereafter."

Heaven will be cheap enough, if we obtain it through suffering. We must deny self all along the way, die to self daily, let Jesus alone appear, and keep His glory continually in view.

The work of salvation is not child's play, to be taken hold of at will and let alone at pleasure. It is the steady purpose, the untiring effort, that will gain the victory at last. It is he who endureth to the end that shall be saved. It is they who patiently continue in well-doing that shall have eternal life and the immortal reward.

NO MORE DEATH—EVER!

And God shall wipe away all tears from their eyes; and there shall be no more death, neither sorrow, nor crying, neither shall there be any more pain; for the former things are passed away. **Rev. 21:4.**

In the home of the redeemed there will be no tears, no funeral trains, no badges of mourning. "The inhabitant shall not say, I am sick: the people that dwell therein shall be forgiven their iniquity." Isa. 33:24. One rich tide of happiness will flow and deepen as eternity rolls on. . . .

Let us consider most earnestly the blessed hereafter. Let our faith pierce through every cloud of darkness and behold Him who died for the sins of the world. He has opened the gates of Paradise to all who receive and believe on Him. . . . Let the afflictions which pain us so grievously become instructive lessons, teaching us to press forward toward the mark of the prize of our high calling in Christ. Let us be encouraged by the thought that the Lord is soon to come. Let this hope gladden our hearts. . . .

We are homeward bound. He who loved us so much as to die for us hath builded for us a city. The New Jerusalem is our place of rest. There will be no sadness in the city of God. No wail of sorrow, no dirge of crushed hopes and buried affections, will evermore be heard. Soon the garments of heaviness will be changed for the wedding garment. Soon we shall witness the coronation of our King. Those whose lives have been hidden with Christ, those who on this earth have fought the good fight of faith, will shine forth with the Redeemer's glory in the kingdom of God.

It will not be long till we shall see Him in whom our hopes of eternal life are centered. And in His presence, all the trials and sufferings of this life will be as nothingness. . . . Look up, look up, and let your faith continually increase. Let this faith guide you along the narrow path that leads through the gates of the city of God into the great beyond, the wide, unbounded future of glory that is for the redeemed.

COMPASSED WITH GOD'S MERCY

Many sorrows shall be to the wicked: but he that trusteth in the Lord, mercy shall compass him about. **Ps. 32:10.**

We often think that those who serve God have more trials than the unbeliever, and that the path marked out for them to travel in is rugged. . . . But does the sinner enjoy his worldly pleasure and enjoyment unalloyed? Oh, no. There are times when the sinner is fearfully troubled. He fears God but does not love Him.

Are the wicked free from disappointment, perplexity, earthly losses, poverty, and distress? Many of them suffer a lingering sickness, yet have no strong and mighty One to lean upon, no strengthening grace from a higher power to support them in their weakness. They lean upon their own strength. They obtain no consolation by looking forward to the future, but a fearful uncertainty torments them; and thus they close their eyes in death, not finding any pleasure in looking forward to the resurrection morn, for they have no cheering hope that they shall have part in the first resurrection. . . .

The Christian is subject to sickness, disappointment, poverty, reproach, and distress. Yet amid all this he loves God, he chooses to do His will, and prizes nothing so highly as His approbation. In the conflicting trials and changing scenes of this life, he knows that there is One who knows it all, One who will bend His ear low to the cry of the sorrowful and distressed, One who can sympathize with every sorrow and soothe the keen anguish of every heart. . . .

Amid all his affliction, the Christian has strong consolation. And if God permits him to suffer a lingering, distressing sickness before he closes his eyes in death, he can with cheerfulness bear it all. . . . He contemplates the future with heavenly satisfaction. A short rest in the grave, and then the Life-giver will break the fetters of the tomb, release the captive, and bring him from his dusty bed immortal, never more to know pain, sorrow, or death. Oh, what a hope is the Christian's! Let this hope of the Christian be mine. Let it be yours.

HOPE FOR THE HOPELESS

Let the wicked forsake his way, and the unrighteous man his thoughts: and let him return unto the Lord, and he will have mercy upon him; and to our God, for he will abundantly pardon. For my thoughts are not your thoughts, neither are your ways my ways, saith the Lord. **Isa. 55:7, 8.**

It is your thought that your mistakes and transgressions have been so grievous that the Lord will not have respect unto your prayers, and will bless and save you. . . . The closer you come to Jesus, the more faulty you will appear in your own eyes; for your vision will be clearer, and your imperfections will be seen in broad and distinct contrast to His perfect nature. But do not be discouraged. This is evidence that Satan's delusions have lost their power; that the vivifying influence of the Spirit of God is arousing you, and your indifference and unconcern are passing away.

No deep-seated love for Jesus can dwell in the heart that does not see and realize its own sinfulness. The soul that is transformed by grace will admire His divine character; but if we do not see our own moral deformity, it is unmistakable evidence that we have not had a view of the beauty and excellence of Christ. The less we see to esteem in ourselves, the more we shall see to esteem in the infinite purity and loveliness of our Saviour. A view of our own sinfulness drives us to Him who can pardon. . . .

God does not deal with us as finite men deal with one another. His thoughts are thoughts of mercy, love, and tenderest compassion. "He will abundantly pardon." He says, "I have blotted out, as a thick cloud, thy transgressions." . . .

Look up, you who are tried, tempted, and discouraged, look up. . . . It is ever safe to look up; it is fatal to look down. If you look down, the earth reels and sways beneath you; nothing is sure. But heaven above you is calm and steady, and there is divine aid for every climber. The hand of the Infinite is reaching over the battlements of heaven to grasp yours in its strong embrace. The mighty Helper is nigh to bless, lift up, and encourage the most erring, the most sinful, if they will look to Him by faith. But the sinner must look up.

ENJOYMENT OF THE TRUTH

Teach me thy way, O Lord; I will walk in thy truth: unite my heart to fear thy name. **Ps. 86:11.**

Say with your whole heart, "I will walk in Thy truth." Every resolution expressed in the fear of God will give strength to purpose and to faith. It will tend to stimulate and to humble, to strengthen and confirm. "I will walk in thy truth." Truth deserves our confidence none the less because the world is flooded with fables. Because error and counterfeit are in circulation it only evidences the fact that there is truth, genuine truth, somewhere. . . .

It is not enough for us to hear the truth only. God requires of us obedience. "Blessed are they that hear the word of God, and keep it." Luke 11:28. "If ye know these things, happy are ye if ye do them." John 13:17.

We may walk in the enjoyment of the truth. It need not be to us a yoke of bondage, but a consolation, a message to us of glad tidings of great joy, animating our hearts and causing us to make melody in our hearts unto God. Through patience and comfort of the Scriptures we have hope. The Christian hope is not gloomy, comfortless. Oh, no, no. It does not shut us up in a prison of doubts and fears. The truth makes free those who love and are sanctified through it. They walk in the glorious liberty of the sons of God.

We who claim to believe the truth should reveal its fruits in our words and character. We are to be far advanced in a knowledge of Jesus Christ, in the reception of His love for God and for our neighbor, in order to have the sunlight of heaven shining in our daily life. Truth must reach down to the deepest recesses of the soul, and cleanse away everything unlike the spirit of Christ, and the vacuum be supplied by the attributes of His character who was pure and holy and undefiled, that all the springs of the heart may be as flowers, fragrant with perfume, a sweet-smelling savor, a savor of life unto life.

It is truth enshrined in the soul that makes one a man of God.

LET JESUS LEAD

Jesus saith unto him I am the way, the truth, and the life: no man cometh unto the Father, but by me. **John 14:6.**

Oh, that we who are pilgrims and strangers in this foreign country . . . might comprehend Christ, the way, the truth, and the life. He says, ''No man cometh unto the Father, but by me.'' The path He has marked out is so plain and distinct that the veriest sinner, loaded with guilt, need not miss his way. Not one trembling seeker need fail of finding the true path, and of walking in pure and holy light, for Jesus leads the way.

The path is so narrow, so holy, that sin cannot be tolerated therein, yet access to the path has been made for all, and not one desponding, doubting, trembling soul needs to say, ''God cares nought for me.'' Every soul is precious in His sight. . . . When Satan was triumphing as the prince of the world, when he claimed the world as his kingdom, when we were all marred and corrupted with sin, God sent His messenger from heaven, even His only begotten Son, to proclaim to all the inhabitants of the world, ''I have found a ransom. I have made a way of escape for all the perishing. I have your emancipation papers provided for you, sealed by the Lord of heaven and earth.'' . . .

It is not because there is any flaw in the title which has been purchased for you that you do not accept it. It is not because the mercy, the grace, the love of the Father and the Son is not ample, and has not been freely bestowed, that you do not rejoice in pardoning love. . . . If you are lost, it will be because you will not come unto Christ that you might have life.

God waits to bestow the blessing of forgiveness of sins, of pardon for iniquity, of the gift of righteousness upon all who will believe in His love, and accept of His salvation. Christ is ready to say to the repenting sinner, ''. . . Behold, I have caused thine iniquity to pass from thee. . . .'' Zech. 3:4-7. Christ is the connecting link between God and man. The blood of Jesus Christ is the eloquent plea that speaks in behalf of sinners.

IN LOVE WITH CHRIST

For such an high priest became us, who is holy, harmless, undefiled, separate from sinners, and made higher than the heavens. **Heb. 7:26.**

The character of Christ was one of unexampled excellence, embracing everything pure, true, lovely, and of good report. We have no knowledge of His ever visiting a party of pleasure or a dance hall, and yet He was the perfection of grace and courtly bearing. Christ was no novice; He was distinguished for the high intellectual powers He possessed even in the morning of His life. His youth was not wasted in indolence, neither was it wasted in sensual pleasure, self-indulgence, or frittered away in things of no profit. Not one of His hours from childhood to manhood was misspent, none was misappropriated. . . .

Jesus was sinless and had no dread of the consequences of sin. With this exception His condition was as yours. You have not a difficulty that did not press with equal weight upon Him, not a sorrow that His heart has not experienced. His feelings could be hurt with neglect, with indifference of professed friends, as easily as yours. Is your path thorny? Christ's was so in a tenfold sense. Are you distressed? So was He. How well fitted was Christ to be an example! . . .

The Inspired Record says of Him: "Jesus increased in wisdom and stature, and in favour with God and man." Luke 2:52. As He grew in years He grew in knowledge. He lived temperately; His precious hours were not wasted in dissipating pleasures. He had a truly healthy body and true powers of mind. The physical and mental powers could be expanded and developed as yours or any other youth's. The Word of God was His study, as it should be yours.

Take Jesus as your standard. Imitate His life. Fall in love with His character. Walk as Christ walked. A new spring will be given to your intellectual faculties, a larger scope to your thoughts, when you bring your powers into vigorous contact with eternal things which are intrinsically grand and great.

THE PRIVILEGE OF ASSURANCE

And hereby we know that we are of the truth, and shall assure our hearts before him. **1 John 3:19.**

I would impress upon our young men and young women the necessity of making their calling and election sure. I would beseech you to do no haphazard or uncertain work where your eternal interests are involved. By so doing you lose happiness, peace, comfort, and hope in this life, and you lose also your immortal inheritance.

My young friends, you are judgment bound, and through the grace of Christ you may render obedience to the commands of God, and daily gain fortitude and strength of character, so that you need not fail or be discouraged. Divine grace has been abundantly provided for every soul, so that each one may engage in the conflict and come off victorious. Do not become sluggish; do not flatter yourselves that you may be saved in walking in accordance with the natural traits of your character—that you may drift with the current of the world, and indulge and please self, and yet be able to withstand the forces of evil in a time of crisis, and come off victorious when the battle waxes hot. . . . You must learn every day to obey the orders of the Captain of the Lord's host.

My young friends, do you pray? Are you educating yourselves to offer petitions for pure thoughts, for holy aspirations, for a pure heart and clean hands? Are you educating your lips to sing the praises of God, and are you seeking to do the will of God? This is the kind of education that will be of the greatest value to you; for it will aid you in the formation of Christlike character.

Do not settle down in Satan's easy chair, and say that there is no use, you cannot cease to sin, that there is no power in you to overcome. There is no power in you apart from Christ, but it is your privilege to have Christ abiding in your heart by faith, and He can overcome sin in you, when you cooperate with His efforts. . . . You may be living epistles, known and read of all men. You are not to be a dead letter, but a living one, testifying to the world that Jesus is able to save.

GOD CALLS FOR
OUR BEST AFFECTIONS

No man can serve two masters: for either he will hate the one, and love the other; or else he will hold to the one, and despise the other. Ye cannot serve God and mammon. Matt. 6:24.

Many are on the enchanted ground of the enemy. Things of the least importance—foolish social parties, singing, jesting, joking—engross their minds and they serve God with a divided heart. . . . The declaration of Christ, "No man can serve two masters," is unheeded.

One of the most marked features of the earth's inhabitants in the days of Noah was their intense worldliness. They made eating and drinking, buying and selling, marrying and giving in marriage, the supreme objects of life. It is not sinful, but the fulfillment of a duty, to eat and drink, if that which is lawful is not carried to excess. . . . God Himself instituted marriage when He gave Eve to Adam. All God's laws are marvelously adapted to meet the nature of man. The sin of the antediluvians was in perverting that which in itself was lawful. They corrupted God's gifts by using them to minister to their selfish desires. . . .

Excessive love and devotion to that which in itself is lawful, proves the ruination of thousands upon thousands of souls. To matters of minor importance is often given the strength of intellect that should be wholly devoted to God. We need always to be guarded against carrying to excess that which, rightly used, is lawful. Many, many souls are lost by engaging in those things which, properly managed, are harmless, but which, perverted and misapplied, become sinful and demoralizing.

If we are constantly thinking of and struggling for the things that pertain to this life, we cannot keep our thoughts fixed on the things of heaven. Satan is seeking to lead our minds away from God, and to center them on the fashions, the customs, and the demands of the world, which bring disease and death. . . .

In this world we are to obtain a fitness for the higher world. God has left a trust with us, and He expects us to use all our faculties in helping and blessing our fellow men. He calls for our best affections, our highest powers.

ABOVE THE FOG
OF DOUBT

Be of good courage, and he shall strengthen your heart, all ye that hope in the Lord. **Ps. 31:24.**

Even Christians of long experience are often assaulted with the most terrible doubts and waverings. . . . You must not consider that for these temptations your case is hopeless. . . . Hope in God, trust in Him and rest in His promises.

When the devil comes with his doubts and unbeliefs, shut the door of your heart. Shut your eyes so that you will not dwell upon his hellish shadow. Lift them up where they can behold the things which are eternal, and you will have strength every hour. The trial of your faith is much more precious than gold. . . . It makes you valiant to fight the battle of the Lord. . . .

Satan connects with everyone that will connect with him. If he can get those that have had an experience in religion, they are his most effectual agents to reach just such men and compass their souls with unbelief. You cannot afford to let any doubts come into your mind. Do not please the devil enough to tell about the terrible burdens you are carrying. Every time you do it, Satan laughs that his soul can control you and that you have lost sight of Jesus Christ your Redeemer. . . .

We are to show forth Him who hath called us out of darkness into His marvelous light. It is by living faith that we rest in that light. It is by living faith that we rejoice in that light every day. We are not to talk our doubts and trials, because they grow bigger every time we talk them. Every time we talk them, Satan has gained the victory; but when we say, "I will commit the keeping of my soul unto Him, as unto a faithful witness," then we testify that we have given ourselves to Jesus Christ without any reservation, and then God gives us light and we rejoice in Him.

The soul that loves God, rises above the fog of doubt; he gains a bright, broad, deep, living experience, and becomes meek and Christlike. His soul is committed to God, hid with Christ in God.

HOW TO MAINTAIN INTEGRITY!

Likewise reckon ye also yourselves to be dead indeed unto sin, but alive unto God through Jesus Christ our Lord. Let not sin therefore reign in your mortal body, that ye should obey it in the lusts thereof. **Rom. 6:11, 12.**

Some regard sin as altogether so light a matter that they have no defense against its indulgence or its consequence. . . .

If you suppose for a moment that God will treat sin lightly, or make provisions or exemptions so that you can go on in committing sin, and the soul suffer no penalty from so doing, you are under a terrible delusion of Satan. Any willful violation of the righteous law of Jehovah exposes your soul to the full assaults of Satan.

When you lose your conscious integrity, your soul becomes a battlefield for Satan; you have doubts and fears enough to paralyze your energies and drive you to discouragement. . . .

Remember that temptation is not sin. Remember that however trying the circumstances in which a man may be placed, nothing can really weaken his soul so long as he does not yield to temptation but maintains his own integrity. The interests most vital to you individually are in your own keeping. No one can damage them without your consent. All the satanic legions cannot injure you unless you open your soul to the arts and arrows of Satan. Your ruin can never take place until your will consents. If there is not pollution of mind in yourself, all the surrounding pollution cannot taint or defile you.

Eternal life is worth everything to us or it is worth nothing. Those only who put forth persevering effort and untiring zeal with intense desire proportionate to the value of the object they are in pursuit of, will gain that life which measures with the life of God. . . .

We have the example of Adam and Eve before us, and the result of their transgression should lead every soul of us to avoid sin, to abhor sin as the hateful thing it is, and to feel, in view of the sufferings which sin is sure to inflict, that it is better to suffer loss of all things than to depart from the least of God's commandments.

"COME UNTO ME"

Come unto me, all ye that labour and are heavy laden, and I will give you rest. **Matt. 11:28.**

Many who hear this invitation, while sighing for rest, yet press on the rugged path, hugging their burdens close to their heart. Jesus loves them, and longs to bear their burdens and themselves also in His strong arms. He would remove the fears and uncertainties that rob them of peace and rest; but they must first come to Him, and tell Him the secret woes of their heart. . . .

Sometimes we pour our troubles into human ears, and tell our afflictions to those who cannot help us, and neglect to confide all to Jesus, who is able to change the sorrowful way to paths of joy and peace. . . .

He proposes to be our friend, to walk with us through all the rough pathways of life. He says to us, I am the Lord thy God; walk with me, and I will fill thy path with light. Jesus, the Majesty of Heaven, proposes to elevate to companionship with Himself those who come to Him with their burdens, their weaknesses, and their cares. . . .

His invitation to us is a call to a pure, holy, and happy life—a life of peace and rest, of liberty and love—and to a rich inheritance in the future, immortal life. . . . It is our privilege to have daily a calm, close, happy walk with Jesus.

Rest is found when all self-justification, all reasoning from a selfish standpoint, is put away. Entire self-surrender, an acceptance of His ways, is the secret of perfect rest in His love. . . . Do just what He has told you to do, and be assured that God will do all that He has said He would do. . . . Have you come to Him, renouncing all your makeshifts, all your unbelief, all your self-righteousness? Come just as you are, weak, helpless, and ready to die.

What is the "rest" promised?—It is the consciousness that God is true, that He never disappoints the one who comes to Him. His pardon is full and free, and His acceptance means rest to the soul, rest in His love.

TIME FOR MEDITATION

But his delight is in the law of the Lord; and in his law doth he meditate day and night. Ps. 1:2.

Your last thought at night, your first thought in the morning, should be of Him in whom is centered your hope of eternal life.

Many seem to begrudge moments spent in meditation, and the searching of the Scriptures, and prayer, as though the time thus occupied was lost. I wish you could all view these things in the light God would have you; for you would then make the kingdom of heaven of the first importance. . . . As exercise increases the appetite, and gives strength and healthy vigor to the body, so will devotional exercises bring an increase of grace and spiritual vigor.

The affections should center upon God. Contemplate His greatness, His mercy and excellences. Let His goodness and love and perfection of character captivate your heart. Converse upon His divine charms, and the heavenly mansions He is preparing for the faithful. He whose conversation is in heaven, is the most profitable Christian to all around him. His words are useful and refreshing. They have a transforming power upon those who hear them.

There is constant need of private communion with God. We must take in the spirit of Christ if we would impart it to others. We cannot meet satanic and human agencies combined unless we spend much time in intercourse with the Source of all strength. There are times when we should get away from the sounds of earthly toil and human voices, and in retired places listen to the voice of Jesus. Thus we may taste of His love and imbibe His spirit. Thus we shall learn to crucify self. This course of action may seem impossible to the human mind. "I have not time," you may say. But when you consider the matter as it really is, you lose no time; for when you secure the power and grace that come alone from God, *you* do not accomplish the work. It is Jesus who is the real worker. "Without me," says Christ, "ye can do nothing." John 15:5. . . . Reflection and earnest prayer will inspire to holy endeavor.

SEEKING GOD
WITH ALL THE HEART

Turn you to the strong hold, ye prisoners of hope: even to day do I declare that I will render double unto thee. Zech. 9:12.

We need to educate the soul to lay hold, and hold fast the rich promises of Christ. The Lord Jesus knows that it is not possible for us to resist the many temptations of Satan, only as we shall have divine power given us from God. He well knows that in our own human strength we should surely fail. Therefore every provision has been made, that in every emergency and trial we shall flee to the Stronghold. . . . We have the word of promise from lips that will not lie. . . . We must individually cherish the faith that we receive of Him the things He hath promised.

God will be to us everything we will let Him be. Our languid, half-hearted prayers will not bring us returns from heaven. Oh, we need to press our petitions! Ask in faith, wait in faith, receive in faith, rejoice in hope, for everyone that seeketh findeth. Be in earnest in the matter. Seek God with all the heart. People put soul and earnestness into everything they undertake in temporal things, until their efforts are crowned with success. With intense earnestness learn the trade of seeking the rich blessings that God has promised, and with persevering, determined effort you shall have His light and His truth and His rich grace.

In sincerity, in soul hunger, cry after God. Wrestle with the heavenly agencies until you have the victory. Put your whole being into the Lord's hands, soul, body, and spirit, and resolve to be His loving, consecrated agency, moved by His will, controlled by His mind, infused by His Spirit.

Tell Jesus your wants in the sincerity of your soul. You are not required to hold a long controversy with, or preach a sermon to, God, but with a heart of sorrow for your sins, say, "Save me, Lord, or I perish." There is hope for such souls. They will seek, they will ask, they will knock, and they will find. When Jesus has taken away the burden of sin that is crushing the soul, you will experience the blessedness of the peace of Christ.

April 13

HUMBLE,
PERSEVERING PRAYER

Elias was a man subject to like passions as we are, and he prayed earnestly that it might not rain: and it rained not on the earth by the space of three years and six months. And he prayed again, and the heaven gave rain, and the earth brought forth her fruit. **James 5:17, 18.**

Important lessons are presented to us in the experience of Elijah. When upon Mount Carmel he offered the prayer for rain, his faith was tested, but he persevered in making known his request unto God.

The servant watched while Elijah prayed. Six times he returned from the watch, saying, There is nothing, no cloud, no sign of rain. But the prophet did not give up in discouragement. He kept reviewing his life, to see where he had failed to honor God. . . . As he searched his heart, he seemed to be less and less, both in his own estimation and in the sight of God. It seemed to him that he was nothing, and that God was everything; and when he reached the point of renouncing self, while he clung to the Saviour as his only strength and righteousness, the answer came. The servant appeared, and said, "Behold, there ariseth a little cloud out of the sea, like a man's hand." 1 Kings 18:34.

We have a God whose ear is not closed to our petitions; and if we prove His word, He will honor our faith. He wants us to have all our interests interwoven with His interests, and then He can safely bless us; for we shall not then take glory to self when the blessing is ours, but shall render all the praise to God. God does not always answer our prayers the first time we call upon Him; for should He do this, we might take it for granted that we had a right to all the blessings and favors He bestowed upon us. Instead of searching our hearts to see if any evil was entertained by us, any sin indulged, we should become careless, and fail to realize our dependence upon Him. . . .

Elijah humbled himself until he was in a condition where he would not take the glory to himself. This is the condition upon which the Lord hears prayer, for then we shall give the praise to Him. . . . God alone is worthy to be glorified.

April 14 Our High Calling

THE WORK
OF HEART-KEEPING

Keep thy heart with all diligence; for out of it are the issues of life. **Prov. 4:23.**

Diligent heart-keeping is essential to a healthy growth in grace. The heart in its natural state is a habitation for unholy thoughts and sinful passions. When brought into subjection to Christ, it must be cleansed by the Spirit from all defilement. This can not be done without the consent of the individual.

When the soul has been cleansed, it is the duty of the Christian to keep it undefiled. Many seem to think that the religion of Christ does not call for the abandonment of daily sins, the breaking loose from habits which have held the soul in bondage. They renounce some things condemned by the conscience, but they fail to represent Christ in the daily life. They do not bring Christlikeness into the home. They do not show a thoughtful care in their choice of words. Too often, fretful, impatient words are spoken, words which stir the worst passions of the human heart. Such ones need the abiding presence of Christ in the soul. Only in His strength can they keep guard over the words and actions.

In the work of heart-keeping we must be instant in prayer, unwearied in petitioning the throne of grace for assistance. Those who take the name of Christian should come to God in earnestness and humility, pleading for help. . . . The Christian cannot always be in the position of prayer, but his thoughts and desires can always be upward.

To keep your heart in heaven will give vigor to all your graces and put life into all your duties. To discipline the mind to dwell upon heavenly things will put life and earnestness into all our endeavors. Our efforts are languid, and we run the Christian race slowly, and manifest indolence and sloth, because we so little value the heavenly prize. We are dwarfs in spiritual attainments. It is the privilege and duty of the Christian to be increasing in the knowledge of the Son of God, "unto a perfect man."

Our High Calling

April 15

THE COURT
OF HOLY LIFE

But ye are a chosen generation, a royal priesthood, an holy nation, a peculiar people; that ye should shew forth the praises of him who hath called you out of darkness into his marvellous light. **1 Peter 2:9.**

The church of Christ on earth is amid the moral darkness of a disloyal world, which is trampling upon the law of Jehovah. But their Redeemer, who has purchased their ransom with the price of His own precious blood, has made every provision that His church shall be a transformed body, illumined with the Light of the world, possessing the glory of Emmanuel. The bright beams of the Sun of Righteousness, shining through His church, will gather into His fold every lost, straying sheep who will come unto Him and find refuge in Him. They will find peace and light and joy in Him who is peace and righteousness forever.

The members of the church should individually keep the light of God's love burning brightly in their own souls, that it may also shine forth to others. We have too much at stake to allow spiritual lethargy to creep over us. Let us beware of indulging a disrelish for religious services and religious duties. Let us resolutely battle against that sluggishness of soul which is so fatal to the growth and even the life of the Christian. That church will be healthy and prosperous whose members are putting forth active, personal effort to do good to others, to save souls. This will be a constant incentive to every good work. Such Christians will labor with greater earnestness to secure their own salvation. The dormant energies will be aroused, the whole soul inspired with an inconquerable determination to win the Saviour's plaudit of "Well done," and to wear the victor's crown.

Christ makes His church a beautiful temple for God. "Where two or three are gathered together in my name," He declared, "there am I in the midst of them." Matt. 18:20. His church is the court of holy life, filled with varied gifts, and endowed with the Holy Spirit. Appropriate duties are assigned by Heaven to each member of the church on earth, and all are to find their happiness in the happiness of those whom they help and bless.

THE SMILES OF GOD

The blessing of the Lord, it maketh rich, and he addeth no sorrow with it. **Prov. 10:22.**

Nothing can do us real good without the blessing of God. What God blesses is blessed. Therefore "a little that a righteous man hath is better than the riches of many wicked." Ps. 37:16. The little with the blessing of God is more efficient, and it will extend farther. The grace of God will make a little go a great ways. When we devote ourselves to the affairs of the kingdom of God, He will mind our affairs.

The Lord has given us precious blessings in the simple flowers of the field, in the fragrance so grateful to our senses. He has tinted every flower with beauty; for He is the great Master Artist. He who has created the beautiful things in nature will do far greater things for the soul. God is a lover of the beautiful, and He would adorn our characters with His own rich graces. He would have our words as fragrant as the flowers of the field. He has given us blessings in daily provision for our physical needs. The very bread we eat has upon it the image and superscription of the cross.

They only are truly blessed whose chief concern is to secure those blessings which will nourish the soul and endure forever. Our Saviour says to us, "Seek ye first the kingdom of God, and his righteousness; and all these things shall be added unto you." Matt. 6:33. God has a care for us, even to bestow His temporal blessings upon us. Our earthly good is not beneath the notice of our heavenly Father. He knoweth that we have need of these things. . . . When God smiles upon our efforts it is worth more than any earthly income.

> "How sweet our daily comforts prove
> When they are seasoned with His love."

Every deliverance, every blessing, that God in the past has granted to His people, should be kept fresh in memory's hall as a sure pledge of further and richer, increasing blessings that He will bestow.

There is no limit to the blessings that it is our privilege to receive.

WITH EYES OF FAITH

The eyes of your understanding being enlightened; that ye may know what is the hope of his calling, and what the riches of the glory of his inheritance in the saints. Eph. 1:18.

The highest qualifications of the mind will not, cannot, supply the place of true simplicity, of genuine piety. The Bible may be studied as a branch of human science would be; but its beauty, the evidence of its power to save the soul that believes, is a lesson that is never thus learned. If the practice of the Word is not brought into the life, then the sword of the Spirit has not wounded the natural heart. It has been shielded in poetic fancy. Sentimentalism has so wrapped it about that the heart has not sufficiently felt the keenness of its edge, piercing and cutting away the sinful shrines where self is worshiped. . . .

The eyes of the understanding must be enlightened, and the heart and mind brought into harmony with God, who is truth. He who beholds Jesus with the eye of faith sees no glory in himself, for the glory of the Redeemer is reflected into the mind and heart. The atonement of His blood is realized, and the taking away of sin stirs the heart with gratitude.

Being justified by Christ, the receiver of truth is constrained to make an entire surrender to God, and is admitted into the school of Christ, that he may learn of Him who is meek and lowly of heart. A knowledge of the love of God is shed abroad in his heart. He exclaims, Oh, what love! What condescension! Grasping the rich promises by faith, he becomes a partaker of the divine nature. His heart being emptied of self, the waters of life flow in; the glory of the Lord shines forth. Perpetually looking unto Jesus, the human is assimilated by the divine. The believer is changed into His likeness. . . . The human character is changed into the divine.

Christ looks upon His people in their purity and perfection as the reward of all His sufferings, His humiliation, and His love, and the supplement of His glory—Christ the great center, from whom radiates all glory.

HOW TO GROW IN GRACE

But grow in grace, and in the knowledge of our Lord and Saviour Jesus Christ. To him be glory both now and for ever. Amen. **2 Peter 3:18.**

How is it possible that we may grow in grace? It is possible to us only as we empty our hearts of self, and present them to Heaven, to be molded after the Divine Pattern. We may have a connection with the living channel of light; we may be refreshed with the heavenly dew, and have the showers of heaven descend upon us. As we appropriate the blessing of God, we shall be able to receive greater measures of His grace.

As little children we are to sit at the feet of Christ, learning of Him. . . . We should not allow a day to pass without gaining an increase of knowledge in temporal and spiritual things. We are to plant no stakes that we are not willing to take up and plant further on, nearer the heights we hope to ascend. The highest education is to be found in training the mind to advance day by day. The close of each day should find us a day's march nearer the overcomer's reward. Day by day our understanding is to ripen. Day by day we are to work out conclusions that will bring a rich reward in this life and in the life to come. Looking daily to Jesus, instead of to what we ourselves have done, we shall make decided advancement in temporal as well as spiritual knowledge.

The end of all things is at hand. What we have done must not be allowed to place the period to our work. The Captain of our salvation says, "Advance. The night cometh, in which no man can work." Constantly we are to increase in usefulness. Our lives are always to be under the power of Christ. Our lamps are to be kept burning brightly. . . . He who places himself where God can enlighten him, advances, as it were, from the partial obscurity of dawn to the full radiance of noonday.

We must put to the stretch every spiritual nerve and muscle. . . . God . . . does not desire you to remain novices. He wants you to reach the very highest round of the ladder, and then step from it into the kingdom of our Lord and Saviour Jesus Christ.

GREAT
IN GOD'S SIGHT

He that is faithful in that which is least is faithful also in much: and he that is unjust in the least is unjust also in much. **Luke 16:10.**

Life is not made up of great things alone; it is the little things that make the sum of life's happiness or miseries. It is the little things in life that reveal a person's real character. Oh, if all youth and those of mature age could see as I have seen the mirror of persons' lives presented before them, they would look more gravely upon even the little duties of life. Every mistake, every error, unimportant though it may be regarded, leaves a scar in this life and a blot on the heavenly records.

Life is full of duties that are not agreeable, but all these unpleasant duties will be made agreeable by a cheerful performance of them because it is right. Taking an interest in the duties which someone must do, and striving to do them with the heart, will make the most disagreeable duties pleasant.

There are many who undervalue the small events of life, the little deeds that are to be performed day by day; but these are not to be estimated as small, as every action tells either for the blessing or the injuring of someone. Every action tells its own story, it bears its own history to the throne of God. It is known whether it is on the side of right or on the side of wrong. It is only by acting in accordance with the principles of God's Word in the small transactions of life, that we place ourselves on the right side. We are tried and tested by these small occurrences, and our character will be estimated according as our work shall be.

It is the conscientious attention to what the world calls little things that makes the great beauty and success of life.

> Little deeds of charity,
> Little words of kindness,
> Little acts of self-denial,
> A wise improvement of opportunities,
> A diligent cultivation of little talents,
> Make great men in God's sight.

HOLD HIGH THE STANDARD

Go through, go through the gates; prepare ye the way of the people; cast up, cast up the highway; gather out the stones; lift up a standard for the people. **Isa. 62:10.**

The Word of God not only sets forth the great principles of truth and duty which should govern our lives, but it presents also, for our encouragement, the history of many who have exemplified these principles. . . . Except the one perfect Pattern, there is not described in the Sacred Pages a single character more worthy of emulation than that of the prophet Daniel. Exposed in youth to all the allurements of a royal court, he became a man of unbending integrity and fervent devotion to God. He was subjected to the fierce temptations of Satan, yet his character was not vacillating, nor his course changeable. He was firm where many would be yielding; he was true where they would be false; he was strong where they would be weak. Daniel was a lofty cedar of Lebanon. . . . Would that the faith, integrity, and devotion of the prophet Daniel might live in the hearts of God's people of today. Never were these noble qualities more needed in the world than now. . . .

In the records of those who have done and suffered for the name of Jesus, there is no name that shines with a brighter or purer luster than the name of Paul, the apostle of the Gentiles. The love of Jesus, glowing in his heart, made him self-forgetful, self-denying. He had seen the risen Christ, and the Saviour's image was impressed upon his soul, and shone forth in his life. With faith, courage, and fortitude, that would not be daunted by danger or stayed by obstacles, he pressed his way from land to land to spread the knowledge of the cross. . . .

Are the professed followers of Christ thus exemplifying the principles of their faith? Where are the deep, living, holy experiences which men of God were wont to recount? Has the standard of Christianity been lowered? . . . No; that standard remains just where God placed it. Holy men of ages past were required to give up all for Christ, to cherish His spirit, and to imitate His example. Nothing less than this will He accept now. . . . When called to give up all for Christ, who will stand the test?

REMINDERS OF
OUR HEAVENLY HOME

Thou, even thou, art Lord alone; thou hast made heaven, the heaven of heavens, with all their host, the earth, and all things that are therein, the seas, and all that is therein, and thou preservest them all; and the host of heaven worshippeth thee. Neh. 9:6.

There is beauty in the valley's awful grandeur, in the solemn, massive, cleft rocks; there is majesty in the towering mountains that look as if they touched the heavens. There are the lofty trees with their delicately formed leaves; the spires of grass, the opening bud and blossoming flower, the forest trees, and every living thing. They all point the mind to the great and living God. Every faculty of our being testifies that there is a living God, and we may learn from the open book of nature the most precious lessons in regard to the Lord of heaven.

In this study the mind expands, is elevated and uplifted, and becomes hungry to know more of God and His majesty. We have awakened in our hearts feelings not only of reverence and awe but of love, of faith, of trust and entire dependence upon One who is the giver of all good. And as I look at His marvelous works and see the evidences of His power I instinctively inquire, "What is man that thou are mindful of him? and the son of man, that thou visitest him?" Ps. 8:4.

All the greatness and glory of these wonderful things in God's house can only be appreciated as they are, in the mind, associated with God and the future home of bliss He is preparing for those who love Him. . . . While we talk freely of other countries, why should we be reticent in regard to the heavenly country, and the house not built with hands, eternal in the heavens? This heavenly country is of more consequence to us than any other city or country on the globe, therefore we should think and talk of this better—even an heavenly—country. And why should we not converse more earnestly, and in a heavenly frame of mind, in regard to God's gifts in nature? He has made all these things, and designs that we shall see God in His created works. These things are to keep God in our remembrance and to lift our hearts from sensual things and bind them in bonds of love and gratitude to our Creator.

THE SACRED TEMPLE
OF THE BODY

What? know ye not that your body is the temple of the Holy Ghost which is in you, which ye have of God, and ye are not your own? For ye are bought with a price: therefore glorify God in your body, and in your spirit, which are God's. 1 Cor. 6:19, 20.

That perfection of character which the Lord requires is the fitting up of the whole being as a temple for the indwelling of the Holy Spirit. God will accept of nothing less than the service of the entire human organism. It is not enough to bring into action certain parts of the living machinery. All parts must work in perfect harmony, or the service will be deficient. It is thus that man is qualified to cooperate with God in representing Christ to the world. Thus God desires to prepare a people to stand before Him pure and holy, that He may introduce them into the society of heavenly angels.

We have been entrusted with the most solemn message ever given to our world, and the object to be kept plainly and distinctly before our minds is the glory of God. Let us take care that we do nothing which will weaken physical, mental, or spiritual healthfulness, for God will not accept a tainted, diseased, corrupted sacrifice. Care must be exercised in eating, in drinking, in dressing, and in working, lest we detract from our efficiency and fail of doing our most exalted work in the best manner, in order that the results of our labor may be as lasting as eternity.

It is our duty to train and discipline the body in order that we shall render to the Master the highest possible service. Inclination must not control us. We are not to pamper the appetite and indulge in the use of that which is not for our good, simply because it gratifies the palate; neither are we to seek to live by the starvation plan, with the idea that we shall become spiritually-minded, and that God shall be glorified. We must use the intelligence that God has given in order that we may be perfect in body, soul, and spirit, that we may have a symmetrical character, a well-balanced mind, and do perfect work for the Master.

April 23

THE BEAUTY
OF CHRISTLIKENESS

Shewing all good fidelity; that they may adorn the doctrine of God our Saviour in all things. Titus 2:10.

Everyone who names the name of Christ is to adorn the doctrine of Christ our Saviour by a well-ordered life and a godly conversation, even the ornament of a meek and quiet spirit. . . . Possessing this, you will have favor both with God and with men.

Words spoken hastily wound and bruise souls, and the deepest wound is made upon the soul of the speaker. Christ's gift, the ornament of a meek and quiet spirit, is authoritatively declared by Him who can make no mistake to be of great price. We must each find out its worth for ourselves by seeking it from God. However men may estimate us, if we wear this ornament, we bear the sign of our discipleship with Christ. We are esteemed by the Most High; for the ornament we wear is in His sight of great price. This precious gem is to be sought for. . . .

To every soul things will come to provoke, to stir up anger, and if you are not under the full control of God, you will be provoked when these things come. But the meekness of Christ calms the ruffled spirit, controls the tongue, and brings the whole being into subjection to God. Thus we learn how to bear with the censure of others. We shall be misjudged, but the precious ornament of a meek and quiet spirit teaches us how to bear, how to have pity for those who utter hasty, unadvised words. Any unpleasant spirit displayed is sure to arouse the demon of passion in unguarded hearts. Unholy anger need not to be strengthened, but bridled. It is a spark which will set on fire untamed human nature. Avoid speaking words which will stir up strife. Rather suffer wrong than do wrong. God requires every one of His followers, as far as is possible, to live peaceably with all men. . . .

We must be Christlike. Let us strive to make our lives what Christ designs them to be, full of the fragrance of love to God and our fellow men, full of Christ's own divine Spirit, full of holy aspirations toward God, rich in the beauty of Christlikeness.

Our High Calling   April 24

HEAVEN CHEAP AT ANY PRICE

And whosoever doth not bear his cross, and come after me, cannot be my disciple. **Luke 14:27.**

It is too true that the great mass who possess ability and talent do not choose to travel the Christian road. Are their talent and ability too precious to devote to the Giver, the Lord of heaven and earth? . . .

Many would be followers of Christ if He would come down from the cross and appear to them in such a manner as they desire. If He would come with riches and pleasure, many would receive Him gladly and would be in haste to crown Him Lord of all. If He would only lay aside His humiliation and sufferings and cry, "If any man will come after Me, let him please himself and enjoy the world and he shall be My disciple," multitudes would believe on Him.

But the blessed Jesus will come to us in no other character than the meek and lowly Crucified One. We must partake of His self-denial and suffering here if we would take the crown hereafter. . . .

The Word of God has not widened the narrow way, and if the multitude have found a path where they can wear a form of godliness and not bear the cross or suffer tribulation, they have found a way where our Saviour did not walk and they follow another example than that which Christ set before us. Is it not enough that Jesus left the felicity and glory of heaven, endured a life of poverty and deep affliction, and died a cruel, shameful death to provide for us the joys of holiness and heaven? And can it be that we, the worthless objects of so great a condescension and love, will seek after a better portion in this life than was given to our Redeemer?

How easy would be the way to heaven if there was no self-denial or cross! How worldlings would rush in the way, and hypocrites would travel in it without number! Thank God for the cross, the self-denial. The ignominy and shame our Saviour endured for us is none too humiliating for those saved by the purchase of His blood. Heaven will indeed be cheap enough.

LET YOUR LIGHT SHINE

Let your light so shine before men, that they may see your good works, and glorify your Father which is in heaven. **Matt. 5:16.**

To every soul born into Christ's kingdom is given a solemn charge, Let your light so shine before men that they, by seeing your good works, shall glorify your Father which is in heaven. Pour forth upon your neighbors the rich rays of light received from the Sun of Righteousness; flash upon your friends in the world the bright gems of light and truth imparted to you abundantly from the throne of God. This is trading upon the talents entrusted. Go on from light to a greater light, catching more and more the bright beams from the Sun of Righteousness, and shine more and more unto the perfect day.

Jesus does not bid the Christian to strive to shine, but just to let his light shine in clear and distinct rays to the world. Do not blanket your light. Do not sinfully withhold your light. Do not let the mist and fog and malaria of the world put out your light. Do not hide it under a bed or under a bushel, but set it on a candlestick, that it may give light to all that are in the house. . . . God bids you shine, penetrating the moral darkness of the world.

Many do not know what is the matter with them. They want light and see no ray. They are calling for help and they hear no response. Shall doubt and unbelief be perpetuated because I do not gather the divine rays of light from Jesus Christ and let them shine forth to others? . . .

The deep struggles of my own soul against temptations, the earnest longings of my mind and heart to know God and Jesus Christ as my personal Saviour, and to have assurance, peace, and rest in their love, lead me to desire every day to be where the beams of the Sun of Righteousness can shine upon me. Without this experience, I shall indeed meet with great loss, and all with whom I associate will be affected by the loss of the light I ought to be receiving from the Source of all light and comfort, and to be flashing into their pathway. Shall I be indeed a light unto the world, or a shadow of darkness?

A JEWEL
OR A PEBBLE?

In that day, saith the Lord of hosts, will I take thee, O Zerubbabel, my servant, the son of Shealtiel, saith the Lord, and will make thee as a signet: for I have chosen thee, saith the Lord of hosts. **Haggai 2:23.**

Christians are Christ's jewels. They are to shine brightly for Him, shedding forth the light of His loveliness. Their luster depends on the polishing they receive. They may choose to be polished or to remain unpolished. But everyone who is pronounced worthy of a place in the Lord's temple must submit to the polishing process. Without the polishing that the Lord gives they can reflect no more light than a common pebble.

Christ says to man, "You are mine. I have bought you. You are now only a rough stone, but if you will place yourself in my hands, I will polish you, and the luster with which you shall shine will bring honor to My name. No man shall pluck you out of My hand. I will make you My peculiar treasure. On My coronation day, you will be a jewel in My crown of rejoicing."

The divine Worker spends little time on worthless material. Only the precious jewels does He polish after the similitude of a palace, cutting away all the rough edges. This process is severe and trying; it hurts human pride. Christ cuts deep into the experience that man is his self-sufficiency has regarded as complete, and takes away self-uplifting from the character. He cuts away the surplus surface, and putting the stone to the polishing wheel, presses it close, that all roughness may be worn away. Then, holding the jewel up to the light, the Master sees in it a reflection of Himself, and He pronounces it worthy of a place in His casket. "In that day, saith the Lord of hosts, will I take thee, . . . and will make thee as a signet: for I have chosen thee, saith the Lord of hosts." Blessed be the experience, however severe, that gives new value to the stone, and causes it to shine with living brightness.

God will not suffer one of His truehearted workers to be left alone to struggle against great odds and be overcome. He preserves as a precious jewel every one whose life is hid with Christ in God.

ROOTED IN CHRIST

The righteous shall flourish like the palm tree: he shall grow like a cedar in Lebanon. **Ps. 92:12.**

The Christian is likened to the cedar of Lebanon. I have read that this tree does more than send down a few short roots into the yielding loam. It sends strong roots deep down into the earth, and strikes down farther and still farther in search of a still stronger hold. And in the fierce blast of the tempest, it stands firm, held by its network of cables beneath.

So the Christian strikes root deep into Christ. He has faith in his Redeemer. He knows in whom he believes. He is fully persuaded that Jesus is the Son of God and the Saviour of sinners. . . . The roots of faith strike deep down. Genuine Christians, like the cedar of Lebanon, do not grow in the soft surface soil, but are rooted in God, riveted in the clefts of the mountain rocks.

If the Christian thrives and progresses at all, he must do so amid strangers to God, amid scoffing, subject to ridicule. He must stand upright like the palm tree in the desert. The sky may be as brass, the desert sand may beat about the palm tree's roots, and pile itself in heaps about its trunk. Yet the tree lives as an evergreen, fresh and vigorous amid the burning desert sands. Remove the sand till you reach the rootlets of the palm tree, and you discover the secret of its life; it strikes down deep beneath the surface, to the secret waters hidden in the earth.

As the palm tree, drawing nourishment from fountains of living water, is green and flourishing in the midst of the desert, so the Christian may draw rich supplies of grace from the fountain of God's love, and may guide weary souls, that are full of unrest and ready to perish in the desert of sin, to those waters of which they may drink, and live. The Christian is ever pointing his fellow men to Jesus, who invites, "If any man thirst, let him come unto me, and drink." John 7:37. This fountain never fails us; we may draw, and draw again.

NO PATCHWORK
RELIGION!

But he that shall endure unto the end, the same shall be saved. **Matt. 24:13.**

The religion that is built on self is worthless; for God makes no compromise with selfishness. . . .

The religion of Christ is a firm fabric, composed of innumerable threads, woven together with tact and skill. Only by the wisdom that God gives can we weave this fabric. Trusting to ourselves, we draw into it threads of selfishness, and the pattern is spoiled.

There are many kinds of cloth which at first have a fine appearance, but they do not endure test. The colors are not fast. They wash out. Under the heat of summer they fade, and are lost. Such a fabric cannot endure rough handling, and is worth very little.

So it is with religion. When the warp and woof of religion will not stand the test of trial, the material of which it is composed is worthless. And an effort to patch the old cloth with a new piece does not better the condition of things; for the worn-out, flimsy material breaks away from the new, leaving the rent much larger than before. Patching will not do. The only way is to discard the old garment and procure a new one. The religion of self, composed of threads that fade and give way under the stress of temptation, must be cast aside, to be replaced by the religion woven by Him in whose life no selfishness found place.

Christ's plan is the only safe one. He declares, "Behold, I make all things new." Rev. 21:5. "If any man be in Christ, he is a new creature." 2 Cor. 5:17. The Saviour gives no encouragement to any to think that He will accept a patchwork religion. Such a religion is of no value in His sight. There may at first seem to be some of self and some of Christ; but it is soon seen that there is none of Christ. The patches of selfishness increase till the entire garment is covered with them. . . .

A religion formed after the divine pattern is the only one that will endure. Only by striving to live the life of Christ here can we prepare ourselves to live with Him through the eternal ages.

THE UNSEARCHABLE
RICHES OF CHRIST

That he would grant you, according to the riches of his glory, to be strengthened with might by his Spirit in the inner man. **Eph. 3:16.**

The themes of redemption are momentous themes, and only those who are spiritually-minded can discern their depth and significance. It is our safety, our joy, to dwell upon the truths of the plan of salvation. Faith and prayer are necessary in order that we may behold the deep things of God. Our minds are so bound about by narrow ideas that we catch but limited views of the experience it is our privilege to have. . . .

Why is it that many who profess to have faith in Christ have no strength to stand against the temptations of the enemy?—It is because they are not strengthened with might by His Spirit in the inner man. The apostle prays "that ye, being rooted and grounded in love, may be able to comprehend with all saints what is the breadth, and length, and depth, and height; and to know the love of Christ, which passeth knowledge, that ye might be filled with all the fulness of God." Eph. 3:17-19. If we had this experience, we should know something of the cross of Calvary. We would know what it means to be partakers with Christ in His sufferings. The love of Christ would constrain us, and though we would not be able to explain how the love of Christ warmed our hearts, we would manifest His love in fervent devotion to His cause.

Paul opens before the Ephesian church, in the most comprehensive language, the marvelous power and knowledge they might possess as sons and daughters of the Most High. It was theirs "to be strengthened with might . . . ," to be "rooted and grounded in love," . . . "to know the love of Christ, which passeth knowledge." . . .

Jehovah Emmanuel—He in whom are hid all the treasures of wisdom and knowledge—to be brought into sympathy with Him, to possess Him, as the heart opens more and more to receive His attributes: to know His love and power, to possess the unsearchable riches of Christ . . . this is the heritage of the servants of the Lord, and "their righteousness is of me, saith the Lord." Isa. 54:17.

ALMOST HOME!

And if I go and prepare a place for you, I will come again, and receive you unto myself; that where I am, there ye may be also. **John 14:3.**

More than eighteen hundred years have passed since the Saviour gave the promise of His coming. Throughout the centuries His words have filled with courage the hearts of His faithful ones. The promise has not yet been fulfilled; . . . but none the less sure is the word that has been spoken.

Christ will come in His own glory, in the glory of His Father, and in the glory of the holy angels. Ten thousand times ten thousand and thousands of thousands of angels, the beautiful, triumphant sons of God, possessing surpassing loveliness and glory, will escort Him on His way. In the place of a crown of thorns, He will wear a crown of glory—a crown within a crown. In the place of that old purple robe, He will be clothed in a garment of whitest white, "so as no fuller on earth can white" (Mark 9:3) it. And on His vesture and on His thigh a name will be written, "King of kings, and Lord of lords." Rev. 19:16. . . .

To His faithful followers Christ has been a daily companion, a familiar friend. They have lived in close, constant communion with God. Upon them the glory of the Lord has risen. In them the light of the knowledge of the glory of God in the face of Jesus Christ has been reflected. Now they rejoice in the undimmed rays of the brightness and glory of the King in His majesty. They are prepared for the communion of heaven, for they have heaven in their hearts.

With uplifted heads, with the bright beams of the Sun of Righteousness shining upon them, with rejoicing that their redemption draweth nigh, they go forth to meet the Bridegroom, saying, "Lo, this is our God; we have waited for him, and he will save us." . . .

The time of tarrying is almost ended. The pilgrims and strangers who have so long been seeking a better country are almost home. I feel as if I must cry aloud, Homeward bound! . . . "Wherefore, beloved, seeing that ye look for such things, be diligent that ye may be found of him in peace, without spot, and blameless." 2 Peter 3:14.

SUPERFICIAL KNOWLEDGE NOT ENOUGH

To whom God would make known what is the riches of the glory of this mystery among the Gentiles; which is Christ in you, the hope of glory. **Col. 1:27.**

There are many mysteries in the Word of God that we do not comprehend, and many of us are content to stop our investigation when we have just begun to receive a little knowledge concerning Christ. When there begins to be a little unfolding of the divine purposes to the mind, and we begin to obtain a slight knowledge of the character of God, we become satisfied and think that we have received about all the light that there is for us in the Word of God. But the truth of God is infinite. With painstaking effort we should work in the mines of truth, discovering the precious jewels that have been hidden. . . . Jesus meant just what He said when He directed His disciples to *"search* the Scriptures"* (John 5:39). Searching means to compare scripture with scripture, and spiritual things with spiritual. We should not be satisfied with a superficial knowledge.

We do not half realize what the Lord is willing to do for His people. . . . Our petitions, mingled with faith and contrition, should go up to God for an understanding of the mysteries that God would make known to His saints. . . . An angel's pen could not portray all the glory of the revealed plan of redemption. The Bible tells how Christ bore our sins and carried our sorrows. Here is revealed how mercy and truth have met together at the cross of Calvary, how righteousness and peace have kissed each other, how the righteousness of Christ may be imparted to fallen man. There infinite wisdom, infinite justice, infinite mercy, and infinite love were displayed. Depths, heights, lengths, and breadths of love and wisdom, all passing knowledge, are made known in the plan of salvation.

He who desires the truth in his heart, who longs for the working of its power upon the life and character, will be sure to have it. Says the Saviour, "Blessed are they which do hunger and thirst after righteousness: for they shall be filled" (Matt 5:6).

OUR DIVINE REDEEMER

Who, being in the form of God, thought it not robbery to be equal with God. **Phil. 2:6.**

Jesus Christ "counted it not a thing to be grasped to be equal with

God.'' Because divinity alone could be efficacious in the restoration of man from the poisonous bruise of the serpent, God Himself, in His only begotten Son, assumed human nature, and in the weakness of human nature sustained the character of God, vindicated His holy law in every particular, and accepted the sentence of wrath and death for the sons of men. What a thought is this! He who was one with the Father before the world was made had such compassion for a world lost and ruined by transgression that He gave His life a ransom for it. He who was the brightness of the Father's glory, the express image of His person, bore our sins in His own body on the tree, suffering the penalty of man's transgression until justice was satisfied and required no more. How great is the redemption that has been worked out for us! So great that the Son of God died the cruel death of the cross to bring to us life and immortality through faith in Him.

This wonderful problem—how God could be just and yet the justifier of sinners—is beyond human ken. As we attempt to fathom it, it broadens and deepens beyond our comprehension. When we look with the eye of faith upon the cross of Calvary, and see our sins laid upon the victim hanging in weakness and ignominy there—when we grasp the fact that this is God, the everlasting Father, the Prince of Peace—we are led to exclaim, ''Behold, what manner of love the Father hath bestowed upon us'' (1 John 3:1)! . . .

When man can measure the exalted character of the Lord of hosts, and distinguish between the eternal God and finite humanity, he will know how great has been the sacrifice of Heaven to bring man from where he has fallen through disobedience to become part of the family of God. . . . The divinity of Christ is our assurance of eternal life. . . . He, the Sin Bearer of the world, is our only medium of reconciliation with a holy God.

TENDER, LOVING, COMPASSIONATE

But thou, O Lord, art a God full of compassion, and gracious, long-suffering, and plenteous in mercy and truth. Ps. 86:15.

God has ordained according to the law of ministry that we should comfort one another in tenderness and love when great sorrows come upon us. No man liveth unto himself. No one dieth unto himself. Life and death both mean something to every human being. . . . God has enjoined the duty upon His human agents to communicate the character of God, testifying to His grace, His wisdom, and His benevolence, by manifesting His refined, tender, merciful love. . . . Jesus . . . was ever touched with human woe, and our hearts should be softened and subdued by His Holy Spirit, that we may be like Him. . . .

Our work is to restore the moral image of God in man through the abundant grace given us of God by Jesus Christ. Everywhere we shall find souls ready to die, and how essential it is that the compassion of Christ shall be given us of Him, in order that we may never place one soul in defiance by not manifesting long forbearance and pitying tenderness. . . . I inquire, Will we ever learn the gentleness of Christ? Oh, how much we need to know Jesus and our heavenly Father that we may represent Him in character! . . .

Jesus calls us to Himself not simply to refresh us with His grace and presence for a few hours, and then to send us forth from His light to walk apart from Him in sadness and gloom. No, no. He tells us that we must abide with Him and He with us. Wherever His work is to be done He is present—tender, loving, and compassionate. He has prepared for you and me an abiding dwelling place in Himself. He is our refuge. Our experience should broaden and deepen. Jesus has opened up all the divine fullness of His inexpressible love, and He declares to you, Ye "are labourers together with God" (1 Cor. 3:9). O what meaning these words have—"Abide in me" (John 15:4), "Take my yoke upon you" (Matt. 11:29). Will we take it? for the promise is, "Ye shall find rest unto your souls." There is rest, complete rest in abiding in Christ.

THE HOLY SPIRIT
OUR HELPER

For as many as are led by the Spirit of God, they are the sons of God.
Rom. 8:14.

Through the ministry of the angels the Holy Spirit is enabled to work upon the mind and heart of the human agent and draw him to Christ. . . . But the Spirit of God does not interfere with the freedom of the human agent. The Holy Spirit is given to be a helper, so that man may cooperate with the Divine, and it is given to Him to draw the soul but never to force obedience.

Christ is ready to impart all heavenly influences. He knows every temptation that comes to man, and the capabilities of each. He weighs his strength. He sees the present and the future, and presents before the mind the obligations that should be met, and urges that common, earthly things shall not be permitted to be so absorbing that eternal things shall be lost out of the reckoning. The Lord has fullness of grace to bestow on every one that will receive of the heavenly gift. The Holy Spirit will bring the

God-entrusted capabilities into Christ's service, and will mold and fashion the human agent according to the divine Pattern.

The Holy Spirit is our efficiency in the work of character building, in forming characters after the divine similitude. When we think ourselves capable of molding our own experience, we make a great mistake. We can never of ourselves obtain the victory over temptation. But those who have genuine faith in Christ will be worked by the Holy Spirit. The soul in whose heart faith abides will grow into a beautiful temple for the Lord. He is directed by the grace of Christ. Just in proportion as he depends on the Holy Spirit's teaching he will grow.

The influence of the Holy Spirit is the life of Christ in the soul. We do not now see Christ and speak to Him, but His Holy Spirit is just as near us in one place as another. It works in and through every one who receives Christ. Those who know the indwelling of the Spirit reveal the fruit of the Spirit—love, joy, peace, long-suffering, gentleness, goodness, faith.

"DESPISED AND REJECTED"

He is despised and rejected of men; a man of sorrows, and acquainted with grief: and we hid as it were our faces from him; he was despised, and we esteemed him not. Isa. 53:3.

How few have any conception of the anguish which rent the heart of the Son of God during His thirty years of life upon earth. The path from the manger to Calvary was shadowed by sorrow and grief. He was the Man of Sorrows, and endured such heartache as no human language can portray. He could have said in truth, "Behold, and see if there be any sorrow like unto my sorrow" (Lam. 1:12). His suffering was the deepest anguish of the soul; and what man could have sympathy with the soul anguish of the Son of the infinite God? Hating sin with a perfect hatred, He yet gathered to His soul the sins of the whole world, as He trod the path to Calvary, suffering the penalty of the transgressor. Guiltless, He bore the punishment of the guilty; innocent, yet offering Himself to bear the penalty of the transgression of the law of God. The punishment of the sins of every soul was borne by the Son of the infinite God. The guilt of every sin pressed its weight upon the divine soul of the world's Redeemer. He who knew no sin became sin for us that we might be made the righteousness of God in Him. In assuming the nature of man, He placed Himself where He was wounded for our transgressions, bruised for our iniquities, that by His stripes we might be healed.

In His humanity Christ was tried with as much greater temptation, with as much more persevering energy than man is tried by the evil one, as His nature was greater than man's. This is a deep mysterious truth, that Christ is bound to humanity by the most sensitive sympathies. The evil works, the evil thoughts, the evil words of every son and daughter of Adam press upon His divine soul. The sins of men called for retribution upon Himself, for He had become man's substitute, and took upon Him the sins of the world. He bore the sins of every sinner, for all transgressions were imputed unto Him. . . . "How shall we escape, if we neglect so great salvation?" (Heb. 2:3).

AN ADVOCATE
CLOTHED IN OUR NATURE

My little children, these things write I unto you, that ye sin not. And if any man sin, we have an advocate with the Father, Jesus Christ the righteous. 1 John 2:1.

God's appointments and grants in our behalf are without limit. The throne of grace itself is occupied by One who permits us to call Him Father. . . . He has placed at His altar an Advocate clothed in our nature. As our Intercessor, Christ's office work is to introduce us to God as His sons and daughters. He intercedes in behalf of those who receive Him. With His own blood He has paid their ransom. By virtue of His merits He gives them power to become members of the royal family, children of the heavenly King. And the Father demonstrates His infinite love for Christ by receiving and welcoming Christ's friends as His friends. He is satisfied with the atonement made. He is glorified by the incarnation, the life, death, and mediation of His Son.

In Christ's name our petitions ascend to the Father. He intercedes in our behalf, and the Father lays open all the treasures of His grace for our appropriation, for us to enjoy and impart to others. . . .

Christ is the connecting link between God and man. . . . He places the whole virtue of His righteousness on the side of the suppliant. He pleads for man, and man, in need of divine help, pleads for himself in the presence of God, using the influence of the One who gave His life for the life of the world. As we acknowledge before God our appreciation of Christ's merits, fragrance is given to our intercessions. As we approach God through the virtue of the Redeemer's merits, Christ places us close by His side, encircling us with His human arm, while with His divine arm He grasps the throne of the Infinite. He puts His merits, as sweet incense, in the censer in our hands, in order to encourage our petitions. . . .

Yes, Christ has become the medium of prayer between man and God. He has also become the medium of blessing between God and man.

THE PRICELESS PEARL

Again, the kingdom of heaven is like unto a merchant man, seeking goodly pearls: who, when he had found one pearl of great price, went and sold all that he had, and bought it. **Matt. 13:45, 46.**

This goodly pearl represents the priceless treasure of Christ, as does the gold hid in the field. In Christ we have everything that is needful for us in this life, and that which will make up the joy of the world to come. All the money in the world will not buy the gift of peace and rest and love. These gifts are provided for us through faith in Christ. We cannot purchase these gifts from God; we have nothing with which to buy them. We are the property of God, for mind, soul, and body have been purchased by the ransom of the life of the Son of God. . . .

Then what is it to buy the eternal treasure? It is simply to give back to Jesus His own, to receive Him into the heart by faith. It is cooperation with God; it is bearing the yoke with Christ; it is lifting His burdens. . . . The Lord Jesus laid aside His royal crown, He left His high command, He clothed His divinity with humanity, in order that through humanity He might uplift the human race. He so appreciated the possibility of the human race that He became man's substitute and surety. He places upon man His own merit, and thus elevates him in the scale of moral value with God.

Christ is the atoning sacrifice. He left the glory of heaven, He parted with His riches, He laid aside His honor, not in order to create love and interest for man in the heart of God, but to be an exponent of the love that existed in the heart of the Father. . . . Jesus paid the price of all His riches, He assumed humanity, He condescended to a life of poverty and humiliation, in order that He might seek and save that which was lost.

Through the grace of Christ we may be strengthened and matured, so that though now imperfect we may become complete in Him. We have mortgaged ourselves to Satan, but Christ came to ransom and redeem us. We cannot purchase anything from God. It is only by grace, the free gift of God in Christ, that we are saved.

PROVISION FOR EVERY EMERGENCY

How shall we escape, if we neglect so great salvation; which at the first began to be spoken by the Lord, and was confirmed unto us by them that heard him. **Heb. 2:3.**

The divine Author of salvation left nothing incomplete in the plan; every phase of it is perfect. The sin of the whole world was laid upon Jesus, and divinity gave its highest value to the suffering of humanity in Jesus that the whole world might be pardoned through faith in the Substitute. The most guilty need have no fear but that God will pardon, for because of the efficacy of the divine sacrifice the penalty of the law will be remitted. Through Christ the sinner may return to allegiance to God.

How wonderful is the plan of redemption in its simplicity and fullness. It not only provides for the full pardon of the sinner but also for the restoration of the transgressor, making a way whereby he may be accepted as a son of God. Through obedience he may be the possessor of love and peace and joy. His faith may unite him in his weakness to Christ, the source of divine strength, and through the merits of Christ he may find the approval of God, because Christ has satisfied the demands of the law, and He imputes His righteousness to the penitent, believing soul. . . .

What love, what wonderful love, was displayed by the Son of God. . . . Christ takes the sinner from the lowest degradation, and purifies, refines, and ennobles him. By beholding Jesus as He is, the sinner is transformed and elevated to the very summit of dignity, even to a seat with Christ upon His throne. . . .

The plan of redemption provides for every emergency and for every want of the soul. If it were deficient in any way, the sinner might find some excuse to plead for neglect of its terms, but the infinite God had a knowledge of every human necessity, and ample provision has been made to supply every need. . . . What, then, can the sinner say in the great day of final judgment as to why he refused to give attention, the most thorough and earnest, to the salvation proffered him?

A FAITH THAT
PURIFIES THE LIFE

But thou, O man of God, flee these things; and follow after righteousness, godliness, faith, love, patience, meekness. Fight the good fight of faith, lay hold on eternal life, whereunto thou art also called, and hast professed a good profession before many witnesses. **1 Tim. 6:11, 12.**

Many teach that all that is necessary to salvation is to believe in Jesus, but what saith the word of truth?—"Faith without works is dead" (James 2:26). We are to "fight the good fight of faith, lay hold on eternal life," take up the cross, deny self, war against the flesh, and follow daily in the footsteps of the Redeemer. . . .

It is a fatal mistake to think that there is nothing for you to do in obtaining salvation. You are to cooperate with the agencies of heaven. . . . There is a cross to be lifted in the pathway, a wall to be scaled before you enter the eternal city, a ladder to be climbed before the gate of pearl is reached, and as you realize your inability and weakness and cry for help, a divine voice will come to you from the battlements of heaven saying, "take hold of my strength" (Isa. 27:5). . . .

The controversy that was waged between Christ and Satan is renewed over every soul that leaves the black banner of the prince of darkness to march under the blood-stained banner of Prince Emmanuel. The evil one will present the most subtle allurements to draw those away from their allegiance who would be true to Heaven, but we must yield all the powers of our being into the service of God, and then we shall be kept from falling into the snares of the enemy. . . .

Any course of action that weakens your physical or mental power unfits you for the service of your Creator. We are to love God with all our hearts, and if we have an eye single to His glory we shall eat, drink, and clothe ourselves with reference to His divine will. Every one who has a realizing sense of what it means to be a Christian will purify himself from everything that weakens and defiles. All the habits of his life will be brought into harmony with the requirements of the Word of truth, and he will not only believe, but will work out his own salvation with fear and trembling, while submitting to the molding of the Holy Spirit.

CHILDREN, NOT SLAVES

Wherefore we receiving a kingdom which cannot be moved, let us have grace, whereby we may serve God acceptably with reverence and godly fear. Heb. 12:28.

There are many who profess to be Christ's followers and yet are not doers of His Word. They do not relish this Word because it presents service which is not agreeable to them. They do not relish the wholesome reproofs and close, earnest appeals. They do not love righteousness, but are mastered and tyrannized over by their own erratic, human impulses.

It makes every difference how we do service for God. The boy who drudges through his lessons because he must learn will never become a real student. The man who claims to keep the commandments of God because he thinks he must do it will never enter into the enjoyment of obedience.

The essence and flavor of all obedience is the outworking of a principle within—the love of righteousness, the love of the law of God. The essence of all righteousness is loyalty to our Redeemer, doing right because it is right. When the Word of God is a burden because it cuts directly across human inclinations, then the religious life is not a Christian life, but a tug and a strain, an enforced obedience. All the purity and godliness of religion are set aside.

But adoption into the family of God makes us children, not slaves. When the love of Christ enters the heart we strive to imitate the character of Christ. . . . The more we study the life of Christ with a heart to learn, the more Christlike we become. Into the heart of every true doer of the Word the Holy Spirit infuses clear understanding. The more we crucify selfish practices by imparting our blessings to others and by exercising our God-given ability, the more the heavenly graces will be strengthened and increased in us. We will grow in spirituality, in patience, in fortitude, in meekness, in gentleness. . . . A train of cars is not merely attached to the engine; they follow on the same track as the engine. Whom are we following?

ABIDING IN CHRIST

Abide in me, and I in you. As the branch cannot bear fruit of itself, except it abide in the vine; no more can ye, except ye abide in me. **John 15:4.**

"Abide in me" are words of great significance. Abiding in Christ means a living, earnest, refreshing faith that works by love and purifies the soul. It means a constant receiving of the spirit of Christ, a life of unreserved surrender to His service. Where this union exists, good works will appear. The life of the vine will manifest itself in fragrant fruit on the branches. The continual supply of the grace of Christ will bless you and make you a blessing, till you can say with Paul, "I am crucified with Christ: nevertheless I live; yet not I, but Christ liveth in me" (Gal. 2:20).

The sacred union with Christ will unite the brethren in the most endearing bonds of Christian fellowship. Their hearts will be touched with divine compassion one for another. . . . Coldness, variance, strife, are entirely out of place among the disciples of Christ. They have accepted the one faith. They have joined to serve the one Lord, to endure in the same warfare, to strive for the same object, and to triumph in the same cause. They have been bought with the same precious blood, and have gone forth to preach the same message of salvation. . . .

Those who are constantly drawing strength from Christ will possess His spirit. They will not be careless in word or deportment. An abiding sense of how much their salvation has cost in the sacrifice of the beloved Son of God will rest upon their souls. Like a fresh and vivid transaction the scenes of Calvary will present themselves to their minds and their hearts will be subdued and made tender by this wonderful manifestation of the love of Christ to them. They will look upon others as the purchase of His precious blood, and those who are united with Him will seem noble and elevated and sacred because of this connection. The death of Christ on Calvary should lead us to estimate souls as He did. His love has magnified the value of every man, woman, and child.

A LIFE OF STRENGTH

I must work the works of him that sent me, while it is day: the night cometh, when no man can work. **John 9:4.**

The Christian life does not consist merely in the exercise of meekness, patience, humility, and kindness. One may possess these precious and amiable traits and yet be nerveless and spiritless, and almost useless when the work goes hard. Such persons lack the positiveness and energy, the solidity and strength of character, which would enable them to resist evil, and would make them a power in the cause of God.

Jesus was our example in all things, and He was an earnest and constant worker. He commenced His life of usefulness in childhood. At the age of twelve He was "about his Father's business." Between the ages of twelve and thirty, before entering upon His public ministry, He led a life of active industry. In His ministry Jesus was never idle. Said He, "I must work the works of him that sent me. . . ." The suffering who came to Him were not turned away unrelieved. He was acquainted with each heart and knew how to minister to its needs. Loving words fell from His lips to comfort, encourage, and bless, and the great principles of the kingdom of heaven were set before the multitudes in words so simple as to be understood by all.

Jesus was a silent and unselfish worker. He did not seek fame, riches, or applause, neither did He consult His own ease and pleasure. . . . He did not shirk care and responsibility, as many do who profess to be His followers. . . .

The claims of Christ upon our service are new every day. However complete may have been our consecration at conversion, it will avail us nothing unless it be renewed daily, but a consecration that embraces the actual present is fresh, genuine, and acceptable to God. We have not weeks and months to lay at His feet; tomorrow is not ours, for we have not yet received it, but today we may work for Jesus. Today we may lay our plans and purposes before Him for His inspection and approval. . . . This is God's day, and you are His hired servant.

JESUS OUR ALL

But of him are ye in Christ Jesus, who of God is made unto us wisdom, and righteousness, and sanctification, and redemption. **1 Cor. 1:30.**

It is growth in knowledge of the character of Christ that sanctifies the soul. To discern and appreciate the wonderful work of the atonement transforms him who contemplates the plan of salvation. By beholding Christ he becomes changed into the same image, from glory to glory, as by the Spirit of the Lord. The beholding of Jesus becomes an ennobling, refining process. . . . The perfection of Christ's character is the Christian's inspiration. . . . Christ should never be out of the mind. The angels said concerning Him, "Thou shalt call his name Jesus: for he shall save his people from their sins" (Matt. 1:21). Jesus, precious Saviour! assurance, helpfulness, security, and peace are all in Him. He is the dispeller of all our doubts, the earnest of all our hopes. How precious is the thought that we may indeed become partakers of the divine nature, whereby we may overcome as Christ overcame! Jesus is the fullness of our expectation. He is the melody of our songs, the shadow of a great rock in a weary land. He is living water to the thirsty soul. He is our refuge in the storm. He is our righteousness, our sanctification, our redemption.

The power of Christ is to be the comfort, the hope, the crown of rejoicing, of every one that follows Jesus in his conflict, in his struggles in life. He who truly follows the Lamb of God which taketh away the sin of the world, can shout as he advances, "This is the victory that overcometh the world, even our faith" (1 John 5:4).

What kind of faith is it that overcomes the world? It is that faith which makes Christ your own personal Saviour—that faith which, recognizing your helplessness, your utter inability to save yourself, takes hold of the Helper who is mighty to save, as your only hope. It is faith that will not be discouraged, that hears the voice of Christ saying, "Be of good cheer, I have overcome the world, and my divine strength is yours." . . . "Lo, I am with you alway."

May 14

THE COMING
OF THE COMFORTER

And I will pray the Father, and he shall give you another Comforter, that he may abide with you for ever; even the Spirit of truth; whom the world cannot receive, because it seeth him not, neither knoweth him: but ye know him; for he dwelleth with you, and shall be in you. **John 14:16, 17.**

Christ was about to depart to His home in the heavenly courts, but He assured His disciples that He would send them the Comforter, who would abide with them forever. To the guidance of this Comforter all may implicitly trust. He is the Spirit of truth; but this truth the world can neither see nor receive. . . .

Christ desired His disciples to understand that He would not leave them orphans. "I will not leave you comfortless," He declared: "I will come to you" (John 14:18, 19). . . . Precious, glorious assurance of eternal life! Even though He was to be absent, their relation to Him was to be that of a child to its parent. . . .

The words spoken to the disciples come to us through their words. The Comforter is ours as well as theirs, at all times and in all places, in all sorrows and in all affliction, when the outlook seems dark and the future perplexing and we feel helpless and alone. These are times when the Comforter will be sent in answer to the prayer of faith.

There is no comforter like Christ, so tender and so true. He is touched with the feeling of our infirmities. His Spirit speaks to the heart. Circumstances may separate us from our friends; the broad, restless ocean may roll between us and them. Though their sincere friendship may still exist, they may be unable to demonstrate it by doing for us that which would be gratefully received. But no circumstances, no distance, can separate us from the heavenly Comforter. Wherever we are, wherever we may go, He is always there, one given in Christ's place, to act in His stead. He is always at our right hand, to speak soothing, gentle words, to support, sustain, uphold, and cheer. The influence of the Holy Spirit is the life of Christ in the soul. This Spirit works in and through every one who receives Christ. Those who know the indwelling of this spirit reveal its fruit—love, joy, peace, long-suffering, gentleness, goodness, faith.

BUILDING UP ONE ANOTHER

We then that are strong ought to bear the infirmities of the weak, and not to please ourselves. **Rom. 15:1.**

God does not want us to place ourselves upon the judgment seat and judge each other. . . . When we see errors in others, let us remember that we have faults graver, perhaps, in the sight of God than the fault we condemn in our brother. Instead of publishing his defects, ask God to bless him and to help him to overcome his error. Christ will approve of this spirit and action, and will open the way for you to speak a word of wisdom that will impart strength and help to him who is weak in the faith.

The work of building one another up in the most holy faith is a blessed work, but the work of tearing down is a work full of bitterness and sorrow. Christ identifies Himself with His suffering children, for He says, "Inasmuch as ye have done it unto one of the least of these my brethren, ye have done it unto me" (Matt. 25:40). . . . Every heart has its own sorrows and disappointments, and we should seek to lighten one another's burdens by manifesting the love of Jesus to those around us. If our conversation were upon heaven and heavenly things, evil speaking would soon cease to have any attraction for us. . . .

Instead of finding fault with others, let us be critical with ourselves. The question with each one of us should be, Is my heart right before God? Will this course of action glorify my Father which is in heaven? If you have cherished a wrong spirit, let it be banished from the soul. It is your duty to eradicate from your heart everything that is of a defiling nature. Every root of bitterness should be plucked up, lest others be contaminated by its baleful influence. Do not allow one poisonous plant to remain in the soil of your heart. Root it out this very hour, and plant in its stead the plant of love. Let Jesus be enshrined in the soul. Christ is our example. He went about doing good. He lived to bless others. Love beautified and ennobled all His actions, and we are commanded to follow in His steps.

OPENING THE MYSTERIES
OF REDEMPTION

Then opened he their understanding, that they might understand the scriptures. **Luke 24:45.**

The Lord wants every one of us to have a deeper, richer experience in the knowledge of our Lord and Saviour Jesus Christ. He desires that we shall grow in knowledge—not earthward, but heavenward, upward to Christ our living Head. How high, how great, is this knowledge to be? To the full stature of men and women in Christ Jesus. We cannot grow too much, we cannot gather up too many of the precious rays of light that God sends us. . . .

We know falsehoods are coming in like a swift current, and that is just the reason why we want every ray of light that God has for us, that we may be able to stand amid the perils of the last days. . . .

O how Christ longs to open before us the mysteries of redemption! He longed to do this for His disciples when He was among them on earth, but they were not far enough advanced in spiritual knowledge to comprehend

His words. He had to say to them, "I have yet many things to say unto you, but ye cannot bear them now" (John 16:12). O how much better could they have borne the terrible ordeal through which they had to pass at His trial and crucifixion if they had advanced and been able to bear the instruction of Christ! Shall we not let Jesus open our understanding? . . .

We are on the borders of the eternal world, and we must have a testimony with which all heaven shall be in harmony.

The Lord is coming, and we must be ready! Every moment I want His grace—I want the robe of Christ's righteousness. We must humble our souls before God as never before, come low to the foot of the cross, and He will put a word in our mouths to speak for Him, even praise unto our God. He will teach us a strain from the song of the angels, even thanksgiving to our heavenly Father. We can do nothing of ourselves, but God wants to touch our lips with a living coal from off the altar. He wants to sanctify our tongues—to sanctify our whole being.

TRUTHS THAT TRANSFORM

The word of God is quick, and powerful, and sharper than any two-edged sword, piercing even to the dividing asunder of soul and spirit, and of the joints and marrow, and is a discerner of the thoughts and intents of the heart. Heb. 4:12.

The truths of the Bible, treasured in the heart and mind and obeyed in the life, convince and convert the soul, transform the character, and comfort and uplift the heart. . . . The Word makes the proud humble, the perverse meek and contrite, the disobedient obedient. The sinful habits natural to man are interwoven with the daily practice. But the Word cuts away the fleshly lusts. It is a discerner of the thoughts and intents of the mind. It divides the joints and marrow, cutting away the lusts of the flesh, making men willing to suffer for their Lord.

The service of Christ is a heavenly and holy and blessed thing. The Word is to be diligently searched, for the ministry of the Word discovers the imperfections in our characters and teaches us that the sanctification of the Spirit is a work of heavenly devising, presenting in Christ Jesus the true perfection that if maintained will become a perfect whole in behalf of every soul. We are educated in Bible lines to become complete in Christlikeness and to see His Father's face in Him who gave His own life for the saving of the soul.

If you are an intelligent Christian you will maintain religious vitality and will not be deterred by difficulties. . . . You will work the works of God in gloom as well as in glory, in shade as well as in sunshine, in trial as well as in peace. The truth must be treasured up in your heart as well as incorporated in your being, so that no temptation and no argument can induce you to yield to Satan's suggestions or devices. The truth is precious. It has wrought important changes upon the life and upon the character, exerting a masterly influence over words, deportment, thoughts, and experience. The soul who appreciates the truth lives under its influence and senses the tremendous realities of eternal things. He lives not to himself, but to Jesus Christ who died for him. To him, God lives and is very cognizant of all his words and actions.

A NEVER-FAILING REFUGE

Be careful for nothing; but in every thing by prayer and supplication with thanksgiving let your requests be made known unto God. **Phil. 4:6.**

It is not the will of God that His people should be weighed down with care. But our Lord does not deceive us. He does not say to us, "Do not fear; there are no dangers in your path." He knows there are trials and dangers, and He deals with us plainly. He does not propose to take His people out of a world of sin and evil, but He points them to a never-failing refuge. . . .

How can we remain in doubt, questioning whether Jesus loves us, sinful though we be and compassed with infirmities? He gave Himself for us that He might redeem us from all iniquity and purify unto Himself a peculiar people, zealous of good works. He came to our world in the humble guise of a man, that He might become acquainted with the griefs and temptations that beset man's pathway, and that He might know how to help the weary with His offer of rest and peace. But thousands upon thousands refuse His assistance and only cling more firmly to their burden of care. He comes to the afflicted, and offers to soothe their grief and heal their sorrow. . . . To the disappointed, the unbelieving, and the unhappy He offers contentment, while pointing to mansions that He is preparing for them. . . . Jesus, our precious Saviour, should be first in our thoughts and affections, and we should trust Him with entire confidence. . . .

As each day comes we must in the strength of Jesus meet its trials and temptations. If we fail one day we add to the burdens of the next, and have less strength. We should not cloud the future by our carelessness in the present, but by thoughtful and careful performance of today's duties be preparing to meet the emergencies of tomorrow.

We need to cultivate a spirit of cheerfulness. . . . Let us ever look on the bright side of life and be hopeful, full of love and good works, rejoicing in the Lord always. "Let the peace of God rule in your hearts," and "be ye thankful" (Col. 3:15).

A PROGRESSIVE FAITH

But without faith it is impossible to please him: for he that cometh to God must believe that he is, and that he is a rewarder of them that diligently seek him. **Heb. 11:6.**

The time has come when we are to expect large blessings from the Lord. We must rise to a higher standard on the subject of faith. We have too little faith. The Word of God is our endorsement. We must take it, simply believing every word. With this assurance we may claim large things, and according to our faith it will be unto us. . . .

The work of faith means more than we think. It means genuine reliance upon the naked word of God. By our actions we are to show that we believe that God will do just as He has said. The wheels of nature and of providence are not appointed to roll backward now to stand still. We must have an advancing, working faith, a faith that works by love and purifies the soul from every vestige of selfishness. It is not self, but God, that we must depend upon. We must not cherish unbelief. We must have that faith that takes God at His word. . . .

True faith consists in doing just what God has enjoined, not manufacturing things He has not enjoined. Justice, truth, mercy, are the fruit of faith. We need to walk in the light of God's law; then good works will be the fruit of our faith, the proceeds of a heart renewed every day. The tree must be made good before the fruit can be good. We must be wholly consecrated to God. Our will must be made right before the fruit can be good. We must have no fitful religion. "Whatsoever ye do, do all to the glory of God" (1 Cor. 10:31).

O what a field is opened before me! Our people must have the deep working of the Spirit of God every day. They must have a faith that works by love, a faith that emanates from God. There must not be a thread of selfishness drawn into the fabric. When our faith works by love, just such a love as Christ revealed in His life, it will be of a firm texture; it will be the fruit of a will subdued. But not until self dies can Christ live in us. Not until self dies can we possess a faith that works by love and purifies the soul.

THE MIGHTY DELIVERER

I have spread out my hands all the day unto a rebellious people, which walketh in a way that was not good, after their own thoughts. **Isa. 65:2.**

The Lord God through Christ holds out His hand all the day long in invitations to the needy. He will receive all. He welcomes all. He rejects none. It is His glory to pardon the chief of sinners. He will take the prey from the mighty, He will deliver the captive, He will pluck the brand from the burning. He will lower the golden chain of His mercy to the greatest depths of human wretchedness and guilt and lift up the debased soul contaminated with sin. But man must will to come, and cooperate in the work of saving his soul by availing himself of opportunities given him of God. The Lord forces no one. The spotless wedding robe of Christ's righteousness is prepared to clothe the sinner, but if he refuses it he must perish.

The record of the past can be blotted out with His [Christ's] blood, the page made clean and white. "Come now, and let us reason together, saith the Lord: though your sins be as scarlet, they shall be as white as snow; though they be red like crimson, they shall be as wool" (Isa. 1:18). . . .

The words falling from the lips of Jesus, "Thy sins be forgiven thee" (Matt. 9:2), are worth everything to us. He saith, I have borne your sins in My own body on Calvary's cross. He sees your sorrows. His hand is laid upon the head of every contrite soul, and Jesus becomes our Advocate before the Father, and our Saviour. The lowly, contrite heart will make very much of forgiveness and pardon. . . .

We may repeat His tender compassion for us to others who are wandering in the mazes of sin. The grace of Christ revealed to us must be tenderly revealed to others. A great tenderness and compassion will fill the soul for human beings who are still under the control of Satan. Christ is to be multiplied in every man and woman who believes in Him, for they are to live over the life of Christ in blessing and enlightening and bringing hope and peace and joy to other hearts.

May 21

HOW TO GET RID OF GUILT

Who is a God like unto thee, that pardoneth iniquity, and passeth by the transgression of the remnant of his heritage? he retaineth not his anger for ever, because he delighteth in mercy. **Micah 7:18.**

I am glad indeed that our feelings are no evidence that we are not children of God. The enemy will tempt you to think that you have done things that have separated you from God, and that He no longer loves you, but our Lord loves us still. . . .

Look away from yourself to the perfection of Christ. We cannot manufacture a righteousness for ourselves. Christ has in His hands the pure robes of righteousness, and He will put them upon us. He will speak sweet words of forgiveness and promise. He presents to our thirsty souls fountains of living water whereby we may be refreshed. He bids us come unto Him with all our burdens, all our griefs, and He says we shall find rest. . . .

Jesus sees the guilt of the past, and speaks pardon, and we must not dishonor Him by doubting His love. This feeling of guiltiness must be laid at the foot of the cross of Calvary. The sense of sinfulness has poisoned the springs of life and of true happiness. Now Jesus says, "Lay it all on Me. I will take your sins; I will give you peace. Banish no longer your self-respect, for I have bought you with the price of My own blood. You are Mine. Your weakened will I will strengthen; your remorse for sin I will remove." Then turn your grateful heart, trembling with uncertainty, to Him and lay hold on the hope set before you. God accepts your broken, contrite heart, and extends to you free pardon. He offers to adopt you into His family, with His grace to help your weakness, and the dear Saviour will lead you on step by step, you placing your hand in His and letting Him guide you.

Search for the precious promises of God. If Satan thrusts threatenings before your mind, turn from them and cling to the promises, and let your soul be comforted by their brightness. The cloud is dark in itself, but when filled with the light it is turned to the brightness of gold, for the glory of God is upon it.

THE ONLY PATH
OF SAFETY

And thine ears shall hear a word behind thee, saying, This is the way, walk ye in it, when ye turn to the right hand, and when ye turn to the left. **Isa. 30:21.**

I know that human beings suffer much because they step out of the path that God has chosen for them to follow. They walk in the sparks of the fire they have kindled themselves, and the sure result is affliction, unrest, and sorrow, which they might have avoided if they had submitted their will to God and had permitted Him to control their ways. God sees that it is necessary to oppose our will and our way, and bring our human will into subjection.

Whatever path God chooses for us, whatever way He ordains for our feet, that is the only path of safety. We are daily to cherish a spirit of childlike submission, and pray that our eyes may be anointed with the heavenly eyesalve in order that we may discern the indications of the divine will, lest we become confused in our ideas, because our will seems to be all-controlling. With the eye of faith, with childlike submission as obedient children, we must look to God, to follow His guidance, and difficulties will clear away. The promise is, "I will instruct thee and teach thee . . . : I will guide thee with mine eye" (Ps. 32:8). . . .

If we come to God in a humble and teachable spirit, not with our plans all formed before we ask Him, and shaped according to our own will, but in submission, in willingness to be taught, in faith, it is our privilege to claim the promise every hour of the day. We may distrust ourselves, and we need to guard against our own inclinations and strong tendencies lest we shall follow our mind and plans and think it is the way of the Lord. . . .

Our heavenly Father is our Ruler, and we must submit to His discipline. We are members of His family. He has a right to our service, and if one of the members of His family would persist in having his own way, persist in doing just that which he pleased, that spirit would bring about a disordered and perplexing state of things. We must not study to have our own way, but God's way and God's will.

THE MARCH TO VICTORY

But thanks be to God, which giveth us the victory through our Lord Jesus Christ. 1 Cor. 15:57.

Nothing can be more helpless, nothing can be more dependent, than the soul that feels its nothingness and relies wholly upon the merits of the blood of a crucified and risen Saviour. The Christian life is a life of warfare, of continual conflict. It is a battle and a march. But every act of obedience to Christ, every act of self-denial for His sake, every trial well endured, every victory gained over temptation, is a step in the march to the glory of final victory.

If we take Christ for our guide, He will lead us safely along the narrow way. The road may be rough and thorny; the ascent may be steep and dangerous; there may be pitfalls upon the right hand and upon the left; we may have to endure toil in our journey; when weary, when longing for rest, we may have to toil on; when faint, we may have to fight; when discouraged, we may be called upon to hope; but with Christ as our Guide we shall not lose the path to immortal life, we shall not fail to reach the desired haven at last.

Christ Himself has trod the rough pathway before us and has smoothed the path for our feet. The narrow path of holiness, the way cast up for the ransomed of the Lord to walk in, is illuminated by Him who is the light of the world. As we follow in His steps, His light will shine upon us, and as we reflect the light borrowed from the glory of Christ, the path will grow brighter and brighter unto the perfect day.

We may think it pleasant at first to follow pride and worldly ambition, but the end is pain and sorrow. Selfish plans may present flattering promises and hold out the hope of enjoyment, but we shall find that our happiness is poisoned and our life embittered by hopes that center in self. In following Christ we are safe, for He will not suffer the powers of darkness to hurt one hair of our heads. He will keep that which is committed to His trust, and we shall be more than conquerors through Him that loved us.

"COME YE YOURSELVES APART"

Wait on the Lord: be of good courage, and he shall strengthen thine heart: wait, I say, on the Lord. **Ps. 27:14.**

No other life was ever so crowded with labor and responsibility as was that of Jesus, yet how often He was found in prayer! How constant was His communion with God! . . . As one with us, a sharer in our needs and weaknesses, He was wholly dependent upon God, and in the secret place of prayer He sought divine strength that He might go forth braced for duty and trial. In a world of sin Jesus endured struggles and torture of soul. In communion with God He could unburden the sorrows that were crushing Him. . . .

In Christ the cry of humanity reached the Father of infinite pity. As a man He supplicated the throne of God till His humanity was charged with a heavenly current that should connect humanity with divinity. Through continual communion He received life from God, that He might impart life to the world. His experience is to be ours. "Come ye yourselves apart" (Mark 6:31), He bids us. If we would give heed to His Word we should be stronger and more useful. . . . If today we would take time to go to Jesus and tell Him our needs we should not be disappointed; He would be at our right hand to help us. . . .

In all who are under the training of God is to be revealed a life that is not in harmony with the world, its customs, or its practices, and everyone needs to have a personal experience in obtaining a knowledge of the will of God. We must individually hear Him speaking to the heart. When every other voice is hushed, and in quietness we wait before Him, the silence of the soul makes more distinct the voice of God. He bids us, "Be still, and know that I am God" (Ps. 46:10). Here alone can true rest be found. And this is the effectual preparation for all who labor for God. Amid the hurrying throng and the strain of life's intense activities, the soul that is thus refreshed will be surrounded with an atmosphere of light and peace. The life will breathe out fragrance and will reveal a divine power that will reach men's hearts.

THE PRECIOUSNESS OF SECRET PRAYER

Trust in him at all times; ye people, pour out your heart before him: God is a refuge for us. **Ps. 62:8.**

A deep sense of our need and a great desire for the things for which we ask must characterize our prayers, else they will not be heard. But we are not to become weary and cease our petitions because the answer is not immediately received. "The kingdom of heaven suffereth violence, and the violent take it by force" (Matt. 11:12). The violence here meant is a holy earnestness, such as Jacob manifested. We need not try to work ourselves up into an intense feeling, but calmly, persistently, we are to press our petitions at the throne of grace. Our work is to humble our souls before God, confessing our sins, and in faith drawing nigh unto God. . . . It is the design of God to reveal Himself in His providence and in His grace. The object of our prayers must be the glory of God, not the glorification of ourselves. . . .

God has honored us by showing how greatly He values us. We are bought with a price, even the precious blood of the son of God. When His heritage shall conscientiously follow the Word of the Lord, His blessing will rest upon them in answer to their prayers. "Therefore also now, saith the Lord, turn ye even to me with all your heart, and with fasting, and with weeping, and with mourning: and rend your heart, and not your garments, and turn unto the Lord your God: for he is gracious and merciful, slow to anger, and of great kindness" (Joel 2:12, 13).

In secret prayer the soul should be laid bare to the inspecting eye of God. . . . How precious is secret prayer—the soul communing with God! Secret prayer is to be heard only by the prayer-hearing God. No curious ear is to receive the burden of petitions. Calmly, yet fervently, the soul is to reach out after God; and sweet and abiding will be the influence emanating from Him who sees in secret, whose ear is open to the prayer arising from the heart. He who in simple faith holds communion with God will gather to himself divine rays of light to strengthen and sustain him in the conflict with Satan.

THE MOTIVE
FOR OBEDIENCE

For this is the love of God, that we keep his commandments: and his commandments are not grievous. **1 John 5:3.**

It is the keeping of the commandments of God that honors and glorifies Him in His chosen. Wherefore every soul to whom God has given reasoning faculties is under obligation to God to search the Word and ascertain all that is enjoined upon us as God's purchased possession. We should seek to understand all that the Word requires of us. . . . We cannot show greater honor to our God, whose we are by creation and redemption, than to give evidence to the beings of heaven, to the worlds unfallen, and to fallen men, that we diligently hearken unto all His commandments, which are the laws that govern His kingdom.

We need to study diligently that we may gain a knowledge of the laws of God. How can we be obedient subjects if we fail to understand the laws that govern the kingdom of God? Then open your Bibles and search for everything that will enlighten you in regard to the precepts of God; and when you discern a Thus saith the Lord, ask not the opinion of men, but whatever the cost to yourself, obey cheerfully. Then the blessing of God will rest upon you. . . .

Often ask prayerfully, "Lord, what wilt thou have me to do? Am I in any way disregarding the divine precepts? Am I in any way placing my influence on the enemy's side? Am I showing a careless disregard of God's commandments? Am I willing to yoke up with Christ, to lift the burdens, and to be a co-laborer with Him? Am I studying out possible excuses for neglecting obedience to a Thus saith the Lord? Am I risking the consequences of neglect to obey the clearly revealed precepts of Jehovah because I am not willing to come out from the world and be separate? Shall the fear of man have a greater influence over me than the fear of God?"

Surrender yourself to God, saying, " 'Here, Lord, I give myself away; 'tis all that I can do.' I will not be found in disobedience to Thy law, for that would place me in the enemy's ranks."

FILLED WITH HIS FULLNESS

And to know the love of Christ, which passeth knowledge, that ye might be filled with all the fulness of God. **Eph. 3:19.**

There are many who think that it is impossible to escape from the power of sin, but the promise is that we may be filled with all the fullness of God. We aim too low. The mark is much higher. Our minds need expansion, that we may comprehend the significance of the provision of God. We are to reflect the highest attributes of the character of God. We should be thankful that we are not to be left to ourselves. The law of God is the exalted standard to which we are to attain. . . . We are not to walk according to our own ideas . . . , but we are to follow in the footsteps of Christ.

The work of overcoming is in our hands, but we are not to overcome in our own name or strength, for of ourselves we cannot keep the commandments of God. The Spirit of God must help our infirmities. Christ has become our sacrifice and surety. He has become sin for us that we might become the righteousness of God in Him. Through faith in His name He imputes unto us His righteousness, and it becomes a living principle in our life. . . . Christ imputes to us His sinless character and presents us to the Father in His own purity.

We cannot provide a robe of righteousness for ourselves, for the prophet says, "All our righteousnesses are as filthy rags" (Isa. 64:6). There is nothing in us from which we can clothe the soul so that its nakedness shall not appear. We are to receive the robe of righteousness woven in the loom of heaven, even the spotless robe of Christ's righteousness. We are to say, "He died for me. He bore my soul's disgrace, that in His name I might be an overcomer and be exalted to His throne."

It is the privilege of the children of God to be filled with all the fullness of God. "Now unto him that is able to do exceeding abundantly above all that we ask or think, according to the power that worketh in us, unto him be glory in the church by Christ Jesus throughout all ages, world without end" (Eph. 3:20, 21).

AN EXAMPLE
OF THE BELIEVERS

For the grace of God that bringeth salvation hath appeared to all men, teaching us that, denying ungodliness and worldly lusts, we should live soberly, righteously, and godly, in this present world. **Titus 2:11, 12.**

There is a great work for us to do if we would inherit eternal life. We are to deny ungodliness and worldly lusts, and live a life of righteousness. . . . There is no salvation for us except in Jesus, for it is through faith in Him that we receive power to become the sons of God. But it is not merely a passing faith, it is faith that works the works of Christ. . . . Living faith makes itself manifest by exhibiting a spirit of sacrifice and devotion toward the cause of God. Those who possess it stand under the banner of Prince Emmanuel and wage a successful warfare against the powers of darkness. They stand ready to do whatsoever their Captain commands. Each one is exhorted to be "an example of the believers, in word, in conversation, in charity, in spirit, in faith, in purity" (1 Tim. 4:12), for we are to "live soberly, righteously, and godly" in this present evil world, representing the character of Christ, and manifesting His spirit. . . .

Those who are connected with Jesus are in union with the Maker and Upholder of all things. They have a power that the world cannot give nor take away. But while great and exalted privileges are given to them, they are not simply to rejoice in their blessings. As stewards of the manifold grace of God they are to become a blessing to others. They are entrusted with great truth, and "unto whomsoever much is given, of him shall be much required" (Luke 12:48). There are weighty responsibilities resting upon all who have received the message for this time. They are to exert an influence that will draw others to the light of God's Word. . . . We are our brother's keeper. . . .

If we are true believers in Jesus we shall be gathering rays from glory, and we shall shed light on the darkened pathway of those around us. We shall reveal the gracious character of our Redeemer, and many will be drawn by our influence to "behold the Lamb of God, which taketh away the sin of the world" (John 1:29).

139

PUTTING OUR GIFTS
TO WORK

But every man hath his proper gift of God, one after this manner, and another after that. **1 Cor. 7:7.**

God gives more than money to His stewards. Your talent of imparting is a gift. What are you communicating of the gifts of God, in your words, in your tender sympathy? . . . The knowledge of truth is a talent. There are many souls in darkness that might be enlightened by true, faithful words from you. There are hearts that are hungering for sympathy, perishing away from God. Your sympathy may help them. The Lord has need of your words, dictated by His Holy Spirit. . . .

The first work for all Christians to do is to search the Scriptures with most earnest prayer, that they may have that faith that works by love and purifies the soul from every thread of selfishness. If the truth is received into the heart, it works like good leaven, until every power is brought into subjection to the will of God. Then you can no more help shining than can the sun. . . .

All natural gifts are to be sanctified as precious endowments. They are to be consecrated to God, that they may minister for the Master. All social advantages are talents. They are not to be devoted to self-pleasing, amusement, or self-gratification. . . . The gift of correct example is a great thing. But many gather about the soul an atmosphere that is malarious. . . .

The gifts of speech, of knowledge, of sympathy and love, communicate a knowledge of Christ. All these gifts are to be converted to God. The Lord stands in need of them, He calls for them. All are to act a part in preparing their own souls and the souls of others to rededicate their talents to God. Every soul, every gift, is to be laid under contribution to God. All are to cooperate with God in the work of saving souls. The talents you possess are given you of God to make you efficient colaborers with Christ. There are hearts hungering for sympathy, perishing for the help and assistance God has given you to give to them.

May 30

EXALTING THE
MAN OF CALVARY

And as Moses lifted up the serpent in the wilderness, even so must the Son of man be lifted up: that whosoever believeth in him should not perish, but have eternal life. **John 3:14, 15.**

I point you to the cross of Calvary. I ask you to consider the infinite sacrifice made in your behalf that through faith in Jesus Christ you may not perish but have everlasting life. . . . I point you to Jesus. You are safe in committing to Him the innermost working of your mind. The Lord Jesus hath purchased you with an infinite price. You may commit the keeping of your soul to Jesus. You may trust Him as your Counselor. . . . Constantly draw nigh unto God. He will help you.

O be sure you receive your illumination from the Source of all light. He is the great central Light of the universe of heaven and the great Light of the world. He will enlighten every man that cometh into the world. Reach no cheap, low standard. Cultivate the gentleness of Christ. Secure the highest attainments, and draw your inspiration from Jesus Christ. He is your Friend. You may always depend upon Him and find Him faithful and true. When you need His sympathy in your greatest perplexity, wounded and bruised, He will not pass you by on the other side. To Him you may come in the simplicity of children. To Him you may come with joy and rejoicing. With everything that is flattering to your hopes, every success which attends your labors in the Lord, look up to Jesus and lay every honor at His feet. Everything depends upon your walking in all humility of mind. Write the name of Christ upon your banner and never dishonor your colors.

All heaven was given to us in Christ Jesus. . . . O honor Jesus by giving to Him the heart's best and holiest services! He has given His life for you. Who is He that hath done this? The only begotten Son of God, He that was One with the Father before the world was.

Lift up your banner, lift it up higher. Never, never let it trail in the dust of the earth. Exalt Jesus. Lift Him up, the Man of Calvary, higher and still higher.

WE SHALL
SEE HIS FACE

And they shall see his face; and his name shall be in their foreheads.
Rev. 22:4.

We cannot now see the glory of God, but it is only by receiving Him here that we shall be able by and by to see Him face to face. God would have us keep our eyes fixed on Him, that we may lose sight of the things of this world. We have . . . no time for any of us to delay that preparation which will enable us to see the face of God. . . .

Only by looking to Jesus, the Lamb of God, and following in His steps, can you prepare to meet God. Follow Him, and you will one day walk the golden streets of the city of God. You will see Him who laid aside His royal garments and His kingly crown, and disguising Himself with humanity, came to our world and bore our sins, that He might lift us up and give us a revelation of His glory and majesty. We shall see Him face to face if we now give ourselves up to be molded and fashioned by Him and prepared for a place in the kingdom of God.

Those who consecrate their lives to the service of God will live with Him through the ceaseless ages of eternity. "God himself shall be with them, and be their God" (Rev. 21:3). . . .

Their minds were given to God in this world; they served Him with their heart and intellect, and now He can put His name in their foreheads. "And there shall be no night there; . . . for the Lord God giveth them light: and they shall reign for ever and ever" (Rev. 22:5). They do not go in as those that beg a place there, for Christ says to them, "Come, ye blessed of my Father, inherit the kingdom prepared for you from the foundation of the world" (Matt. 25:34). He takes them as His children, saying, Enter ye into the joy of your Lord. The crown of immortality is placed on the brow of the overcomers. They take their crowns and cast them at the feet of Jesus, and touching their golden harps, they fill all heaven with rich music in songs of praise to the Lamb. Then "they shall see his face; and his name shall be in their foreheads."

LEARNING OF GOD
THROUGH HIS WORKS

The Lord is good to all: and his tender mercies are over all his works. All thy works shall praise thee, O Lord; and thy saints shall bless thee. Ps. 145:9, 10.

We love to contemplate the character and love of God in His created works. What evidences has He given the children of men of His power, as well as of His parental love! He has garnished the heavens and made grand and beautiful the earth.

"O Lord our Lord, how excellent is thy name in all the earth! . . . When I consider thy heavens, the work of thy fingers, the moon and the stars, which thou hast ordained; what is man, that thou art mindful of him? and the son of man, that thou visitest him?" "All thy works praise thee, O Lord; and thy saints shall bless thee" (Ps. 8:1, 3, 4; 145:10).

Had our world been formed with a perfectly level surface the monotony would have fatigued the eye and wearied the senses. God has adorned our world with grand mountains, hills, valleys, and ranges of mountains. The rugged granite, bare mountains, also the mountains decorated with evergreens and verdure, and the valleys with their softened beauty make the world a mirror of loveliness. The goodness, wisdom, and power of God are manifest everywhere. In mountains, rocks, hills, and valleys, I see the works of divine power. I can never be lonely while viewing the grand scenery of nature. On the journey over the plains and mountains I have had feelings of the deepest reverence and awe while viewing the frowning precipice and snow-capped mountain heights.

The mountains, hills, and valleys should be to us as schools in which to study the character of God in His created works. The works of God which we may view in the ever-varying scenes—in mountains, hills, and valleys, in trees, shrubs, and flowers, in every leaf, every spire of grass—should teach us lessons of the skill and love of God and of His infinite power.

Those who study nature cannot be lonesome. They love the quiet hours of meditation, for they feel that they are brought in close communion with God while tracing His power in His created works.

NOT TO CONDEMN BUT TO SAVE

For God sent not his Son into the world to condemn the world; but that the world through him might be saved. **John 3:17.**

There are souls who are trembling in unbelief. They ask, "How can I know that God is reconciled to me? How can I be assured that He loves and pardons me?" It is not for you, dear youth, to make yourselves just with God. Jesus invites you to come to Him with all your burdens and perplexities. . . . Accept the promise and the provision that God has made. . . . Look away from self to Jesus; for in Christ the character of the Father is revealed.

The blood of Christ in ever-abiding efficacy is our only hope, for through His merits alone we have pardon and peace.

The character of God as revealed by Christ invites our faith and love, for we have a Father whose mercy and compassion fail not. At every step of our journey heavenward He will be with us to guide in every perplexity, to give us help in every temptation.

Your reason and imagination should be touched with the life-giving power of Christ, that forms of beauty and truth may be impressed thereon. There are great and precious truths that demand your contemplation, in order that you may have a sound foundation for your faith by having a correct knowledge of God. O that the superficial, vain seeker for truth would learn that the world by wisdom, however much acquired, knew not God.

It is proper to seek to learn all that is possible from nature, but do not fail to look from nature to Christ for the complete representation of the character of the living God. By contemplation of Christ, by conformity to the divine likeness, your conceptions of the divine character will expand, and your mind and heart will be elevated, refined, and ennobled. Let the youth aim high, not relying upon human wisdom, but living day by day as seeing Him who is invisible, doing their work as in the sight of the intelligences of heaven. . . .

He who constantly depends upon God through simple trust and prayerful confidence, will be surrounded by the angels of heaven. He who lives by faith in Christ, will be strengthened and upheld, able to fight the good fight of faith, and lay hold upon eternal life.

THE HEAVENLY ELECTION

Wherefore the rather, brethren, give diligence to make your calling and election sure: for if ye do these things, ye shall never fall. **2 Peter 1:10.**

This is the only election regarding which the Bible speaks. Fallen in sin, we may become partakers of the divine nature and attain to a knowledge far in advance of any scientific learning. By partaking of the flesh and the blood of our crucified Lord, we shall gain life eternal. In the sixth of John we read: "Whoso eateth my flesh, and drinketh my blood, hath eternal life" (John 6:54). "It is the spirit that quickeneth; the flesh profiteth nothing: the words that I speak unto you, they are spirit, and they are life" (verse 63).

None need lose eternal life. Everyone who chooses daily to learn of the heavenly Teacher will make his calling and election sure. Let us humble our hearts before God and follow on to know Him whom to know aright is life eternal.

"Give diligence to make your calling and election *sure:* for if ye do these things, ye shall never fall: for so an entrance shall be ministered unto you abundantly into the everlasting kingdom of our Lord and Saviour Jesus Christ" (2 Peter 1:10, 11).

Here are your life-insurance papers. This is not an insurance policy the value of which someone else will receive after your death; it is a policy that assures *you* a *life* measuring with the life of God—even eternal life. O what an assurance! what a hope! Let us ever reveal to the world that we are seeking for a better country, even a heavenly. Heaven has been made for us, and we want a part in it. We cannot afford to allow anything to separate us from God and heaven. In this life we must be partakers of the divine nature. Brethren and sisters, you have only one life to live. O let it be a life of virtue, a life hid with Christ in God!

Unitedly we are to help one another gain perfection of character. To this end, we are to cease all criticism. Onward and still onward we may advance toward perfection, until at last there will be ministered unto us an abundant entrance into the heavenly kingdom.

OUR SURE FOUNDATION

For other foundation can no man lay than that is laid, which is Jesus Christ. Now if any man build upon this foundation gold, silver, precious stones, wood, hay, stubble; every man's work shall be made manifest: for the day shall declare it, because it shall be revealed by fire; and the fire shall try every man's work of what sort it is. **1 Cor. 3:11-13.**

As fire reveals the difference between gold, silver, and precious stones, and wood, hay, and stubble, so the day of judgment will test characters, showing the difference between characters formed after Christ's likeness and characters formed after the likeness of the selfish heart. All selfishness, all false religion, will then appear as it is. The worthless material will be consumed; but the gold of true, simple, humble faith will never lose its value. It can never be consumed; for it is imperishable.

Character is not obtained by receiving an education. Character is not obtained by amassing wealth or by gaining worldly honor. Character is not obtained by having others fight the battle of life for us. It must be sought, worked for, fought for; and it requires a purpose, a will, a determination. To form a character which God will approve, requires persevering effort. It will take a continual resisting of the powers of darkness to . . . have our names retained in the book of life. Is it not worth more to have our names registered in that book, have them immortalized among the heavenly angels, than to have them sounded in praise throughout the whole earth?

In the probationary time granted us here we are each building a structure that is to have the inspection of the Judge of all the earth. This work is the molding of our characters. Every act of our lives is a stone in that building, every faculty is a worker, every blow that is struck is for good or for evil. The words of inspiration warn us to take heed how we build, to see that our foundation is sure. If we build upon the solid rock, pure, noble, upright deeds, the structure will go up beautiful and symmetrical, a fit temple for the indwelling of the Holy Spirit.

THE HAPPIEST PEOPLE

Thou wilt shew me the path of life: in thy presence is fulness of joy; at thy right hand there are pleasures for evermore. **Ps. 16:11.**

Do not think that when you walk with Jesus you must walk in the shadow. The happiest people in the world are those who trust in Jesus and gladly do His bidding. From the lives of those who follow Him, unrest and discontent are banished. . . . They may meet with trial and difficulty, but their lives are full of joy; for Christ walks beside them, and His presence makes the pathway bright. . . .

When you arise in the morning, rise with the praise of God on your lips, and when you go out to work, go with a prayer to God for help. . . . Wait for a leaf from the tree of life. This will soothe and refresh you, filling your heart with peace and joy. Fix your thoughts upon the Saviour. Go apart from the bustle of the world and sit under Christ's shadow. Then, amid the din of daily toil and conflict, your strength will be renewed. It is positively necessary for us to sit down sometimes and think of how the Saviour descended from heaven, from the throne of God, to show what human beings may become if they will unite their weakness to His strength. Having gained renewal of strength by communion with God, we may go on our way rejoicing, praising Him for the privilege of bringing the sunshine of Christ's love into the lives of those we meet. . . .

Heavenly intelligences are waiting to cooperate with human instrumentalities, that the world may see what human beings may become through a union with the divine. Those who consecrate body, soul, and spirit to God's service will constantly receive a new endowment of physical, mental, and spiritual power. The inexhaustible supplies of heaven are at their command. Christ gives them the life of His life. The Holy Spirit puts forth its highest energies to work in mind and heart. Through the grace given us we may achieve victories which, because of our defects of character and the smallness of our faith, may have seemed to us impossible.

To every one who offers himself to the Lord for service, withholding nothing, is given power for the attainment of measureless results.

LET US ASK OF GOD

If any of you lack wisdom, let him ask of God, that giveth to all men liberally, and upbraideth not; and it shall be given him. **James 1:5.**

It is the privilege of every believer first to talk with God in his closet, and then as God's mouthpiece to talk with others. In order that we may have something to impart, we must daily receive light and blessing. Men and women who commune with God, who have an abiding Christ, who, because they cooperate with holy angels, are surrounded with holy influences, are needed at this time. The cause needs those who have power to draw with Christ, power to express the love of God in words of encouragement and sympathy.

As the believer bows in supplication before God, and in humility and contrition offers his petition from unfeigned lips, he loses all thought of self. His mind is filled with the thought of what he must have in order to build up a Christlike character. He prays, "Lord, if I am to be a channel through which Thy love is to flow day by day and hour by hour, I claim by faith the grace and power that Thou hast promised." He fastens his hold firmly on the promise, "If any of you lack wisdom, let him ask of God, . . . and it shall be given him."

How this dependence pleases the Master! How He delights to hear the steady, earnest pleading! . . . With wonderful and ennobling grace the Lord sanctifies the humble petitioner, giving him power to perform the most difficult duties. All that is undertaken is done unto the Lord, and this elevates and sanctifies the lowliest calling. It invests with new dignity every word, every act, and links the humblest worker . . . with the highest of the angels in the heavenly courts. . . .

The sons and daughters of God have a great work to do in the world. They are to accept the Word of God as the man of their counsel and to impart it to others. They are to diffuse light. All who have received the engrafted word will be faithful in giving that word to others. They will speak the words of Christ. In conversation and in deportment they will give evidence of a daily conversion to the principles of truth. Such believers will be a spectacle to the world, to angels, and to men, and God will be glorified in them.

NOTHING TOO SMALL

The Lord is good unto them that wait for him, to the soul that seeketh him. **Lam. 3:25.**

There are few who rightly appreciate or improve the precious privilege of prayer. We should go to Jesus and tell Him all our needs. We may bring Him our little cares and perplexities as well as our greater troubles. Whatever arises to disturb or distress us, we should take it to the Lord in prayer.

We lose many precious blessings by failing to bring our needs and cares and sorrows to our Saviour. He is the wonderful Counselor. He looks upon His church with intense interest and with a heart full of tender sympathy. He enters into the depth of our necessities. But our ways are not always His ways. He sees the result of every action, and He asks us to trust patiently in His wisdom, not in the supposedly wise plans of our own making.

Do not cease to pray. If the answer tarry, wait for it. Lay all your plans at the feet of the Redeemer. Let your importunate prayers ascend to God. If it be for His name's glory, the soothing words will be spoken, "Be it unto thee according to thy word."

We can never weary Christ by earnest supplications. We do not depend on God as we should. Let us leave unsaid every word of complaint. Talk faith and courage while waiting for God. . . . Be afraid to doubt, lest this become a habit that will destroy faith. The dealing of the heavenly Father may seem dark and mysterious and unexplainable; nevertheless we are to trust in Him.

Oh, how precious is Jesus to the soul who trusts in Him! But many are walking in darkness because they bury their faith in the shadow of Satan. . . . Never for a moment should we allow Satan to think that his power to distress and annoy is greater than the power of Christ to uphold and strengthen. . . .

Every sincere prayer that is offered is mingled with the efficacy of Christ's blood. If the answer is deferred, it is because God desires us to show a holy boldness in claiming the pledged word of God. He is faithful who hath promised. He will never forsake the soul who is wholly surrendered to Him.

OUR PERSONAL INTERCESSOR

Who is he that condemneth? It is Christ that died, yea rather, that is risen again, who is even at the right hand of God, who also maketh intercession for us. **Rom. 8:34.**

The Lord Jesus is your personal intercessor. . . . Repeat over and over many times through the day, "Jesus has died for me. He saw me in peril, exposed to destruction, and poured out His life to save me. He does not behold the soul as a trembling suppliant prostrate at His feet without pity, and He will not fail to raise me up." He has become the advocate for man. He has lifted up those who believe in Him and placed a treasurehouse of blessing at their demand. Men cannot bestow one blessing upon their fellows, they cannot remove one stain of sin. It is only the merit and righteousness of Christ that will avail anything, but this is placed to our account in rich fullness. We may draw upon God every moment. As we turn to Him, He answers, "Here I am."

Christ proclaims Himself our Intercessor. He would have us know that He has graciously engaged to be our Substitute. He places His merit in the golden censer to offer up with the prayers of His saints, so that the prayers of His dear children may be mingled with the fragrant merit of Christ as they ascend to the Father in the cloud of incense.

The Father hears every prayer of His contrite children. The voice of supplication from the earth unites with the voice of our Intercessor, who pleads in heaven, whose voice the Father always hears. Let our prayers therefore continually ascend to God. Let them not come up in the name of any human being, but in the name of Him who is our Substitute and Surety. Christ has given us His name to use. . . .

Jesus receives and welcomes you as His own friend. He loves you; He has pledged Himself to open before you all the treasures of His grace for your appropriation. He says, "At that day ye shall ask in my name: and I say not unto you, that I will pray the Father for you: for the Father himself loveth you, because ye have loved me, and have believed that I came out from God" (John 16:26, 27). He virtually says, Make use of My name, and it will be your passport to the heart of My Father, and to all the riches of His grace.

ANGELS IN THE HOME

For he shall give his angels charge over thee, to keep thee in all thy ways. They shall bear thee up in their hands, lest thou dash thy foot against a stone. **Ps. 91:11, 12.**

Angels of God are watching over us. Upon this earth there are thousands and tens of thousands of heavenly messengers commissioned by the Father to prevent Satan from obtaining any advantage over those who refuse to walk in the path of evil. And these angels who guard God's children on earth are in communication with the Father in heaven. "Take heed that ye despise not one of these little ones," Christ said; "for I say unto you, That in heaven their angels do always behold the face of my Father which is in heaven" (Matt. 18:10).

Scarcely any of us realize that angels are about us; and these precious angels, who minister to those who shall be heirs of salvation, are saving from us many, many temptations and difficulties. The whole family of heaven is interested in the families here below; and how thankful we should be for this interest manifested for us day and night.

Words spoken in our homes which are impatient and unkind, angels hear; and do you want to find in the books of heaven a record of the impatient and passionate words you have uttered in your family? Impatience brings the enemy of God and man into your family and drives out the angels of God. If you are abiding in Christ, and Christ in you, you cannot speak angry words.

Fathers and mothers, I beseech you for Christ's sake, to be kind, tender, and patient in your homes. Then light and sunshine will enter your homes, and you will feel that bright beams from the Sun of Righteousness are indeed shining into your hearts.

It is the absence of the graces of God's Spirit that leaves the home in a dark, unhappy condition. Your home should be a blessed sanctuary where God can come in, and where His holy angels can minister unto you. If impatience and unkindness are manifested one to another, angels cannot be attracted to your home; but where love and peace abide, these heavenly ones love to come and bring still more of the holy influence of the home above.

THE ACT OF FAITH

Now faith is the substance of things hoped for, the evidence of things not seen. **Heb. 11:1.**

Faith is not the ground of our salvation, but it is the great blessing—the eye that sees, the ear that hears, the feet that run, the hand that grasps. It is the means, not the end. If Christ gave His life to save sinners, why shall I not take that blessing? My faith grasps it, and thus my faith is the substance of things hoped for, the evidence of things unseen. Thus resting and believing, I have peace with God through the Lord Jesus Christ.

Faith, saving faith . . . is the act of the soul by which the whole man is given over to the guardianship and control of Jesus Christ. He abides in Christ and Christ abides in the soul by faith as supreme. The believer commits his soul and body to God, and with assurance may say, Christ is able to keep that which I have committed unto Him against that day. All who will do this will be saved unto life eternal. There will be an assurance that the soul is washed in the blood of Christ and clothed with His righteousness and precious in the sight of Jesus.

Remember that the exercise of faith is the one means of preserving it. Should you sit always in one position, without moving, your muscles would become strengthless and your limbs would lose the power of motion. The same is true in regard to your religious experience. You must have faith in the promises of God. . . . Faith will perfect itself in exercise and activity.

It is of the greatest importance to us that we surround the soul with the atmosphere of faith. Every day we are deciding our own eternal destiny in harmony with the atmosphere that surrounds the soul. We are individually accountable for the influence that we exert, and consequences that we do not see will result from our words and actions. If God would have saved Sodom for the sake of ten righteous persons, what would be the influence for good that might go out as the result of the faithfulness of the people of God if every one who professed the name of Christ were also clothed with His righteousness?

A WORKING FAITH

And be found in him, not having mine own righteousness, which is of the law, but that which is through the faith of Christ, the righteousness which is of God by faith. **Phil. 3:9.**

It is one thing to read and teach the Bible, and another thing to have by practice its life-giving, sanctifying principles engrafted on the soul. . . . "By grace are ye saved through faith" (Eph. 2:8). The mind should be educated to exercise faith rather than to cherish doubt, suspicion, and jealousy. We are too prone to regard obstacles as impossibilities. To have faith in the promises of God, to go forward by faith, pressing on without being governed by circumstances, is a lesson hard to learn. Yet it is a positive necessity that every child of God should learn this lesson. The grace of God through Christ is ever to be cherished, for it is given us as the only way of approaching God. . . .

The faith mentioned in God's Word calls for a life in which faith in Christ is an active, living principle. It is God's will that faith in Christ shall be made perfect by works; He connects the salvation and eternal life of those who believe, with these works, and through them provides for the light of truth to go to all countries and peoples. This is the fruit of the workings of God's Spirit.

We show our faith in God by obeying His commands. Faith is always expressed in words and actions. It produces practical results, for it is a vital element in the life. The life that is molded by faith develops a determination to advance, to go forward, following in the footsteps of Christ.

We have been taken as rough stones out of the quarry of the world by the cleaver of truth and placed in the workshop of God. He who has genuine faith in Christ as his personal Saviour will find that the truth accomplishes a definite work for him. His faith is a working faith. . . . We cannot create our faith, but we can be co-laborers with Christ in promoting the growth and triumph of faith.

The faith that works by love and purifies the soul produces the fruit of humility, patience, forbearance, long-suffering, peace, joy, and willing obedience.

OUR EXAMPLE IN OBEDIENCE

For even hereunto were ye called: because Christ also suffered for us, leaving us an example, that ye should follow his steps: who did no sin, neither was guile found in his mouth. 1 Peter 2:21, 22.

Before us is held out the wonderful possibility of being like Christ—obedient to all the principles of the law of God. But of ourselves we are utterly powerless to attain to this condition. All that is good in man comes to him through Christ. The holiness that God's Word declares we must have before we can be saved is the result of the working of divine grace as we bow in submission to the discipline and restraining influence of the Spirit of truth.

Man's obedience can be made perfect only by the incense of Christ's righteousness, which fills with divine fragrance every act of true obedience. The part of the Christian is to persevere in overcoming every fault. Constantly he is to pray to the Saviour to heal the disorders of his diseased soul. He has not the wisdom and strength without which he cannot overcome. They belong to the Lord, and He bestows them on those who in humiliation and contrition seek Him for help.

The work of transformation from unholiness to holiness is a continuous work. Day by day God labors for man's sanctification, and man is to cooperate with Him by putting forth persevering efforts in the cultivation of right habits. . . .

God will more than fulfill the highest expectations of those who put their trust in Him. He desires us to remember that when we are humble and contrite, we stand where He can and will manifest Himself to us. He is well pleased when we urge past mercies and blessings as a reason why He should bestow on us higher and greater blessings. He is honored when we love Him and bear testimony to the genuineness of our love by keeping His commandments. He is honored when we set apart the seventh day as sacred and holy. To those who do this, the Sabbath is a sign, . . . God declares, "that I am the Lord that sanctify them" (Eze. 20:12). Sanctification means habitual communion with God. There is nothing so great and powerful as God's love for those who are His children.

THE HIGHEST CULTURE

Happy is the man that findeth wisdom, and the man that getteth understanding. **Prov. 3:13.**

The fear of the Lord is the beginning of wisdom, and the man who consents to be molded and fashioned after the divine similitude is the noblest specimen of the work of God. . . .

The experimental knowledge of true godliness, in daily consecration and service to God, ensures the highest culture of the mind, soul, and body. . . . The impartation of divine power honors our sincere striving after wisdom for the conscientious use of our highest faculties to honor God and bless our fellow men. As these faculties are derived from God, and not self-created, they should be appreciated as talents from God to be employed in His service.

The Heaven-entrusted faculties of the mind are to be treated as the higher powers, to rule the kingdom of the body. The natural appetites and passions are to be brought under the control of the conscience and the spiritual affections. . . .

The religion of Jesus Christ never degrades the receiver; it never makes him coarse or rough, discourteous or self-important, passionate or hardhearted. On the contrary, it refines the taste, sanctifies the judgment, purifies and ennobles the thoughts by bringing them into captivity to Jesus Christ.

God's ideal for His children is higher than the highest human thought can reach. The living God has given in His holy law a transcript of His character. The greatest Teacher the world has ever known is Jesus Christ. And what is the standard He has given for all who believe in Him to reach? "Be ye therefore perfect, even as your Father which is in heaven is perfect" (Matt. 5:48). As God is perfect in His high sphere of action, so man may be perfect in his human sphere. The ideal of Christian character is Christlikeness. There is opened before us a path of continual advancement. We have an object to reach, a standard to gain which includes everything good and pure and noble and elevated. There should be continual striving and constant progress onward and upward toward perfection of character.

CHRIST IN ALL OUR THOUGHTS

Search me, O God, and know my heart: try me, and know my thoughts: and see if there be any wicked way in me, and lead me in the way everlasting. **Ps. 139:23, 24.**

Few realize that it is a duty to exercise control over the thoughts and imaginations. It is difficult to keep the undisciplined mind fixed upon profitable subjects. But if the thoughts are not properly employed, religion cannot flourish in the soul. The mind must be preoccupied with sacred and eternal things, or it will cherish trifling and superficial thoughts. Both the intellectual and the moral powers must be disciplined, and they will . . . improve by exercise.

In order to understand this matter aright, we must remember that our hearts are naturally depraved, and we are unable of ourselves to pursue a right course. It is only by the grace of God, combined with the most earnest effort on our part, that we can gain the victory. The intellect, as well as the heart, must be consecrated to the service of God. He has claims upon all there is of us.

Few believe that humanity has sunk so low as it has or that it is so thoroughly bad, so desperately opposed to God, as it is. . . . When the mind is not under the direct influence of the Spirit of God, Satan can mold it as he chooses. All the rational powers which he controls he will carnalize. He is directly opposed to God in his tastes, views, preferences, likes and dislikes, choice of things and pursuits; there is no relish for what God loves or approves, but a delight in those things which He despises. . . .

If Christ is abiding in the heart, He will be in all our thoughts. Our deepest thoughts will be of Him, His love, His purity. He will fill all the chambers of the mind. Our affections will center about Jesus. All our hopes and expectations will be associated with Him. To live the life we now live by faith in the Son of God, looking forward to and loving His appearing, will be the soul's highest joy. He will be the crown of our rejoicing.

Those who have trained the mind to delight in spiritual exercises are the ones who can be translated and not be overwhelmed with the purity and transcendent glory of heaven.

THE GOLD OF CHRISTIAN CHARACTER

A good name is rather to be chosen than great riches, and loving favour rather than silver and gold. Prov. 22:1.

Men may aspire to renown. They may desire to possess a great name. With some the possession of houses and lands and plenty of money, that which will make them great according to the measure of the world, is the height of their ambition. They desire to reach the place where they can look down with a sense of superiority upon those who are poor. All such are building on the sand, and their house will fall suddenly. Superiority of position is not true greatness. That which does not increase the value of the soul is of no real value in itself. That which alone is worth obtaining is greatness of soul in the sight of Heaven. The true and exalted nature of your work you may never know. The value of your own being you can only measure by the value of that Life given to save all who will receive it.

Every man will have some estimate of his own worth when he becomes a laborer together with Christ, doing the work that Christ did, filling the world with Christ's righteousness, bearing a commission from the Most High. . . . The commission given to the disciples is given to all who are connected with Christ. They are to make any and every sacrifice for the joy of seeing souls saved who are perishing out of Christ. . . .

The highest honor that can be conferred upon human beings, be they young or old, rich or poor, is to be permitted to lift up the oppressed, to comfort the feeble-minded. The world is full of suffering. Go, and preach the gospel to the poor; heal the sick. This is the work to be connected with the gospel message. "The poor have the gospel preached to them" (Matt. 11:5). Colaborers with God are to fill the space they occupy in the world with the love of Jesus. . . . The love of Christ in the heart is expressed in the actions. If love for Christ is dull the love for those for whom Christ died will degenerate. . . .

True riches are genuine faith and genuine love. These make the character complete in Christ. If there were more faith, simple, trusting faith in Jesus, there would be love, pure love, which is the gold of Christian character.

KIND AND
COURTEOUS WORDS

The Lord God hath given me the tongue of the learned, that I should know how to speak a word in season to him that is weary: he wakeneth morning by morning, he wakeneth mine ear to hear as the learned. **Isa. 50:4.**

What Christ was in His life on this earth, that every Christian is to be. He is our example, not only in His spotless purity, but in His patience, gentleness, and winsomeness of disposition. He was firm as a rock where truth and duty were concerned, but He was invariably kind and courteous. His life was a perfect illustration of true courtesy. . . . His presence brought a purer atmosphere into the home, and His life was as leaven working amid the elements of society. Harmless and undefiled, He walked among the thoughtless, the rude, the uncourteous; amid the unjust publicans, the unrighteous Samaritans, the heathen soldiers, the rough peasants, and the mixed multitude.

He spoke a word of sympathy here and a word there as He saw men weary and compelled to bear heavy burdens. He shared their burdens and repeated to them the lessons He had learned from nature, of the love, the kindness, the goodness of God. He sought to inspire with hope the most rough and unpromising, setting before them the assurance that they might become blameless and harmless, attaining such a character as would make them manifest as children of God. . . . Jesus sat an honored guest at the table of the publicans, by His sympathy and social kindliness showing that He recognized the dignity of humanity; and men longed to become worthy of His confidence. Upon their thirsty souls His words fell with blessed, life-giving power. New impulses were awakened, and the possibility of a new life opened to these outcasts of society.

The religion of Jesus softens whatever is hard and rough in the temper and smooths off whatever is rugged and sharp in the manners. It is this religion that makes the words gentle and the demeanor winning. Let us learn from Christ how to combine a high sense of purity and integrity with sunniness of disposition. A kind, courteous Christian is the most powerful argument that can be produced in favor of the gospel.

THE TEST OF APPETITE

But I keep under my body, and bring it into subjection: lest that by any means, when I have preached to others, I myself should be a castaway. **1 Cor. 9:27.**

After His baptism the Son of God entered the dreary wilderness, there to be tempted by the devil. For nearly six weeks He endured the agonies of hunger. . . . He realized the power of appetite upon man; and in behalf of sinful man He bore the closest test possible upon that point. Here a victory was gained which few can appreciate. The controlling power of depraved appetite and the grievous sin of indulging it can only be understood by the length of the fast which our Saviour endured that He might break its power. . . .

Intemperance lies at the foundation of all the moral evils known to man. Christ began the work of redemption just where the ruin began. The fall of our first parents was caused by the indulgence of appetite. In redemption, the denial of appetite is the first work of Christ.

The Son of God saw that man could not of himself overcome this powerful temptation. . . . He came to earth to unite His divine power with our human efforts, that through the strength and moral power which He imparts, we might overcome in our own behalf. Oh! what matchless condescension for the King of glory to come down to this world to endure the pangs of hunger and the fierce temptations of a wily foe, that He might gain an infinite victory for man. Here is love without a parallel. Yet this great condescension is but dimly comprehended by those for whom it was made.

It was not the gnawing pangs of hunger alone which made the sufferings of our Redeemer so inexpressibly severe. It was the sense of guilt which had resulted from the indulgence of appetite that had brought such terrible woe into the world, which pressed so heavily upon His divine soul. . . .

With man's nature, and the terrible weight of his sins pressing upon Him, our Redeemer withstood the power of Satan upon this great leading temptation, which imperils the souls of men. If man should overcome this temptation, he could conquer on every other point.

KEEPING LOVE ALIVE

Wives, submit yourselves unto your own husbands, as it is fit in the Lord. Husbands, love your wives, and be not bitter against them. **Col. 3:18, 19.**

How much trouble and what a tide of woe and unhappiness would be saved if men, and women also, would continue to cultivate the regard, attention, and kind words of appreciation and little courtesies of life which kept love alive and which they felt were necessary in gaining the companions of their choice. If the husband and wife would only continue to cultivate these attentions which nourish love, they would be happy in each other's society and would have a sanctifying influence upon their families. They would have in themselves a little world of happiness and would not desire to go outside this world for new attractions and new objects of love. . . .

Many women pine for words of love and kindness and the common attentions and courtesies due them from their husbands who have selected them as their life companions. . . . It is these little attentions and courtesies which make up the sum of life's happiness. . . .

If the hearts were kept tender in our families, if there were a noble, generous deference to each other's tastes and opinions, if the wife were seeking opportunities to express her love by actions in her courtesies to her husband, and the husband were manifesting the same consideration and kindly regard for the wife, the children would partake of the same spirit. The influence would pervade the household, and what a tide of misery would be saved in families! . . .

Every couple who unite their life interest should seek to make the life of each as happy as possible. That which we prize we seek to preserve and make more valuable if we can. In the marriage contract men and women have made a trade, an investment for life, and they should do their utmost to control their words of impatience and fretfulness, even more carefully than they did before their marriage, for now their destinies are united for life as husband and wife, and each is valued in exact proportion to the amount of painstaking effort put forth to retain and keep fresh the love so eagerly sought for and prized before marriage.

THE VOICE OF DUTY

Whatsoever thy hand findeth to do, do it with thy might. **Eccl. 9:10.**

The voice of duty is the voice of God—an inborn, heaven-sent guide. Whether it be pleasing or unpleasing, we are to do the duty that lies directly in our pathway. If the Lord would have us bear a message to Nineveh, it will not be pleasing to Him for us to go to Joppa or Capernaum. God has reasons for sending us to the place to which our feet are directed. . . .

It is the little foxes that spoil the vines; the little neglects, the little deficiencies, the little dishonesties, the little departures from principle, that blind the soul and separate it from God.

It is the little things of life that develop the spirit and determine the character. Those who neglect the little things will not be prepared to endure severe tests when they are brought to bear upon them. Remember that the character building is not finished till life ends. Every day a good or bad brick is placed in the structure. You are either building crookedly or with the exactness and correctness that will make a beautiful temple for God. Therefore, in looking for great things to do, neglect not the little opportunities that come to you day by day. He who neglects the little things, and yet flatters himself that he is ready to do wonderful things for the Master, is in danger of failing altogether. Life is made up, not of great sacrifices and of wonderful achievements, but of little things.

Whatever your hands find to do, do it with your might. Make your work pleasant with songs of praise. If you would have a clean record in the books of heaven, never fret or scold. Let your daily prayer be, ''Lord, help me to do my best. . . . Give me energy and cheerfulness. Help me to bring into my service the loving ministry of the Saviour.''

Look upon every duty, however humble, as sacred because it is part of God's service. Do not allow anything to make you forgetful of God. Bring Christ into all that you do. Then your lives will be filled with brightness and thanksgiving. You will do your best, moving forward cheerfully in the service of the Lord, your hearts filled with His joy.

June 20

LIVING FOR OTHERS

Even as the Son of man came not to be ministered unto, but to minister, and to give his life a ransom for many. **Matt. 20:28.**

We are not to live for ourselves. Christ came to this world to live for others—not to be ministered unto, but to minister. If you strive to live as

He lived you are saying to the world, "Behold the Man of Calvary." By precept and example you are leading others in the way of righteousness.

The sin which is indulged to the greatest extent, and which separates us from God and produces so many contagious spiritual disorders, is selfishness. There can be no returning to the Lord except by self-denial. Of ourselves we can do nothing; but through God strengthening us we can live to do good to others, and in this way shun the evil of selfishness. We need not go to heathen lands to manifest our desire to devote all to God in a useful, unselfish life. We should do this in the home circle, in the church, among those with whom we associate and with whom we do business. Right in the common walks of life is where self is to be denied and kept in subordination.

Paul could say: "I die daily" (1 Cor. 15:31). It is the daily dying to self in the little transactions of life that makes us overcomers. We should forget self in the desire to do good to others. With many there is a decided lack of love for others. Instead of faithfully performing their duty, they seek rather their own pleasure.

God positively enjoins upon all His followers a duty to bless others with their influence and means. . . . In doing for others, a sweet satisfaction will be experienced, an inward peace which will be a sufficient reward. When actuated by a high and noble desire to do others good, they will find true happiness in a faithful discharge of life's manifold duties. This will bring more than an earthly reward; for every faithful, unselfish performance of duty is noticed by the angels and shines in the life record. In heaven none will think of self, nor seek their own pleasure; but all, from pure, genuine love, will seek the happiness of the heavenly beings around them. If we wish to enjoy heavenly society in the earth made new, we must be governed by heavenly principles here.

NO ONE FREE
FROM TEMPTATION

Who are kept by the power of God through faith unto salvation ready to be revealed in the last time. Wherein ye greatly rejoice, though now for a season, if need be, ye are in heaviness through manifold temptations. **1 Peter 1:5, 6.**

Do not think that the Christian life is free from temptation. Temptations will come to every Christian. Both the Christian and the one who does not accept Christ as his leader will have trials. The difference is that the latter is serving a tyrant, doing his mean drudgery, while the Christian is serving the One who died to give him eternal life. Do not look upon trial as something strange, but as the means by which we are to be purified and strengthened. "Count it all joy when ye fall into divers temptations," James admonishes; "knowing this, that the trying of your faith worketh patience" (James 1:2, 3).

In the future life we shall understand things that here greatly perplex us. We shall realize how strong a helper we had and how angels of God were commissioned to guard us as we followed the counsel of the Word of God.

To all who receive Him, Christ will give power to become the sons of God. He is a present help in every time of need. Let us be ashamed of our wavering faith. Those who are overcome have only themselves to blame for their failure to resist the enemy. All who choose can come to Christ and find the help they need.

There stands among you the mighty Counselor of the ages, inviting you to place your confidence in Him. Shall we turn away from Him to uncertain human beings, who are as wholly dependent on God as we ourselves are? Have we fallen so far below our privileges? Have we not been guilty of expecting so little that we have not asked for what God is longing to give?

"I will mention the lovingkindnesses of the Lord, and the praises of the Lord, according to all that the Lord hath bestowed on us, and the great goodness toward the house of Israel. . . . For he said, Surely they are my people, children that will not lie: so he was their Saviour. In all their affliction he was afflicted, and the angel of his presence saved them" (Isa. 63:7-9).

STRENGTH FOR TODAY

And I will bring the third part through the fire, and will refine them as silver is refined, and will try them as gold is tried: they shall call on my name, and I will hear them: I will say, It is my people: and they shall say, The Lord is my God. Zech. 13:9.

By trial the Lord proves the strength of His children. Is the heart strong to bear? Is the conscience void of offense? Does the Spirit bear witness with our spirit that we are the children of God? This the Lord ascertains by trying us. In the furnace of affliction He purifies us from all dross. He sends us trials, not to cause needless pain, but to lead us to look to Him, to strengthen our endurance, to teach us that if we do not rebel, but put our trust in Him, we shall see of His salvation. . . .

Christ's love for His children is as strong as it is tender. It is a love stronger than death, for He died for us. It is a love more true than that of a mother for her children. The mother's love may change, but Christ's love is changeless. "I am persuaded," Paul says, "that neither death, nor life, nor angels, nor principalities, nor powers, nor things present, nor things to come, nor height, nor depth, nor any other creature, shall be able to separate us from the love of God, which is in Christ Jesus our Lord" (Rom. 8:38, 39).

In every trial we have strong consolation. Is not our Saviour touched with the feeling of our infirmities? Has He not been tempted in all points like as we are? And has He not invited us to take every trial and perplexity to Him? Then let us not make ourselves miserable over tomorrow's burdens. Bravely and cheerfully carry the burdens of today. Today's trust and faith we must have. But we are not asked to live more than a day at a time. He who gives strength for today will give strength for tomorrow. . . .

Nothing wounds the soul like the sharp darts of unbelief. When trial comes, as it will, do not worry or complain. Silence in the soul makes more distinct the voice of God. "Then are they glad because they be quiet" (Ps. 107:30). Remember that underneath you are the everlasting arms. "Rest in the Lord, and wait patiently for him" (Ps. 37:7). He is guiding you into a harbor of gracious experience.

MEMBERS OF
GOD'S HOUSEHOLD

Now therefore ye are no more strangers and foreigners, but fellowcitizens with the saints, and of the household of God; and are built upon the foundation of the apostles and prophets, Jesus Christ himself being the chief corner stone. **Eph. 2:19, 20.**

The Lord Jesus is making experiments on human hearts through the exhibition of His mercy and abundant grace. He is affecting transformations so amazing that Satan . . . stands viewing them as a fortress impregnable to his sophistries and delusions. They are to him an incomprehensible mystery. The angels of God . . . look on with astonishment and joy, that fallen men, once children of wrath, are through the training of Christ developing characters after the divine similitude, to be sons and daughters of God, to act an important part in the occupations and pleasures of heaven.

The Lord has provided His church with capabilities and blessings, that they may present to the world an image of His own sufficiency, and that His church may be complete in Him, a continual representation of another, even the eternal world, of laws that are higher than earthly laws. His church is to be a temple built after the divine similitude. . . .

To His church, Christ has given ample facilities, that He may receive a large revenue of glory from His redeemed, purchased possession. The church, being endowed with the righteousness of Christ, is His depository, in which the wealth of His mercy, His love, His grace, is to appear in full and final display. The declaration in His intercessory prayer, that the Father's love is as great toward us as toward Himself, the only-begotten Son, and that we shall be with Him where He is, forever one with Christ and the Father, is a marvel to the heavenly host, and it is their great joy. The gift of His Holy Spirit, rich, full, and abundant, is to be to His church as an encompassing wall of fire, which the powers of hell shall not prevail against. In their untainted purity and spotless perfection, Christ looks upon His people as the reward of all His suffering, His humiliation, and His love, and the supplement of His glory—Christ, the great center from which radiates all glory.

REMEMBER
YOUR HIGH CALLING

Wherefore I will not be negligent to put you always in remembrance of these things, though ye know them, and be established in the present truth. **2 Peter 1:12.**

No matter how long we may have been traveling in the way of life eternal we need often to recount the mercies of our heavenly Father toward us and gather hope and courage from the promises of His Word. . . . Peter realized the value of constant vigilance in the Christian life, and he felt impelled by the Holy Spirit to urge upon the believers the importance of exercising great carefulness in the daily life. . . .

"Always in remembrance." Oh, if only we were to keep before our minds those things that pertain to our eternal welfare, we should not engage in any foolishness or idle speaking! Our lifework is before us. It is for us to give diligence to make our calling and election sure, by giving heed to the plain instruction contained in God's Holy Word. . . .

There are many wrong things which we allow to pass by unnoticed, when by our godly conversation we might set an example of rightdoing that would be a standing rebuke to the evildoers. We cannot afford by our example to seem to sanction wrongdoing. There is a heaven to win and a hell to shun. In large churches of believers . . . there is special danger of lowering the standard. Where many are gathered together some are more liable to grow careless and indifferent than they would be if isolated and made to stand alone. But even under adverse circumstances we may watch unto prayer and set an example in godly conversation that will be a powerful testimony for the right. . . . We cannot afford to speak words that would discourage our fellow pilgrims in the Christian pathway. Christ has given His life in order that we might live with Him in glory. Throughout eternity He will bear in His hands the prints of the cruel nails by which He was transfixed to the cross of Calvary. . . .

We are now fitting up for the future, eternal life; and soon, if faithful, we shall see the gates of the city of our God swing back on their glittering hinges that the nations who have kept the truth may enter in to their eternal inheritance.

OUR MISSION TO THE WORLD

As thou hast sent me into the world, even so have I also sent them into the world. John 17:18.

Will separation from the world, in obedience to the divine command, unfit us for the work the Lord has left us? Will it hinder us from doing good to those around us? No; the firmer hold we have on heaven, the greater will be our power for usefulness. We should study the Pattern, that the spirit which dwelt in Christ may dwell in us. The Saviour was not found among the exalted and honorable of the world. He did not spend His time among those who were seeking their ease and pleasure. He worked to help those who needed help, to save the lost and perishing, to lift up the bowed down, to break the yoke of oppression from those in bondage, to heal the afflicted, and to speak words of sympathy and consolation to the distressed and sorrowing. We are required to follow this example. The more we partake of the spirit of Christ, the more we shall seek to do for our fellow men. We shall bless the needy and comfort the distressed. . . .

Probation is about to close. . . . Soon the last prayer for sinners will have been offered, the last tear shed, the last warning given, the last entreaty made, and the sweet voice of mercy will be heard no more. This is why Satan is making such mighty efforts to secure men and women in his snare. . . . The enemy is playing the game of life for every soul. He is working to remove from us everything of a spiritual nature, and in the place of the precious graces of Christ to crowd our hearts with the evil traits of the carnal nature—hatred, evil surmising, jealousy, love of the world, love of self, love of pleasure, and the pride of life. We need to be fortified against the incoming foe, . . . for unless we are watchful and prayerful these evils will enter the heart and crowd out all that is good.

How great is the responsibility placed upon the disciple of Christ. How imperative the duty to reflect the light of heaven upon a world enshrouded in darkness. The deeper the surrounding gloom, the brighter should shine out the light of Christian faith and Christian example.

THE MOST POWERFUL ARGUMENT

I, even I, am the Lord; and beside me there is no saviour. . . . Therefore ye are my witnesses, saith the Lord, that I am God. **Isa. 43:11, 12.**

Of His true followers the Lord says, "This people have I formed for myself; they shall shew forth my praise" (verse 21). They are My witnesses, My chosen representatives, in an apostate world. . . .

God calls for our cooperation. His requirements are just and reasonable. . . . When we take the name of Christ we pledge ourselves to represent Him. In order for us to be true to our pledge, Christ must be formed within, the hope of glory. The daily life must become more and more like the Christ life. We must be Christians in deed and in truth. Christ will have nothing to do with pretense. He will welcome to the heavenly courts those only whose Christianity is genuine. The lives of professed Christians who do not live the life of Christ are a mockery to religion.

God does not ask us to purchase His favor by any costly sacrifice. He asks only for the service of a humble, contrite heart, which has gladly and thankfully accepted His free gift. The one who receives Christ as his personal Saviour has in his possession the salvation provided by Christ. And he is never to forget that as he has freely received, so he is freely to impart.

Do you realize your value in the sight of God? He says, Ye are laborers together with Me. Are you letting your light shine in clear rays to a fallen world? Are you seeking to exercise every faculty and every power which God has given you? You may not be a minister, but you can be a witness. You may not be an eloquent speaker, but you can be eloquent in living Christ, you can be eloquent in letting your light shine before men.

A true, lovable Christian is the most powerful argument that can be advanced in favor of Bible truth. Such a man is Christ's representative. His life is the most convincing evidence that can be borne to the power of divine grace. When God's people bring the righteousness of Christ into the daily life, sinners will be converted and victories over the enemy will be gained.

OUR OBLIGATIONS
TO THE POOR

For I was an hungred, and ye gave me meat: I was thirsty, and ye gave me drink: I was a stranger, and ye took me in: naked, and ye clothed me: I was sick, and ye visited me: I was in prison, and ye came unto me. **Matt. 25:35, 36.**

While the world needs sympathy, while it needs the prayers and assistance of God's people, while it needs to see Christ in the lives of His followers, the people of God are equally in need of opportunities that draw out their sympathies, give efficiency to their prayers, and develop in them a character like that of the divine pattern.

It is to provide these opportunities that God has placed among us the poor, the unfortunate, the sick, and the suffering. They are Christ's legacy to His church, and they are to be cared for as He would care for them. In this way God takes away the dross and purifies the gold, giving us that culture of heart and character which we need.

The Lord could carry forward His work without our cooperation. He is not dependent on us for our money, our time, or our labor. But the church is very precious in His sight. It is the case which contains His jewels, the fold which encloses His flock, and He longs to see it without spot or blemish or any such thing. He yearns after it with unspeakable love. This is why He has given us opportunities to work for Him, and He accepts our labors as tokens of our love and loyalty.

In placing among us the poor and the suffering, the Lord is testing us to reveal to us what is in our hearts. . . . The culture of the mind and heart is more easily accomplished when we feel such tender sympathy for others that we bestow our benefits and privileges to relieve their necessities. . . .

Good works cost us a sacrifice, but it is in this very sacrifice that they provide discipline. These obligations bring us into conflict with natural feelings and propensities, and in fulfilling them we gain victory after victory over the objectionable traits of our characters.

The world will be convinced not so much by what the pulpit teaches as by what the church lives. The preacher announces the theory of the gospel, but the practical piety of the church demonstrates its power.

A WORK
OF PREPARATION

Being confident of this very thing, that he which hath begun a good work in you will perform it until the day of Jesus Christ. **Phil. 1:6.**

There is an earnest work of preparation to be done by Seventh-day Adventists if they would stand firm in the trying experiences just before them. If they remain true to God in the confusion and temptation of the last days, they must seek the Lord in humility of heart for wisdom to resist the deceptions of the enemy. . . .

Ever are we to keep in mind the solemn thought of the Lord's soon return, and in view of this to recognize the individual work to be done. Through the aid of the Holy Spirit we are to resist natural inclinations and tendencies to wrong, and weed out of the life every un-Christlike element. Thus we shall prepare our hearts for the reception of God's blessing, which will impart to us grace and bring us into harmony with the faith of Jesus. For this work of preparation great advantages have been granted to this people in light bestowed, in messages of warning and instruction, sent through the agency of the Spirit of God.

Because of the increasing power of Satan's temptations, the times in which we live are full of peril for the children of God, and we need to learn constantly of the Great Teacher, that we may take every step in surety and righteousness. Wonderful scenes are opening before us, and at this time a living testimony is to be borne in the lives of God's professing people, so that the world may see that in this age when evil reigns on every side, there is yet a people who are laying aside their will and are seeking to do God's will—a people in whose hearts and lives the law of God is written. There are strong temptations before us, sharp tests. The commandment-keeping people of God are to prepare for this time of trial by obtaining a deeper experience in the things of God and a practical knowledge of the righteousness of Christ. . . . Not to unbelievers only, but to church members the words are spoken, "Seek ye the Lord while he may be found, call ye upon him while he is near" (Isa. 55:6). . . .

Let your daily lives witness to the faith you profess.

IF CHRIST
SHOULD COME TODAY

Watch ye therefore, and pray always, that ye may be accounted worthy to escape all these things that shall come to pass, and to stand before the Son of man. **Luke 21:36.**

Christ bids us watch, that we may be accounted worthy to escape the things that are coming on the earth. It is of the greatest importance that we heed this warning. The enemy of all righteousness is on our track, seeking to lead us to forget God.

We should be filled with joy at the thought of Christ's soon appearing. To those that love His appearing He will come without sin unto salvation. But if our minds are filled with thoughts of earthly things, we cannot look forward with joy to His appearing.

"If I knew that Christ were coming in a few years," one says, "I should live very differently." But if we believe that He is coming at all, we should live just as faithfully as if we knew that He would appear in a few years. We cannot see the end from the beginning, but Christ has provided sufficient help for every day in the year.

All we have to do with is this one day. Today we must be faithful to our trust. Today we must love God with all the heart and our neighbor as ourselves. Today we must resist the temptations of the enemy, and through the grace of Christ gain the victory. Thus we shall watch and wait for Christ's coming. Each day we should live as if we knew that this would be our last day on this earth. If we knew that Christ would come tomorrow, would we not crowd into today all the kind words, all the unselfish deeds, that we could? We should be patient and gentle, and intensely in earnest, doing all in our power to win souls to Christ. . . .

I urge you to turn your thoughts from worldly things and center them on the things of eternity. Christ has placed everlasting life within your reach, and He has promised to give you help in every time of need. . . . We should never rest satisfied with present attainments. If we put mind and heart into the work of reaching God's ideal for us, if we go to Christ, the mighty helper, for aid, He will give us the very assistance that we need. He will bestow on us the very power that will enable us to be victorious in the struggle against evil.

BY THE TREE OF LIFE

And they sung a new song, saying, Thou art worthy to take the book, and to open the seals thereof: for thou wast slain, and hast redeemed us to God by thy blood out of every kindred, and tongue, and people, and nation. **Rev. 5:9.**

Do we expect to get to heaven at last and join the heavenly choir? Just as we go into the grave we will come up, as far as the character is concerned. . . . Now is the time for washing and ironing. . . .

John saw the throne of God and around that throne a company, and he inquired, Who are these? The answer came, "These are they which . . . have washed their robes, and made them white in the blood of the Lamb" (Rev. 7:14). Christ leads them to the fountains of living waters, and there is the tree of life and there is the previous Saviour. Here is presented to us a life that measures with the life of God. There is no pain, sorrow, sickness, or death there. All is peace and harmony and love. . . .

Now is the time to receive grace and strength and power to combine with our human efforts that we can form characters for everlasting life. When we do this we will find that the angels of God will minister unto us, and we shall be heirs of God and joint heirs with Jesus Christ. And when the last trump shall sound, and the dead shall be called from their prison house and changed in a moment, in the twinkling of an eye, the crowns of immortal glory shall be placed upon the heads of the overcomers. The pearly gates will swing back for the nations that have kept the truth and they will enter in. The conflict is ended.

"Come, ye blessed of my Father, inherit the kingdom prepared for you from the foundation of the world" (Matt. 25:34). Do we want this benediction? I do, and I believe you do. May God help you that you may fight the battles of this life and gain a victory day by day and at last be among the number that shall cast their crowns at Jesus' feet and touch the golden harps and fill all heaven with sweetest music. I want you to love my Jesus. . . . Do not reject my Saviour, for He has paid an infinite price for you. I see in Jesus matchless charms, and I want you to see these charms.

ONE EXPENSIVE MISTAKE

God hath made man upright; but they have sought out many inventions. **Eccl. 7:29.**

The book of Genesis gives quite a definite account of social and individual life, and yet we have no record of an infant's being born blind, deaf, crippled, deformed, or imbecile. There is not an instance upon record of a natural death in infancy, childhood, or early manhood. There is no account of men and women dying of disease. Obituary notices in the book of Genesis run thus: "And all the days that Adam lived were nine hundred and thirty years: and he died." "And all the days of Seth were nine hundred and twelve years: and he died." . . .

God endowed man with so great vital force that he has withstood the accumulation of disease brought upon the race in consequence of perverted habits, and has continued for six thousand years. This fact of itself is enough to evidence to us the strength and electrical energy that God gave to man at his creation. . . . If Adam, at his creation, had not been endowed with twenty times as much vital force as men now have, the race, with their present habits of living in violation of natural law, would have become extinct. . . .

God did not create the race in its present feeble condition. This state of things is not the work of Providence, but the work of man; it has been brought about by wrong habits and abuses, by violating the laws that God has made to govern man's existence.

God created man for His own glory, that after test and trial the human family might become one with the heavenly family, if they would show themselves obedient to His every word.

To Eve it seemed a small thing to disobey God by tasting the fruit of the forbidden tree, and to tempt her husband also to transgress; but their sin opened the floodgates of woe upon the world. Who can know, in the moment of temptation, the terrible consequences that will result from one wrong step?

ADAM HOME AGAIN!

For as in Adam all die, even so in Christ shall all be made alive. But every man in his own order: Christ the firstfruits; afterward they that are Christ's at his coming. **1 Cor. 15:22, 23.**

Amid the reeling of the earth, the flash of lightning, and the roar of thunder, the voice of the Son of God calls forth the sleeping saints. . . . The dead shall hear that voice, and they that hear shall live. And the whole earth shall ring with the tread of the exceeding great army of every nation, kindred, tongue, and people. . . .

All come forth from their graves the same in stature as when they entered the tomb. Adam, who stands among the risen throng, is of lofty height and majestic form, in stature but little below the Son of God. He presents a marked contrast to the people of later generations; in this one respect is shown the great degeneracy of the race. But all arise with the freshness and vigor of eternal youth. . . .

All blemishes and deformities are left in the grave. Restored to the tree of life in the long-lost Eden, the redeemed will "grow up" to the full stature of the race in its primeval glory. . . .

As the ransomed ones are welcomed to the City of God, there rings out upon the air an exultant cry of adoration. The two Adams are about to meet. The Son of God is standing with outstretched arms to receive the father of our race—the being whom He created, who sinned against his Maker, and for whose sin the marks of the crucifixion are borne upon the Saviour's form. As Adam discerns the prints of the cruel nails, he does not fall upon the bosom of his Lord, but in humiliation casts himself at His feet, crying: "Worthy, worthy is the Lamb that was slain!" Tenderly the Saviour lifts him up and bids him look once more upon the Eden home from which he has so long been exiled. . . .

This reunion is witnessed by the angels who wept at the fall of Adam and rejoiced when Jesus, after His resurrection, ascended to heaven, having opened the grave for all who should believe on His name. Now they behold the work of redemption accomplished, and they unite their voices in the song of praise.

AN OPEN DOOR

By faith Enoch was translated that he should not see death; and was not found, because God had translated him: for before his translation he had this testimony, that he pleased God. Heb. 11:5.

When we learn to walk by faith and not by feeling, we shall have help from God just when we need it, and His peace will come into our hearts. It was this simple life of obedience and trust that Enoch lived. If we learn this lesson of simple trust, ours may be the testimony that he received, that he pleased God.

In every phase of your character building you are to please God. This you may do; for Enoch pleased Him through living in a degenerate age. And there are Enochs in this our day.

For three hundred years Enoch had been seeking purity of heart, that he might be in harmony with heaven. For three centuries he had walked with God. Day by day he had longed for a closer union; nearer and nearer had grown the communion, until God took him to Himself. He had stood at the threshold of the eternal world, only a step between him and the land of the blest; and now the portals opened, the walk with God, so long pursued on earth, continued, and he passed through the gates of the holy city,—the first from among men to enter there.

With the word of God in his hands, every human being, wherever his lot in life may be cast, may have such companionship as he shall choose. In its pages he may hold converse with the noblest and best of the human race, and may listen to the voice of the Eternal as He speaks with men. . . . He may dwell in this world in the atmosphere of heaven, imparting to earth's sorrowing and tempted ones thoughts of hope and longings for holiness; . . . like him of old who walked with God, drawing nearer and nearer to the threshold of the eternal world, until the portals shall open, and he shall enter there. He will find himself no stranger. The voices that will greet him are the voices of the holy ones, who, unseen, were on earth his companions—voices that here he learned to distinguish and to love. He who through the word of God has lived in fellowship with heaven, will find himself at home in heaven's companionship.

SAFE INSIDE

And the Lord said unto Noah, Come thou and all thy house into the ark; for thee have I seen righteous before me in this generation. **Gen. 7:1.**

Noah had faithfully followed the instructions which he had received from God. The ark was finished in every part as the Lord had directed, and was stored with food for man and beast. And now the servant of God made his last solemn appeal to the people. With an agony of desire that words cannot express, he entreated them to seek a refuge while it might be found. Again they rejected his words, and raised their voices in jest and scoffing. Suddenly a silence fell upon the mocking throng. Beasts of every description, the fiercest as well as the most gentle, were seen coming from mountain and forest and quietly making their way toward the ark. A noise as of a rushing wind was heard, and lo, birds were flocking from all directions, their numbers darkening the heavens, and in perfect order they passed to the ark. Animals obeyed the command of God, while men were disobedient.

When they saw the beasts come from the forests to the door of the ark, and Noah take them in, they had so long resisted, so long denied the message that God had given them, that . . . conscience had become unimpressible.

Mercy had ceased its pleadings for the guilty race. The beasts of the field and the birds of the air had entered the place of refuge. Noah and his household were within the ark, "and the Lord shut him in." . . . The massive door, which it was impossible for those within to close, was slowly swung to its place by unseen hands. Noah was shut in, and the rejecters of God's mercy were shut out. The seal of Heaven was on that door; God had shut it, and God alone could open it. So when Christ shall cease His intercession for guilty men, before His coming in the clouds of heaven, the door of mercy will be shut. Then divine grace will no longer restrain the wicked, and Satan will have full control of those who have rejected mercy. They will endeavor to destroy God's people; but as Noah was shut into the ark, so the righteous will be shielded by divine power.

A HOME GOD CAN BLESS

For I know him, that he will command his children and his household after him, and they shall keep the way of the Lord, to do justice and judgment. **Gen. 18:19.**

In God's sight, a man is just what he is in his family. The life of Abraham, the friend of God, was signalized by a strict regard for the word of the Lord. He cultivated home religion. The fear of God pervaded his household. He was the priest of his home. He looked upon his family as a sacred trust. His household numbered more than a thousand souls, and he directed them all, parents and children, to the divine Sovereign. He suffered no parental oppression on the one hand or filial disobedience on the other. By the combined influence of love and justice, he ruled his household in the fear of God, and the Lord bore witness to his faithfulness.

He "will command . . . his household." There would be no sinful neglect to restrain the evil propensities of his children, no weak, unwise, indulgent favoritism, no yielding of his conviction of duty to the claims of mistaken affection. Abraham would not only give right instruction, but he would maintain the authority of just and righteous laws.

How few there are in our day who follow this example. On the part of too many parents there is a blind and selfish sentimentalism, which is manifested in leaving children with their unformed judgment and undisciplined passions, to the control of their own will. This is the worst cruelty to the youth and a great wrong to the world. Parental indulgence causes disorder in families and in society. It confirms in the young the desire to follow inclination, instead of submitting to the divine requirements.

Parents and children alike belong to God to be ruled by Him. By affection and authority combined, Abraham ruled his house. God's word has given us rules for our guidance. These rules form the standard from which we cannot swerve if we would keep the way of the Lord. God's will must be paramount. The question for us to ask is not: What have others done? What will my relatives think? or, What will they say of me if I pursue this course? but, What has God said? Neither parent nor child can truly prosper in any course excepting in the way of the Lord.

HOW CAN I DO IT?

How then can I do this great wickedness, and sin against God? **Gen. 39:9.**

It is always a critical period in a young man's life when he is separated from home influences and wise counsels and enters upon new scenes and trying tests. But if he does not of his own accord place himself in these positions of danger and remove himself from parental restraint; if, without will or choice of his own, he is placed in dangerous positions and relies upon God for strength—cherishing the love of God in his heart—he will be kept from yielding to temptation by the power of God who placed him in that trying position. God will protect him from being corrupted by the fierce temptation. God was with Joseph in his new home. He was in the path of duty, suffering wrong but not doing wrong. He therefore had the love and protection of God for he carried his religious principle into everything he undertook.

Joseph's faith and integrity were to be tested by fiery trials. His master's wife endeavored to entice the young man to transgress the law of God. Heretofore he had remained untainted by the corruption teeming in that heathen land; but this temptation, so sudden, so strong, so seductive—how should it be met? Joseph knew well what would be the consequence of resistance. On the one hand were concealment, favor, and rewards; on the other, disgrace, imprisonment, perhaps death. His whole future life depended upon the decision of the moment. Would principle triumph? Would Joseph still be true to God? With inexpressible anxiety, angels looked upon the scene.

Joseph's answer reveals the power of religious principle. He would not betray the confidence of his master on earth, and, whatever the consequences, he would be true to his Master in heaven. Under the inspecting eye of God and holy angels many take liberties of which they would not be guilty in the presence of their fellow men, but Joseph's first thought was of God. "How can I do this great wickedness, and sin against God?" he said.

If we were to cherish an habitual impression that God sees and hears all that we do and say and keeps a faithful record of our words and actions, and that we must meet it all, we would fear to sin.

POWER GUARANTEED

As a prince hast thou power with God and with men, and hast prevailed. **Gen. 32:28.**

Had not Jacob previously repented of his sin in obtaining the birthright by fraud, God could not have heard his prayer and mercifully preserved his life. So in the time of trouble, if the people of God had unconfessed sins to appear before them while tortured with fear and anguish, they would be overwhelmed; despair would cut off their faith, and they could not have confidence to plead with God for deliverance. But while they have a deep sense of their unworthiness, they will have no concealed wrongs to reveal. Their sins will have been blotted out by the atoning blood of Christ, and they cannot bring them to remembrance. . . .

All who endeavor to excuse or conceal their sins, and permit them to remain upon the books of heaven, unconfessed and unforgiven, will be overcome by Satan. The more exalted their profession, and the more honorable the position which they hold, the more grievous is their course in the sight of God, and the more certain the triumph of the great adversary.

Yet Jacob's history is an assurance that God will not cast off those who have been betrayed into sin, but who have returned unto Him with true repentance. It was by self-surrender and confiding faith that Jacob gained what he had failed to gain by conflict in his own strength. God thus taught His servant that divine power and grace alone could give him the blessing he craved. Thus it will be with those who live in the last days. As dangers surround them, and despair seizes upon the soul, they must depend solely upon the merits of the atonement. . . . None will ever perish while they do this. . . .

Jacob prevailed because he was persevering and determined. . . . It is now that we are to learn this lesson of prevailing prayer, of unyielding faith. The greatest victories to the church of Christ or to the individual Christian are not those that are gained by talent or education, by wealth or the favor of men. They are those victories that are gained in the audience chamber with God, when earnest, agonizing faith lays hold upon the mighty arm of power.

SEEING THE INVISIBLE

By faith he forsook Egypt, not fearing the wrath of the king: for he endured, as seeing him who is invisible. **Heb. 11:27.**

Moses had a deep sense of the personal presence of God. He was not only looking down through the ages for Christ to be made manifest in the flesh, but he saw Christ in a special manner accompanying the children of Israel in all their travels. God was real to him, ever present in his thoughts. When misunderstood, when called upon to face danger and to bear insult for Christ's sake, he endured without retaliation. Moses believed in God as one whom he needed and who would help him because of his need. God was to him a present help.

Much of the faith which we see is merely nominal: the real, trusting, persevering faith is rare. Moses realized in his own experience the promise that God will be a rewarder to those who diligently seek Him. He had respect unto the recompense of the reward. Here is another point in regard to faith which we wish to study: God will reward the man of faith and obedience. If this faith is brought into the life experience, it will enable everyone who fears and loves God to endure trials. Moses was full of confidence in God because he had appropriating faith. He needed help, and he prayed for it, grasped it by faith, and wove into his experience the belief that God cared for him. He believed that God ruled his life in particular. He saw and acknowledged God in every detail of his life and felt that he was under the eye of the All-seeing One, who weighs motives, who tries the heart. He looked to God and trusted in Him for strength to carry him uncorrupted through every form of temptation. . . . The presence of God was sufficient to carry him through the most trying situations in which a man could be placed.

Moses did not merely think of God: he saw Him. God was the constant vision before him: he never lost sight of His face. He saw Jesus as his Saviour, and he believed that the Saviour's merits would be imputed to him. This faith was to Moses no guesswork: it was a reality. This is the kind of faith we need, faith that will endure the test. Oh, how often we yield to temptation because we do not keep our eye upon Jesus!

CLOUD AND FIRE

He spread a cloud for a covering; and fire to give light in the night. **Ps. 105:39.**

"And the Lord went before them by day in a pillar of cloud, to lead them the way: and by night in a pillar of fire, to give them light." . . . The standard of their invisible Leader was ever with them. By day the cloud directed their journeyings or spread as a canopy above the host. It served as a protection from the burning heat, and by its coolness and moisture afforded grateful refreshment in the parched, thirsty desert. By night it became a pillar of fire, illuminating their encampment and constantly assuring them of the divine presence.

In one of the most beautiful and comforting passages of Isaiah's prophecy, reference is made to the pillar of cloud and of fire to represent God's care for His people in the great final struggle with the powers of evil: "The Lord will create upon every dwelling place of Mount Zion, and upon her assemblies, a cloud and smoke by day, and the shining of a flaming fire by night: for above all the glory shall be a covering. And there shall be a tabernacle for a shadow in the daytime from the heat, and for a place of refuge, and for a covert from storm and from rain" (Isa. 4:5, 6, margin).

In the time of trial before us God's pledge of security will be placed upon those who have kept the word of His patience. Christ will say to His faithful ones: "Come, my people, enter thou into thy chambers, and shut thy doors about thee: hide thyself as it were for a little moment until the indignation be overpast" (Isa. 26:20). The Lion of Judah, so terrible to the rejectors of His grace, will be the Lamb of God to the obedient and faithful. The pillar of cloud which speaks wrath and terror to the transgressor of God's law is light and mercy and deliverance to those who have kept his commandments. The arm strong to smite the rebellious will be strong to deliver the loyal. Every faithful one will surely be gathered. "He shall send his angels with a great sound of a trumpet, and they shall gather together his elect from the four winds, from one end of heaven to the other" (Matt. 24:31).

Conflict and Courage   July 10

WHY WAIT?

Let us go up at once, and possess it; for we are well able to overcome it. **Num. 13:30.**

It was Caleb's faith in God that gave him courage: that . . . enabled him to stand boldly and unflinchingly in defense of the right. From the same exalted source, the mighty General of the armies of heaven, every true soldier of the cross of Christ must receive strength and courage to overcome obstacles that often seem insurmountable. . . . those who would do their duty must be ever ready to speak the words that God gives them, and not the words of doubt, discouragement, and despair. . . .

While the doubting ones talk of impossibilities, while they tremble at the thought of high walls and strong giants, let the faithful Calebs, who have "another spirit," come to the front. The truth of God, which bringeth salvation, will go forth to the people if ministers and professed believers will not hedge up its way, as did the unfaithful spies. . . .

Human agencies are to be employed in this work. Zeal and energy must be intensified: talents that are rusting from inaction must be pressed into service. The voice that would say, "Wait: do not allow yourself to have burdens imposed upon you," is the voice of the cowardly spies. We want Calebs now who will press to the front—chieftains in Israel who with courageous words will make a strong report in favor of immediate action. When the selfish, ease-loving, panic-stricken people, fearing tall giants and inaccessible walls, clamor for retreat, let the voice of the Calebs be heard, even though the cowardly ones stand with stones in their hands, ready to beat them down for their faithful testimony.

It is when the unbelieving cast contempt upon the Word of God that the faithful Calebs are called for. It is then that they will stand firm at the post of duty, without parade, and without swerving because of reproach. The unbelieving spies stood ready to destroy Caleb. He saw the stones in the hands of those who had brought a false report, but this did not deter him: he had a message, and he would bear it. The same spirit will be manifested today by those who are true to God.

THE ONLY WAY TO WIN

This book of the law shall not depart out of thy mouth; but thou shalt meditate therein day and night, that thou mayest observe to do according to all that is written therein: for then thou shalt make thy way prosperous, and then thou shalt have good success. Joshua 1:8.

If men will walk in the path that God has marked out for them, they will have a counselor whose wisdom is far above any human wisdom. Joshua was a wise general because God was his guide. The first sword that Joshua used was the sword of the Spirit, the Word of God. . . .

It was because the strongest influences were to be brought to bear against his principles of righteousness that the Lord in mercy charged him not to turn to the right hand or to the left. He was to follow a course of strictest integrity. . . . If there had been no peril before Joshua, God would not over and over again have charged him to be of good courage. But amid all his cares, Joshua had his God to guide him.

There is no greater deception than for man to suppose that in any difficulty he can find a better guide than God, a wiser counselor in any emergency, a stronger defense under any circumstance. . . .

The Lord has a great work to be done in our world. To every man he has given *His* work for man to do. But man is not to make man his guide, lest he be led astray; this is always unsafe. While Bible religion embodies the principles of activity in service, at the same time there is the necessity of asking for wisdom daily from the Source of all wisdom. What was Joshua's victory? Thou shalt meditate upon the Word of God day and night. The word of the Lord came to Joshua just before he passed over Jordan. . . . This was the secret of Joshua's victory. He made God his Guide.

Those holding the positions of counselors should be unselfish men, men of faith, men of prayer, men that will not dare to rely upon their own human wisdom, but will seek earnestly for light and intelligence as to what is the best manner of conducting their business. Joshua, the commander of Israel, searched the books diligently in which Moses had faithfully chronicled the directions given by God,—His requirements, reproofs, and restrictions,—lest he should move unadvisedly.

Conflict and Courage   July 12

TOO MANY SOLDIERS

And the Lord said unto Gideon, The people that are with thee are too many for me to give the Midianites into their hands, lest Israel vaunt themselves against me, saying, Mine own hand hath saved me. **Judges 7:2.**

It had been made a law in Israel that before they went to battle the following proclamation should be made throughout the army: "What man is there that hath built a new house, and hath not dedicated it? let him go and return to his house, lest he die in the battle, and another man dedicate it. And what man is he that hath planted a vineyard, and hath not yet eaten of it? let him also go and return unto his house, lest he die in the battle, and another man eat of it. And what man is there that hath betrothed a wife, and hath not taken her? let him go and return unto his house, lest he die in the battle, and another man take her." And the officers were to speak further to the people, saying, "What man is there that is fearful and fainthearted? let him go and return unto his house, lest his brethren's heart faint as well as his heart" (Deut. 20:5-8).

Because his numbers were so few compared with those of the enemy, Gideon had refrained from making the usual proclamation. He was filled with astonishment at the declaration that his army was too large. But the Lord saw the pride and unbelief existing in the hearts of His people. Aroused by the stirring appeals of Gideon, they had readily enlisted; but

179

many were filled with fear when they saw the multitudes of the Midianites. Yet, had Israel triumphed, those very ones would have taken the glory to themselves instead of ascribing the victory to God.

Gideon obeyed the Lord's direction, and with a heavy heart he saw twenty-two thousand, or more than two thirds of his entire force, depart for their homes.

The Lord is willing to do great things for us. We shall not gain the victory through numbers, but through the full surrender of the soul to Jesus. We are to go forward in His strength, trusting in the mighty God of Israel. There is a lesson for us in the story of Gideon's army. . . . The Lord is just as willing to work through human efforts now, and to accomplish great things through weak instrumentalities.

NO GENERATION GAP

And the child Samuel ministered unto the Lord before Eli. **1 Sam. 3:1.**

Young as he was when brought to minister in the tabernacle, Samuel had even then duties to perform in the service of God, according to his capacity. These were at first very humble, and not always pleasant; but they were performed to the best of his ability, and with a willing heart. . . .

If children were taught to regard the humble round of everyday duties as the course marked out for them by the Lord, as a school in which they were to be trained to render faithful and efficient service, how much more pleasant and honorable would their work appear. To perform every duty as unto the Lord, throws a charm around the humblest employment and links the workers on earth with the holy beings who do God's will in heaven.

The life of Samuel from early childhood had been a life of piety and devotion. He had been placed under the care of Eli in his youth, and the loveliness of his character drew forth the warm affection of the aged priest. He was kind, generous, diligent, obedient, and respectful. The contrast between the course of the youth Samuel and that of the priest's own sons was very marked, and Eli found rest and comfort and blessing in the presence of his charge. It was a singular thing that between Eli, the chief magistrate of the nation, and the simple child so warm a friendship should exist. Samuel was helpful and affectionate, and no father ever loved his child more tenderly than did Eli this youth. As the infirmities of age came upon Eli, he felt more keenly the disheartening, reckless, profligate course of his own sons, and he turned to Samuel for comfort and support.

How touching to see youth and old age relying one upon the other, the youth looking up to the aged for counsel and wisdom, the aged looking to the youth for help and sympathy. This is as it should be. God would have the young possess such qualifications of character that they shall find delight in the friendship of the old, that they may be united in the endearing bonds of affection to those who are approaching the borders of the grave.

PREPARING TO LEAD

When there came a lion, or a bear, and took a lamb out of the flock, I went out after him, and smote him, and delivered it out of his mouth: and when he arose against me, I caught him by his beard, and smote him, and slew him. 1 Sam. 17:34, 35, R.V.

David was growing in favor with God and man. He had been instructed in the way of the Lord, and he now set his heart more fully to do the will of God than ever before. He had new themes for thought. He had been in the court of the king and had seen the responsibilities of royalty. He had discovered some of the temptations that beset the soul of Saul and had penetrated some of the mysteries in the character and dealings of Israel's first king. He had seen the glory of royalty shadowed with a dark cloud of sorrow, and he knew that the household of Saul, in their private life, were far from happy. All these things served to bring troubled thoughts to him who had been anointed to be king over Israel. But while he was absorbed in deep meditation, and harassed by thoughts of anxiety, he turned to his harp, and called forth strains that elevated his mind to the Author of every good, and the dark clouds that seemed to shadow the horizon of the future were dispelled.

God was teaching David lessons of trust. As Moses was trained for his work, so the Lord was fitting the son of Jesse to become the guide of His chosen people. In his watchcare for his flocks, he was gaining an appreciation of the care that the Great Shepherd has for the sheep of His pasture.

The lonely hills and the wild ravines where David wandered with his flocks were the lurking place of beasts of prey. Not infrequently the lion from the thickets by the Jordan, or the bear from his lair among the hills, came, fierce with hunger, to attack the flocks. According to the custom of his time, David was armed only with his sling and shepherd's staff; yet he clearly gave proof of his strength and courage in protecting his charge. . . .

His experience in these matters proved the heart of David and developed in him courage and fortitude and faith.

181

SATAN'S STEALTHY WORK

For our fight is not against any physical enemy: it is against organizations and powers that are spiritual. We are up against the unseen power that controls this dark world, and spiritual agents from the very headquarters of evil. **Eph. 6:12, Phillips.**

The Bible has little to say in praise of men. Little space is given to recounting the virtues of even the best men who have ever lived. This silence is not without purpose; it is not without a lesson. All the good qualities that men possess are the gift of God; their good deeds are performed by the grace of God through Christ. Since they owe all to God the glory of whatever they are or do belongs to Him alone; they are but instruments in His hands. More than this—as all the lessons of Bible history teach—it is a perilous thing to praise or exalt men; for if one comes to lose sight of his entire dependence on God, and to trust to his own strength, he is sure to fall. . . .

It is impossible for us in our own strength to maintain the conflict; and whatever diverts the mind from God, whatever leads to self-exaltation or to self-dependence, is surely preparing the way for our overthrow. The tenor of the Bible is to inculcate distrust of human power and to encourage trust in divine power.

It was the spirit of self-confidence and self-exaltation that prepared the way for David's fall. Flattery and the subtle allurements of power and luxury were not without effect upon him. Intercourse with surrounding nations also exerted an influence for evil. According to the customs prevailing among Eastern rulers, crimes not to be tolerated in subjects were uncondemned in the king; the monarch was not under obligation to exercise the same self-restraint as the subject. All this tended to lessen David's sense of the exceeding sinfulness of sin. And instead of relying in humility upon the power of Jehovah, he began to trust to his own wisdom and might.

As soon as Satan can separate the soul from God, the only Source of strength, he will seek to arouse the unholy desires of man's carnal nature. The work of the enemy is not abrupt; it is not, at the outset, sudden and startling; it is a secret undermining of the strongholds of principle.

A LATE AWAKENING

Then I looked on all the works that my hands had wrought, and on the labour that I had laboured to do: and, behold, all was vanity and vexation of spirit, and there was no profit under the sun. **Eccl. 2:11.**

By his own bitter experience, Solomon learned the emptiness of a life that seeks in earthly things its highest good. He erected altars to heathen gods, only to learn how vain is their promise of rest to the spirit. Gloomy and soul-harassing thoughts troubled him night and day. For him there was no longer any joy of life or peace of mind, and the future was dark with despair.

Yet the Lord forsook him not. By messages of reproof and by severe judgments, He sought to arouse the king to a realization of the sinfulness of his course. . . . At last the Lord, through a prophet, delivered to Solomon the startling message: . . . "I will surely rend the kingdom from thee, and will give it to thy servant. Notwithstanding in thy days I will not do it for David thy father's sake: but I will rend it out of the hand of thy son."

Awakened as from a dream by this sentence of judgment pronounced against him and his house, Solomon with quickened conscience began to see his folly in its true light. Chastened in spirit, with mind and body enfeebled, he turned wearied and thirsting from earth's broken cisterns, to drink once more at the fountain of life. . . . He could never hope to escape the blasting results of sin; he could never free his mind from all remembrance of the self-indulgent course he had been pursuing; but he would endeavor earnestly to dissuade others from following after folly. . . .

The true penitent does not put his past sins from his remembrance. He does not, as soon as he has obtained peace, grow unconcerned in regard to the mistakes he has made. He thinks of those who have been led into evil by his course, and tries in every possible way to lead them back into the true path. The clearer the light that he has entered into, the stronger is his desire to set the feet of others in the right way.

A VOICE
IN THE WILDERNESS

And Elijah the Tishbite, . . . said unto Ahab, As the Lord God of Israel liveth, before whom I stand, there shall not be dew nor rain these years, but according to my word. **1 Kings 17:1.**

Among the mountains of Gilead, east of the Jordan, there dwelt in the days of Ahab a man of faith and prayer whose fearless ministry was destined to check the rapid spread of apostasy in Israel. Far removed from any city of renown, and occupying no high station in life, Elijah the Tishbite nevertheless entered upon his mission confident in God's purpose to prepare the way before him and to give him abundant success. The word of faith and power was upon his lips, and his whole life was devoted to the work of reform. His was the voice of one crying in the wilderness to rebuke sin and press back the tide of evil. And while he came to the people as a reprover of sin, his message offered the balm of Gilead to the sin-sick souls of all who desired to be healed. . . .

To Elijah was entrusted the mission of delivering to Ahab Heaven's message of judgment. He did not seek to be the Lord's messenger; the word of the Lord came to him. And jealous for the honor of God's cause, he did not hesitate to obey the divine summons, though to obey seemed to invite swift destruction at the hand of the wicked king.

It was only by the exercise of strong faith in the unfailing power of God's word that Elijah delivered his message. Had he not possessed implicit confidence in the One whom he served, he would never have appeared before Ahab. On his way to Samaria, Elijah had passed by ever-flowing streams, hills covered with verdure, and stately forests that seemed beyond the reach of drought. Everything on which the eye rested was clothed with beauty. The prophet might have wondered how the streams that had never ceased their flow could become dry, or how those hills and valleys could be burned with drought. But he gave no place to unbelief. He fully believed that God would humble apostate Israel, and that through judgments they would be brought to repentance. The fiat of Heaven had gone forth; God's word could not fail; and at the peril of his life Elijah fearlessly fulfilled his commission.

THE BATTLE SONG

And when he had consulted with the people, he appointed singers unto the Lord, and that should praise the beauty of holiness, as they went out before the army, and to say, Praise the Lord; for his mercy endureth for ever. **2 Chron. 20:21.**

It was a singular way of going to battle against the enemy's army—praising the Lord with singing, and exalting the God of Israel. This was their battle song. They possessed the beauty of holiness. If more praising of God were engaged in now, hope and courage and faith would steadily increase. And would not this strengthen the hands of the valiant soldiers who today are standing in defense of truth?

They praised God for the victory, and four days thereafter the army returned to Jerusalem, laden with the spoils of their enemies, singing praise for the victory won.

When we have a deeper appreciation of the mercy and loving-kindness of God, we shall praise Him, instead of complaining. We shall talk of the loving watchcare of the Lord, of the tender compassion of the Good Shepherd. The language of the heart will not be selfish murmuring and repining. Praise, like a clear, flowing stream, will come from God's truly believing ones. . . .

Why not awake the voice of spiritual song in the days of our pilgrimage? . . . We need to study God's Word, to meditate and pray. Then we shall have spiritual eyesight to discern the inner courts of the celestial temple. We shall catch the notes of thanksgiving sung by the heavenly choir around the throne. When Zion shall arise and shine, her light will be most penetrating, and songs of praise and thanksgiving will be heard in the assembly of the saints. Little disappointments and difficulties will be lost sight of.

The Lord is our helper. . . . No one ever trusted God in vain. He never disappoints those who put their dependence on Him. If we would only do the work that the Lord would have us do, walking in the footsteps of Jesus, our hearts would become sacred harps, every chord of which would send forth praise and thanksgiving to the One sent by God to take away the sin of the world.

ALL ON THE ALTAR

No man, having put his hand to the plough, and looking back, is fit for the kingdom of God. **Luke 9:62.**

We are not all asked to serve as Elisha served, nor are we all bidden to sell everything we have; but God asks us to give His service the first place in our lives, to allow no day to pass without doing something to advance His work in the earth. He does not expect from all the same kind of service. One may be called to ministry in a foreign land; another may be asked to give of his means for the support of gospel work. God accepts the offering of each. It is the consecration of the life and all its interests, that is necessary. Those who make this consecration will hear and obey the call of Heaven. . . .

It was no great work that was at first required of Elisha; commonplace duties still constituted his discipline. He is spoken of as pouring water on the hands of Elijah, his master. He was willing to do anything that the Lord directed, and at every step he learned lessons of humility and service. . . . Elisha's life after uniting with Elijah was not without temptations. Trials he had in abundance; but in every emergency he relied on God. He was tempted to think of the home that he had left, but to this temptation he gave no heed. Having put his hand to the plow, he was resolved not to turn back, and through test and trial he proved true to this trust. . . .

As Elisha accompanied the prophet . . . his faith and resolution were once more tested. At Gilgal, and again at Bethel and Jericho, he was invited by the prophet to turn back. . . . But . . . he would not be diverted from his purpose. . . . "And . . . Elijah said unto Elisha, Ask what I shall do for thee, before I be taken away from thee."

Elisha asked not for worldly honor, or for a high place among the great men of earth. That which he craved was a large measure of the Spirit that God had bestowed so freely upon the one about to be honored with translation. He knew that nothing but the Spirit which had rested upon Elijah, could fit him to fill the place in Israel to which God had called him; and so he asked, "I pray thee, let a double portion of thy Spirit be upon me."

RELUCTANT PROPHET

Arise, go to Nineveh, that great city, and cry against it; for their wickedness is come up before me. **Jonah 1:2.**

Nineveh, wicked though it had become, was not wholly given over to evil. He who "beholdeth all the sons of men" (Psalm 33:13) . . . perceived in that city many who were reaching out after something better and higher. . . . God revealed Himself to them in an unmistakable manner, to lead them, if possible, to repentance.

The instrument chosen for this work was the prophet Jonah. . . . Had the prophet obeyed unquestioningly, he would have been spared many bitter experiences, and would have been blessed abundantly. Yet in the hour of Jonah's despair the Lord did not desert him. Through a series of trials and strange providences, the prophet's confidence in God and in his infinite power to save was to be revived. . . .

Once more the servant of God was commissioned to warn Nineveh. . . . As Jonah entered the city, he began at once to "cry against" it the message, "Yet forty days, and Nineveh shall be overthrown." From street to street he went, sounding the note of warning.

The message was not in vain. The cry that rang through the streets of the godless city was passed from lip to lip until all the inhabitants had heard the startling announcement. The Spirit of God pressed the message home to every heart and caused multitudes to tremble because of their sins and to repent in deep humiliation. . . . their doom was averted, the God of Israel was exalted and honored throughout the heathen world, and his law was revered. Not until many years later was Nineveh to fall a prey to the surrounding nations through forgetfulness of God and through boastful pride. . . .

The lesson is for God's messengers today, when the cities of the nations are as verily in need of a knowledge of the attributes and purposes of the true God as were the Ninevites of old. . . . The only city that will endure is the city whose builder and maker is God. . . . the Lord Jesus is calling upon men to strive with sanctified ambition to secure the immortal inheritance.

Conflict and Courage   July 21

JEREMIAH,
GOD'S MOUTHPIECE

It is good that a man should both hope and quietly wait for the salvation of the Lord. **Lam. 3:26.**

Among those who had hoped for a permanent spiritual revival as the result of the reformation under Josiah was Jeremiah, called of God to the prophetic office while still a youth. . . .

In the youthful Jeremiah, God saw one who would be true to his trust and who would stand for the right against great opposition. . . . "Say not, I am a child," the Lord bade His chosen messenger; "for thou shalt go to all that I shall send thee, and whatsoever I command thee thou shalt speak. Be not afraid of their faces: for I am with thee to deliver thee." . . .

For forty years Jeremiah was to stand before the nation as a witness for truth and righteousness. In a time of unparalleled apostasy he was to exemplify in life and character the worship of the only true God. During the terrible sieges of Jerusalem he was to be the mouthpiece of Jehovah.

Naturally of a timid and shrinking disposition, Jeremiah longed for the peace and quiet of a life of retirement, where he need not witness the continued impenitence of his beloved nation. His heart was wrung with anguish over the ruin wrought by sin. . . .

The experiences through which Jeremiah passed in the days of his youth and also in the later years of his ministry, taught him the lesson that "the way of man is not in himself: it is not in man that walketh to direct his steps." He learned to pray, "O Lord, correct me, but with judgment; not in thine anger, lest thou bring me to nothing" (Jer. 10:23, 34).

When called to drink of the cup of tribulation and sorrow, and when tempted in his misery to say, "My strength and my hope is perished from

187

the Lord," he recalled the providences of God in his behalf and triumphantly exclaimed, "It is of the Lord's mercies that we are not consumed, because his compassions fail not. . . . The Lord is my portion, saith my soul; therefore will I hope in him."

FAITH AND GOD'S PROMISES

Behold, his soul which is lifted up is not upright in him: but the just shall live by his faith. Hab. 2:4.

At the time Josiah began to rule, and for many years before, the truehearted in Judah were questioning whether God's promises to ancient Israel could ever be fulfilled. . . .

These anxious questionings were voiced by the prophet Habakkuk. Viewing the situation of the faithful in his day, he expressed the burden of his heart in the inquiry: "O Lord, how long shall I cry, and thou wilt not hear!" . . . And then, his faith reaching out beyond the forbidding prospect of the immediate future, and laying fast hold on the precious promises that reveal God's love for His trusting children, the prophet added, "We shall not die." With this declaration of faith he rested his case, and that of every believing Israelite, in the hands of a compassionate God. . . .

The faith that strengthened Habakkuk and all the holy and the just in those days of deep trial was the same faith that sustains God's people today. In the darkest hours, under circumstances the most forbidding, the Christian believer may keep his soul stayed upon the source of all light and power. Day by day, through faith in God, his hope and courage may be renewed. "The just shall live by his faith." . . .

We must cherish and cultivate the faith of which prophets and apostles have testified—the faith that lays hold on the promises of God and waits for deliverance in His appointed time and way. The sure word of prophecy will meet its final fulfillment in the glorious advent of our Lord and Saviour Jesus Christ, as King of kings and Lord of lords. . . . With the prophet who endeavored to encourage Judah in a time of unparalleled apostasy, let us confidently declare, "The Lord is in his holy temple: let all the earth keep silence before him." Let us ever hold in remembrance the cheering message, "The vision is yet for an appointed time, but at the end it shall speak, and not lie: though it tarry, wait for it; because it will surely come."

DANIEL,
GOD'S AMBASSADOR

Then the presidents and princes sought to find occasion against Daniel concerning the kingdom; but they could find none occasion nor fault; forasmuch as he was faithful, neither was there any error or fault found in him. **Dan. 6:4.**

Daniel, the prime minister of the greatest of earthly kingdoms, was at the same time a prophet of God, receiving the light of heavenly inspiration. A man of like passions as ourselves, the pen of inspiration describes him as without fault. His business transactions, when subjected to the closest scrutiny of his enemies, were found to be without one flaw. He was an example of what every businessman may become when his heart is converted and consecrated, and when his motives are right in the sight of God. . . .

Unwavering in his allegiance to God, unyielding in his master of self, Daniel, by his noble dignity and unswerving integrity, while yet a young man, won the "favor and tender love" of the heathen officer in whose charge he had been placed. . . . He rose speedily to the position of prime minister of the kingdom of Babylon. Through the reign of successive monarchs, the downfall of the nation, and the establishment of another world empire, such were his wisdom and statesmanship, so perfect his tact, his courtesy, his genuine goodness of heart, his fidelity to principle, that even his enemies were forced to the confession that "they could find none occasion nor fault; forasmuch as he was faithful."

Honored by men with the responsibilities of state and with the secrets of kingdoms bearing universal sway, Daniel was honored by God as His ambassador, and was given many revelations of the mysteries of ages to come. His wonderful prophecies, as recorded by him in chapters 7 to 12 of the book bearing his name, were not fully understood even by the prophet himself; but before his life labors closed, he was given the blessed assurance that "at the end of the days"—in the closing period of this world's history—he would again be permitted to stand in his lot and place. . . .

We may, like Daniel and his fellows, live for that which is true and noble and enduring. And learning in this life the principles of the kingdom of our Lord and Saviour, . . . we may be prepared at His coming to enter with him into its possession.

KNOWLEDGE REQUIRES ACTION

Ezra . . . was a ready scribe in the law of Moses, which the Lord God of Israel had given. **Ezra 7:6.**

More than two thousand years have passed since Ezra "prepared his heart to seek the law of the Lord, and to do it," yet the lapse of time has not lessened the influence of his pious example. Through the centuries the record of his life of consecration has inspired many with the determination "to seek the law of the Lord, and to do it."

Ezra's motives were high and holy; in all that he did he was actuated by a deep love for souls. The compassion and tenderness that he revealed toward those who had sinned, either willfully or through ignorance, should be an object lesson to all who seek to bring about reforms. . . .

There is no such thing as weakening or strengthening the law of Jehovah. As it has been, so it is. It always has been, and always will be, holy, just, and good, complete in itself. It cannot be repealed or changed. To "honor" or "dishonor" it is but the speech of men. . . .

Christians should be preparing for what is soon to break upon the world as an overwhelming surprise, and this preparation they should make by diligently studying the word of God and striving to conform their lives to its precepts. The tremendous issues of eternity demand of us something besides an imaginary religion, a religion of words and forms, where truth is kept in the outer court. . . .

If the saints of the Old Testament bore so bright a testimony of loyalty, should not those upon whom is shining the accumulated light of centuries, bear a still more signal witness to the power of truth?

Shall we let the example of Ezra teach us the use we should make of our knowledge of the Scriptures? The life of this servant of God should be an inspiration to us to serve the Lord with heart and mind and strength. We each have an appointed work to do, and this can be accomplished only by consecrated effort. We need first to set ourselves to know the requirements of God, and then to practice them. Then we can sow seeds of truth that will bear fruit into eternal life.

NONE WERE PERFECT

This priceless treasure we hold, so to speak, in a common earthenware jar—to show that the splendid power of it belongs to God and not to us. **2 Cor. 4:7, Phillips.**

All the disciples had serious faults when Jesus called them to his service. Even John, who came into closest association with the meek and lowly One, was not himself naturally meek and yielding. He and his brother were called "the sons of thunder." While they were with Jesus, any slight shown to Him aroused their indignation and combativeness. Evil temper, revenge, the spirit of criticism, were all in the beloved disciple. He was proud, and ambitious to be first in the kingdom of God. But day by day, in contrast with his own violent spirit, he beheld the tenderness and forbearance of Jesus, and heard His lessons of humility and patience. He opened his heart to the divine influence, and became not only a hearer but a doer of the Saviour's words. Self was hid in Christ. He learned to wear the yoke of Christ and to bear His burden.

Jesus reproved His disciples, He warned and cautioned them; but John and his brethren did not leave Him; they chose Jesus, notwithstanding the reproofs. The Saviour did not withdraw from them because of their weakness and errors. They continued to the end to share his trials and to learn the lessons of his life. By beholding Christ, they became transformed in character. . . .

As His representatives among men, Christ does not choose angels who have never fallen, but human beings, men of like passions with those they seek to save. . . .

Having been in peril themselves, they are acquainted with the dangers and difficulties of the way, and for this reason are called to reach out for others in like peril. There are souls perplexed with doubt, burdened with infirmities, weak in faith, and unable to grasp the Unseen; but a friend whom they can see, coming to them in Christ's stead, can be a connecting link to fasten their trembling faith upon Christ.

We are to be laborers together with the heavenly angels in presenting Jesus to the world.

IT HAS TO BE PERSONAL

If I may but touch his garment, I shall be whole. **Matt. 9:21.**

It was a poor woman who spoke these words—a woman who for twelve years had suffered from a disease that made her life a burden. She had spent all her means upon physicians and remedies, only to be pronounced incurable. But as she heard of the Great Healer, her hopes revived. . . . Again and again she had tried in vain to get near Him.

She had begun to despair, when, in making His way through the multitude, He came near where she was. . . . But amid the confusion she could not speak to Him, nor catch more than a passing glimpse of His figure. . . . As He was passing, she reached forward, and succeeded in barely touching the border of His garment. But in that moment she knew that she was healed. In that one touch was concentrated the faith of her life, and instantly her pain and feebleness gave place to the vigor of perfect health.

With a grateful heart she then tried to withdraw from the crowd; but suddenly Jesus stopped. . . . The Saviour could distinguish the touch of faith from the casual contact of the careless throng. Such trust should not be passed without comment. . . . Finding concealment vain, she came forward tremblingly, and cast herself at His feet. With grateful tears she told the story of her suffering, and how she had found relief. Jesus gently said, "Daughter, be of good comfort: thy faith hath made thee whole; go in peace." He gave no opportunity for superstition to claim healing virtue for the mere act of touching His garments. It was not through the outward contact with Him, but through the faith which took hold on His divine power, that the cure was wrought. . . .

So in spiritual things. To talk of religion in a casual way, to pray without soul hunger and living faith, avails nothing. A nominal faith in Christ, which accepts Him merely as the Saviour of the world, can never bring healing to the soul. . . . It is not enough to believe *about* Christ; we must believe *in* Him. The only faith that will benefit us is that which embraces Him as a personal Saviour; which appropriates His merits to ourselves.

NOTHING TOO COSTLY

For the love of Christ constraineth us. **2 Cor. 5:14.**

Christ delighted in the earnest desire of Mary to do the will of her Lord. He accepted the wealth of pure affection which His disciples did not, would not, understand. The desire that Mary had to do this service for her Lord was of more value to Christ than all the precious ointment in the world, because it expressed her appreciation of the world's Redeemer. It was the love of Christ that constrained her. The matchless excellence of the character of Christ filled her soul. That ointment was a symbol of the heart of the giver. It was the outward demonstration of a love fed by heavenly streams until it overflowed.

The work of Mary was just the lesson the disciples needed to show them that the expression of their love for Him would be pleasing to Christ. He had been everything to them, and they did not realize that soon they would be deprived of His presence, that soon they could offer Him no token of their gratitude for His great love. The loneliness of Christ, separated from the heavenly courts, living the life of humanity, was never understood or appreciated by the disciples as it should have been. . . .

Their afterknowledge gave them a true sense of the many things they might have done for Jesus expressive of the love and gratitude of their hearts. . . . When Jesus was no longer with them, . . . they began to see how they might have shown Him attentions that would have brought gladness to His heart. They no longer cast blame upon Mary, but upon themselves. Oh, if they could have taken back their censuring, their presenting the poor as more worthy of the gift than was Christ! They felt the reproof keenly as they took from the cross the bruised body of their Lord.

The same want is evident in our world today. But few appreciate all that Christ is to them. If they did, the great love of Mary would be expressed, the anointing would be freely bestowed. The expensive ointment would not be called a waste. Nothing would be thought too costly to give for Christ, no self-denial or self-sacrifice too great to be endured for His sake.

JUST FOR ONE MAN

And the angel of the Lord spake unto Philip, saying, Arise, and go toward the south unto the way that goeth down from Jerusalem unto Gaza, which is desert. And he arose and went. **Acts 8:26, 27.**

Notice how much effort was put forth for just one man, an Ethiopian.

This Ethiopian was a man of good standing and of wide influence. God saw that when converted he would give others the light he had received and would exert a strong influence in favor of the gospel. Angels of God were attending this seeker for light, and he was being drawn to the Saviour. By the ministration of the Holy Spirit the Lord brought him into touch with one who could lead him to the light.

Philip was directed to go to the Ethiopian and explain to him the prophecy that he was reading. "Go near," the Spirit said, "and join thyself to this chariot." . . . The man's heart thrilled with interest as the Scriptures were explained to him; and when the disciple had finished, he was ready to accept the light given. He did not make his high worldly position an excuse for refusing the gospel. . . .

This Ethiopian represented a large class who need to be taught by such missionaries as Philip—men who will hear the voice of God and go where He sends them. There are many who are reading the Scriptures who cannot understand their true import. All over the world men and women are looking wistfully to heaven. Prayers and tears and inquiries go up from souls longing for light, for grace, for the Holy Spirit. Many are on the verge of the kingdom, waiting only to be gathered in.

An angel guided Philip to the one who was seeking for light and who was ready to receive the gospel, and today angels will guide the footsteps of those workers who will allow the Holy Spirit to sanctify their tongues and refine and ennoble their hearts.

He who sent Philip to the Ethiopian councilor, Peter to the Roman centurion, and the little Israelitish maiden to the help of Naamah, the Syrian captain, sends men and women and youth today as His representatives to those in need of divine help and guidance.

SAUL TO PAUL

And he trembling and astonished said, Lord, what wilt thou have me to do? And the Lord said unto him, Arise, and go into the city, and it shall be told thee what thou must do. **Acts 9:6.**

In the wonderful conversion of Paul we see the miraculous power of God. . . . Jesus, whose name of all others he most hated and despised, revealed Himself to Paul for the purpose of arresting his mad yet honest career, that he might make this most unpromising instrument a chosen vessel to bear the gospel to the Gentiles. . . . The light of heavenly illumination had taken away Paul's eyesight; but Jesus, the Great Healer of the blind, does not restore it. He answers the question of Paul in these words: "Arise, and go into the city, and it shall be told thee what thou must do." Jesus could not only have healed Paul of his blindness, but he could have forgiven his sins and told him his duty by marking out his future course. From Christ all power and mercies were to flow; but He did not give Paul an experience, in his conversion to truth, independent of his church recently organized upon the earth.

The marvelous light given Paul upon that occasion astonished and confounded him. He was wholly subdued. This part of the work man could not do for Paul, but there was a work still to be accomplished which the servants of Christ could do. Jesus directs him to his agents in the church for a further knowledge of duty. Thus He gives authority and sanction to his organized church. Christ had done the work of revelation and conviction, and now Paul was in a condition to learn of those whom God had ordained to teach the truth. Christ directs Paul to His chosen servants, thus placing him in connection with his church. The very men whom Paul was purposing to destroy were to be his instructors in the very religion that he had despised and persecuted. . . .

An angel is sent to Ananias, directing him to go to a certain house where Saul is praying to be instructed in what he is to do next. . . . In Christ's stead Ananias touches his eyes that they may receive sight; in Christ's stead he lays his hands upon him, prays in Christ's name, and Saul receives the Holy Ghost.

TOWARD THE MARK

This one thing I do, forgetting those things which are behind, and reaching forth unto those things which are before, I press toward the mark for the prize of the high calling of God in Christ Jesus. **Phil. 3:13, 14.**

Paul did many things. He was a wise teacher. His many letters are full of instructive lessons setting forth correct principles. He worked with his hands, for he was a tent-maker, and in this way earned his daily bread. . . . He carried a heavy burden for the churches. He strove most earnestly to present their errors before them, that they might correct them, and not be deceived and led away from God. He was always seeking to help them in their difficulties; and yet he declares, "One thing I do." . . . The responsibilities of his life were many, yet he kept always before him this "one thing." The constant sense of the presence of God constrained him to keep his eye ever looking unto Jesus, the Author and Finisher of his faith.

The great purpose that constrained Paul to press forward in the face of hardship and difficulty should lead every Christian worker to consecrate himself wholly to God's service. Worldly attractions will be presented to draw his attention from the Saviour, but he is to press on toward the goal, showing to the world, to angels, and to men that the hope of seeing the face of God is worth all the effort and sacrifice that the attainment of this hope demands.

The lowliest disciple of Christ may become an inhabitant of heaven, an heir of God to an inheritance incorruptible, and that fadeth not away. O that every one might make choice of the heavenly gift, become an heir of God to that inheritance whose title is secure from any destroyer, world without end! O, choose not the world, but choose the better inheritance! Press, urge your way toward the mark for the prize of your high calling in Christ Jesus.

Soon we shall witness the coronation of our King. Those whose lives have been hidden with Christ, those who on this earth have fought the good fight of faith, will shine forth with the Redeemer's glory in the kingdom of God.

HITHERTO HATH
THE LORD HELPED US

O give thanks unto the Lord; call upon his name: make known his deeds among the people. Sing unto him, sing psalms unto him: talk ye of all his wondrous works. Ps. 105:1, 2.

The dealings of God with His people should be often repeated. How frequently were the waymarks set up by the Lord in His dealings with ancient Israel! Lest they should forget the history of the past, He commanded Moses to frame these events into song, that parents might teach them to their children. They were to gather up memorials and to lay them up in sight. Special pains were taken to preserve them, that when the children should inquire concerning these things, the whole story might be repeated. Thus the providential dealings and the marked goodness and mercy of God in His care and deliverance of His people were kept in mind. We are exhorted to "call to remembrance the former days, in which, after ye were illuminated, ye endured a great fight of afflictions" (Heb. 10:32). For His people in this generation the Lord has wrought as a wonder-working God. . . . We need often to recount God's goodness and to praise Him for his wonderful works.

Let us not cast away our confidence, but have firm assurance, firmer than ever before. "Hitherto hath the Lord helped us," and He will help us to the end (1 Sam. 7:12). Let us look to the monumental pillars, reminders of what the Lord has done to comfort us and to save us from the hand of the destroyer. Let us keep fresh in our memory all the tender mercies that God has shown us—the tears He has wiped away, the pains He has soothed, the anxieties removed, the fears dispelled, the wants supplied, the blessings bestowed—thus strengthening ourselves for all that is before us through the remainder of our pilgrimage.

We cannot but look forward to new perplexities in the coming conflict, but we may look on what is past as well as on what is to come, and say, "Hitherto hath the Lord helped us." "As thy days, so shall they strength be" (Deut. 33:25). The trial will not exceed the strength that shall be given us to bear it. Then let us take up our work just where we find it, believing that whatever may come, strength proportionate to the trial will be given.

196

GOD'S KINGDOM
IN THE HEART

Behold, the kingdom of God is within you. Luke 17:21.

The government under which Jesus lived was corrupt and oppressive; on every hand were crying abuses—extortion, intolerance, and grinding cruelty. Yet the Saviour attempted no civil reforms. He attacked no national abuses, nor condemned the national enemies. He did not interfere with the authority or administration of those in power. He who was our example kept aloof from earthly governments. Not because He was indifferent to the woes of men, but because the remedy did not lie in merely human and external measures. To be efficient, the cure must reach men individually, and must regenerate the heart.

Some of the Pharisees had come to Jesus demanding "when the kingdom of God should come" (Luke 17:20). More than three years had passed since John the Baptist gave the message that like a trumpet call had sounded through the land, "The kingdom of heaven is at hand" (Matt. 3:2). And as yet these Pharisees saw no indication of the establishment of the kingdom. . . .

Jesus answered, "The kingdom of God cometh not with outward show [margin]: neither shall they say, Lo here! or lo there! for, behold, the kingdom of God is within you." The kingdom of God begins in the heart. Look not here or there for manifestations of earthly power to mark its coming.

The works of Christ not only declared Him to be the Messiah, but showed in what manner His kingdom was to be established. . . . It comes through the gentleness of the inspiration of His word, through the inward working of His spirit, the fellowship of the soul with Him who is its life. The greatest manifestation of its power is seen in human nature brought to the perfection of the character of Christ. . . .

When God gave His Son to our world, He endowed human beings with imperishable riches—riches compared with which the treasured wealth of men since the world began is nothingness. Christ came to the earth and stood before the children of men with the hoarded love of eternity, and this is the treasure that, through our connection with Him, we are to receive, to reveal, and to impart.

LIKE YEAST

The kingdom of heaven is like unto leaven, which a woman took, and hid in three measures of meal, till the whole was leavened. **Matt. 13:33.**

In the Saviour's parable, leaven is used to represent the kingdom of heaven. It illustrates the quickening, assimilating power of the grace of God. . . .

The grace of God must be received by the sinner before he can be fitted for the kingdom of glory. All the culture and education which the world can give will fail of making a degraded child of sin a child of heaven. The renewing energy must come from God. . . . As the leaven, when mingled with the meal, works from within outward, so it is by the renewing of the heart that the grace of God works to transform the life. . . .

The leaven hidden in the flour works invisibly to bring the whole mass under its leavening process; so the leaven of truth works secretly, silently, steadily, to transform the soul. The natural inclinations are softened and subdued. New thoughts, new feelings, new motives, are implanted. A new standard of character is set up—the life of Christ. The mind is changed; the faculties are roused to action in new lines. . . . The conscience is awakened. . . .

The heart of him who receives the grace of God overflows with love for God and for those for whom Christ died. Self is not struggling for recognition. . . . He is kind and thoughtful, humble in his opinion of himself, yet full of hope, always trusting in the mercy and love of God. . . .

The grace of Christ is to control the temper and the voice. Its working will be seen in politeness and tender regard shown by brother for brother, in kind, encouraging words. An angel presence is in the home. The life breathes a sweet perfume, which ascends to God as holy incense. Love is manifested in kindness, gentleness, forbearance, and long-suffering. The countenance is changed. Christ abiding in the heart shines out in the faces of those who love Him and keep His commandments. . . . As these changes are effected, angels break forth in rapturous song, and God and Christ rejoice over souls fashioned after the divine similitude.

THE ROYAL ROBE

And to her was granted that she should be arrayed in fine linen, clean and white: for the fine linen is the righteousness of saints. **Rev. 19:8.**

The parable of the wedding garment [Matt. 22:1-14] opens before us a lesson of the highest consequence. . . . By the wedding garment in the parable is represented the pure, spotless character which Christ's true followers will possess. . . . The fine linen, says the Scripture, "is the righteousness of saints." It is the righteousness of Christ, his own unblemished character, that through faith is imparted to all who receive Him as their personal Saviour.

The white robe of innocence was worn by our first parents when they were placed by God in holy Eden. They lived in perfect conformity to the will of God. . . . A beautiful soft light, the light of God, enshrouded the holy pair. . . . But when sin entered, they severed their connection with God, and the light that had encircled them departed. Naked and ashamed, they tried to supply the place of the heavenly garments by sewing together fig leaves for a covering.

We cannot provide a robe of righteousness for ourselves, for the prophet says, "All our righteousnesses are as filthy rags" (Isa. 64:6). There is nothing in us from which we can clothe the soul so that its nakedness shall not appear. We are to receive the robe of righteousness woven in the loom of heaven, even the spotless robe of Christ's righteousness.

God has made ample provision that we may stand perfect in His grace, wanting in nothing, waiting for the appearing of our Lord. Are you ready? Have you the wedding garment on? That garment will never cover deceit, impurity, corruption, or hypocrisy. The eye of God is upon you. It is a discerner of the thoughts and intents of the heart. We may conceal our sins from the eyes of men, but we can hide nothing from our Maker.

Let the youth and the little children be taught to choose for themselves that royal robe woven in heaven's loom—the "fine linen, clean and white," which all the holy ones of earth will wear. This robe, Christ's own spotless character, is freely offered to every human being. But all who receive it will receive and wear it here.

GOD WITH US

They shall call his name Emmanuel, which being interpreted is, God with us. **Matt. 1:23.**

From the days of eternity the Lord Jesus Christ was one with the Father; He was "the image of God," the image of His greatness and majesty, "the outshining of his glory." It was to manifest this glory that He came to our world. To this sin-darkened earth He came to reveal the light of God's love—to be "God with us.". . .

Our little world is the lesson book of the universe. God's wonderful purpose of grace, the mystery of redeeming love, is the theme into which "angels desire to look," and it will be their study throughout endless ages. Both the redeemed and the unfallen beings will find in the cross of Christ their science and their song. It will be seen that the glory shining in the face of Jesus is the glory of self-sacrificing love. In the light from Calvary it will be seen that the law of self-renouncing love is the law of life for earth and heaven; that the love which "seeketh not her own" has its source in the heart of God. . . .

Jesus might have remained at the Father's side. He might have retained the glory of heaven, and the homage of the angels. But He chose to give back the scepter into the Father's hands, and to step down from the throne of the universe, that he might bring light to the benighted, and life to the perishing. . . .

This great purpose had been shadowed forth in types and symbols. The burning bush, in which Christ appeared to Moses, revealed God. . . . The all-merciful God shrouded His glory in a most humble type, that Moses could look upon it and live. So in the pillar of cloud by day and the pillar of fire by night, God communicated with Israel, revealing to men His will, and imparting to them His grace. God's glory was subdued, and His majesty veiled, that the weak vision of finite men might behold it. So Christ was to come in "the body of our humiliation" (Phil. 3:21, R.V.), "in the likeness of men." . . . His glory was veiled, His greatness and majesty were hidden, that He might draw near to sorrowful, tempted men.

ADOPTED SONS AND DAUGHTERS

Having predestinated us unto the adoption of children by Jesus Christ to himself, according to the good pleasure of his will, to the praise of the glory of his grace, wherein he hath made us accepted in the beloved. **Eph. 1:5, 6.**

Before the foundations of the earth were laid the covenant was made that all who were obedient, all who should through the abundant grace provided become holy in character and without blame before God by appropriating that grace, should be children of God.

We owe everything to grace, free grace, sovereign grace. Grace in the covenant ordained our adoption. Grace in the Saviour effected our redemption, our regeneration, and our adoption to heirship with Christ.

As we fully believe that we are His by adoption, we may have a foretaste of heaven. . . . We have a nearness to Him, and can hold sweet communion with Him. We obtain distinct views of His tenderness and compassion, and our hearts are broken and melted with contemplation of the love that is given to us. We feel indeed an abiding Christ in the soul. We abide in Him, and feel at home with Jesus. . . . We have a realizing sense of the love of God, and we rest in His love. No language can describe it, it is beyond knowledge. We are one with Christ, our life is hid with Christ in God. We have the assurance that when He who is our life shall appear, then shall we also appear with Him in glory. With strong confidence we can call God our Father.

All who have been born into the heavenly family are in a special sense the brethren of our Lord. The love of Christ binds together the members of His family, and wherever that love is manifest there the divine relationship is revealed. . . .

Love to man is the earthward manifestation of the love of God. It was to implant this love, to make us children of one family, that the King of glory became one with us. And when His parting words are fulfilled, "Love one another, as I have loved you" (John 15:12); when we love the world as He has loved it, then for us His mission is accomplished. We are fitted for heaven; for we have heaven in our hearts.

BLESSINGS
THROUGH OBEDIENCE

I delight to do thy will, O my God: yea, thy law is within my heart. **Ps. 40:8.**

What a God is our God! He rules over His kingdom with diligence and care, and He has built a hedge—the Ten Commandments—about His subjects to preserve them from the results of transgression. In requiring obedience to the laws of His kingdom, God gives His people health and happiness, peace and joy. He teaches them that the perfection of character He requires can be attained only by becoming familiar with His Word.

The true seeker, who is striving to be like Jesus in word, life, and character, will contemplate his Redeemer and, by beholding, become changed into his image, because he longs and prays for the same disposition and mind that was in Christ Jesus. . . . He longs after God. The history of his Redeemer, the immeasurable sacrifice that He made, becomes full of meaning to him. Christ, the Majesty of heaven, became poor, that we through His poverty might become rich; not rich merely in endowments, but rich in attainments.

These are the riches that Christ earnestly longs that His followers shall possess. As the true seeker after the truth reads the Word and opens his mind to receive the Word, he longs after truth with his whole heart. The love, the pity, the tenderness, the courtesy, the Christian politeness, which will be the elements in the heavenly mansions that Christ has gone to prepare for those that love Him, take possession of his soul. His purpose is steadfast. He is determined to stand on the side of righteousness. Truth has found its way into the heart, and is planted there by the Holy Spirit, who is the truth. When truth takes hold of the heart, the man gives sure evidence of this by becoming a steward of the grace of Christ.

Each steward has his own special work to do for the advancement of God's kingdom. . . . The talents of speech, memory, influence, property, are to accumulate for the glory of God and the advancement of His kingdom. He will bless the right use of His gifts.

IN THE MOST HOLY PLACE

The Lord is in his holy temple: let all the earth keep silence before him. **Hab. 2:20.**

I saw a throne, and on it sat the Father and the Son. I gazed on Jesus' countenance and admired His lovely person. The Father's person I could not behold, for a cloud of glorious light covered Him. I asked Jesus if His Father had a form like Himself. He said He had, but I could not behold it, for said He, "If you should once behold the glory of His person, you would cease to exist." . . .

I saw the Father rise from the throne, and in a flaming chariot go into the holy of holies within the veil, and sit down. . . . then a cloudy chariot, with wheels like flaming fire, surrounded by angels, came to where Jesus was. He stepped into the chariot and was borne to the holiest, where the Father sat. There I beheld Jesus, a great High Priest, standing before the Father.

Two lovely cherubs, one on each side of the ark, stood with their wings outstretched above it, and touching each other above the head of Jesus as He stood before the mercy seat. Their faces were turned toward each other, and they looked downward to the ark, representing all the angelic host looking with interest at the law of God. Between the cherubim was a golden censer, and as the prayers of the saints, offered in faith, came up to Jesus, and he presented them to His Father, a cloud of fragrance arose from the incense, looking like smoke of the most beautiful colors. Above the place where Jesus stood, before the ark, was exceedingly bright glory that I could not look upon; it appeared like the throne of God.

Our crucified Lord is pleading for us in the presence of the Father at the throne of grace. His atoning sacrifice we may plead for our pardon, our justification, and our sanctification. The lamb slain is our only hope. Our faith looks up to Him, grasps Him as the One who can save to the uttermost, and the fragrance of the all-sufficient offering is accepted of the Father. . . . Christ's glory is concerned in our success. He has a common interest in all humanity. He is our sympathizing Saviour.

SOURCE OF
COMPASSION AND MERCY

Thy throne, O God, is for ever and ever: the sceptre of thy kingdom is a right sceptre. **Ps. 45:6.**

Though now He has ascended to the presence of God, and shares the throne of the universe, Jesus has lost none of His compassionate nature. Today, the same tender, sympathizing heart is open to all the woes of humanity. Today the hand that was pierced is reached forth to bless more abundantly His people that are in the world. . . .

Through all our trials we have a never-failing Helper. He does not leave us alone to struggle with temptation, to battle with evil, and be finally crushed with burdens and sorrow. Though now He is hidden from mortal sight, the ear of faith can hear His voice saying, Fear not; I am with you. "I am he that liveth, and was dead; and, behold, I am alive forevermore" (Rev. 1:18).

Those who put away iniquity from their hearts and stretch out their hands in earnest supplication unto God will have that help which God alone can give them. A ransom has been paid for the souls of men, that they may have an opportunity to escape from the thralldom of sin and obtain pardon, purity, and heaven. . . . Those who frequent the throne of grace, offering up sincere, earnest petitions for divine wisdom and power, will not fail to become active, useful servants of Christ. They may not possess great talents, but with humility of heart and firm reliance upon Jesus they may do a good work in bringing souls to Christ. . . .

Thousands have a false conception of God and His attributes. . . . God is a God of truth. Justice and mercy are the attributes of His throne. He is a God of love, of pity and tender compassion. Thus He is represented in His Son, our Saviour. He is a God of patience and long-suffering. If such is the being whom we adore and to whose character we are seeking to assimilate, we are worshiping the true God.

If we are following Christ, His merits, imputed to us, come up before the Father as sweet odor. And the graces of our Saviour's character, implanted in our hearts, will shed around us a precious fragrance.

TO DRAW US TO GOD

I have loved thee with an everlasting love: therefore with lovingkindness have I drawn thee. **Jer. 31:3.**

The Lord of life and glory clothed His divinity with humanity to demonstrate to man that God through the gift of Christ would connect us with Him. Without a connection with God no one can possibly be happy. Fallen man is to learn that our Heavenly Father cannot be satisfied until His love embraces the repentant sinner, transformed through the merits of the spotless Lamb of God.

The work of all the heavenly intelligences is to this end. Under the command of their General they are to work for the reclaiming of those who by transgression have separated themselves from their Heavenly Father. A plan has been devised whereby the wondrous grace and love of Christ shall stand revealed to the world. In the infinite price paid by the Son of God to ransom man, the love of God is revealed. This glorious plan of redemption is ample in its provisions to save the whole world. Sinful and fallen man may be made complete in Jesus through the forgiveness of sin and the imputed righteousness of Christ.

In all the gracious deeds that Jesus did, He sought to impress upon men the parental, benevolent attributes of God. . . . Jesus would have us understand the love of the Father, and He seeks to draw us to Him by presenting His parental grace. He would have the whole field of our vision filled with the perfection of God's character. . . . It was only by living among men that He could reveal the mercy, compassion, and love of His heavenly Father; for it was only by actions of benevolence that He could set forth the grace of God.

Christ came to manifest the love of God to the world, to draw the hearts of all men to Himself. . . . The first step toward salvation is to respond to the drawing of the love of Christ. . . . It is that men may understand the joy of forgiveness, the peace of God, that Christ draws them through the manifestation of His love. If they respond to His drawing, yielding their hearts to His grace, He will lead them on step by step, to a full knowledge of Himself, and this is life eternal.

TERMS OF THE COVENANT

If ye will obey my voice indeed, and keep my covenant, then ye shall be a peculiar treasure unto me above all people. **Ex. 19:5.**

In the beginning, God gave His law to mankind as a means of attaining happiness and eternal life.

The ten commandments, Thou shalt, and Thou shalt not, are ten promises, assured to us if we render obedience to the law governing the universe. "If ye love me, keep my commandments" (John 14:15). Here is the sum and substance of the law of God. The terms of salvation for every son and daughter of Adam are here outlined. . . .

That law of ten precepts of the greatest love that can be presented to man is the voice of God from heaven speaking to the soul in promise, "This do, and you will not come under the dominion and control of Satan." There is not a negative in that law, although it may appear thus. It is DO and Live.

The condition of eternal life is now just what it always has been—just what it was in Paradise before the fall of our first parents—perfect obedience to the law of God, perfect righteousness. If eternal life were granted on any condition short of this, then the happiness of the whole universe would be imperiled. The way would be open for sin, with all its train of woe and misery, to be immortalized.

Christ does not lessen the claims of the law. In unmistakable language He presents obedience to it as the condition of eternal life—the same condition that was required of Adam before his fall. . . . the requirement under the covenant of grace is just as broad as the requirement made in Eden—harmony with God's law, which is holy, just, and good.

The standard of character presented in the Old Testament is the same that is presented in the New Testament. This standard is not one to which we cannot attain. In every command or injunction that God gives there is a promise, the most positive, underlying the command. God has made provision that we may become like unto Him, and He will accomplish this for all who do not interpose a perverse will and thus frustrate His grace.

WRITTEN ON THE HEART

After those days, saith the Lord, I will put my law in their inward parts, and write it in their hearts. . . . I will forgive their iniquity, and I will remember their sin no more. **Jer. 31:33, 34.**

The same law that was engraved upon the tables of stone, is written by the Holy Spirit upon the tables of the heart. Instead of going about to establish our own righteousness we accept the righteousness of Christ. His blood atones for our sins. His obedience is accepted for us. Then the heart renewed by the Holy Spirit will bring forth "the fruits of the Spirit." Through the grace of Christ we shall live in obedience to the law of God written upon our hearts. Having the Spirit of Christ, we shall walk even as He walked.

There are two errors against which the children of God—particularly those who have just come to trust in His grace—especially need to guard. The first . . . is that of looking to their own works, trusting to anything they can do, to bring themselves into harmony with God. He who is trying to become holy by his own works in keeping the law, is attempting an impossibility. . . .

The opposite and no less dangerous error is, that belief in Christ releases men from keeping the law of God; that since by faith alone we become partakers of the grace of Christ, our works have nothing to do with our redemption. . . . If the law is written in the heart, will it not shape the life? . . . Instead of releasing man from obedience, it is faith, and faith only, that makes us partakers of the grace of Christ, which enables us to render obedience. . . .

Where there is not only a belief in God's Word, but a submission of the will to Him; where the heart is yielded to Him, the affections fixed upon Him, there is faith—faith that works by love, and purifies the soul. Through this faith the heart is renewed in the image of God. And the heart that in its unrenewed state is not subject to the law of God, neither indeed can be, now delights in its holy precepts, exclaiming with the psalmist, "O how love I thy law! it is my meditation all the day" (Ps. 119:97). And the righteousness of the law is fulfilled in us, "who walk not after the flesh, but after the Spirit" (Rom. 8:1).

GOD'S ETERNAL PLEDGE

He hath remembered his covenant forever, the word which he commanded to a thousand generations. **Ps. 105:8.**

God stands back of every promise He has made. With your Bibles in your hands, say: "I have done as Thou hast said. I present Thy promise, 'Ask, and it shall be given you; seek, and ye shall find; knock, and it shall be opened unto you' (Matt. 7:7). . . .

The rainbow about the throne is an assurance that God is true; that in Him is no variableness, neither shadow of turning. We have sinned against Him and are undeserving of His favor; yet He Himself has put into our lips that most wonderful of pleas: "Do not abhor us, for thy name's sake, do not disgrace the throne of thy glory: remember, break not thy covenant with us" (Jer. 14:21). He has pledged Himself to give heed to our cry when we come to him confessing our unworthiness and sin. The honor of His throne is staked for the fulfillment of His word to us.

To everyone who offers himself to the Lord for service, withholding nothing, is given power for the attainment of measureless results. The Lord God is bound by an eternal pledge to supply power and grace to everyone who is sanctified through obedience to the truth.

Nehemiah pressed into the presence of the King of kings and won to his side a power that can turn hearts as rivers of waters are turned. [See Nehemiah 1 and 2.]

To pray as Nehemiah prayed in his hour of need is a resource at the command of the Christian under circumstances when other forms of prayer may be impossible. Toilers in the busy walks of life, crowded and almost overwhelmed with perplexity, can send up a petition to God for divine guidance. . . . In times of sudden difficulty or peril the heart may send up its cry for help to One who has pledged Himself to come to the aid of His faithful, believing ones whenever they call upon Him. In every circumstance, under every condition, the soul weighed down with grief and care, or fiercely assailed by temptation, may find assurance, support, and succor in the unfailing love and power of a covenant-keeping God.

UNUTTERABLE LONELINESS

I have trodden the winepress alone; and of the people there was none with me. **Isa. 63:3.**

Through childhood, youth, and manhood, Jesus walked alone. In His purity and His faithfulness, He trod the winepress alone, and of the people there was none with Him. He carried the awful weight of responsibility for the salvation of men. He knew that unless there was a decided change in the principles and purposes of the human race, all would be lost. This was the burden of His soul, and none could appreciate the weight that rested upon Him.

Throughout His life His mother and His brothers did not comprehend His mission. Even His disciples did not understand Him. He had dwelt in eternal light, as one with God, but His life on earth must be spent in solitude. As one with us, He must bear the burden of our guilt and woe. The Sinless One must feel the shame of sin. The peace lover must dwell with strife, the truth must abide with falsehood, purity with vileness. Every sin, every discord, every defiling lust that transgression had brought, was torture to His spirit.

Alone He must tread the path; alone He must bear the burden. Upon Him who had laid off His glory and accepted the weakness of humanity the redemption of the world must rest. He saw and felt it all, but His purpose remained steadfast. Upon His arm depended the salvation of the fallen race, and He reached out His hand to grasp the hand of Omnipotent love.

The loneliness of Christ, separated from the heavenly courts, living the life of humanity, was never understood or appreciated by the disciples as it should have been. . . . When Jesus was no longer with them, . . . they began to see how they might have shown Him attentions that would have brought gladness to His heart. . . .

The same want is evident in our world today. But few appreciate all that Christ is to them. If they did, the great love of Mary [Matt. 26:6-13] would be expressed, the anointing would be freely bestowed. . . . Nothing would be thought too costly to give for Christ, no self-denial or self-sacrifice too great to be endured for His sake.

THE SINS OF THE WORLD

He was wounded for our transgressions, he was bruised for our iniquities: the chastisement of our peace was upon him; and with his stripes we are healed. Isa. 53:5.

Some have limited views of the atonement. They think that Christ suffered only a small portion of the penalty of the law of God; they suppose that, while the wrath of God was felt by His dear Son, He had, through all His painful sufferings, the evidence of His Father's love and acceptance; that the portals of the tomb before Him were illuminated with bright hope, and that He had the abiding evidence of His future glory. Here is a great mistake. Christ's keenest anguish was a sense of His Father's displeasure. His mental agony because of this was of such intensity that man can have but faint conception of it.

With many the story of the condescension, humiliation, and sacrifice of our divine Lord awakens no deeper interest . . . than does the history of the death of the martyrs of Jesus. Many have suffered death by slow tortures; others have suffered death by crucifixion. In what does the death of God's dear Son differ from these? . . . If the sufferings of Christ consisted in physical pain alone, then His death was no more painful than that of some of the martyrs. But bodily pain was but a small part of the agony of God's dear Son. The sins of the world were upon Him, also the sense of His Father's wrath as He suffered the penalty of the law transgressed. It was these that crushed His divine soul. . . . The separation that sin makes between God and man was fully realized and keenly felt by the innocent, suffering Man of Calvary. He was oppressed by the powers of darkness. He had not one ray of light to brighten the future. . . . It was in this terrible hour of darkness, the face of His Father hidden, legions of evil angels enshrouding Him, the sins of the world upon Him, that the words were wrenched from His lips: "My God, my God, why hast thou forsaken me?" . . .

In comparison with the enterprise of everlasting life, every other sinks into insignificance.

SO COSTLY—AND YET FREE

By the righteousness of one the free gift came upon all men unto justification of life. **Rom. 5:18.**

Money cannot buy it, intellect cannot grasp it, power cannot command it; but to all who will accept it, God's glorious grace is freely given. But men may feel their need, and, renouncing all self-dependence, accept salvation as a gift. Those who enter heaven will not scale its walls by their own righteousness, nor will its gates be opened to them for costly offerings of gold or silver, but they will gain an entrance to the many mansions of the Father's house through the merits of the cross of Christ.

For sinful men, the highest consolation, the greatest cause of rejoicing, is that Heaven has given Jesus to be the sinner's Saviour. . . . He offered to go over the ground where Adam stumbled and fell; to meet the tempter on the field of battle, and conquer him in man's behalf. Behold Him in the wilderness of temptation. Forty days and forty nights He fasted, enduring the fiercest assaults of the powers of darkness. He trod the "winepress alone; and of the people there was none with'' Him (Isa. 63:3). It was not for Himself, but that He might break the chain that held the human race in slavery to Satan.

As Christ in His humanity sought strength from His Father, that He might be enabled to endure trial and temptation, so are we to do. We are to follow the example of the sinless Son of God. Daily we need help and grace and power from the Source of all power. We are to cast our helpless souls upon the One who is ready to help us in every time of need. Too often we forget the Lord. Self gives way to impulse, and we lose the victories that we should gain.

If we are overcome let us not delay to repent, and to accept the pardon that will place us on vantage ground. If we repent and believe, the cleansing power from God will be ours. His saving grace is freely offered. His pardon is given to all who will receive it. . . . Over every sinner that repents the angels of God rejoice with songs of joy. Not one sinner need be lost. Full and free is the gift of saving grace.

A COMFORTER LIKE CHRIST

Nevertheless I tell you the truth; it is expedient for you that I go away: for if I go not away, the Comforter will not come unto you; but if I depart, I will send him unto you. John 16:7.

The Comforter that Christ promised to send after He ascended to heaven, is the Spirit in all the fullness of the Godhead, making manifest the power of divine grace to all who receive and believe in Christ as a personal Saviour.

With the consecrated worker for God, in whatever place he may be, the Holy Spirit abides. The words spoken to the disciples are spoken also to us. The Comforter is ours as well as theirs.

There is no comforter like Christ, so tender and so true. He is touched with the feeling of our infirmities. His Spirit speaks to the heart. Circumstances may separate us from our friends; the broad, restless ocean may roll between us and them. Though their sincere friendship may still exist, they may be unable to demonstrate it. . . . But no circumstances, no distance, can separate us from the heavenly Comforter. Wherever we are, wherever we may go, He is always there, one given in Christ's place, to act in His stead. He is always at our right hand, to speak soothing, gentle words; to support, sustain, uphold, and cheer. The influence of the Holy Spirit is the life of Christ in the soul. This Spirit works in and through every one who receives Christ. Those who know the indwelling of this

Spirit reveal its fruit—love, joy, peace, long-suffering, gentleness, goodness, faith.

The Holy Spirit ever abides with him who is seeking for perfection of Christian character. The Holy Spirit furnishes the pure motive, the living, active principle, that sustains striving, wrestling, believing souls in every emergency and under every temptation. The Holy Spirit sustains the believer amid the world's hatred, amid the unfriendliness of relatives, amid disappointment, amid the realization of imperfection, and amid the mistakes of life. Depending upon the matchless purity and perfection of Christ, the victory is sure to him who looks unto the Author and Finisher of our faith. . . . He has borne our sins, in order that through Him we might have moral excellence, and attain unto the perfection of Christian character.

PURIFYING, VITALIZING POWER

Create in me a clean heart, O God; and renew a right spirit within me. **Ps. 51:10.**

The Lord purifies the heart very much as we air a room. We do not close the doors and windows, and throw in some purifying substance; but we open the doors and throw wide the windows, and let heaven's purifying atmosphere flow in. . . . The windows of impulse, of feeling must be opened up toward heaven, and the dust of selfishness and earthliness must be expelled. The grace of God must sweep through the chambers of the mind, the imagination must have heavenly themes for contemplation, and every element of the nature must be purified and vitalized by the Spirit of God.

He who lives the principles of Bible religion, will not be found weak in moral power. Under the ennobling influence of the Holy Spirit, the tastes and inclinations become pure and holy. Nothing takes so strong a hold upon the affections, nothing reaches so fully down to the deepest motives of action, nothing exerts so potent an influence upon the life, and gives so great firmness and stability to the character, as the religion of Christ. It leads its possessor ever upward, inspiring him with noble purposes, teaching him propriety of deportment, and imparting a becoming dignity to every action.

The church is the object of God's tenderest love and care. If the members will allow Him, He will reveal His character through them. He says to them, "Ye are the light of the world" (Matt. 5:14). Those who walk and talk with God practice the gentleness of Christ. In their lives, forbearance, meekness, and self-restraint are united with holy earnestness

211

and diligence. As they advance heavenward, the sharp, rough edges of character are worn off, and godliness is seen. The Holy Spirit, full of grace and power, works upon mind and heart.

The heart in which Jesus makes His abode will be quickened, purified, guided, and ruled by the Holy Spirit, and the human agent will make strenuous efforts to bring his character into harmony with God. He will avoid everything that is contrary to the revealed will and mind of God.

THE LATTER RAIN

Ask ye of the Lord rain in the time of the latter rain; so the Lord shall make bright clouds, and give them showers of rain, to every one grass in the field. **Zech. 10:1.**

Under the figure of the early and the latter rain, that falls in Eastern lands at seedtime and harvest, the Hebrew prophets foretold the bestowal of spiritual grace in extraordinary measure upon God's church. The outpouring of the Spirit in the days of the apostles was the beginning of the early, or former rain, and glorious was the result. . . . But near the close of earth's harvest, a special bestowal of spiritual grace is promised to prepare the church for the coming of the Son of man. This outpouring of the Spirit is likened to the falling of the latter rain; and it is for this added power that Christians are to send their petitions to the Lord of the harvest "in the time of the latter rain."

As Christ was glorified on the day of Pentecost so will He again be glorified in the closing work of the gospel, when He shall prepare a people to stand the final test, in the closing conflict of the great controversy.

Many . . . will be seen hurrying hither and thither, constrained by the Spirit of God to bring the light to others. The truth, the Word of God, is as a fire in their bones, filling them with a burning desire to enlighten those who sit in darkness. Many, even among the uneducated, now proclaim the words of the Lord. Children are impelled by the Spirit to go forth and declare the message from heaven. The Spirit is poured out upon all who will yield to its promptings, and . . . they will declare the truth with the might of the Spirit's power.

But unless the members of God's church today have a living connection with the Source of all spiritual growth, they will not be ready for the time of reaping. Unless they keep their lamps trimmed and burning, they will fail of receiving added grace in times of special need.

Divine grace is needed at the beginning, divine grace at every step of advance, and divine grace alone can complete the work. . . . By prayer and faith we are continually to seek more of the Spirit.

IT TAKES TIME

I the Lord do keep it; I will water it every moment: lest any hurt it, I will keep it night and day. **Isa. 27:3.**

The mind of a man or a woman does not come down in a moment from purity and holiness to depravity, corruption, and crime. It takes time to transform the human to the divine, or to degrade those formed in the image of God to the brutal or the satanic. By beholding we become changed. Though formed in the image of his Maker, man can so educate his mind that sin which he once loathed will become pleasant to him. As he ceases to watch and pray, he ceases to guard the citadel, the heart. . . . Constant war against the carnal mind must be maintained; and we must be aided by the refining influence of the grace of God, which will attract the mind upward and habituate it to meditate upon pure and holy things.

Character does not come by chance. It is not determined by one outburst of temper, one step in the wrong direction. It is the repetition of the act that causes it to become habit, and molds the character either for good or for evil. Right characters can be formed only by persevering, untiring effort, by improving every entrusted talent and capability to the glory of God.

God expects us to build characters in accordance with the pattern set before us. We are to lay brick by brick, adding grace to grace, finding our weak points and correcting them in accordance with the directions given.

God gives us strength, reasoning power, time, in order that we may build characters on which He can place His stamp of approval. He desires each child of His to build a noble character, by the doing of pure, noble deeds, that in the end he may present a symmetrical structure, a fair temple, honored by man and God. . . .

He who would grow into a beautiful building for the Lord must cultivate every power of the being. It is only by the right use of the talents that the character can be developed harmoniously. Thus we bring to the foundation that which is represented in the Word as gold, silver, precious stones—material that will stand the test of God's purifying fires.

213

PERFECTION NOW?

Be ye therefore perfect, even as your Father which is in heaven is perfect. **Matt. 5:48.**

When God gave His Son to the world, He made it possible for men and women to be perfect by the use of every capability of their beings to the glory of God. In Christ He gave to them the riches of His grace, and a knowledge of His will. As they would empty themselves of self, and learn to walk in humility, leaning on God for guidance, men would be enabled to fulfill God's high purpose for them.

Perfection of character is based upon that which Christ is to us. If we have constant dependence on the merits of our Saviour, and walk in His footsteps, we shall be like Him, pure and undefiled.

Our Saviour does not require impossibilities of any soul. He expects nothing of His disciples that He is not willing to give them grace and strength to perform. He would not call upon them to be perfect if He had not at His command every perfection of grace to bestow on the ones upon whom He would confer so high and holy a privilege. . . .

Our work is to strive to attain in our sphere of action the perfection that Christ in His life on the earth attained in every phase of character. He is our example. In all things we are to strive to honor God in character. . . . We are to be wholly dependent on the power that He has promised to give us.

Jesus revealed no qualities, and exercised no powers, that men may not have through faith in Him. His perfect humanity is that which all His followers may possess, if they will be in subjection to God as He was.

Our Saviour is a Saviour for the perfection of the whole man. He is not the God of part of the being only. The grace of Christ works to the disciplining of the whole human fabric. He made all. He has redeemed all. He has made the mind, the strength, the body as well as the soul, partaker of the divine nature, and all is His purchased possession. He must be served with the whole mind, heart, soul, and strength. Then the Lord will be glorified in His saints in even the common, temporal things with which they are connected. "Holiness unto the Lord" will be in the inscription placed upon them.

AWAITING OUR DEMAND

Ask, and ye shall receive, that your joy may be full. **John 16:24.**

Prayer is heaven's ordained means of success in the conflict with sin and the development of Christian character. The divine influences that come in answer to the prayer of faith will accomplish in the soul of the suppliant all for which he pleads. For the pardon of sin, for the Holy Spirit, for a Christlike temper, for wisdom and strength to do His work, for any gift He has promised, we may ask; and the promise is, "Ye shall receive."

Jesus is our helper; in Him and through Him we must conquer. . . . The grace of Christ is waiting your demand upon it. He will give you grace and strength as you need it if you ask Him. . . . The religion of Christ will bind and restrain every unholy passion, will stimulate to energy, to self-discipline, and industry, even in the matters of homely, everyday life, leading us to learn economy, tact, and self-denial, and to endure even privation without a murmur. The Spirit of Christ in the heart will be revealed in the character, will develop noble qualities and powers. "My grace is sufficient" (2 Cor. 12:9) says Christ.

Make every effort to keep open the communion between Jesus and your own soul. . . . We should pray in the family circle, and above all we must not neglect secret prayer; for this is the life of the soul. It is impossible for the soul to flourish while prayer is neglected. Family or public prayer alone is not sufficient. In solitude let the soul be laid open to the inspecting eye of God. Secret prayer is to be heard only by the prayer-hearing God. No curious ear is to receive the burden of such petitions. In secret prayer the soul is free from surrounding influences, free from excitement. . . . By calm, simple faith, the soul holds communion with God, and gathers to itself rays of divine light to strengthen and sustain it in the conflict with Satan. . . .

Pray in your closet, and as you go about your daily labor, let your heart be often uplifted to God. It was thus that Enoch walked with God. These silent prayers rise like precious incense before the throne of grace. Satan cannot overcome him whose heart is thus stayed upon God.

ANGEL REINFORCEMENTS

Behold, I give unto you power to tread on serpents and scorpions, and over all the power of the enemy. **Luke 10:19.**

Fallen man is Satan's lawful captive. The mission of Christ was to rescue him from the power of his great adversary. Man is naturally inclined to follow Satan's suggestions, and he cannot successfully resist so terrible a foe unless Christ, the mighty Conqueror, dwells in him, guiding his desires, and giving him strength. God alone can limit the power of Satan. . . . Satan knows better than God's people the power that they can have over him when their strength is in Christ. When they humbly entreat the mighty Conqueror for help, the weakest believer in the truth, relying firmly upon Christ, can successfully repulse Satan and all his host. . . .

Satan will call to his aid legions of his angels to oppose the advance of even one soul, and, if possible, wrest it from the hand of Christ. . . . But if the one in danger perseveres, and in his helplessness casts himself upon the merits of the blood of Christ, our Saviour listens to the earnest prayer of faith, and sends a reinforcement of those angels that excel in strength to deliver him. Satan cannot endure to have his powerful rival appealed to, for he fears and trembles before His strength and majesty. At the sound of fervent prayer, Satan's whole host trembles.

Nothing but Christ's loving compassion, His divine grace, His almighty power, can enable us to baffle the relentless foe, and subdue the opposition of our own hearts. What is our strength? The joy of the Lord. Let the love of Christ fill our hearts, and then we shall be prepared to receive the power that He has for us. . . .

Beholding Christ for the purpose of becoming like Him, the seeker after truth sees the perfection of the principles of God's law, and he becomes dissatisfied with everything but perfection. . . . A battle must be fought with the attributes that Satan has been strengthening for his own use. . . . But he knows that with the Redeemer there is saving power that will gain for him the victory in the conflict. The Saviour will strengthen and help him as he comes pleading for grace and efficiency.

August 23   God's Amazing Grace

THE CHRISTIAN'S BADGE

Now unto him that is able to do exceeding abundantly above all that we ask or think, according to the power that worketh in us. **Eph. 3:20.**

The Lord is waiting to manifest through His people His grace and power. But He requires that those who engage in His service shall keep their minds ever directed to Him. Every day they should have time for reading the Word of God and for prayer. . . .

Individually we are to walk and talk with God; then the sacred influence of the gospel of Christ in all its preciousness will appear in our lives.

There is an eloquence far more powerful than the eloquence of words in the quiet, consistent life of a pure, true Christian. What a man is has more influence than what he says.

The officers who were sent to Jesus came back with the report that never man spoke as He spoke. But the reason for this was that never man lived as He lived. Had His life been other than it was, He could not have spoken as He did. His words bore with them a convincing power, because they came from a heart pure and holy, full of love and sympathy, benevolence and truth.

It is our own character and experience that determine our influence upon others. In order to convince others of the power of Christ's grace, we must know its power in our own hearts and lives. The gospel we present for the saving of souls must be the gospel by which our own souls are saved. Only through a living faith in Christ as a personal Saviour is it possible to make our influence felt in a skeptical world. If we would draw sinners out of the swift-running current, our own feet must be firmly set upon the Rock, Christ Jesus.

The badge of Christianity is not an outward sign, not the wearing of a cross or a crown, but it is that which reveals the union of man with God. By the power of His grace manifested in the transformation of character the world is to be convinced that God has sent His son as its Redeemer. No other influence that can surround the human soul has such power as the influence of an unselfish life. The strongest argument in favor of the gospel is a loving and lovable Christian.

CONDITIONS OF CHRISTIAN GROWTH

And this I pray, that your love may abound yet more and more in knowledge and in all judgment; . . . being filled with the fruits of righteousness, which are by Jesus Christ, unto the glory and praise of God. **Phil. 1:9-11.**

Where there is life, there will be growth and fruit-bearing; but unless we grow in grace, our spirituality will be dwarfed, sickly, fruitless. It is only by growing, by bearing fruit, that we can fulfill God's purpose for us. "Herein is my Father glorified," Christ said, "that ye bear much fruit" (John 15:8). In order to bear much fruit, we must make the most of our privileges. We must use every opportunity granted us for obtaining strength.

A pure, noble character, with all its grand possibilities, has been provided for every human being. But there are many who have not an earnest longing for such a character. They are not willing to part with the evil that they may have the good. . . . They neglect to grasp the blessings that would place them in harmony with God. . . . They cannot grow.

One of the divine plans for growth is impartation. The Christian is to gain strength by strengthening others. "He that watereth shall be watered also himself" (Prov. 11:25). This is not merely a promise; it is a divine law, a law by which God designs that the streams of benevolence, like the waters of the great deep, shall be kept in constant circulation, continually flowing back to their source. In the fulfilling of this law is the secret of spiritual growth. . . .

If we come to God in faith, He will receive us and give us strength to climb upward to perfection. If we watch every word and action, that we may do nothing to dishonor the One who has trusted us, if we improve every opportunity granted us, we shall grow into the full stature of men and women in Christ. . . .

Christians, is Christ revealed in us? Are we doing all in our power to gain a body that is not easily enfeebled, a mind that looks beyond self to the cause and effect of every movement, that can wrestle with hard problems and conquer them, a will that is firm to resist evil and defend the right? Are we crucifying self? Are we growing up into the full stature of men and women in Christ, preparing to endure hardness as good soldiers of the cross?

IN KINDNESS

Put on therefore, as the elect of God, holy and beloved, bowels of mercies, kindness, humbleness of mind, meekness, longsuffering. **Col. 3:12.**

Let the law of kindness be upon your lips and the oil of grace in your heart. This will produce wonderful results. You will be tender, sympathetic, courteous. You need all these graces. The Holy Spirit must be received and brought into your character; then it will be as holy fire, giving forth incense which will rise up to God, not from lips that condemn, but as a healer of the souls of men. Your countenance will express the image of the divine. . . . By beholding the character of Christ you will become changed into His likeness. The grace of Christ alone can change your heart and then you will reflect the image of the Lord Jesus. God calls upon us to be like Him—pure, holy, and undefiled. We are to bear the divine image. . . .

The Lord Jesus is our only helper. Through His grace we shall learn to cultivate love, to educate ourselves to speak kindly and tenderly. Through His grace our cold, harsh manners will be transformed. The law of kindness will be upon our lips, and those who are under the precious influences of the Holy Spirit, will not feel that it is an evidence of weakness to weep with those who weep, to rejoice with them that rejoice. We are to cultivate heavenly excellences of character. We are to learn what it means to have good-will toward all men, a sincere desire to be as sunshine and not as shadow in the lives of others.

Seize every opportunity to contribute to the happiness of those around you, sharing with them your affection. Words of kindness, looks of sympathy, expressions of appreciation, would to many a struggling, lonely one be as a cup of cold water to a thirsty soul. . . .

Live in the sunshine of the Saviour's love. Then your influence will bless the world. Let the Spirit of Christ control you. Let the law of kindness be ever on your lips. Forbearance and unselfishness mark the words and actions of those who are born again, to live the new life in Christ.

A DIVINE PRESCRIPTION

That the name of our Lord Jesus Christ may be glorified in you, and ye in him, according to the grace of our God and the Lord Jesus Christ. 2 Thess. 1:12.

Many are longing to grow in grace; they pray over the matter, and are surprised that their prayers are not answered. The Master has given them a work to do whereby they shall grow. Of what value is it to pray when there is need of work? The question is, Are they seeking to save souls for whom Christ died? Spiritual growth depends upon giving to others the light that God has given to you. You are to put forth your best thoughts in active labor to do good, and only good, in your family, in your church, and in your neighborhood.

In place of growing anxious with the thought that you are not growing in grace, just do every duty that presents itself, carry the burden of souls on your heart, and by every conceivable means seek to save the lost. Be kind, be courteous, be pitiful; speak in humility of the blessed hope; talk of the love of Jesus; tell of His goodness, His mercy, and His righteousness; and cease to worry as to whether or not you are growing. Plants do not grow through any conscious effort. . . . The plant is not in continual worriment about its growth; it just grows under the supervision of God.

If we will consecrate heart and mind to the service of God, doing the work He has for us to do and walking in the footsteps of Jesus, our hearts will become sacred harps, every chord of which will send forth praise and thanksgiving to the Lamb sent by God to take away the sins of the world. . . .

The Lord Jesus is our strength and happiness, the great storehouse from which, on every occasion, men may draw strength. As we study Him, talk of Him, become more and more able to behold Him—as we avail ourselves of His grace and receive the blessings He proffers us, we have something with which to help others. Filled with gratitude, we communicate to others the blessings that have been freely given us. Thus receiving and imparting, we grow in grace.

UNION WITH CHRIST

But put ye on the Lord Jesus Christ, and make not provision for the flesh, to fulfil the lusts thereof. **Rom. 13:14.**

To effect the salvation of men, God employs various agencies. He speaks to them by His word and by His ministers, and He sends by the Holy Spirit messages of warning, reproof, and instruction. These means are designed to enlighten the understanding of the people, to reveal to them their duty and their sins, and the blessings which they may receive; to awaken in them a sense of spiritual want, that they may go to Christ and find in Him the grace they need. . . .

Every individual, by his own act, either puts Christ from him by refusing to cherish His spirit and follow His example, or he enters into a personal union with Christ by self-renunciation, faith, and obedience. We must, each for himself, choose Christ, because He has first chosen us. This union with Christ is to be formed by those who are naturally at enmity with Him. It is a relation of utter dependence, to be entered into by a proud heart. This is close work, and many who profess to be followers of Christ know nothing of it. They nominally accept the Saviour, but not as the sole ruler of their hearts. . . .

To renounce their own will, perhaps their chosen objects of affection or pursuit, requires an effort, at which many hesitate and falter and turn back. Yet this battle must be fought by every heart that is truly converted. We must war against temptations without and within. We must gain the victory over self, crucify the affections and lusts; and then begins the union of the soul with Christ. . . . After this union is formed, it can be preserved only by continual, earnest, painstaking effort. Christ exercises His power to preserve and guard this sacred tie, and the dependent, helpless sinner must act his part with untiring energy, or Satan by his cruel, cunning power will separate him from Christ. . . .

Your birth, your reputation, your wealth, your talents, your virtues, your piety, your philanthropy, . . . will not form a bond of union between your soul and Christ. Your connection with the church . . . will be of no avail unless you believe in Christ. It is not enough to believe *about* him. You must believe *in* Him. You must rely wholly upon His saving grace.

PRAISE GOD!

I will mention the lovingkindness of the Lord, and the praises of the Lord, according to all that the Lord hath bestowed on us, and the great goodness toward the house of Israel. Isa. 63:7.

When a sense of the loving-kindness of God is constantly refreshing the soul, it will be revealed in the countenance by an expression of peace and joy. It will be manifest in the words and works. And the generous, holy Spirit of Christ, working upon the heart, will yield in the life a converting influence upon others. . . .

Have we not reason to talk of God's goodness and to tell of His power? When friends are kind to us we esteem it a privilege to thank them for their kindness. How much more should we count it a joy to return thanks to the Friend who has given us every good and perfect gift. Then let us, in every church, cultivate thanksgiving to God. Let us educate our lips to praise God in the family circle. . . . Let our gifts and offerings declare our gratitude for the favors we daily receive. In everything we should show forth the joy of the Lord. . . .

David declares, "I love the Lord, because he hath heard my voice and my supplications. Because he hath inclined his ear unto me, therefore will I call upon him as long as I live" (Ps. 116:1, 2). God's goodness in hearing and answering prayer places us under heavy obligation to express our thanksgiving for the favors bestowed upon us. We should praise God much more than we do. The blessings received in answer to prayer should be promptly acknowledged. . . .

We grieve the Spirit of Christ by our complaints and murmurings and repinings. We should not dishonor God by the mournful relation of trials that appear grievous. All trials that are received as educators will produce joy. The whole religious life will be uplifting, elevating, ennobling, fragrant with good words and works.

Let the peace of God reign in your soul. Then you will have strength to bear all suffering, and you will rejoice that you have grace to endure. Praise the Lord; talk of His goodness; tell of His power. Sweeten the atmosphere that surrounds your soul. . . . Praise with heart and soul and voice, Him who is the health of your countenance, your Saviour, and your God.

WHILE WE WAIT

Let your loins be girded about, and your lights burning; and ye yourselves like unto men that wait for their lord. **Luke 12:35, 36.**

Now is the time to prepare for the coming of our Lord. Readiness to meet Him cannot be attained in a moment's time. Preparatory to that solemn scene there must be vigilant waiting and watching, combined with earnest work. So God's children glorify Him. Amid the busy scenes of life their voices will be heard speaking words of encouragement, faith, and hope. All they have and are is consecrated to the Master's service. . . .

Christ tells us when the day of His kingdom shall be ushered in. He does not say that all the world will be converted, but that "this gospel of the kingdom shall be preached in all the world for a witness unto all nations; and then shall the end come" (Matt. 24:14). By giving the gospel to the world, it is in our power to hasten the coming of the day of God. Had the church of Christ done her appointed work as the Lord ordained, the whole world would before this have been warned, and the Lord Jesus would have come to the earth in power and great glory.

Living power must attend the message of Christ's second appearing. We must not rest until we see many souls converted to the blessed hope of the Lord's return. In the days of the apostles the message that they bore wrought a real work, turning souls from idols to serve the living God. The work to be done today is just as real, and the truth is just as much truth; only we are to give the message with as much more earnestness as the coming of the Lord is nearer. The message for this time is positive, simple, and of the deepest importance. We must act like men and women who believe it. Waiting, watching, working, praying, warning the world—this is our work.

I have been deeply impressed by scenes that have recently passed before me in the night season. There seemed to be a great movement—a work of revival—going forward in many places. Our people were moving into line, responding to God's call. My brethren, the Lord is speaking to us. Shall we not heed His call? Shall we not trim our lamps, and act like men who look for their Lord to come?

WHAT A REWARD!

If any man's work abide . . . , he shall receive a reward. **1 Cor. 3:14.**

Glorious will be the reward bestowed when the faithful workers gather about the throne of God and of the Lamb. When John in his mortal state beheld the glory of God, he fell as one dead; he was not able to endure the sight. But when the children of God shall have put on immortality, they will "see him as he is" (1 John 3:2). They will stand before the throne, accepted in the Beloved. All their sins have been blotted out, all their transgressions borne away. Now they can look upon the undimmed glory of the throne of God. They have been partakers with Christ in His sufferings, they have been workers together with Him in the plan of redemption, and they are partakers with Him in the joy of seeing souls saved in the kingdom of God, there to praise God through all eternity. . . .

In that day the redeemed will shine forth in the glory of the Father and the Son. The angels, touching their golden harps, will welcome the King and His trophies of victory. . . . A song of triumph will peal forth, filling all heaven. Christ has conquered. He enters the heavenly courts, accompanied by His redeemed ones, the witnesses that His mission of suffering and sacrifice has not been in vain. . . .

There are homes for the pilgrims of earth. There are robes for the righteous, with crowns of glory and palms of victory. All that has perplexed us in the providences of God will in the world to come be made plain. The things hard to be understood will then find explanation. The mysteries of grace will unfold before us. Where our finite minds discovered only confusion and broken promises, we shall see the most perfect and beautiful harmony. We shall know that infinite love ordered the experiences that seemed most trying. As we realize the tender care of Him who makes all things work together for our good, we shall rejoice with joy unspeakable and full of glory.

I urge you to prepare for the coming of Christ in the clouds of heaven. . . . Prepare for the judgment, that when Christ shall come, to be admired in all them that believe, you may be among those who will meet Him in peace.

LOOK UP!

Comfort ye, comfort ye my people, saith your God. Speak ye comfortably to Jerusalem, and cry unto her, that her warfare is accomplished, that her iniquity is pardoned. Isa. 40:1, 2.

In the darkest days of her long conflict with evil, the church of God has been given revelations of the eternal purpose of Jehovah. His people have been permitted to look beyond the trials of the present to the triumphs of the future, when, the warfare having been accomplished, the redeemed will enter into possession of the promised land. These visions of future glory, scenes pictured by the hand of God, should be dear to His church today, when the controversy of the ages is rapidly closing and the promised blessings are soon to be realized in all their fullness.

To us who are standing on the very verge of their fulfillment, of what deep moment, what living interest, are these delineations of the things to come—events for which, since our first parents turned their steps from Eden, God's children have watched and waited, longed and prayed!

Fellow pilgrim, we are still amid the shadows and turmoil of earthly activities; but soon our Saviour is to appear to bring deliverance and rest. Let us by faith behold the blessed hereafter as pictured by the hand of God. He who died for the sins of the world is opening wide the gates of Paradise to all who believe on Him. Soon the battle will have been fought, the victory won. Soon we shall see Him in whom our hopes of eternal life are centered. And in His presence the trials and sufferings of this life will seem as nothingness. The former things "shall not be remembered, nor come into mind." "Cast not away therefore your confidence, which hath great recompense of reward. For ye have need of patience, that, after ye have done the will of God, ye might receive the promise. For yet a little while, and he that shall come will come, and will not tarry." "Israel shall be saved . . . with an everlasting salvation: ye shall not be ashamed nor confounded world without end."

Look up, look up, and let your faith continually increase. Let this faith guide you along the narrow path that leads through the gates of the city into the great beyond, the wide, unbounded future of glory that is for the redeemed.

THE CONFLICT OVER

For verily I say unto you, Till heaven and earth pass, one jot or one tittle shall in no wise pass from the law, till all be fulfilled. Matt. 5:18.

When Christ entered upon His campaign, Satan met Him and contested every inch of ground, exerting his utmost powers to conquer Him. Much was involved in this controversy. Intense interests were at stake. The questions to be answered were: "Is God's law imperfect, in need of being amended or abrogated? or is it immutable? Is God's government stable? or is it in need of changes?" Not only before those living in the city of God, but before the inhabitants of all the heavenly universe, were these questions to be answered. . . .

From the manger to the cross Satan followed the Son of God. Temptations beat upon Him like a tempest. But the more fierce the conflict, the more familiar He became with the temptations wherewith man is beset, and the better prepared He was to succor the tempted.

The severity of the trial through which Christ passed was proportionate to the value of the object to be gained or lost by His success or failure. Not merely the interests of one world were involved. This world was the battlefield, but all the worlds that God has created were affected by the result of the conflict. . . . Satan sought to make it appear that he was working for the liberty of the universe. Even while Christ was on the cross, the enemy was determined to make his arguments so varied, so deceptive, so insidious, that all would be convinced that God's law was tyrannical. He himself laid every scheme, planned every evil, inflamed every mind to bring affliction on Christ. He himself instigated the false accusations against One who had done only good. He himself inspired the cruel deeds that added to the suffering of the Son of God—the pure, the holy, the innocent.

By this course of action Satan has forged a chain by which he himself will be bound. The heavenly universe will bear witness to the justice of God in punishing him. Heaven itself saw what heaven would be, if he were in it. . . .

Not merely in the minds of a few finite creatures in this world, but in the minds of all the inhabitants of the heavenly universe, has the immutability of God's law been established. . . . With one voice they extolled God as righteous, merciful, self-denying, just.

AGENTS FOR HEAVEN

Finally, be ye all of one mind, having compassion one of another, love as brethren, be pitiful, be courteous. 1 Peter 3:8.

What great need there is of cultivating tenderness and gentleness. None should be ashamed to manifest a tender, compassionate spirit for those who err; for those who think they make no mistakes are far from being without fault before God. No one need to think that the manifestation of compassion is something for which he need be ashamed. . . .

When a crisis comes in the life of any soul, and another attempts to give advice, that advice and counsel will have only the weight of influence for good that their example and spirit of the adviser has accumulated for him. It is the consistent life, the revelation of a sincere, Christlike interest for the soul in peril, that will make counsel effectual to persuade and win into safe paths. Those who are quick to censure others, who speak words that cut and bruise the already wounded soul, are doing Satan's work, and are laborers with the prince of darkness. . . .

Let the tempted and tried souls remember that when chastisement comes upon them, it is the Lord who would save them from death. Let the souls to whom reproof comes, remember that "as many as I love, I rebuke and chasten" (Rev. 3:19).

The human agent, imbued with the Spirit of Christ, will watch for souls as they that must give an account. The claims of Christ are upon us, and we must understand our duty, and do it in the fear of God with an eye single to His glory, and not prove unfaithful. Let no thought of self or of natural feelings be cherished to keep the lips silent. Speak, and be not afraid. With the heart full of tenderness and love for souls, warn, exhort, and entreat.

Never cease to labor for a soul while there is one ray of hope. Your words may cut to the soul. Oh, then be cautious, and clothe them with the love and tenderness of Jesus. Soften every accent with love and sympathy. . . . As you deal with others, as you judge others, so the Lord will judge and deal with you. Let the agent who claims to be a child of God, practice the lessons of Christ. If he is compelled to wound, let him feel the duty of healing as compulsory upon him. The truth is ever to be spoken in love, with the Spirit of Christ abiding in the soul.

HOW TO MAKE AN IMPACT

Now when they saw the boldness of Peter and John, and perceived that they were unlearned and ignorant men, they marvelled; and they took knowledge of them, that they had been with Jesus. Acts 4:13.

When Jesus Christ was upon this earth, He did not direct fishermen to leave their nets and boats, and go to the Jewish teachers to gain a preparation for the gospel ministry. Walking by the Sea of Galilee, He saw "two brethren, Simon called Peter, and Andrew his brother, casting a net into the sea: for they were fishers. And he saith unto them, Follow me, and I will make you fishers of men. And they straightway left their nets, and followed him. And going on from thence, he saw other two brethren, James the son of Zebedee, and John his brother, in a ship with Zebedee their father, mending their nets; and he called them. And they immediately left the ship and their father, and followed him" (Matt. 4:18-22).

This prompt obedience, without any question, without one promise of wages, seems remarkable. But the words of Christ were an invitation that implied all that He meant it should. There was an impelling influence in His words. There was no long explanation, but what He said had a drawing power. . . .

Christ would make these humble fishermen, in connection with himself, the means of taking men out of the service of Satan, and making them believers in Christ, teaching them in regard to the kingdom of God. In this work they would become His ministers, fishers of men. . . .

Christ chose the foolish things of the world—those whom the world pronounced unlearned and ignorant—to confound the wise men of the world. The disciples were unlearned in the traditions of the rabbis, but with Christ as their example and teacher, they were gaining an education of the highest order; for they had before them a divine Example. Christ was presenting to them truths of the highest character.

Those whom God employs to do service for Him, He would have fitted in His way for that service. Those who preach Christ must learn of Christ daily, in order to understand the mystery of saving and serving the souls for whom He has died. . . . They must pattern after Him in all things, sharing His tender compassion and His sternness against all evil working.

FOR THE FEARFUL, FAINT, AND FEEBLE

Trust in the Lord, and do good; so shalt thou dwell in the land, and verily thou shalt be fed. **Ps. 37:3.**

"Trust in the Lord." Each day has its burdens, its cares, and perplexities; and when we meet, how ready we are to talk of our difficulties and trials. So many borrowed troubles intrude, so many fears are indulged, such a weight of anxiety is expressed, that one might almost suppose that we had no pitying, loving Saviour, ready to hear all our requests, and to be to us a present help in every time of need.

Some are always fearing and borrowing trouble. Every day they are surrounded by the tokens of God's love, every day they are enjoying the bounties of His providence; but they overlook these present blessings. Their minds are continually dwelling upon something disagreeable which they fear may come: or some difficulty may really exist, which, though small, blinds their eyes to the many things which demand gratitude. The difficulties which they encounter, instead of driving them to God, the only source of help, separate them from Him, because they awaken unrest and repining.

Brethren and sisters, do we well to be thus unbelieving? Why should we be ungrateful and distrustful? Jesus is our friend. All heaven is interested in our welfare; and our anxiety and fear grieve the Holy Spirit of God. We should not indulge in a solicitude which only frets and wears us, but does not help us to bear trials. No place should be given to that distrust of God which leads us to make a preparation against future want the chief pursuit of life, as though our happiness consisted in these earthly things, and we could gain them while ignoring the fact that God controls all things.

You may be perplexed in business; your prospects may grow darker and darker, and you may be threatened with loss. But do not become discouraged; cast your care upon God, and remain calm and cheerful. Begin every day with earnest prayer, not omitting to offer praise and thanksgiving. Ask for wisdom to manage your affairs with discretion, and thus prevent loss and disaster. Do all you can on your part to bring about favorable results. Jesus has promised divine aid, but not aside from human efforts.

THE ONLY SECURITY

Verily my sabbaths ye shall keep: for it is a sign between me and you throughout your generations; that ye may know that I am the Lord that doth sanctify you. **Ex. 31:13.**

Let every one seek the Lord for himself. Eternity is before us. You cannot afford to let another day pass without taking your position on the Lord's side. Will you not act the part that God has appointed you to act in the closing scenes of this earth's history?

It is impossible to give any idea of the experience of the people of God who will be alive on the earth when past woes and celestial glory will be blended. They will walk in the light proceeding from the throne of God. By the means of the angels there will be constant communication between heaven and earth. And Satan, surrounded by evil angels, and claiming to be God, will work miracles of all kinds, to deceive, if possible, the very elect. God's people will not find their safety in working miracles; for Satan would counterfeit any miracle that might be worked. God's tried and tested people will find their power in the sign spoken of in Exodus 31:12-18. They are to take their stand on the living Word—"It is written." This is the only foundation upon which they can stand securely. Those who have broken their covenant with God will in that day be without hope and without God in the world.

The worshipers of God will be especially distinguished by their regard for the fourth commandment—since this is the sign of His creative power, and the witness to His claim upon man's reverence and homage. The wicked will be distinguished by their efforts to tear down the Creator's memorial, to exalt the institution of Rome. In the issue of the contest, all Christendom will be divided into two great classes—those who keep the commandments of God and the faith of Jesus, and those who worship the beast and his image and receive his mark. . . .

Fearful tests and trials await the people of God. The spirit of war is stirring the nations from one end of the earth to the other. But in the midst of the time of trouble that is coming—a time of trouble such as has not been since there was a nation—God's chosen people will stand unmoved. Satan and his angels cannot destroy them; for angels that excel in strength will protect them.

OPEN THE
TOP WINDOWS!

Seek the Lord and his strength, seek his face continually. **1 Chron. 16:11.**

Now just now is our opportunity to open the windows of the soul heavenward and to close the windows earthward. Now is the time for every church member to say, I will close my heart to everything that would hinder my communion with Christ; I will open the windows of my soul heavenward that I may understand spiritual things.

Believers need to talk with God in regard to their individual need of the Holy Spirit. The Word of God must be their assurance. All heaven is inviting us to receive the bright beams of the Sun of Righteousness into our lives. If we will talk faith and hope and courage, our souls will be strengthened, and our hope and courage and faith will increase. Let us seek this great gift of the Sun of Righteousness, that it may shine forth in our lives to others. Let us seek the Lord that we may learn how to work His works in the world. This will make us successful missionaries, able to help others to a hopeful, courageous experience.

In our service for the Master, let not the little things be overlooked. Every human being has a life web to weave, and if the pattern is complete and perfected at last, every thread of the pattern must be carefully and faithfully worked. The grace of Christ will enable us to weave skillfully and well. Day by day we are to put forth personal diligent effort to improve. Every day we are to use our Christian intelligence in the work of strengthening the weak, and encouraging the desponding. A great test is coming to every soul. Shall we not then work and watch and pray and praise the Lord? This will give us a most precious experience. Very much has been lost to many believers because they have neglected to seek the Lord with earnestness and with a faith that will not be denied.

Words spoken and works performed in a simple, humble, encouraging way will inspire faith in other hearts. The Lord is soon to come, and the natural heart must be daily converted. We must learn to speak words in the meekness of Christ; our works and our spirit must testify that we are serving the Lord.

ASSURANCE OF VICTORY

Who gave himself for our sins, that he might deliver us from this present evil world, according to the will of God and our Father. **Gal. 1:4.**

By giving His life for the life of the world, Christ bridged the gulf that sin had made, joining this sin-cursed earth to the universe of heaven as a province. God chose this world to be the theater of His mighty works of grace. While the sentence of condemnation was suspended over it because of the rebellion of its inhabitants, while the clouds of wrath were accumulating because of the transgression of the law of God, a mysterious voice was heard in heaven, "Lo, I come . . . to do thy will, O God" (Ps. 40: 7, 8). Our substitute and surety came from heaven declaring that He had brought with him the vast and inestimable donation of eternal life. Pardon is offered to all who will return their allegiance to the law of God. But there are those who refuse to accept a "thus saith the Lord." They will not reverence and respect His law. They make rigorous human enactments in opposition to a "thus saith the Lord," and by precept and example lead men, women, and children into sin. They exalt human enactments above the divine law. But the condemnation and wrath of God are suspended over the disobedient. The clouds of God's justice are gathering. The material of destruction has been piled up for ages; and still apostasy, rebellion, and disloyalty against God is continually increasing. The remnant people of God, who keep His commandments, will understand the word spoken by Daniel, "Many shall be purified, and made white, and tried; but the wicked shall do wickedly: and none of the wicked shall understand; but the wise shall understand" (Dan. 12:10).

Satan has called this world his territory. Here his seat is, and he holds in allegiance to himself all who refuse to keep God's commandments, who reject a plain, "thus saith the Lord." They stand under the enemy's banner; for there are but two parties in the world. All rank either under the banner of the obedient or under the banner of the disobedient.

Jesus is now sending His message to a fallen world. He delights to take apparently hopeless material, those through whom Satan has worked, and make them the subjects of His grace. He rejoices to deliver them from the wrath which is to fall upon the disobedient.

HEAVENLY GUARANTEE

Ask, and it shall be given you; seek, and ye shall find; knock, and it shall be opened unto you. **Matt. 7:7.**

Oh, if every one would only know by personal experience how much of heaven's promised rest can be secured to the soul, even now, by sincere prayer. If one has not learned this lesson, every other lesson of life [had] better not be learned till he shall learn in the school of Christ how to master this lesson.

As Christians we want a new and living experience every day. We want to learn how to trust Jesus, to believe in Him and confide everything to Him. Jacob was raised from a man of feebleness and defects, through faith in God in prayer, to be a prince with God. He prevailed through faith. God is omnipotent. Man is finite. In converse with God, we may lay the most secret thing of the soul open to Him—for He knows it all—but not to man. . . .

Do not become careless and separate from the Source of your strength. Watch your thoughts, watch your words, and in all things you seek to do, seek to glorify God. The more closely you lie at the foot of the cross, the more clearly will you see the matchless charms of Jesus and the unparalleled love He has evidenced for fallen man. . . .

Let not the pressure of business separate you from God, for if you ever need counsel and clear forethought and sharp ideas, it is when you have much work on your hands. It is then that you need to take time to pray, to have increased faith and implicit trust in the counsel of the Physician in Chief. Ask Him to help you. Pray the oftener the more critical the work you have to do. . . .

Oh what a theme to contemplate that man, depraved and lost in his natural condition, may be renewed and saved by the gracious help that Christ gives him in the gospel. The love of Jesus in the soul will drive out the enemy who is seeking to take possession of man. Every trial patiently borne, every blessing thankfully received, every temptation faithfully resisted, will make you a strong man in Jesus Christ. All this grace may be gained in the prayer of faith. . . .

Lay hold upon strength from above. Even Jesus, when preparing for some great trial, would resort to the solitude of the mountains and spend the night in prayer to his Father.

LIVING THE NEW LIFE

Therefore all things whatsoever ye would that men should do to you, do ye even so to them: for this is the law and the prophets. **Matt. 7:12.**

Christ came to teach us, not only what we ought to know and believe, but also what we ought to do in our relations with God and with our fellow men. The golden rule of equity demands that we do unto others as we would they should do unto us. We are to keep their eternal interests in view, saying to ourselves, "They are the purchase of the Saviour's blood, bought with a price."

In all our dealing with our fellow men, whether they be believers or unbelievers, we are to treat them as Christ would treat them were He in our place. If it is for our present and eternal good to obey the law of God, it will be for their present and eternal good also to do this. Our highest aim is to be to them medical missionary workers after Christ's order. . . .

All who enter through the pearly gates into the city of God must have set forth Christ in all their dealings. It is this that constitutes them the messengers of Christ, His witnesses. They are to bear a plain, decided testimony against all evil practices, pointing them to the Lamb of God, which taketh away the sin of the world. He gives to all who receive Him, power to become the sons of God.

Regeneration is the only path by which we can reach the holy city. It is narrow and the gate by which we enter is strait, but along it we are to lead men and women and children, teaching them that in order to be saved, they must have a new heart and a new spirit. The old hereditary traits of character are to be overcome. The natural desires of the soul must be changed. All deception, all falsifying, all evil-speaking must be put away. The new life, which makes men and women Christlike, is to be lived. We are, as it were, to swim against the current of evil.

The way to heaven is narrow, hedged in by the divine law of Jehovah. Those who follow this way must constantly deny self. They must obey the teachings of Christ. . . . Let us not trust in man, but in Jesus Christ, who died that He might win us to righteousness.

September 10

ESSENTIALS
OF SALVATION

For ye were sometimes darkness, but now are ye light in the Lord: walk as children of light. **Eph. 5:8.**

He who commanded the light to shine out of darkness sheds light into the mind of every one who will properly behold Him, loving Him supremely, showing unswerving faith and trust in Him. His light shines into the chambers of the mind and into the soul temple. The heart is filled with the light of the knowledge of the glory that shines in the face of Jesus Christ. And with this light comes spiritual discernment. . . .

Yielding willingly to the evidence of truth, and walking in the light that shines in our pathway, we receive still greater light. Through the power of the manifestation of divine glory, we constantly advance in spiritual understanding.

Christ's knowledge of truth was direct, positive, without a shadow. The closer the acquaintance a man has with Jesus Christ, the more careful he will be to treat his fellow men respectfully, courteously, righteously. He has learned of Christ, and he follows His example in word and action. By faith he is united with Christ. "We are labourers together with God" (1 Cor. 3:9). . . .

Christ's prayer was for unity among His followers. This unity is the evidence that is to convince the world that God sent His Son to save sinners. We serve Christ by revealing true, pure, holy love for one another. Those who are chosen to connect with the Lord's institutions are to be devoted, self-denying, self-sacrificing men, living not to please themselves, but to please the Master. These are the men who will do honor to the Lord's institutions.

A knowledge of God and of Christ is positively essential to salvation. We lose much every day that we do not learn more of the meekness and lowliness of Christ. Those who learn of Christ obtain the very highest class of education. Through faith and dependence on the saving grace of Christ, they increase in knowledge and wisdom. They love and praise the Saviour. . . .

Those who are saved must in this life make it their daily business to receive grace from God, not to hoard in selfishness, but to impart for the blessing of those connected with them, to aid them in obtaining an education in spiritual things.

BEING ALIVE UNTO GOD

Whosoever therefore shall confess me before men, him will I confess also before my Father which is in heaven. But whosoever shall deny me before men, him will I also deny before my Father which is in heaven. **Matt. 10:32, 33.**

How is it? Are we confessing Christ in our daily life? Do we confess

Him in our dress, adorning ourselves with plain and modest apparel? Is our adorning that of the meek and quiet spirit which is of so great price in the sight of God? Are we seeking to advance the cause of the Master? Is the line of demarcation between you and the world distinct, or are you seeking to follow the fashions of this degenerate age? Is there no difference between you and the worldling? Does the same spirit work in you that works in the children of disobedience?

If we are Christians, we shall follow Christ, even though the path in which we are to walk cuts right across our natural inclinations. There is no use in telling you that you must not wear this or that, for if the love of these vain things is in your heart, your laying off your adornments will only be like cutting the foliage off a tree. The inclinations of the natural heart would again assert themselves. You must have a conscience of your own.

O, did we remember that Christ became poor, that we through His poverty might become rich, would we not seek to honor His name, and advance His cause? We are to abide in Him as the branch abides in the vine. Jesus says, "I am the vine, ye are the branches: He that abideth in me, and I in him, the same bringeth forth much fruit: for without me ye can do nothing. . . . Herein is my Father glorified, that ye bear much fruit; so shall ye be my disciples" (John 15:5-8).

If we fulfilled this command of our Lord, there would be a different state of affairs in our churches, and we should know what it is to have the deep movings of the Spirit of God. What we want is to have the ax laid at the root of the tree. We want to be dead to the world, dead to self, and alive unto God. Our life must be hid with Christ in God, that when He shall appear, we also may appear with Him in glory. We need to come close to Christ, that men may know that we have been with Christ and learned of Him. . . . Keep your eye fixed upon Christ. With humility of mind seek for a nearness to God. In words, in conduct, in life, confess Christ.

September 12   This Day With God

THE COMPASSIONATE CHRISTIAN

The prince of this world cometh, and hath nothing in me. **John 14:30.**

In all His habits of life, the Saviour gave an example of what God designs His church on earth to be. Tell this to the people. Christ desires to present His church before the Father without spot or blemish.

From His earliest years the Saviour's life was one of poverty. His childhood days were spent in toil. Working at the carpenter's bench, bearing the burdens that came to Him as a member of the family, He often became weary. He lived in a corrupt age. Yet He was uncorrupted by the evil that surrounded Him, uninfluenced by the characters of those who were artificial and wicked. In the open fields and amid the scenes of nature He found rest from toil and food for spiritual life. Looking beneath the surface, He gathered knowledge from the mysteries of nature that filled Him with peace and joy.

During the years of His public ministry, the Saviour was continually watched by crafty and hypocritical men. Spies were continually upon His track to catch something from His lips which they could use to create prejudice against Him. Again and again they tried to make Him appear guilty of wrong. There were occasions when they laid traps for Him by presenting to Him questions, the answers to which they hoped to use to cause His condemnation by the people. But at every attempt they were compelled to retire from the field confounded; their actions were revealed in their true light by the answers of Christ. The Saviour's discourses presented a power of truth to the multitudes who listened. Even the men who were sent to spy upon His actions were forced to return with the report to those who sent them, "Never man spake like this man" (John 7:46). . . .

Let your conversation be with grace, for Christ is listening to the words you speak. Let compassion for one another be blended with all you say, then you will reveal the character of Christ. The manners of Christ were gentle and unassuming. As His followers we are to partake of His nature. We need to be daily learners of the great Teacher, that the atmosphere surrounding the soul may be filled with spiritual life.

UNRESERVED SURRENDER

I am crucified with Christ: nevertheless I live; yet not I, but Christ liveth in me: and the life which I now live in the flesh I live by the faith of the Son of God, who loved me, and gave himself for me. **Gal. 2:20.**

God will accept nothing less than unreserved surrender. Half-hearted, sinful Christians can never enter heaven. There they would find no happiness; for they know nothing of the high, holy principles that govern the members of the royal family.

The true Christian keeps the windows of the soul open heavenward. He lives in fellowship with Christ. His will is conformed to the will of Christ. His highest desire is to become more and more Christlike. . . .

Earnestly and untiringly we are to strive to reach God's ideal for us. Not as a penance are we to do this, but as the only means of gaining true happiness. The only way to gain peace and joy is to have a living connection with Him who gave His life for us, who died that we might live, and who lives to unite His power with the efforts of those who are striving to overcome.

Holiness is constant agreement with God. Shall we not strive to be that which Christ so greatly desires us to be—Christians in deed and in truth—that the world may see in our lives a revelation of the saving power of truth? This world is our preparatory school. While here we shall meet with trials and difficulties. Continually the enemy of God will seek to draw us away from our allegiance. But while we cleave to Him who gave Himself for us, we are safe.

The whole world was gathered into the embrace of Christ. He died on the cross to destroy him who had the power of death, and to take away the sin of every believing soul. He calls upon us to offer ourselves on the altar of service, a living, consuming sacrifice. We are to make an unreserved consecration to God of all that we have and are.

In this lower school of earth we are to learn the lessons that will prepare us to enter the higher school, where our education will continue under the personal instruction of Christ. Then He will open to us the meaning of His Word. Shall we not, in the few days of probation remaining to us, act like men and women who are seeking for life in the kingdom of God, even an eternity of bliss?

WITHOUT SPOT

Even as Christ also loved the church, and gave himself for it; . . . that he might present it to himself a glorious church, not having spot, or wrinkle, or any such thing; but that it should be holy and without blemish. **Eph. 5:25-27.**

We bear the name of Christian. Let us be true to this name. To be a Christian means to be Christlike. It means to follow Christ in self-denial, bearing aloft His banner of love, honoring Him by unselfish words and deeds. In the life of the true Christian there is nothing of self—self is dead. There was no selfishness in the life that Christ lived while on this earth. Bearing our nature, He lived a life wholly devoted to the good of others. . . .

In word and deed Christ's followers are to be pure and true. In this world—a world of iniquity and corruption—Christians are to reveal the attributes of Christ. All they do and say is to be free from selfishness. Christ desires to present them to the Father "without spot, or wrinkle, or any such thing," purified through his grace, bearing His likeness.

In His great love, Christ surrendered Himself for us. He gave Himself for us to meet the necessities of the striving, struggling soul. We are to surrender ourselves to Him. When this surrender is entire, Christ can finish the work He began for us by the surrender of Himself. Then He can bring to us complete restoration.

Christ gave himself for the redemption of the race, that all who believe in Him may have everlasting life. Those who appreciate this great sacrifice receive from the Saviour that most precious of all gifts—a clean heart. They gain an experience that is more valuable than gold or silver or precious stones. They sit together in heavenly places in Christ, enjoying in communion with Him the joy and peace that he alone can give. They love Him with heart and mind and soul and strength, realizing that they are His blood-bought heritage. Their spiritual eyesight is not dimmed by worldly policy or worldly aims. They are one with Christ as He is one with the Father.

Think you not that Christ values those who live wholly for Him? Think you not that he visits those who, like the beloved John, are for His sake in hard and trying places? He finds His faithful ones, and holds communion with them, encouraging and strengthening them.

TRUTH WILL TRIUMPH

Not walking in craftiness, nor handling the word of God deceitfully; but by manifestation of the truth commending ourselves to every man's conscience in the sight of God. **2 Cor. 4:2.**

There is to be no undermining of the fundamental truths that the Lord has submitted by many miraculous evidences. A voice is to be heard in clear affirmation of the truth, in contradiction to the skepticism and fallacies that have been coming in from the enemy of truth. Reformations will take place, and the working out of the principles of divine truth will reveal growth in grace, for the divine agencies are efficient to enlighten and sanctify the human understanding.

The truth as it is in Jesus, as it was proclaimed by Him when He was enshrouded by the billowy cloud, is verity and truth in this our day, and will just as surely renovate the mind of the receiver as it has renovated minds in the past. Christ has declared, "If they hear not Moses and the prophets, neither will they be persuaded, though one rose from the dead" (Luke 16:31).

As a people, we must prepare the way of the Lord, under the overruling guidance of the Holy Spirit, for the spread of the gospel in its purity. The stream of living water is to deepen and widen in its course. In all fields, nigh and afar off, men will be called from the plow and from the more common commercial business vocations that largely occupy the mind, and will become educated in connection with men who have had experience—men who understand the truth. Through most wonderful workings of God, mountains of difficulty will be removed and cast into the sea. . . .

Those who preach the truth will strive to demonstrate the truth by a well-ordered life and godly conversation. And as they do this, they will become powerful in advocating the truth and in giving it the sure application that God has given it. . . .

The call is to go forth, "Son, go labor today in My vineyard." As this call is obeyed, the message that means so much to the dwellers on the earth, will be heard and understood. Men will know what is truth. Onward, and still onward, will the work advance. And marked events of Providence will be seen and recognized, in judgments and in blessings. The truth will bear away the victory.

MATCHLESS LOVE

And the glory which thou gavest me I have given them; that they may be one, even as we are one: I in them, and thou in me, that they may be made perfect in one; and that the world may know that thou has sent me, and hast loved them, as thou hast loved me. **John 17:22, 23.**

O what love, what matchless love! Fallen human beings may become so closely united with Christ that they are glorified with Him. On this earth they have followed in His footsteps, laboring as He labored for the souls for whom He died, and when He comes to claim His own, they enter in to His joy, sitting with Him at His table in His kingdom. "Where I am," He says, "there shall also my servant be" (John 12:26). . . .

What a wonderful thought it is that we, poor, fallen sinners, can become one with Christ, partakers of His divine nature, through His grace refined, purified, glorified. We may overcome, and sit down with Christ. We are to be conformed to His image. He loves, and He will help us. We are to be passive in his hands.

We have his promise. We hold the title deeds to real estate in the kingdom of glory. Never were title deeds drawn up more strictly according to law, or signed more legibly, than those that give God's people a right to the heavenly mansions. "Let not your heart be troubled," Christ says: "Ye believe in God, believe also in me. In my Father's house are many mansions: if it were not so, I would have told you. I go to prepare a place for you. And if I go and prepare a place for you, I will come again, and receive you unto myself; that where I am, there ye may be also" (chap. 14:1-3). . . .

All who will may come under the covenant promise. Precious is the price paid for our redemption—the blood of the only begotten Son of God. Christ was tried by the sharp proving of affliction. His human nature was tried to the uttermost. He bore the death penalty of man's transgression. He became the sinner's substitute and surety. He is able to show the fruit of His sufferings and death, in His resurrection from the dead. From the rent sepulcher of Joseph rings forth the proclamation, "I am the resurrection and the life. Those who believe in Me, and do the works of righteousness that I do, are justified, sanctified, made white and tried. They have obtained godliness and eternal life."

AN EVER PRESENT HELP

The Lord is good, a strong hold in the day of trouble; and he knoweth them that trust in him. **Nahum 1:7.**

We have rich promises in the Word of God, if we only believe and trust in Him. We are in danger of trusting to our own poor human efforts, and not putting our trust in God. Everyone who has any part to act in this great preparation of the work of God for these last days should come close to God. When God sends out His workers to do a special errand for Him, He has pledged Himself to be one with them, if they will be one with God. But if they draw apart from God, and try to do this work in their own strength, they will find difficulties and discouragements at every step. Here we have the promise that in working for the Lord He is by our right hand to help us and work with us.

It would be the greatest folly in the world for any of us to take any of the credit to ourselves for any success we may have. The more humbly we walk with God, the more will He manifest Himself to us to help us. The Lord never designed to send out His servants to do a work for Him with all the opposition of Satan and evil angels against them unless He gives them divine help. The reason that we do not have greater success in the work is because we depend on our own efforts rather than upon the help God will give us. It is our privilege to feel our weakness, our unworthiness, and then claim the help that God has provided for us. We can take the Word in our distress, and while we feel the burden of souls upon us, and say, "Here, Lord, Thou hast promised, and I believe Thy Word."

We must learn to go to our heavenly Father just as a child goes to its earthly parents. He says, "Or what man is there of you, whom if his son ask bread, will he give him a stone? Or if he ask a fish, will he give him a serpent? If ye then, being evil, know how to give good gifts unto your children, how much more shall your Father which is in heaven give good things to them that ask him?'' (Matt. 7:9-11). . . .

While every one of God's workmen should cultivate his powers to the best of his ability, yet he should not trust in these powers. . . . Make of yourselves everything that it is possible for you to make and then trust the rest to God.

THE DIVINE SUBSTITUTE

For he hath made him to be sin for us, who knew no sin; that we might be made the righteousness of God in him. 2 Cor. 5:21.

''He saved others; himself he cannot save'' (Mark 15:31). It is because Christ would not save Himself that the sinner has any hope of pardon or favor with God. If, in His undertaking to save the sinner, Christ had failed or become discouraged, the last hope of every son and daughter of Adam would have been at an end. The entire life of Christ was one of self-denial and self-sacrifice; and the reason that there are so few stalwart Christians is because of their self-indulgence and self-pleasing in the place of self-denial and self-sacrifice.

Oh, what soul hunger and longing had Christ to save that which was lost! The body crucified upon the cross did not detract from His divinity, His power of God to save through the human sacrifice, all who would accept His righteousness. In dying upon the cross, He transferred the guilt from the person of the transgressor to that of the divine Substitute through faith in Him as his personal Redeemer. The sins of a guilty world, which in figure are represented as ''red as crimson,'' were imputed to the divine Surety. . . .

Divinity was doing its work while humanity was suffering from the hatred and revenge of a God-hating people, because Christ had acknowledged Himself the Son of God. He alone could respond to the poor suffering thief. He alone was free to undertake the suretyship of the guilty criminal. The dying Redeemer saw him to be far less guilty than the ones who had condemned Him to death, far less guilty than the priests, the scribes, and rulers who had taken an active part in demanding the death of the Son of God.

What a faith had that dying thief upon the cross! He accepted Christ when apparently it was an utter impossibility that He should be the Son of God, the Redeemer of the world. In the prayer of the poor thief, there was a note different from that which was sounding on every side; it was a note of faith, and it reached to Christ. The faith of the dying man in Him was as sweetest music in the ears of Christ. The glad note of redemption and salvation was heard amid His dying agonies. God was glorified in and through His Son.

CULTIVATE TENDERNESS IN THE HOME

And above all things have fervent charity among yourselves: for charity shall cover the multitude of sins. **1 Peter 4:8.**

The young man who came to Jesus asked what he should do that he might inherit eternal life. Jesus told him to keep the commandments, and enumerated several of the precepts of the law. The young man said, "All these things have I kept from my youth up: what lack I yet?" (Matt. 19:20). The first four commandments enjoin upon man the duty of loving God supremely and the last six present the requirement of loving our neighbors as ourselves. How many are truly, sincerely, and wholeheartedly doing this?

The Lord is coming in a little while, and are we performing the duties that result from righteousness? Love is the basis of godliness. No man has love to God, no matter what his profession may be, unless he has unselfish love for his brother. As we love God because He first loved us, we shall love all for whom Christ died. We shall not feel like letting the soul who is in the greatest peril, and in the greatest need, go unwarned, unlabored for, and uncared for. We shall not feel like holding the erring off, and being critical and exacting, or letting them alone to plunge into further unhappiness and discouragement, and to fall on Satan's battleground, for God will deal with us as He deals with our brethren or the younger members of the Lord's family.

Cultivate tenderness of heart; surround yourselves in your home life with the atmosphere of love. But the spirit that has largely pervaded the church is an offense to God. Everyone who has been free to condemn, to dishearten, and to discourage, who has failed to give tender kindness, sympathy, and compassion to the tempted and the tried, will in his own experience be brought over the ground which others have passed over, and suffered with their hardheartedness, and will feel what others have suffered because of his want of sympathy, until he shall abhor his hardness of heart and open the door for Jesus to come in.

The converting power of God must come to every soul who has any connection with the work and cause of God that each one may be filled with the love and compassion of Christ or many will never see the kingdom of heaven.

241

TAKE HOLD
OF DIVINE STRENGTH

Then thou spakest in vision to thy holy one, and saidst, I have laid help upon one that is mighty. **Ps. 89:19.**

The Lord loves you. The Lord is of tender compassion. His promise is, "Draw nigh to God, and he will draw nigh to you" (James 4:8). When the enemy comes in like a flood, the Spirit of the Lord shall lift up for you a standard against him. Bear in mind that Jesus Christ is your hope. In the sad, discouraging things that shall come to you at any time, Christ says to you, "Let him take hold of my strength, that he may make peace with me; and he shall make peace with me" (Isa. 27:5).

Your work is to take hold of the strength that is as firm as is the eternal throne. Believe in God. Trust in Him. Be cheerful under all circumstances. Although you may have trials, know that Christ suffered these afflicting things in behalf of His heritage. Nothing is as dear to the Lord as His church. The Lord looks at the heart. He knows who are His. The Lord will test and prove every soul that lives. "Many shall be purified, and made white, and tried; but the wicked shall do wickedly: and none of the wicked shall understand; but the wise shall understand" (Dan. 12:10). . . .

Let those who love God and are doers of His word sing praise and thanksgiving rather than speak words of accusing and faultfinding and murmuring. The Lord will bless those who make for peace. . . .

Trust in the Lord. Let not the feelings, the speeches, or the attitude of any human agent depress you. Be careful that in words or act you do not give others any opportunity to obtain the advantage in hurting you. Keep looking unto Jesus. He is your strength. By beholding Jesus you will become changed into His likeness. He will be the health of your countenance and your God. . . .

The church needs you, and you need to soften and subdue your own feelings for Christ's sake. He wants you to have His Holy Spirit to work you. Then you may impart life and comfort to the church. Let your words be well chosen that you may be a real blessing to the church. Do not afflict your souls over the inconsistencies of others. Take yourselves in hand, and be consistent in all things.

IN THE WORLD,
BUT NOT OF IT

Ye adulterers and adulteresses, know ye not that the friendship of the world is enmity with God? whosoever therefore will be a friend of the world is the enemy of God. **James 4:4.**

The great day of the Lord is near at hand. When Christ appears in the clouds of heaven, those who have not sought Him with all the heart, those who have allowed themselves to be deceived, will surely perish. Our only safety is to be found through repentance and conversion, and the blotting out of sins. Those who will now seek the Lord earnestly, humbling their hearts before Him, and forsaking their sins, will, through the sanctification of the truth, be fitted to unite with the members of the royal family, and will see the King in His beauty. . . .

Whatever his educational attainments, only he who realizes his accountability to God, and who is led by the Holy Spirit, can be an effectual teacher, or be successful in winning to God those who are brought under his influence. Shall those who do not need the divine counsel be acknowledged as leaders in the Lord's institutions?—God forbid. How can we regard as safe guides those who manifest a spirit of unbelief, and who, in words and character, fail of revealing true godliness?

"Verily I say unto you, Except ye be converted, and become as little children [in learning the way of the Lord], ye shall not enter the kingdom of heaven" (Matt. 18:3).

Self needs to be brought into submission to the yoke of Christ. The great Teacher invites all to learn of Him. . . . "The Son of man is come to save that which was lost" (verse 11). But those who desire to be saved must be willing to be saved in the Lord's appointed way, and not in a way of their own choosing. The free grace of God is man's only hope. God is in earnest with every one of us. . . .

We are called to be the Lord's special people in a much higher sense than many have realized. The world lies in wickedness, and God's people are to come out of the world, and be separate. They are to be free from worldly customs and worldly habits. They are not to accord with worldly sentiments, but are to stand out distinct, as the Lord's peculiar people, earnest in all their service. They are to have no fellowship with the works of darkness.

DIVINE GRACE,
OUR GREATEST NEED

Though I preach the gospel, I have nothing to glory of. **1 Cor. 9:16.**

Genuine conversion brings us daily into communion with God. There will be temptations to meet, and a strong undercurrent drawing us from God to our former state of indifference and sinful forgetfulness of God. No human heart can remain strong without divine grace. No man can remain converted unless he takes care of himself and the Master has a care for him. Unless the heart holds fast to God, and God holds fast to him, he will become self-confident and exalted and will surely stumble and fall. The power of God through faith was Paul's dependence. "I live; yet not I," he exclaims in his humility, "but Christ liveth in me" (Gal. 2:20). "I therefore so run, not as uncertainly; so fight I, not as one that beateth the air: but I keep under my body, and bring it into subjection: lest that by any means, when I have preached to others, I myself should be a castaway" (1 Cor. 9:26, 27).

Paul was in such constant dread, lest his evil propensities should get the better of him, that he was constantly battling, with firm resistance, unruly appetites and passions. If the great apostle felt like trembling in view of his weakness, who has a right to feel self-confident and boastful? The moment we begin to feel self-sufficient and confident then we are in danger of a disgraceful failure.

Our only sure defense against besetting sins is prayer, daily and hourly prayer. Not one day zealous and the next careless, but through watchfulness and earnestness becoming vitalized by intercourse with God. Prayer is necessary, and we should not wait for feeling, but pray, earnestly pray, whether we feel like it or not. Heaven is open to our prayers. Prayer is the channel that conducts our gratitude and yearnings of soul for the divine blessing to the throne of God, to be returned to us in refreshing showers of divine grace. With very many, this channel is allowed to freeze up, and then the connection with heaven is interrupted. . . . Oh, that we would spend more time upon our knees and less time in planning for ourselves and in thinking we may do some great thing.

THE BANQUET OF GOD'S WORD

I am the living bread which came down from heaven: . . . and the bread that I will give is my flesh, which I will give for the life of the world. **John 6:51.**

The only safety for any of us is to plant our feet upon the Word of God and study the Scriptures, making God's Word our constant meditation. Tell the people to take no man's word regarding the testimonies, but to read them and study them for themselves, and then they will know that they are in harmony with the truth. The Word of God is the truth. Of a good man the psalmist declares, "His delight is in the law of the Lord; and in his law doth he meditate day and night" (Ps. 1:2). He who puts the mind and heart into this work gains a solid, valuable experience. The Holy Spirit is in the Word of God. Here is the living, undying element so distinctly represented in the sixth chapter of John. . . .

Let us believe the Word. He who thus eats the bread of heaven is nourished every day and will know what these words mean, "Needeth not that any man teach you." We have lessons pure from the lips of Him who owns us, who has bought us with the price of His own blood. The precious Word of God is a solid foundation upon which to build. When men come to you with their suppositions, tell them that the Great Teacher has left you His Word, which is of incalculable value, that he has sent a Comforter in His own name, even the Holy Ghost. "He shall teach you all things, and bring all things to your remembrance, whatsoever I have said unto you" (John 14:26). . . .

Here is presented before us a rich banquet, of which all who believe in Christ as a personal Saviour may eat. He is the Tree of life to all who continue to feed on Him. . . .

All who study these precious utterances may have strong consolation. If they will feed upon the banquet of God's Word, they will gain an experience of the highest value. They will see that in comparison with the word of God, the word of man is as chaff to the wheat.

I am instructed by the Word of God that His promises are for me and for every child of God. The banquet is spread before us; we are invited to eat the Word of God, which will strengthen spiritual muscle and sinew.

THE FINAL BATTLE

Behold, I come as a thief. Blessed is he that watcheth, and keepeth his garments, lest he walk naked, and they see his shame. **Rev. 16:15.**

A terrible contest is before us. We are nearing the battle of the great day of God Almighty. That which has been held in control is to be let loose. The angel of mercy is folding its wings, preparing to step down from the golden throne and leave the world to the control of Satan, the king it has chosen, a murderer and a destroyer from the beginning.

The principalities and powers of earth are in bitter revolt against the God of heaven. They are filled with hatred against all who serve Him, and soon, very soon, is to be fought the last great battle between good and evil. The earth is to be the battlefield—the scene of the final contest and the final victory. Here, where for so long Satan has led men against God, rebellion is to be forever suppressed.

Christ came to this earth in human form that He might stand as the Captain of our salvation, so that we should not be overcome by Satan's power. And when the enemy has seemed to be gaining a signal victory over righteousness, God has been working in mercy and power to counteract his designs.

Determined to efface the image of God in man, Satan works with an intensity of effort to hide God from view. Not openly does he work, but secretly, mingling the human and the divine, the spurious and the genuine, so seeking to bring confusion and distress. But in proportionate power divine mercy is revealed to counteract this wicked working, and bring to light the enemy's hidden purposes.

God's people are to hear a bold, decided testimony for the truth, unfolding the purposes of God by the witness of pen and voice. In place after place they are to proclaim the message of God's Word, arousing men and women to comprehend the truth. . . .

There is a reality in sound doctrine. It is not as a vapor, which passes away. Light is to shine forth from the Word of God. God calls upon His people to draw near to Him. Let no one interpose between Him and His people. Christ is knocking at the door of the heart, seeking for entrance. Will you let Him in?

THINGS WROUGHT BY PRAYER

Let us draw near with a true heart in full assurance of faith. **Heb. 10:22.**

There can be no true prayer without true faith. "Without faith it is impossible to please him" (Heb. 11:6). Prayer and faith are the arms by which the soul hangs upon the neck of infinite love, and grasps the hand of infinite power. God does not recognize dumb children, as far as experience in His truth is concerned. Faith is an active, working power. The newborn faith in Christ is revealed by prayer and praise. Prayer is a relief and a comfort to the troubled soul. The sincere, humble suppliant at the throne of grace may know that he is communing with God, through the divinely appointed means, and that it is his privilege to understand what God is to the believing soul. We must have a realization of our needs. We must hunger and thirst after life in Christ and through Christ. Then we shall come to Him in humility and sincerity, and He will give us the faith that works by love and purifies the soul. . . .

Christ gave Himself willingly and cheerfully to the carrying out of the will of God. "He . . . became obedient unto death, even the death of the cross" (Phil. 2:8). In view of all that He has done, should we feel it a hardship to deny ourselves? Shall we draw back from being partakers of Christ's sufferings? His death ought to stir every fiber of our beings, making us willing to consecrate to His work all that we have and are.

As we think of what He has done for us, our hearts should be filled with gratitude and love, and we should renounce all selfishness and sin. What duty could the heart refuse to perform, under the constraining influence of the love of God and Christ? "I am crucified with Christ," the apostle Paul declared: "nevertheless I live; yet not I, but Christ liveth in me: and the life which I now live in the flesh I live by the faith of the Son of God, who loved me, and gave himself for me" (Gal. 2:20).

Let us relate ourselves to God in self-denying, self-sacrificing obedience. Faith in Christ always leads to willing, cheerful obedience. He died to redeem us from all iniquity, and to purify unto Himself a peculiar people, zealous of good works. There is to be perfect conformity, in thought, word, and deed, to the will of God. Heaven is only for those who have purified their souls through obedience to the truth.

PRESENT ADVANTAGES AND FUTURE BENEFITS

Looking unto Jesus the author and finisher of our faith; who for the joy that was set before him endured the cross, despising the shame, and is set down at the right hand of the throne of God. **Heb. 12:2.**

We should ever cherish feelings of gratitude to those who have shown us favors in times of need. But these feelings that are so readily called into exercise by the kindness and disinterestedness of our friends should respond to the love and compassion of our benevolent heavenly Friend. . . . The friendship expressed by nearest and dearest relatives and friends is so far surpassed by the revelation of Jesus Christ that the former is dumb and expressionless when compared with the latter. It is natural that the heart should entertain sentiments of the warmest affection toward those who have done or suffered something for us.

Let me lead you to the scene of the crucifixion and show you the Son of God dying in your stead. Will not the spectacle of the cross of Christ awaken every feeling of gratitude? Will it not sweep away the coldness and indifference which steels the senses to the great sacrifice made in our behalf? . . .

Satan, the adversary of souls, is constantly at work with his devices and enchantments, stealing away the senses and deadening the feelings to our highest interest. To all the little matters of life the affections are given free play, but in eternal interest the affections are trammeled, bound as by magical cords. . . .

There are so many who endure privation and pursue at considerable sacrifice a course which promises advantages in the future. They forego present comfort for a future inducement as an equivalent, but here Jesus presents eternal life as the reward of obedience, and if paltry things of earthly gain will be sacrificed for some future good, how much more should ease, pleasure, and present worldly advantages be sacrificed for the incomparable riches and glory of the future immortal life. Let not the sorcery of earthly enchantments steal the affections from God and harden the heart to eternal interest. Look at the things that are unseen. Enshrine Jesus in the heart. Love him with your whole soul.

THE HOLY SPIRIT —
THE GIFT OF GIFTS

And being found in fashion as a man, he humbled himself, and
became obedient unto death, even the death of the cross. **Phil. 2:8.**

In proportion to Christ's humiliation and suffering is His exaltation.
He could have become the Saviour, the Redeemer, only by first being the
Sacrifice. What a mystery there is in the godliness of Christ. Having
magnified the law and made it honorable by accepting its conditions in
saving a world from ruin, Christ hastened to heaven to perfect His work,
and to accomplish His mission by sending the Holy Spirit to His disciples.
Thus He would assure His believing ones that he had not forgotten them,
though now in the presence of God, where there is fullness of joy
forevermore.

The Holy Spirit was to descend on those in this world who loved
Christ. By this they would be qualified, in and through the glorification of
their Head, to receive every endowment necessary for the fulfilling of their
mission. The Life-giver held in His hands, not only the keys of death, but
a whole heaven of rich blessings. All power in heaven and earth was given
to Him, and having taken His place in the heavenly courts, He could
dispense these blessings to all who receive Him.

Christ has said to His disciples, "It is expedient for you that I go away:
for if I go not away, the Comforter will not come unto you; but if I depart,
I will send him unto you" (John 16:7). This was the gift of gifts. The Holy
Spirit was sent as the most priceless treasure man could receive. The
church was baptized with the spirit's power. The disciples were fitted to go
forth and proclaim Christ, first in Jerusalem, where the shameful work of
dishonoring the rightful King had been done, and then to the uttermost
parts of the earth. . . .

How full and free are the blessings to be bestowed on all who come to
God in the name of His Son. If they will observe the conditions laid down
in His Word, he will open to them the windows of heaven, and pour them
down a blessing that there will not be room enough to receive it. . . . If
God's people will sanctify themselves by obedience to his precepts, the
Lord will work in their midst. He will renew humble, contrite souls,
making their characters pure and holy.

THE LORD'S PHILOSOPHY

To the law and to the testimony: if they speak not according to this word, it is because there is no light in them. **Isa. 8:20.**

The Lord's philosophy, plainly outlined in His Word, is to be our rule of life. The entire being is to be under the control of the One who knows the end from the beginning. The Bible, and the Bible only is to be our guide. We must follow and obey the life-giving principles of heaven, not only for our inclinations. The wisdom and the power of God, working upon the receptive heart, brings mind and character into harmony with the laws and rules of heaven. Individually we must have the guidance of the Holy Spirit, in order to communicate to the world the great facts of truth and righteousness. . . .

We are bidden to sound an alarm to the people. The watchmen must not fail now. They must watch unto prayer, that they may have a clear perception of their obligation to Him who, though the only begotten Son of God, came to our world to lead men and women away from the guidance of Satan.

We are to instruct and guide souls to look to Christ's example, to realize their obligation to Him, whose they are by creation and by redemption. He is the owner of every man and woman and child who comes into the world. This He became by paying the redemption price. If fallen human beings will consent to become sons and daughters of God in willing obedience, they will become one with Christ. The Saviour has bought them by giving His life to pay the penalty of sin. . . . Those who are truly converted will reveal the saving grace of Christ by laboring for these souls blinded by Satan. In their own lives God's workers are to show forth the power of truth and righteousness. The world is soon to meet the great lawgiver over His broken law. Those only can hope for pardon who turn from transgression to obedience.

We are to raise the banner on which is inscribed, "The commandments of God and the faith of Jesus." This is the great issue. Let it not be put out of sight. We must strive to arouse church members and those who make no profession, to see and obey the claims of the law of heaven. We are to magnify this law and make it honorable. We are to arouse those who are sunk in spiritual slumber.

WHEN TRUTH
CONTROLS THE LIFE

He that followeth me shall not walk in darkness, but shall have the light of life. **John 8:12.**

The Lord Jesus took upon Him the form of sinful man, clothing His divinity with humanity. But He was holy, even as God is holy. If He had not been without spot or stain of sin, He could not have been the Saviour of mankind. He was a Sinbearer, needing no atonement. One with God in purity and holiness of character, he could make a propitiation for the sins of the whole world.

Christ is the light of the world. Through Him light is shining amid the moral darkness. If He were not light, the darkness would not be apparent, because light reveals darkness. The clearer the light, the more manifest the contrast between light and darkness. Let the light be removed, and there is nought but darkness.

Christ has declared our position. "He that followeth me shall not walk in darkness, but shall have the light of life" (John 8:12). He is Himself the bright and morning Star. He is the Sun of Righteousness, the brightness of His Father's glory. He is the "true Light, which lighteth every man that cometh into the world" (chap. 1:9). A Physician, a Healer, He came to restore the moral image of God that was lost by transgression.

When Christ abides in the soul by faith, He makes the one who loves Him all light in the Lord. It is true that many who say they believe the truth have only a nominal faith. They are not doers of the Word. They profess to believe, but their profession will not convert them. . . .

When Christ dwells in the heart, His presence is apparent. Good and pleasant words and actions reveal the Spirit of Christ. Sweetness of temper is manifested. There is no angry passion, no obstinacy, no evil-surmising. There is no hatred in the heart, because . . . ideas and methods . . . are not accepted and appreciated by others. . . .

When the truth controls the life, there is purity and freedom from sin. The glory, the fullness, the completeness of the gospel plan is fulfilled in the life. The light of truth irradiates the soul temple. The understanding takes hold of Christ.

WALK IN
THE FOOTSTEPS OF JESUS

And unto one he gave five talents, to another two, and to another one; to every man according to his several ability. **Matt. 25:15.**

Study the instruction found in Matthew 25:14-46. Compare this instruction with your life record. Let every man put away his boasting. . . . Let us walk in the footsteps of Christ in all the humility of true faith. Let us put away all self-trust, committing ourselves, day by day and hour by hour, to the Saviour, constantly receiving and imparting His grace. I beg those who profess to believe in Christ to walk humbly before God. Pride and self-exaltation are an offense to Him. "If any man will come after me," Christ declares, "let him deny himself, and take up his cross, and follow me" (Matt. 16:24). Those only who obey this word will He recognize as His believing ones. "As many as received him, to them gave he power to become the sons of God, even to them that believe on his name: which were born, not of blood, nor of the will of the flesh, nor of the will of man, but of God" (John 1:12, 13).

"And the Word was made flesh, and dwelt among us" (verse 14). O wonderful condescension! The Prince of heaven, the Commander of the heavenly hosts, stepped down from His high position, laid aside His royal robe and kingly crown, and clothed His divinity with humanity, that he might become the divine Teacher of all classes of men, and live before human beings a life free from all selfishness and sin, setting them an example of what, through His grace, they may become.

"The Word was made flesh, and dwelt among us, (and we beheld his glory, the glory as of the only begotten of the Father,) full of grace and truth" (verse 14). Praise God for this wonderful statement. The possibilities that it presents seem almost too great for us to grasp, and put to shame our weakness and our unbelief. I praise God that I can see my Saviour by faith. My soul grasps the great gift. Our only hope in this life is to reach forth the hand of faith, and grasp the hand outstretched to save. "Behold the Lamb of God, which taketh away the sin of the world" (verse 29). If we would look away from self to Jesus, making Him our Guide, the world would see in our churches a power that it does not now see.

THE NEED FOR A REFORMATION

But now being made free from sin, and become servants to God, ye have your fruit unto holiness, and the end everlasting life. For the wages of sin is death; but the gift of God is eternal life through Jesus Christ our Lord. **Rom. 6:22, 23.**

Paul felt that the Lord's requirements must be obeyed, His judgments avoided. Like Paul, we must make every effort to obtain the crown of life, which brings eternal honor to every victor. We must not be content to live useless lives.

What is humility? That sense of sin and unworthiness which leads to repentance. But we must be assured of the malignity of a disease before we feel our need of a cure. Those who do not realize the sinfulness of sin are not able to appreciate the value of the atonement and the necessity of being cleansed from all sin. The sinner measures himself by himself and by those who like himself are sinners. He does not look at the purity and holiness of Christ. But when the law of God brings conviction to his heart, he says with Paul, "I was alive without the law once: but when the commandment came, sin revived, and I died" (Rom. 7:9). . . .

God created man for His glory. He will not, cannot endure the presence of sin in His dominion. If there are in the church those who are willfully sinning against God, every possible means should be used to bring them to repentance. If this is not done, God's name is dishonored. He is too pure to look upon iniquity with favor. . . .

Adam's sin would be regarded by the churches of today as a simple mistake, to be at once forgiven and no more thought of. But God's standard is high and His word immutable, and all selfish, covetous practices are an abomination in His sight. The hearts of believers need to be purified, sanctified, refined, ennobled. . . .

Look up, my brethren. Has the gospel lost its power to impress hearts? Is it because the regenerating influence of the Spirit of Christ has died away that hearts are not purified, sanctified, and prepared for the Holy Spirit? No; the Sword of the Spirit, the Word of the living God, is with us yet; but it must be wielded with earnestness. Let us use it as did God's sanctified ones of old. By its living, quickening power it will cut its way to hearts. . . .

The Lord calls for a reformation all through our ranks. . . . When the church is awakened, decided changes will be made. Men and women will be converted, and so filled will they be by the Spirit of God that they will pass from country to country, from city to city, proclaiming the message of truth. With hearts filled with earnest love for souls, they will open their Bibles and present the Word.

I AM A CHILD OF GOD

And if children, then heirs; heirs of God, and joint-heirs with Christ;
if so be that we suffer with him, that we may be also glorified together.
Rom. 8:17.

The influence of grace is to soften the heart, to refine and purify the feelings, giving a heaven-born delicacy and sense of propriety. A Christian cannot be self-exalted, for this is not Christlike. The world's Redeemer, the sinner's substitute and surety, says, "Come unto me, all ye that labour and are heavy laden, and I will give you rest" (Matt. 11:28). . . .

But let us continually bear in mind that the meek and lowly Jesus has the spirit and the ambition of a conqueror. The vast dominions over which earthly potentates hold sway form no adequate theater for the exercise of His grace, the expression of His love, and the manifestation of His glory. He who loves the Lord Jesus Christ in truth and sincerity will love those whom Christ died to save, and will eagerly embrace every opportunity to minister to Christ in the person of His disciples.

We must look at our lives as sons and daughters of God, as laborers with Jesus Christ, living for a noble purpose. We are representatives of Jesus Christ, living for a noble purpose. We are representatives of Jesus Christ in character, and are to serve Him with our undivided affections. Not only will we reveal the fact that we love God, but will, in accordance with His holy character, live a pure, perfect life. We must live perfection, because in looking at Jesus we see in Him the embodiment of perfection; and the great Center upon whom our hope of eternal life and happiness is centered will lead us to unity and harmony. . . .

The life we now live must be by faith in Jesus Christ. If we are Christ's followers our lives will not be as pieced out by little cheap spasmodic actions according to circumstances and surroundings—jerking actions, revealing feelings to be our master, indulging in little frettings, envious faultfindings, jealousies, and selfish vanity. These put us all out of harmony with the harmonious life of Jesus Christ, and we cannot be overcomers if we retain these defects. . . .

When exposed to varied scenes in life, and words are spoken that are calculated to cut and bruise the soul, speak to yourself: "I am a child of God, an heir with Jesus Christ, a colaborer with God. I must not therefore have a cheap mind, easily to take offense, always thinking of myself, for this will naturally produce an inharmonious character. It is unworthy of my noble calling. The heavenly Father has given me my work to do; let me be worthy of the trust."

INFALLIBLE ASSURANCE

And they that be wise shall shine as the brightness of the firmament; and they that turn many to righteousness as the stars for ever and ever. **Dan. 12:3.**

Many, very many, will be terribly surprised when the Lord shall come suddenly as a thief in the night. Let us watch and pray, lest coming suddenly He find us sleeping. My soul is deeply stirred as I consider how much we ought to do for perishing souls. The prediction of Daniel, "Many shall run to and fro, and knowledge shall be increased" (Dan. 12:4), is to be fulfilled in our giving of the warning message; many are to be enlightened regarding the sure word of prophecy. . . .

The salvation of souls should be our first consideration. I am troubled when I see many rejoicing in temporal prosperity, for those who possess worldly treasure seldom seek earnestly to secure the heavenly. They are in danger of falling into temptation and a snare, and into many foolish and hurtful lusts, which drown man in destruction. . . .

We need a more firm reliance upon a "Thus saith the Lord." If we have this, we shall not trust to feeling, and be ruled by feeling. God asks us to rest in His love. It is our privilege to know the Word of God as a sure and tried guide, an infallible assurance. Let us work on the faith side of the question. Let us believe and trust, and talk faith and hope and courage. Let the praise of God be in our hearts and on our lips oftener than it is. "Whoso offereth praise glorifieth me" (Ps. 50:23). Keep the mind stayed upon God, and know the love of Christ as the Word of God reveals it. This Word is life. Talk of Christ; call others to behold Him as your Redeemer.

It is our privilege to rest in an active, living faith in Christ as the Life-giver. It is our privilege to comprehend with all saints, what is the length and depth and height, and to know the love of God which passeth knowledge, and be filled with all the fullness of God. Let us contemplate Christ as the One in whom all fullness dwells. Beholding Him as our personal Saviour, we shall appreciate the value of His saving grace. We should think about Jesus more than we do. We should let His praise be in our hearts. We should speak of the love that has been so abundantly expressed for us. We certainly have every reason to praise God with heart and soul and voice, saying, I will praise the Lord for His great love wherewith He hath loved me. . . .

Lift Him up, the Christ of Calvary; lift Him up, that the world may behold Him. Talk of His goodness, sing of His love, and give Him the grateful thanks of your hearts.

GOD'S PLANS ARE PERFECT

By faith he sojourned in the land of promise, as in a strange country, dwelling in tabernacles with Isaac and Jacob, the heirs with him of the same promise: for he looked for a city which hath foundations, whose builder and maker is God. Heb. 11:9, 10.

Jesus ascended to the Father as a representative of the human race, and God will bring those who reflect His image to behold and share with Him His glory. There are homes for the pilgrims of earth. There are robes for the righteous, with crowns of glory and palms of victory. All that perplexed us in the providences of God will then be made plain. The things hard to be understood will then find an explanation. The mysteries of grace will unfold before us. Where our finite minds discovered only confusion and broken purposes, we shall see the most perfect and beautiful harmony. We shall know that infinite love ordered the experiences that seemed most trying and hard to bear. As we realize the tender care of Him who makes all things work together for our good, we shall rejoice with joy unspeakable and full of glory.

Pain cannot exist in the atmosphere of heaven. In the home of the redeemed there will be no tears, no funeral trains, no badges of mourning. "The inhabitant shall not say, I am sick: the people that dwell therein shall be forgiven their iniquity" (Isa. 33:34). One rich tide of happiness will flow and deepen as eternity rolls on. Think of this; tell it to the children of suffering and sorrow, and bid them rejoice in hope.

The nearer we come to Jesus, the more clearly we behold the purity and greatness of His character, the less we shall feel like exalting self. The contrast between our characters and His will lead to humiliation of soul and deep heart searching. The more we love Jesus, the more entirely will self be humbled and forgotten. . . .

He who is meek in spirit, he who is purest and most childlike, will be made strong for the battle. He will be strengthened with might by His Spirit in the inner man. He who feels his weakness, and wrestles with God as did Jacob, and like this servant of old cries, "I will not let thee go, except thou bless me," will go forth with the fresh anointing of the Holy Spirit. The atmosphere of heaven will surround him. He will go about doing good. His influence will be a positive force in favor of the religion of Christ. . . .

Our God is a very present help in time of need. He is acquainted with the most secret thoughts of our hearts, with all the intents and purposes of our souls. When we are in perplexity, even before we open to Him our distresses, he is making arrangements for our deliverance.

CHRIST LIVED A LIFE
OF HUMBLE OBEDIENCE

Though he were a Son, yet learned he obedience by the things which he suffered; And being made perfect, he became the author of eternal salvation unto all them that obey him. Heb. 5:8, 9.

Christ came to our world, and lived in the home of a peasant. He wore the best garments His parents could provide, but they were the humble garments of the peasants. He walked the rough paths, and climbed the steeps of the hillsides and mountains. When He walked the streets He was apparently alone, for human eyes did not behold His heavenly attendants. He learned the trade of a carpenter, that He might stamp all honest labor as honorable and ennobling to all who work with an eye single to the glory of God. . . .

Christ, the Lord of the whole earth, was a humble artisan. He was unrecognized, neglected, and despised. But He held His commission and authority from the highest power, the Sovereign of heaven. Angels were His attendants, for Christ was doing His Father's business just as much when toiling at the bench as a carpenter, as when working miracles for the multitude. But He concealed the secret from the world. He attached no high titles to His name, to make His position understood, but He lived the royal law of God. His work must begin in consecrating the humble trade of the craftsmen who had toiled for their daily bread. Had Christ passed His life among the grand and the rich, the world of toilers would have been deprived of the inspiration which the Lord intended they should have.

Meek and lowly was the life of Christ. He chose this life that He might help the human family. He did not take His place upon a throne as Commander of the whole earth. He laid aside His royal robe, He laid off His kingly crown, that He might be made one of the human family. He took not on Him the nature of angels. His work was not the priestly office after the appointments of men. It was impossible for man to understand His exalted position, unless the Holy Spirit should make it known. For our sake, He clothed His divinity with humanity, and stepped down from the royal throne. He resigned His position as Commander in the heavenly courts, and for our sakes became poor, that we through His poverty might be made rich. Thus, He hid His glory under the guise of humanity, that He might touch humanity with His divine, transforming power. . . .

Those to whom Christ has given a probation in which to form characters for the mansions He has gone to prepare are to enter into His life example.

THE MINISTRY OF ANGELS

And Elisha prayed, and said, Lord, I pray thee, open his eyes, that he may see. And the Lord opened the eyes of the young man; and he saw: and, behold, the mountain was full of horses and chariots of fire round about Elisha. **2 Kings 6:17.**

How few contemplate the unseen agencies. Men are acting their part either for God or for Satan, the Prince of light, or the prince of darkness. All heaven is intensely interested in human beings who seem to be so full of activity, and yet have no thought for the unseen. Their thoughts are not on the Word of God and its instruction. If they would appropriate the Word of God, they would be astonished that there are agencies, good and evil, observing every word and deed. They are in every assembly for business transactions, in councils, and in meetings for the worship of God. There are more listeners in these public assemblies than can be seen with the natural sight, and every man has his work to do. Those unseen agencies are co-laborers with God or with Satan, and they work more mightily and more constantly than do men. Sometimes the heavenly intelligences draw aside the curtain that hides the unseen world, that we may have our minds withdrawn from the hurry and rush, and consider that there are witnesses to all we do and say when we [are] engaged in business, or when we think ourselves alone.

The Lord would have our perceptions keen to understand that these mighty ones who visit our world have borne an active part in all the work which we have called our own. These heavenly beings are ministering angels, and they frequently disguise themselves in the form of human beings. As strangers they converse with those who are engaged in the work of God. In lonely places they have been the companions of the traveler in peril. In tempest-tossed ships angels in human form have spoken words of encouragement to allay fear and inspire hope in the hour of danger, and the passengers have thought that it was one of their number to whom they had never before spoken.

Many, under different circumstances, have listened to the voices of the inhabitants of other worlds. They have come to act a part in this life. They have spoken in assemblies, and opened before assemblies human histories, and have done works which it was impossible for human agencies to do. Time and again have they been the generals of armies. They have been sent forth to cleanse away pestilence. They have eaten at the humble board of families. Often they have appeared as weary travelers in need of shelter for the night.

We need to understand better than we do the work of these angel visitants.

WE MAY OVERCOME
AS CHRIST OVERCAME

[He] was in all points tempted like as we are, yet without sin. **Heb. 4:15.**

Christ, at an infinite cost, by a painful process, mysterious to angels as well as to men, assumed humanity. Hiding His divinity, laying aside His glory, He was born a babe in Bethlehem. In human flesh He lived the law of God, that He might condemn sin in the flesh, and bear witness to heavenly intelligences that the law was ordained to life and to ensure the happiness, peace, and eternal good of all who obey. . . .

This is the mystery of godliness, that One equal with the Father should clothe His divinity with humanity, and laying aside all the glory of His office as Commander in heaven, [should] descend step after step in the path of humiliation, enduring severe and still more severe abasement. Sinless and undefiled, He stood in the judgment hall, to be tried, to have His case investigated and pronounced upon by the very nation He had delivered from slavery. The Lord of glory was rejected and condemned, yea, spat upon. With contempt for what they regarded as His pretentious claims, men smote Him in the face. . . .

Pilate pronounced Christ innocent, declaring that he found no fault in Him. Yet to please the Jews, he commanded Him to be scourged and then delivered Him up, bruised and bleeding, to suffer the cruel death of crucifixion. The Majesty of heaven was led as a lamb to the slaughter, and amid scoffing and jeers, ridicule and false accusation, He was nailed to the cross. The crowd, in whose hearts humanity seemed to be dead, sought to aggravate the cruel sufferings of the Son of God by their revilings. But as a sheep before His shearers is dumb, so He opened not His mouth. He was giving His life for the life of the world, that all who believed in Him should not perish. . . .

Christ bore the sins of the whole world. He endured our punishment—the wrath of God against transgression. His trial involved the fierce temptation of thinking that He was forsaken by God. His soul was tortured by the pressure of a horror of great darkness. . . . He could not have been tempted in all points like as man is tempted had there been no possibility of His failing. He was a free agent, placed on probation, as was Adam and as is man. Unless there is a possibility of yielding, temptation is no temptation. Temptation comes and is resisted when man is powerfully influenced to do a wrong action, and knowing that he can do it, resists by faith, with a firm hold upon divine power.

259

OUR CHRISTIAN EXPERIENCE MUST BE ANIMATED

I counsel thee to buy of me gold tried in the fire, that thou mayest be rich; and white raiment, that thou mayest be clothed, and that the shame of thy nakedness do not appear; and anoint thine eyes with eyesalve, that thou mayest see. As many as I love, I rebuke and chasten: be zealous therefore, and repent. **Rev. 3:18, 19.**

Our conscience must be purged from dead works to serve the living God. Sanctification means perfect love, perfect obedience, entire conformity to the will of God. If our lives are conformed to the life of Christ through the sanctification of mind, soul, and body, our example will have a powerful influence on the world. We are not perfect, but it is our privilege to cut away from the entanglements of self and sin, and go on unto perfection. . . .

Great possibilities, high and holy attainments, are placed within the reach of all who have true faith. Shall we not anoint our eyes with eyesalve, that we may discern the wondrous things here brought before us? Why do we not with persevering earnestness, work out this prayer, advancing onward and upward, reaching the standard of holiness? We are laborers together with God, and we must work in harmony with one another and with God, "for it is God which worketh in . . . [us] both to will and to do of his good pleasure." . . .

The Lord takes no pleasure in seeing us spiritually weak. "God, who commanded the light to shine out of darkness, hath shined in our hearts, to give the light of the knowledge of the glory of God in the face of Jesus Christ. But we have this treasure in earthen vessels, that the excellency of the power may be of God, and not of us." We have conflicts and trials to meet, but we need not fail or be discouraged. . . .

God can only be honored when we who profess to believe in Him are conformed to His image. We are to represent to the world the beauty of Holiness, and we shall never enter the gates of the city of God until we perfect a Christlike character. If we, with trust in God, strive for sanctification, we shall receive it. Then as witnesses for Christ, we are to make known what the grace of God has wrought in us.

The greatest disquietude we can have is uncertainty. The acceptance of the blessings of God brings righteousness and peace. The fruit of righteousness is quietness and assurance forever. We must have simplicity and Godlike sincerity. We must have that wisdom which cometh from above. Our Christian experience must be animated by piety, and instinct with the divine life.

CHRISTLIKE LOVE
BLENDS HEART WITH HEART

With all lowliness and meekness, with longsuffering, forbearing one another in love. **Eph. 4:12.**

God is love. The love of the Father and the Son is an attribute of every believer. The Word of God is the channel through which divine love is communicated to man. God's truth is the medium by which the intellect is reached. The Holy Spirit is given to the human agent who works in cooperation with divine agencies. It transforms mind and character, enabling man to endure as seeing Him who is invisible. Perfect love can be enjoyed only through the belief of the truth and the reception of the Holy Spirit. . . .

Christ prayed that His disciples might realize the importance of the love that He expressed by giving His life for the world. He desired them to understand something in regard to His infinite sacrifice. If they had more fully understood His self-sacrificing love, they would never have engaged in alienation and strife.

I urge all who claim to believe present truth to practice that truth. If they do this, they will have a stronger and more powerful influence for good. The world will see that the love expressed by believers is the central and controlling principle of Christ's followers. Christlike love blends heart with heart. The truth draws men together. It brings into harmony and unity all who have an earnest, living faith in the Saviour. Christ designs those who believe in Him to develop and become strong by association with one another. All who work unselfishly in the Master's service bear credentials to the world that God has sent His Son to this earth.

Although a company of Christians united in church capacity have not all the same talents, yet it is the duty of everyone to work. Talents differ, but to every man is given his work. All are dependent upon Christ in God. He is the glorious Head of all grades and classes of people associated through faith in the Word of God. Bound together by a common belief in heavenly principles, they are all dependent on Him who is the Author and Finisher of their faith. He has created the principles that produce universal oneness, universal love. His followers should meditate upon His love. They should not stop short of reaching the standard set before them. If the principles of Christianity are lived, they will produce universal harmony and perfect peace. When the heart is imbued with the Spirit of Christ, there is no quarreling, no seeking for the supremacy, no striving to be reigning lords.

THINGS THOU KNOWEST NOT

Call unto me, and I will answer thee, and shew thee great and mighty things, which thou knowest not. **Jer. 33:3.**

We do not always consider that the sanctification we so earnestly desire and for which we pray so earnestly is brought about through the truth and, by the providence of God, in a manner we least expect. When we look for joy, behold there is sorrow. When we expect peace, we frequently have distrust and doubt because we find ourselves plunged into trials we cannot avoid. In these trials we are having the answers to our prayers. In order for us to be purified, the fire of affliction must kindle upon us, and our will must be brought into conformity to the will of God. In order to be conformed to the image of our Saviour, we pass through a most painful process of refining. The very ones that we regard the most dear upon the earth may cause us the greatest sorrow and trial. They may view us in the wrong light. They may think us in error, and that we are deceiving and degrading ourselves because we follow the dictates of enlightened conscience in seeking for the truth as for hid treasures. . . .

Our prayers for conformity to the image of Christ may not be answered exactly as we desire. We may be tested and proved, for God sees it best to put us under a course of discipline which is essential for us before we are fit subjects for the blessing we crave. We should not become discouraged and give way to doubt, and think that our prayers are not noticed. We should rely more securely upon Christ and leave our case with God to answer our prayers in His own way. God has not promised to bestow His blessings through the channels we have marked out. God is too wise to err and too regardful of our good to allow us to choose for ourselves.

The plans of God are always the best, although we may not always discern them. Perfection of Christian character can be obtained only through labor, conflict, and self-denial. . . .

How inestimably precious are the gifts of God—the graces of His Spirit—and we shall not shrink from the trying, testing process, be it ever so painful or humiliating to us. How easy would be the way to heaven if there were no self-denial or cross! How worldlings would rush in the way, and hypocrites would travel in it without number! Thank God for the cross, the self-denial. The ignominy and shame our Saviour endured for us is none too humiliating for those saved by the purchase of His blood. Heaven will indeed be cheap enough.

THE WORD OF GOD YOUR GUIDE

Thy word is a lamp unto my feet, and a light unto my path. **Ps. 119:105.**

If we would work wisely and intelligently, our human passions, our hereditary and cultivated tendencies, must be brought under the control of a higher and more commanding generalship than human ability. . . .

"Cease to do evil; learn to do well." This is the lesson everyone should learn day by day. The training due to one's self comes first. The influence exerted by a life of strict integrity will be a continual education to others. Those who are restrained and guided by the moral and religious principles plainly laid down in God's Word walk in accordance with the mind and will of God, who is too wise to err and too good to do us harm.

If you would walk wisely, walk in the way of God's commandments. The Word of God you have in your keeping, right at hand. This Word is so plain that none need go astray unless they allow themselves to be led by their hereditary and cultivated tendencies to wrong. Your Redeemer met Satan's treacherous advances with the words, "It is written," and with the imperative command, "Get thee behind me, Satan." I counsel you to receive with meekness the engrafted Word, which is able to save your soul. The Word of God is your haven. It is a tower of strength, into which you may run and be safe. . . .

The earnest, sincere searcher for truth will not mistake truth for error. The Word of God is the bread of life, of which all may partake and obtain eternal life. Error is falsehood and deception. Those who partake of it must suffer in consequence, as did Adam and Eve in Eden. It is the privilege of all to search with prayerful, eager interest for the truth. Truth is the tree of life, the leaves of which the human family are to eat and live.

Those who try to interpret the Word according to their own ideas, who read it in accordance with their opinions, will never see the truth, and will die in their sins. Those who eat of the forbidden tree accept Satan's fallacies in the place of "Thus saith the Lord," and unless they repent, they will never gain that life which measures with the life of God. As did Adam and Eve, they exclude themselves from the tree of life, the fruit of which perpetuates immortality. . . .

We are living amid the solemnities of the judgment. Our souls should be filled with awe, for we are in God's presence continually. Each one must decide for himself whether he will obey and live or disobey and perish.

To those who obey, the Word of God is the tree of life. It is the word of salvation, received unto eternal life.

CHRIST CALLS FOR UNITY

That they all may be one; as thou, Father, art in me, and I in thee, that they also may be one in us: that the world may believe that thou hast sent me. **John 17:21.**

We each need the help we can receive from other minds. God will work in other minds than ours. The various gifts given to different ones are to blend for the "perfecting of the saints, for the work of the ministry, for the edifying of the body of Christ" (Eph. 4:12). . . .

The Lord Jesus Christ will heal our infirmities and our weaknesses. He owns us. We are His by creation and by redemption. We must all be united in Him. He is the only source of healing. All restoring power comes from Him. He has opened a fountain "to the inhabitants of Jerusalem for sin and for uncleanness." He gives each one an invitation to come and be healed, and to drink of the water of life. Let us not trust in ourselves, but in Jesus.

There will always be obstacles before us, but we are to follow our Leader, and meet our difficulties unitedly, hand in hand. There is only one way to heaven. We must walk in the footsteps of Jesus, doing His works, even as He did the works of His Father. We must study His ways, not man's ways; we must obey His will, not our own. Walk carefully. Do not go ahead of Christ. Make no move without consulting your Leader. Ask in humble prayer, and "ye shall receive." He is the Way, the Truth, the Life.

Read and study carefully the prayer that Christ offered just before His trial, recorded in the seventeenth chapter of John. Follow its teachings, and you will be brought into unity. Our only hope of reaching heaven is to be one with Christ, and then, in and through Christ, we shall be one with one another. No one is called to walk alone. In Christ life and immortality are brought to light. He has opened the way to the kingdom of heaven to those who believe in Him, but He assigns to no one a path different to that which all must travel. He calls for unity, and unity we must have. God asks us to sink self in Christ. For the natural man this is not easy. But through the power of the incarnation of Christ, God manifest in the flesh, the strength of God is revealed in gentleness and beauty. To "as many as received him, to them gave he power to become the sons of God." By this power we may overcome our evil tendencies and so modify our imperfect dispositions that the will of God may be fulfilled in us.

ARE YOU PREPARING FOR HEAVEN?

Eye hath not seen, nor ear heard, neither have entered into the heart of man, the things which God hath prepared for them that love him. **1 Cor. 2:9.**

What a work is before us. We need greater faith in Christ and the Father, for this we must certainly have, else we shall be counted with the unbelievers. We see great opportunities and a great amount of work to do. We want the sanctification of the Holy Spirit. We cannot afford to miss the mark of the prize of the high calling in Christ Jesus. The sanctification of the truth, confirming man's steadfastness in the faith, will constitute men laborers together with God.

United with the Source of all power, persevering in duty, enlarging the apprehension of the love of God in Christ Jesus, they become one with Christ, until they are complete with Christ in God.

The glories that await the faithful overcomer are beyond any description. The Lord will greatly honor and exalt His faithful ones. They shall grow like the cedar, and their comprehension will be certainly increasing. And at every advanced stage of knowledge their anticipation will fall far beneath the reality. "Eye hath not seen, nor ear heard, neither have entered into the heart of man, the things which God hath prepared for them that love him" (1 Cor. 2:9). Our work now is to prepare for those mansions that God is preparing for those who love Him and keep His commandments. . . . The Lord Jesus will enlarge every mind and heart for the reception of the Holy Spirit. . . .

Time is short. Let the little time you have be employed for your own present and eternal good by active Christian service, doing all the good possible. Redeem the time that has been lost; seek first the kingdom of God and His righteousness. Then you will have something to impart in good works, in cheerful, consecrated influence. . . .

What preparation have you made for the future, eternal world? . . . You want something higher and better than you now have. You may exert a conscious and unconscious influence in right doing. God deserves something better from you as His subject than that which you have given Him. Carefully consider: Are you standing under the banner of Prince Emmanuel, or under the black banner of the prince of darkness? There is an obligation resting upon you to return the influence and money that is lent you of the Lord to advance His cause and glorify His name.

The Lord calls upon you, "My son, give me thine heart."

CHRIST INTERCEDES FOR YOU

We have such an high priest, who is set on the right hand of the throne of the Majesty in the heavens; a minister of the sanctuary, and of the true tabernacle, which the Lord pitched, and not man. **Heb. 8:1, 2.**

The natural eye can never behold the comeliness and beauty of Christ. The inward illumination of the Holy Spirit, revealing to the soul its true hopeless, helpless condition without the mercy and pardon of the Sin-bearer—the all-sufficiency of Christ—can alone enable man to discern His infinite mercy, His immeasurable love, benevolence, and glory.

No one ever came to our world on such an errand of grace, infinite compassion, and unspeakable love, as our Saviour; and none ever received such treatment at the hands of fallen man. "Ye are not your own; ye are bought with a price" (see 1 Cor. 6:19, 20). We are Christ's by creation, His by redemption. He is the only sinless Being who endured suffering, shameful humiliation, and rejection in our behalf. . . .

Then, how should those who become new creatures in Christ Jesus, saved by His merits, conduct themselves before the universe of heaven? Shall they complain? Shall they accuse one another? Would not a meek and submissive spirit be more becoming? "Learn of me," said the great Teacher, "for I am meek and lowly in heart: and ye shall find rest unto your souls. For my yoke is easy, and my burden is light." Shall we reveal this spirit in our characters? Shall we wear His yoke, and lift His burdens? . . .

Could all see Christ before the throne, waiting for their prayers, waiting for them to surrender their will, to cease their rebellion and come back to their allegiance to God, in deep penitence they would pray the Father to forgive their transgression of His law, and forgive them for the influence they have exercised in causing others to disregard the law of Jehovah. The confederacies of the enemy's army are triumphing in their delay. Will they longer remain under the condemnation of the law? Or, will they stand on the side of Christ, and with their influence help the betrayed, rebellious race by their own experimental knowledge? Will they now become co-workers with Jesus Christ, who is making personal intercession for them before the Father? Angels are keeping back the destroying agencies, for they have an intense interest for these rebellious sons, and they want to help them to return to the fold in safety and peace, that they may finally be overcomers, and be saved, eternally saved with the family of God in heaven.

GOD'S HAND IS ON THE WHEEL

Finally, my brethren, be strong in the Lord, and in the power of his might. **Eph. 6:10.**

The future is before us, and unforeseen events will surely take place, changing the present aspect of things in the world. Lust and greed are striving for the supremacy. Oppression and hatred will be exercised to destroy. Inspired by a power from beneath, Satan's instrumentalities will work with intensity to carry out his will. "The wicked shall do wickedly: and none of the wicked shall understand; but the wise shall understand" (Dan. 12;10). Every truly converted soul will put on the whole armor of God, and will bravely face the unseen foe. God's servants will realize the necessity of partaking of the divine nature. . . .

Now is our time of peril. Our only safety is in walking in the footsteps of Christ, and wearing His yoke. Troublous times are before us. In many instances, friends will become alienated. Without cause, men will become our enemies. The motives of the people of God will be misinterpreted, not only by the world, but by their own brethren. The Lord's servants will be put in hard places. A mountain will be made out of a molehill to justify men in pursuing a selfish, unrighteous course.

The work that men have done faithfully will be disparaged and underrated, because apparent prosperity did not attend their efforts. By misrepresentation, these men will be clothed in the dark vestments of dishonesty, because circumstances beyond their control made their work perplexing. They will be pointed to as men that cannot be trusted. And this will be done by the members of the church. God's servants must arm themselves with the mind of Christ. They must not expect to escape insult and misjudgment. They will be called enthusiasts and fanatics. But let them not become discouraged. God's hand is on the wheel of His providence, guiding His work to the glory of His name.

God calls upon His people to be bright lights in the world shining amid the darkness of sin. Living the life of the Life-giver brings its reward. He went about doing good. This, every true follower of His will do, filled with a sacred sense of his loyalty to God and his duty to his fellow beings. Through the knowledge of the truth as it is in Jesus, Christians are to grow in grace, constantly drawing nearer perfection of character.

LET GOD WORK HIS WILL IN YOU

The God of peace . . . make you perfect in every good work to do his will, working in you that which is wellpleasing in his sight, through Jesus Christ; to whom be glory for ever and ever. **Heb. 13:20, 21.**

By studying the Word of God, and carrying out its precepts in all their business transactions, men may carefully discern the spirit that controls the actions. In the place of following human impulse and natural inclination, they may learn, by diligent study, the principles that should control the sons and daughters of Adam.

The Bible is the guidebook that is to decide the many difficult problems that rise in minds that are selfishly inclined. It is a reflection of the wisdom of God, and not only furnishes great and important principles, but supplies practical lessons for the life and conduct of man toward his fellow man. It gives minute particulars that decide our relation to God and to each other. It is a complete revelation of the attributes and will of God in the person of Jesus Christ, and in it is set forth the obligation of the human agent to render wholehearted service to God, and to inquire at every step of the way, "Is this the way of the Lord?" . . .

A deceiving crookedness is discernible in the minds of those whose eyes are not anointed with the heavenly eyesalve that they may see all things in the light of God's Word. The will becomes enslaved, bound to pursue a course which the Word of God will not justify. The will of the human agent is not to be given into the control of any other man. When merged into the will of other men, it is misleading. . . .

If the human agent consents, God can and will so identify His will with all our thoughts and aims, so blend our hearts and minds into conformity to His Word, that when obeying His will, we are only carrying out the impulses of our minds. All such will not possess an unsanctified, selfish disposition, ready to carry out their own wills, but will have a jealous, earnest, determined zeal for the glory of God. They will not want to do anything in their own strength, and will guard strictly against the danger of promoting self.

All who would perfect a Christian character must wear the yoke of Christ. If they would sit together in heavenly places in Christ Jesus, they must learn of Him while on this earth. Our natures are in need of discipline. They must be conformed to the nature of Jesus Christ, that He may accomplish the good He designs to do for all who will submit to be molded by yielding their natures to His authority. The great Teacher will yoke up with every soul who will bear His yoke.

CHRIST'S LOVE
CANNOT BE MEASURED

For I am persuaded, that neither death, nor life, nor angels, nor principalities, nor powers, nor things present, nor things to come, nor height, nor depth, nor any other creature, shall be able to separate us from the love of God, which is in Christ Jesus our Lord. **Rom. 8:38, 39.**

Christ might, because of our guilt, have moved far from us. But instead of moving farther away from us, He came and dwelt among us, filled with all the fullness of the Godhead, to be one with us, that through His grace we might attain to perfection. By a death of shame and suffering He paid man's ransom. What self-sacrificing love is this! From the highest excellency He came, His divinity clothed with humanity, descending step by step to the very depths of humiliation. No line can measure the depth of this love. Christ has shown us how much God can love and our Redeemer suffer in order to secure our complete restoration. He desires His children to reveal His character, to exert His influence, that other minds may be drawn into harmony with His mind.

Christ, our Saviour, in whom dwelt absolute perfection, became sin for the fallen race. He did not know sin by the experience of sinning, but He bore the terrible weight of the guilt of the whole world. He became our propitiation, that all who receive Him may become sons of God. The cross was erected to save man. Christ lifted on the cross, was the means devised in heaven for awakening in the repenting soul a sense of the sinfulness of sin. By the cross Christ sought to draw all to Himself. He died as the only hope of saving those who, because of sin, were in the gall of bitterness. Through the agency of the Holy Spirit, a new principle of mental and spiritual power was to be brought to man, who, through association with divinity, was to become one with God.

To break down the barriers that Satan had erected between God and man, Christ made a full and complete sacrifice, revealing unexampled self-denial. He revealed to the world the amazing spectacle of God living in human flesh, and sacrificing Himself to save fallen man. What wonderful love! As I consider it, I weep to think that so many of those who claim to believe the truth are encrusted with selfishness. . . .

I marvel that professing Christians do not grasp the divine resources; that they do not see the cross more clearly as the medium of forgiveness and pardon, the means of bringing the proud, selfish heart of man into direct contact with the Holy Spirit, that the riches of Christ may be poured into the mind, and the human agent be adorned with the graces of the Spirit, that Christ may be commended to those who know Him not.

STANDING BY PRINCIPLE

O how love I thy law! it is my meditation all the day. **Ps. 119:97.**

Let those who talk of principle as if they would not on any account depart from it be sure that they understand the principles laid down in the Word of God for our guidance. There are some who follow false principles. Their idea of principle is misleading. Following right principle means the faithful doing of the first four and the last six commandments. In obedience to these divine commands, we eat the flesh and drink the blood of Christ, appropriating all that is embraced in the atonement made on Calvary. Christ will stand by the side of all who receive Him as their Saviour. To them He will give power to become the sons of God. "The Word was made flesh, and dwelt among us, (and we beheld his glory, the glory as of the only begotten of the Father,) full of grace and truth" (John 1:14).

The One here referred to as the Word is the Son of God, who was the Commander in the heavenly courts, and who came to this world to open heavenly things to fallen human beings. He is the Way, the Truth, and the Life. He is the Word that was with God before the world was. In clothing His divinity with humanity, He became possessed of two natures, the divine and the human. And because of this, He was fully able to accomplish for the human race their complete redemption, and their restoration to the privileges of the higher life.

He began His earthly life as human beings begin theirs, coming to this world as a helpless babe. And while here, He lived the life that every human being may live who will receive the great gift that the Lord made to our world in sending His son to work out the plan of salvation.

Christ bore the penalty of sin, the stroke of divine justice, that human beings might not be left to perish. He bore in His body the sentence pronounced against sinners. This is the science of salvation, which can safely be searched into, and which it is profitable to strive to understand. . . .

Those who continue in transgression will be judged according to their refusal of light. They choose to stand on the side of the prince of darkness, to become the helping hand of him who, if it were possible, would deceive the very elect. They refuse the wonderful gift of heaven, and though they may profess righteousness, and talk of "adherence to principle," they are at the same time following principles opposed to the noble principles of heaven, and they teach others to follow the same corrupting principles.

OUR SANCTUARY DOCTRINE

Unto two thousand and three hundred days; then shall the sanctuary be cleansed. **Dan. 8:14.**

God bids us give our time and strength to the work of preaching to the people the messages that stirred men and women in 1843 and 1844. . . .

My brethren, take your position where God bids you. Leave alone those who, after light has been repeatedly given them, have taken a stand on the opposite side. . . . Take up the work which has been given us. With the Word of God as your message, stand on the platform of truth and proclaim the soon coming of Christ. Truth, eternal truth, will prevail.

For more than half a century [i.e., since 1844] the different points of present truth have been questioned and opposed. New theories have been advanced as truth, which were not truth, and the Spirit of God revealed their error. As the great pillars of our faith have been presented, the Holy Spirit has borne witness to them, and especially is this so regarding the truths of the sanctuary question. Over and over again the Holy Spirit has in a marked manner endorsed the preaching of this doctrine. But today, as in the past, some will be led to form new theories and to deny the truths upon which the Spirit of God has placed His approval.

Any man who seeks to present theories which would lead us from the light that has come to us on the ministration in the heavenly sanctuary should not be accepted as a teacher. A true understanding of the sanctuary question means much to us as a people. When we were earnestly seeking the Lord for light on that question, light came. In vision I was given such a view of the heavenly sanctuary, and the ministration connected with the holy place, that for many days I could not speak of it.

I know from the light that God has given me that there should be a revival of the messages that have been given in the past, because men will seek to bring in new theories, and will try to prove that these theories are scriptural, whereas they are error, which, if allowed a place, will undermine faith in the truth. We are not to accept these suppositions and pass them along as truth. No, no; we must not move from the platform of truth on which we have been established.

There will always be those who are seeking for something new, and who stretch and strain the Word of God to make it support their ideas and theories. Let us, brethren, take the things that God has given us, and which His Spirit has taught us is truth, and believe them, leaving alone those theories which His Spirit has not endorsed.

271

EATING THE LEAVES OF
THE TREE OF LIFE

In the midst of the street of it, and on either side of the river, was there the tree of life, which bare twelve manner of fruits, and yielded her fruit every month: and the leaves of the tree were for the healing of the nations. **Rev. 22:2.**

Must we wait until we are translated before we eat of the leaves of the tree of life? He who receives into his heart the words of Christ knows what it means to eat the leaves of the tree of life. . . .

The knowledge that comes from God is the bread of life. It is the leaves of the tree of life which are for the healing of the nations. The current of spiritual life thrills the soul as the words of Christ are believed and practiced. Thus it is that we are made one with Christ. The experience that was weak and feeble becomes strong. It is eternal life to us if we hold the beginning of our confidence firm unto the end.

All truth is to be received as the life of Jesus. Truth cleanses us from all impurity, and prepares the soul for Christ's presence. Christ is formed within, the hope of glory. . . .

It is essential that those who pledge themselves to keep God's commandments have an intelligent knowledge of the Scriptures. Thus we learn to deny self and to be strictly honest with God in using His goods. It was in order that we might understand the divine will that God gave us the Bible. We cannot obey His commandments until we know what these commandments are.

Parents are without excuse if they fail to obtain a clear understanding of God's will, that they may obey the laws of His kingdom. Only thus can they lead their children to heaven. My brethren and sisters, it is your duty to understand God's requirements. How can you educate your children in the things of God unless you first know yourselves what is right and what is wrong, unless you realize that obedience means eternal life and disobedience eternal death?

We must make it our lifework to understand the will of God. Only as we do this can we train our children aright. Your every word and action is to be in accordance with the will of God, irrespective of the opinions and practices of those who refuse to obey God. . . .

"The law of the Lord is perfect, converting the soul" (Ps. 19:7). The Lord has kept back nothing that is necessary for the enlightenment of His children. No one can plead in excuse for transgression that he was left in ignorance, that the way to heaven was not clearly marked out. We have not been left to serve God in a vague, uncertain way.

ONLY ONE LIGHT
TO ILLUMINATE THE WAY

But the path of the just is as the shining light, that shineth more and more unto the perfect day. **Prov. 4:18.**

Christ's love in the heart, revealing through the life its wondrous power—this is the greatest miracle that can be performed before a fallen, quarrelling world. Let us try to work this miracle, not in our own power, but in the name of the Lord Jesus Christ, whose we are and whom we serve. Let us put on Christ, and the miracle-working power of His grace will be so plainly revealed in the transformation of character that the world will be convinced that God has sent His Son into the world to make men as angels in the character and life.

Those who truly believe in Christ sit together with Him in heavenly places. Let us accept the badge of Christianity. This is not an outward sign, not the wearing of a cross or a crown, but it is something that reveals the union of man with God. Let us "put off the old man with his deeds; and . . . put on the new man, which is renewed in knowledge after the image of him that created him" (Col. 3:9, 10). The beauty of holiness is revealed as Christians draw near together, blending in Christlike love.

"Having therefore, brethren, boldness to enter into the holiest by the blood of Jesus, by a new and living way, which he hath consecrated for us, through the veil, that is to say, his flesh; and having an high priest over the house of God; let us draw near with a true heart in full assurance of faith, having our hearts sprinkled from an evil conscience, and our bodies washed with pure water. Let us hold fast the profession of our faith without wavering; (for he is faithful that promised;) and let us consider one another to provoke unto love and to good works: not forsaking the assembling of ourselves together, as the manner of some is, but exhorting one another: and so much the more, as ye see the day approaching" (Heb. 10:19-25).

There is only one true religion, only one way to heaven; only one light to illuminate the way as the pilgrims press on. As we follow on to know the Lord, we shall acknowledge at every step that Christ is the Light of the world, that He is the Way, the Truth, and the Life; and we shall find that the path that He bids us follow is "as the shining light, that shineth more and more unto the perfect day" (Prov. 4:18). . . .

The Lord is good and greatly to be praised. . . . How blest, how doubly blest, is the home in which father, mother, and children are consecrated to the service of Christ.

CHRIST HAS POWER FOR US

And ye are complete in him, which is the head of all principality and power. **Col. 2:10.**

We are to live in the warm, genial rays of the Sun of Righteousness. Nothing but His loving compassion, His divine grace, His almighty power, can enable us to baffle the relentless foe and subdue the opposition of the human heart. What is our strength? The joy of the Lord. Let the melting love of Christ fill the heart, and we are softened and subdued, prepared to receive the power that He has for us.

Let us thank God every day for the blessings that are ours. If the human agent will humble himself before God, realizing how inappropriate it is for him to cherish a feeling of self-sufficiency; realizing his utter inability to do the work that needs to be done in order for his soul to be purified, casting away, making of no account, his own righteousness, Christ will engrave His own image upon his soul. . . .

Christ will never neglect the work that has been placed in His hands. He will inspire the resolute disciple with a sense of the perversity, the sin-stained condition, the depravity, of the heart upon which He is working. The true penitent has learned the uselessness of self-importance. Looking to Jesus, comparing his own defective character with the Saviour's perfect character, he can say,

In my hand no price I bring;
Simply to Thy cross I cling.

With Isaiah he declares, "Lord, thou wilt ordain peace for us: for thou also hast wrought all our works in us. O Lord our God, other lords beside thee have had dominion over us: but by thee only will we make mention of thy name" (Isa. 26:12, 13).

Beholding Christ for the purpose of becoming like Him, the seeker after truth sees the perfection of the principles of God's law, and he becomes dissatisfied with everything but perfection. Hiding his life in the life of Christ, he sees that the holiness of the divine law is revealed in the character of Christ, and more and more earnestly he strives to be like Him. A warfare may be expected at any time, for the tempter sees that he is losing one of his subjects. A battle must be fought with the attributes which Satan has been strengthening for his own use.

The human agent sees what he has to contend with—a strange power opposed to the idea of attaining the perfection that Christ holds out. But with Christ there is saving power that will gain for him victory in the conflict. The Saviour will strengthen and help him as he comes pleading for grace and efficiency.

HELP FOR THE CONFLICT PROMISED

Thus saith the Lord that created thee, O Jacob, and he that formed thee, O Israel, Fear not: for I have redeemed thee, I have called thee by thy name; thou art mine. **Isa. 43:1.**

Every obstacle to the redemption of the people of God is to be removed by the opening of the Word of God and the presentation of a plain "Thus saith the Lord." The true light is to shine forth, for darkness covers the earth and gross darkness the people. The truth of the living God is to appear in contrast with error. Proclaim the glad tidings: We have a Saviour who has given His life that all who believe in Him should not perish, but have everlasting life.

Obstacles to the advancement of the work of the Lord will appear, but fear not. To the omnipotence of the King of kings, our covenant-keeping God unites the gentleness and care of a tender shepherd. Nothing can stand in His way. His power is absolute, and is the pledge of the sure fulfillment of His promises to His people. He can remove all obstructions to the advancement of His work. . . .

The church of Christ is God's agency for the proclamation of truth, empowered by Him to do a special work, and if she is loyal to God, obedient to all His commandments, there will dwell within her the excellency of divine power. If she will honor the Lord God of Israel, there is no power that can stand against her. If she will be true to her allegiance, the forces of the enemy will be no more able to overpower her than is the chaff to resist the whirlwind.

There is before the church the dawn of a bright, glorious day, if she will put on the robe of Christ's righteousness, withdrawing from all alliance with the world. The members of the church need now to confess their backslidings, and press together. My brethren and sisters, allow nothing to come in that will separate you from one another and from God. Talk not of differences of opinion, but unite in the love of the truth as it is in Jesus. Come before God and plead the shed blood of the Saviour as a reason that you should receive help in the warfare against evil. I assure you that you will not plead in vain. As you draw near to God, with heartfelt contrition and in full assurance of faith, the enemy who seeks to destroy you will be overcome.

Turn to the Lord, ye prisoners of hope. Seek strength from God, the living God. Show an unwavering, humble faith in His power and willingness to save. From Christ is flowing the living stream of salvation. He is the Fountain of life and the Source of all power.

SERVICE TO GOD
BEGINS ON EARTH

That the trial of your faith, being much more precious than of gold that perisheth, though it be tried with fire, might be found unto praise and honour and glory at the appearing of Jesus Christ. **1 Peter 1:7.**

Those who work against the natural laws of the being must suffer the penalty of transgression. But the Saviour pities us, even when we suffer from infirmities caused by our own wrong course of action. In Him there is a healing power for us. Let us praise God for the tree of life, the leaves of which are for the healing of the nations. . . .

Everywhere the effects of the curse are seen. Let us praise God that in the earth made new "there shall be no more curse: but the throne of God and of the Lamb shall be in it; and his servants shall serve him" (Rev. 22:3). Some little know what true service means. Those who expect to sing in an entertainment spend time in practicing, to familiarize themselves with the music and the words. That we may learn how to serve the Lord in heaven, we must enter His service now, becoming acquainted with Him and learning to be faithful servants. . . .

It is our privilege to understand the blessed Word of God. We have fallen, it is true, but we are not always to remain in sin. We have been placed on vantage ground. The Lord God of heaven "so loved the world, that he gave his only begotten Son, that whosoever believeth in him should not perish, but have everlasting life" (John 3:16). What a precious hope we have in Christ! . . .

Temptations will come. But when Satan throws his hellish shadow before us, we should reach in faith through the shadow to the light of life—to Him who has not only created man but who by His own blood has redeemed him. We are Christ's cherished heritage. In living faith we must cooperate with Him in working out our own salvation. Amid trials and temptations His hand upholds and sustains us. Those who rest in Christ Jesus are never restless or uneasy. He means just what He says when He bids us commit the keeping of our souls unto Him, as to a faithful Creator.

Those who hold fast their faith unto the end will come forth from the furnace of trial as fine gold seven times purified. Of this work the prophet Isaiah says, "I will make a man more precious than fine gold; even a man than the golden wedge of Ophir" (Isa. 13;12). When in trouble, remember that faith tried in the furnace of affliction is more precious than gold tried with fire. Remember that there is One watching every movement, to see when the last particle of dross is taken away from your character.

THE MEANING OF
COMMUNION WITH GOD

That which we have seen and heard declare we unto you, that ye also may fellowship with us: and truly our fellowship is with the Father, and with his Son Jesus Christ. 1 John 1:3.

Communion with God is the life of the soul. It is not something that we cannot interpret, something that we can clothe with beautiful words but which does not give us the genuine experience that makes our words of real value. Communion with God gives a daily experience that does indeed make our joy full.

Those who have this union with Christ will declare it in spirit and word and work. Profession is nothing unless in word and work good fruit is manifest. Unity, fellowship with one another and with Christ—this is the fruit borne on every branch of the living vine. The cleansed soul, born again, has a clear, distinct testimony to bear. . . .

To know God is, in the scriptural sense of the term, to be one with Him in heart and mind, having an experimental knowledge of Him, holding reverential communion with Him as the Redeemer. Only through sincere obedience can this communion be obtained. Where this communion is lacking, the heart is not in any sense a temple of God, but is controlled by the foe, who is working out his own purposes through the human agency. Such a man, whatever his profession or claims, is not a temple of the Holy Spirit.

The experience is perfected by fruit bearing. He who does not bear good fruit in words and deeds, in the strength of elevated, ennobling principle, is a bad tree. The fruit that he bears is unpalatable to God. His professed knowledge of Christ is a falsehood, a deception. . . .

In the light of the love of Christ, the gospel is an open book. This is the true light, which Christ came to bring to the world. The Saviour's true disciples have received this love. . . .

From the light that God has given me, I know that men's great danger is in being self-deceived. Satan is watching his chance. He will come to men in human form, and will speak to them most entrancing words. He will bring against them the same temptations that he brought against Christ. Unless their minds and hearts are filled with the pure, unselfish, sanctified love that Christ revealed, they will fall under Satan's power, and will do and say and write strange things, to deceive, if it were possible, the very elect. . . .

Following Christ's example of unselfish service, trusting like little children in His merits, and obeying His commands, we shall receive the approval of God.

HEAVEN, THE CHRISTIAN'S SUMMER

Looking for that blessed hope, and the glorious appearing of the great God and our Saviour Jesus Christ. **Titus 2:13.**

Christ is soon to come the second time. Of this we should often talk. It should be the uppermost thought in our minds. He is coming, with power and great glory, and every eye shall see Him. All the holy angels will accompany Him. Of this company John writes, "I beheld, and heard the voice of many angels round about the throne and the beast and the elders: and the number of them was ten thousand times ten thousand, and thousands of thousands" (Rev. 5:11).

The trumpet has not yet sounded. Those who have gone down into the grave have not yet cried, "O death, where is thy sting? O grave, where is thy victory?" (1 Cor. 15:55). The righteous dead have not yet been caught up with the living saints to meet their Lord in the air. But the time is near when the words spoken by the apostle Paul will have their fulfillment, "For the Lord himself shall descend from heaven with a shout, with the voice of the archangel, and with the trump of God: and the dead in Christ shall rise first: then we which are alive and remain shall be caught up together with them in the clouds, to meet the Lord in the air: and so shall we ever be with the Lord" (1 Thess. 4:16-18).

In order for us to be like the Saviour, we must be changed (see Phil. 3:20, 21). Now is the time for us to bring into the daily life the virtues of Christ's life. We have no time to lose. Should we fail in our character building, we shall lose eternal life. We must build on the true foundation. . . . We must do the work of Christ, and be constantly watching and praying. Then we shall be ready for His appearing, prepared to receive eternal life.

All who will can be overcomers. Let us strive earnestly to reach the standard set before us. Christ knows our weakness, and to Him we can go daily for help. It is not necessary for us to gain strength a month ahead. We are to conquer from day to day.

This earth is the place of preparation for heaven. The time spent here is the Christian's winter. Here the chilly winds of affliction blow upon us, and the waves of trouble roll against us. But in the near future, when Christ comes, sorrow and sighing will be forever ended. Then will be the Christian's summer. All trials will be over, and there will be no more sickness or death. "God shall wipe away all tears from their eyes; and there shall be no more death, neither sorrow, nor crying, neither shall there be any more pain: for the former things are passed away" (Rev. 21:4).

WE HAVE THE BLESSED ASSURANCE

I will never leave thee, nor forsake thee. **Heb. 13:5.**

We have but one life to live, and through our daily connection with God we have, in and through the merits of the Lord Jesus Christ, a constant sustenance in doing the things that will represent Christ to the world. We may not have all the conveniences that some have in ease and comfort and in earthly goods, but we have the blessed assurance which Christ gave to His believing disciples. . . . To them He said, "Let not your heart be troubled: ye believe in God, believe also in me. In my Father's house are many mansions: if it were not so, I would have told you. I go to prepare a place for you. And if I go and prepare a place for you, I will come again, and receive you unto myself; that where I am, there ye may be also" (John 14:1-3). . . .

Blessed words! We may receive Him into our hearts, and He will be unto us hope and courage and sustaining grace. The Lord would have us trust fully and entirely in Him. Then we will, in the simplicity of our faith, believe that Christ will do for us all that He has promised. Let all come to the Saviour in full assurance that He will do all that He has promised.

We cannot please our Saviour more than by having faith in His promises. His mercies can come to you, and your prayers can come to Him. Nothing can break this line of communication. We must learn to bring all perplexities to Jesus Christ, for He will help us. He will listen to our requests. We may come to Him in full assurance of faith, nothing doubting, for He is the living Way. . . .

The more we press our petitions to His throne, the more sure we are of constantly receiving the great grace of our Lord Jesus Christ. You do not give strength to the road you are traveling by [having] faith. But you increase in strength and in assurance because you have a Guide right by your side, and you can ask Him with perfect faith to guide your steps aright.

Then trust in the Lord Jesus to lead you step by step into the right path. You can derive assurance and strength at every step you advance, for you can be assured that your hand is in His hand. You can "run and not be weary"; you can "walk and not faint," for you can realize by faith that you have your hand in the hand of Christ. You will not sink under discouragement, for as you follow on to know the Lord, trusting in Him, you will have the assurance that the One who never forsakes those who fully trust Him is your constant Helper.

DROP SELF INTO GOD'S HANDS

My Father, which gave them me, is greater than all; and no man is able to pluck them out of my Father's hand. **John 10:29.**

We must rise to a higher standard on the subject of faith. We have too little faith. The Word of God is our endorsement. We must take it, simply believing every word. With this assurance, we may claim large things, and according to our faith it will be unto us. . . . If we humble our hearts before God, if we seek to abide in Christ, we shall have a higher, holier experience. . . .

True faith consists in doing just what God has enjoined, not manufacturing things He has not enjoined. Justice, truth, mercy, are the fruit of faith. We need to walk in the light of God's law; then good works will be the fruit of our faith, the proceeds of a heart renewed every day. . . .

We must not in any way make self our god. God has given Himself to die for us, that He might purify us from all iniquity. The Lord will carry on this work of perfection for us if we will allow ourselves to be controlled by Him. . . .

The work of righteousness cannot be carried forward unless we exercise implicit faith. Move every day under God's mighty working power. The fruit of righteousness is quietness and assurance forever. If we had exercised more faith in God and had trusted less to our own ideas and wisdom, God would have manifested His power in a marked manner on human hearts. By a union with Him, by living faith, we are privileged to enjoy the virtue and efficacy of His mediation. Hence we are crucified with Christ, dead with Christ, risen with Christ, to walk in newness of life with Him.

We are not to hold ourselves in our own hands. We are to drop self into the hands of God. . . . Our lack of faith is the reason that we have not seen more of the power of God. We exercise more faith in our own working than in God's working for us. God designs that everything possible shall be done to enable us to stand heart to heart, mind to mind, shoulder to shoulder. This lack of love and confidence in one another weakens our faith in God.

We need to pray as we never have prayed before for the baptism of the Holy Spirit, for if there was ever a time when we needed this baptism, it is now. There is nothing the Lord has more frequently told us He would bestow upon us, and nothing by which His name would be more glorified in bestowing, than the Holy Spirit. When we partake of this Spirit, men and women will be born again. . . . Souls once lost will be found, and brought back.

THE MEANING OF
CHRISTIAN PERFECTION

I can do all things through Christ which strengtheneth me. **Phil. 4:13.**

What does God require? Perfection; nothing less than perfection. But if we would be perfect, we must put no confidence in self. Daily we must know and understand that self is not to be trusted. We need to grasp God's promises with firm faith. We need to ask for the Holy Spirit with a full realization of our own helplessness. Then when the Holy Spirit works, we shall not give self the glory. The Holy Spirit will graciously take the heart into His keeping, bringing to it all the bright beams of the Sun of Righteousness. We shall be kept by the power of God through faith.

When we are daily under the control of God's Spirit, we shall be commandment-keeping people. We may show to the world that obedience to God's commands brings its own reward, even in this life, and in the future life eternal blessedness. Notwithstanding our profession of faith, the Lord by whom our actions are weighed sees but an imperfect representation of Christ. He has declared that such a condition of things cannot glorify Him.

It means much to commit the keeping of the soul to God. It means that we are to live and walk by faith, not trusting in or glorifying self, but looking to Jesus our Advocate as the Author and Finisher of our faith. The Holy Spirit will do its work upon a heart that is contrite, but never can He work upon a self-important, self-righteous soul. In his own wisdom such a one would mend himself. He interposes between his soul and the Holy Spirit. The Holy Spirit will work if self will not interpose. . . .

The Holy Spirit is ready to cooperate with all who will receive Him and be taught by Him. All who lay hold on the truth and are sanctified through the truth are so united with Christ that they can represent Him in word and action. . . . May the Holy Spirit speak to the hearts of God's chosen people, that their words may be as choice as gold as they give the bread of life to those in transgression and sin. . . .

It is God's pleasure and will that the blessings bestowed on man shall be given in perfect completeness. He has made provision that every difficulty may be overcome, every want supplied through the Holy Spirit. Thus He designs that man shall perfect a Christian character. God would have us contemplate His love, His promises, given so freely to those who have no merit in themselves. He would have us depend fully, gratefully, rejoicingly in the righteousness provided for us in Christ. To all who come to God in His appointed way, He freely listens.

SHINE WITH
LIVING BRIGHTNESS

And they shall be mine, saith the Lord of hosts, in that day when I make up my jewels; and I will spare them, as a man spareth his own son that serveth him. **Mal. 3:17.**

Christians are Christ's jewels, bought with an infinite price. They are to shine brightly for Him, shedding forth the light of His loveliness. And ever they are to remember that all the luster that Christian character possesses is received from the Sun of Righteousness.

The luster of Christ's jewels depends on the polishing that they receive. God does not compel us to be polished. We are left free to choose to be polished or to remain unpolished. But everyone who is pronounced worthy of a place in the Lord's temple must submit to the polishing process. He must consent to have the sharp edges cut away from his character, that it may be shapely and beautiful, fitted to represent the perfection of Christ's character. . . .

The divine Worker spends little time on worthless material. Only the precious jewels does He polish after the similitude of a palace. With hammer and chisel He cuts away the rough edges, preparing us for a place in God's temple. The process is severe and trying. It hurts human pride. Christ cuts deep into the experience that man in his self-sufficiency regarded as complete, and takes away self-uplifting from the character. He cuts away the surplus surface, and putting the stone to the polishing wheel, presses it close, that all roughness may be worn off. Then holding the jewel up to the light the Master sees in it a reflection of His own image, and it is pronounced worthy of a place in His temple.

Blessed be the experience, however severe, that gives new value to the stone, enabling it to shine with living brightness!

[The Lord] has workers whom He will call forth from poverty and obscurity. Engaged in the common duties of life, and clothed with coarse raiment, they are looked upon by men as of little value. But Christ sees in them infinite possibilities, and in His hands they will become precious jewels, to shine brightly in the kingdom of God. "They shall be mine, saith the Lord of Host, in that day when I make up my jewels" (Mal. 3:17).

Christ's perfect knowledge of human character fits Him to deal with minds. God knows just how to treat each soul. He judges not as man judges. He knows the real value of the material upon which He is working in fitting men and women for positions of trust.

WE ARE OBJECTS OF
INFINITE LOVE

But God, who is rich in mercy, for his great love wherewith he loved us, even when we were dead in sins, hath quickened us together with Christ. **Eph. 2:4, 5.**

The heart surrendered to God's wise discipline will trust every working out of His providence. . . . Temptation will come to discourage, but what is gained by yielding to any such temptations? Is the soul made any better by murmuring and complaining of its only source of strength? Is the anchor cast within the vail. Will it hold in sickness? Will it be the testimony borne in the last closing scenes of life when the lips are becoming palsied with death? The anchor holds! I know that my Redeemer liveth. . . .

O Precious, loving, long-suffering, long-forbearing Jesus, how my soul adores Thee! That a poor, unworthy, sin-polluted soul can stand before the Holy God, complete in the righteousness of our Substitute and Surety! Wonder, O Heavens, and be astonished, O earth, that fallen man is the object of His infinite love and delight. He rejoices over them with celestial songs, and man defiled with sin, having become cleansed through the righteousness of Christ, is presented to the Father free from every spot and stain of sin, "not having spot, or wrinkle, or any such thing" (Eph. 5:27). "Who shall lay any thing to the charge of God's elect? It is God that justifieth" (Rom. 8:33).

Let every weak, tempest-tossed soul find anchorage in Jesus Christ and not become so self-centered that he can think only of his little disappointments and the interruption of his plans and hopes. Is not the subject of the plan of salvation all-absorbing? If the infinite God justifies me, "who is he that condemneth? It is Christ that died" (verse 34). He has in His dying for man revealed how much He loves man—enough to die for him! The law condemns the sinner and drives him to Christ. It is God that justifies and pardons.

Satan will accuse and seek permission to destroy, but it is God that opens the door of refuge. It is God that justifieth him that entereth that door. Then if God be for us, who can be against us? Oh, the bright glorious truth. Why do not men discern it? Why not walk in its bright beams? Why do not all who believe talk of Christ's matchless love? . . .

God lives and reigns. All who are saved must fight manfully as soldiers of Jesus Christ; then they will be registered in heaven's books as true and faithful. They are to work the works of Jesus Christ, fight the good fight of faith.

CHRIST'S COMPASSION KNEW NO LIMIT

This was to fulfil what was spoken by the prophet Isaiah, "He took our infirmities and bore our diseases." Matt. 8:17, RSV.

Our Lord Jesus Christ came to this world as the unwearied servant of man's necessity. He "took our infirmities, and bare our sicknesses," that He might minister to every need of humanity. The burden of disease and wretchedness and sin He came to remove. It was His mission to bring to man complete restoration; He came to give them health and peace and perfection of character.

Varied were the circumstances and needs of those who besought His aid, and none who came to Him went away unhelped. From Him flowed a stream of healing power, and in body and mind and soul men were made whole.

The Saviour's work was not restricted to any time or place. His compassion knew no limit. On so large a scale did He conduct His work of healing and teaching that there was no building in Palestine large enough to receive the multitudes that thronged to Him. On the green hill slopes of Galilee, in the thoroughfares of travel, by the seashore, in the synagogues, and in every place where the sick could be brought to Him was to be found His hospital. In every city, every town, every village through which He passed, He laid His hands upon the afflicted ones, and healed them. Wherever there were hearts ready to receive His message, He comforted them with the assurance of their heavenly Father's love. All day He ministered to those who came to Him; in the evening He gave attention to such as through the day must toil to earn a pittance for the support of their families.

Jesus carried the awful weight of responsibility for the salvation of men. He knew that unless there was a decided change in the principles and purposes of the human race, all would be lost. This was the burden of His soul, and none could appreciate the weight that rested upon Him. Through childhood, youth, and manhood, He walked alone. . . .

Day by day He met trials and temptations; day by day He was brought into contact with evil, and witnessed its power upon those whom He was seeking to bless and to save. Yet He did not fail nor become discouraged.
. . .

He was always patient and cheerful, and the afflicted hailed Him as a messenger of life and peace. He saw the needs of men and women, children and youth, and to all He gave the invitation, "Come unto me."
. . .

As He passed through the towns and cities, He was like a vital current, diffusing life and joy.

CHRIST A PERFECT EXAMPLE FOR ALL

And Jesus increased in wisdom and stature, and in favour with God and man. **Luke 2:52.**

Man has fallen. God's image in him is defaced. By disobedience he is depraved in inclination and weakened in power, unable, apparently, to look forward to anything but tribulation and wrath. But God, through Christ, has wrought out a way of escape, and He says to everyone, "Be ye therefore perfect." It is His purpose that man shall stand before Him upright and noble, and He will not be defeated. He sent His Son to this world to bear the penalty of sin, and to show man how to live a sinless life.

Christ is our ideal. He has left a perfect example for childhood, youth, and manhood. He came to this earth, and passed through the different phases of human experience. In His life sin found no place. From the beginning to the close of His earthly life, He preserved unsullied His loyalty to God. The Word says of Him, "The child grew, and waxed strong in spirit, filled with wisdom: and the grace of God was upon Him." He "increased in wisdom and stature, and in favour with God and man."

The Saviour lived not to please Himself. . . . He had no home in this world, only as the kindness of His friends provided Him one, yet it was heaven to be in His presence. Day by day He met trials and temptations, yet He did not fail or become discouraged. He was always patient and cheerful, and the afflicted hailed Him as a messenger of life and peace and health. His life held nothing that was not pure and noble. . . .

God's promise is, "Ye shall be holy; for I am holy." Holiness is the reflection of God's glory. But in order to reflect this glory, we must cooperate with God. Heart and mind must be emptied of all that leads to wrong. The Word of God must be read and studied with a sincere desire to gain from it spiritual strength. This Word is the Bread of heaven. Those who receive it, and make it a part of their lives, grow strong in the strength of God. Our sanctification is God's object in all His dealing with us. He has chosen us from eternity, that we may be holy. Christ declares, "This is the will of God, even your sanctification." Is it your will, also, that your desires and inclinations shall be brought into conformity to the divine will? . . .

Living the life of the Saviour, overcoming every selfish desire, fulfilling bravely and cheerfully our duty to God and to those around us—this makes us more than conquerors. This prepares us to stand before the great white throne free from spot or wrinkle, having washed our robes of character, and made them white in the blood of the lamb.

JESUS PROVIDED A MODEL OF CHARACTER

For ye are dead, and your life is hid with Christ in God. When Christ who is our life, shall appear, then shall ye also appear with him in glory. **Col. 3:3, 4.**

Let your light shine forth in good works. Said Christ, "Ye are the salt of the earth: but if the salt have lost his savour, wherewith shall it be salted? it is thenceforth good for nothing, but to be cast out, and to be trodden under foot of men." I fear that there are many who are in this condition. All have not the same work to do; different circumstances and talents qualify individuals for different kinds of work in God's vineyard. There are some who fill more responsible positions than do others; but to each one is given his work, and if he does his work with fidelity and zeal, he is a faithful steward of the grace of God.

God does not intend that your light shall so shine that your good words or works shall bring the praise of men to yourself; but that the Author of all good shall be glorified and exalted. Jesus, in His life, gave to men a model of character. How little power did the world have over Him to mold Him according to its standard! All its influence was thrown off. He declared, "My meat is to do the will of him that sent me, and to finish his work!" If we had this devotion to the work of God, doing it with an eye single to His glory, we should be able to say with Christ, "I seek not mine own glory." His life was full of good works, and it is our duty to live as our great Example lived. Our life must be hid with Christ in God, and then the light will be reflected from Jesus to us, and we shall reflect it upon those around us, not in mere talk and profession, but in good works, and by manifesting the character of Christ. Those who are reflecting the light of God will cherish a loving disposition. They will be cheerful, willing, obedient to all the requirements of God. They will be meek and self-sacrificing, and will work with devoted love for the salvation of souls. . . .

All who are true lightbearers will reflect light upon the pathway of others. Let those who have named the name of Christ, depart from all iniquity. If you yield to the claims of God, and become permeated with His love, and filled with His fullness, children, youth, and young disciples will look to you for their impressions of what constitutes practical godliness; and you may thus be the means of leading them in the path of obedience to God. You will then be exerting an influence which will bear the test of God, and your work will be compared to gold, silver, and precious stones, for it will be of an imperishable nature.

TRUE FOLLOWERS OBEY GOD'S LAW

Sin is the transgression of the law. **1 John 3:4.**

The desire for an easy religion that requires no striving, no self-denial, no divorce from the follies of the world, has made the doctrine of faith, and faith only, a popular doctrine; but what saith the Word of God? Says the apostle James: "What doth it profit, my brethren, though a man say he hath faith, and have not works? can faith save him? . . . Wilt thou know, O vain man, that faith without works is dead? Was not Abraham our father justified by works, when he had offered Isaac his son upon the altar? Seest thou how faith wrought with his works, and by works was faith made perfect? . . . Ye see then how that by works a man is justified, and not by faith only" (James 2:14-24).

The testimony of the Word of God is against this ensnaring doctrine of faith without works. It is not faith that claims the favor of Heaven without complying with the conditions upon which mercy is to be granted, it is presumption; for genuine faith has its foundation in the promises and provisions of the Scriptures. . . .

The commission of a known sin silences the witnessing voice of the spirit and separates the soul from God. "Sin is the transgression of the law." And "whosoever sinneth [transgresseth the law] hath not seen him, neither known him" (1 John 3:6). Though John in his Epistles dwells so fully upon love, yet he does not hesitate to reveal the true character of that class who claim to be sanctified while living in transgression of the law of God. "He that saith, I know him, and keepeth not his commandments, is a liar, and the truth is not in him. But whoso keepeth his word, in him verily is the love of God perfected" (chap. 2:4, 5).

Here is the test of every man's profession. We cannot accord holiness to any man without bringing him to the measurement of God's only standard of holiness in heaven and in earth. If men feel no weight of the moral law, if they belittle and make light of God's precepts, if they break one of the least of these commandments, and teach men so, they shall be of no esteem in the sight of Heaven, and we may know that their claims are without foundation.

And the claim to be without sin is, in itself, evidence that he who makes this claim is far from holy. It is because he has no true conception of the infinite purity and holiness of God or of what they must become who shall be in harmony with His character; because he has not true conception of the purity and exalted loveliness of Jesus, and the malignity and evil of sin, that man can regard himself as holy.

It was the righteousness revealed in His [Christ's] life that distinguished Him from the world.

HOW WE MAY KEEP GOD'S LAW

His work is honourable and glorious: and his righteousness endureth for ever. Ps. 111:3.

One ray of the glory of God, one gleam of the purity of Christ, penetrating the soul, makes every spot of defilement painfully distinct, and lays bare the deformity and defects of the human character. How can anyone who is brought before the holy standard of God's law, which makes apparent the evil motives, the unhallowed desires, the infidelity of the heart, the impurity of the lips, and that lays bare the life, make any boast of holiness? His acts of disloyalty in making void the law of God are exposed to his sight, and his spirit is stricken and afflicted under the searching influences of the Spirit of God. He loathes himself as he views the greatness, the majesty, the pure and spotless character of Jesus Christ.

When the Spirit of Christ stirs the heart with its marvelous awakening power, there is a sense of deficiency in the soul, that leads to contrition of mind, and humiliation of self, rather than to proud boasting of what has been acquired. When Daniel beheld the glory and majesty surrounding the heavenly messenger that was sent unto him, he exclaimed, as he described the wonderful scene, "Therefore I was left alone, and saw this great vision, and there remained no strength in me: for my comeliness was turned in me into corruption, and I retained no strength."

The soul that is thus touched will never wrap itself about with self-righteousness, or a pretentious garb of holiness; but will hate its selfishness, abhor its self-love, and will seek, through Christ's righteousness, for that purity of heart which is in harmony with the law of God and the character of Christ. He will then reflect the character of Christ, the hope of glory. It will be the greatest mystery to him that Jesus should have made so great a sacrifice to redeem him.

He will exclaim, with humble mien and quivering lip, "He loved me. He gave Himself for me. He became poor that I, through His poverty, might be made rich. The Man of Sorrows did not spurn me, but poured out His inexhaustible, redeeming love that my heart might be made clean; and He has brought me back into loyalty and obedience to all His commandments. His condescension, His humiliation, His crucifixion, are the crowning miracles in the marvelous exhibition of the plan of salvation. . . . All this He has done to make it possible to impart to me His own righteousness, that I may keep the law I have transgressed. For this I adore Him. I will proclaim Him to all sinners.''

THE REPENTANT SINNER ACCEPTED IN CHRIST

For Christ is not entered into the holy places made with hands, which are the figures of the true; but into heaven itself, now to appear in the presence of God for us. **Heb. 9:24.**

Christ is our sacrifice, our substitute, our surety, our divine intercessor; He is made unto us righteousness, sanctification, and redemption. ''For Christ is not entered into the holy places made with hands, which are the figures of the true; but into heaven itself, now to appear in the presence of God for us.''

The intercession of Christ in our behalf is that of presenting His divine merits in the offering of Himself to the Father as our substitute and surety; for He ascended up on high to make an atonement for our transgressions. . . . ''Herein is love, not that we loved God, but that he loved us, and sent his Son to be the propitiation for our sins'' (1 John 4:10). ''He is able also to save them to the uttermost that come unto God by him, seeing he ever liveth to make intercession for them'' (Heb. 7:25).

From these scriptures it is evident that it is not God's will that you should be distrustful, and torture your soul with the fear that God will not accept you because you are sinful and unworthy. . . . Present your case before Him, pleading the merits of the blood shed for you upon Calvary's cross. Satan will accuse you of being a great sinner, and you must admit this, but you can say: ''I know I am a sinner, and that is the reason I need a Saviour. Jesus came into the world to save sinners. 'The blood of Jesus Christ his Son cleanseth us from all sin.' . . . I have no merit or goodness whereby I may claim salvation, but I present before God the all-atoning blood of the spotless Lamb of God, which taketh away the sin of the world. This is my only plea. The name of Jesus gives me access to the Father. His ear, His heart, is open to my faintest pleading, and He supplies my deepest necessities.''

It is the righteousness of Christ that makes the penitent sinner acceptable to God and works his justification. However sinful has been his life, if he believes in Jesus as his personal Saviour, he stands before God in the spotless robes of Christ's imputed righteousness.

The sinner so recently dead in trespasses and sins is quickened by faith in Christ. He sees by faith that Jesus is his Saviour, and alive forevermore, able to save unto the uttermost all that come unto God by Him. In the atonement made for him the believer sees such breadth, and length, and height, and depth of efficiency, sees such completeness of salvation, purchased at such an infinite cost, that his soul is filled with praise and thanksgiving.

JUSTIFIED SOULS WALK IN THE LIGHT

God presented him [Christ Jesus] as a sacrifice of atonement, through faith in his blood. . . . He did it to demonstrate his justice at the present time, so as to be just and the one who justifies the man who has faith in Jesus. **Rom. 3:25, 26, NIV.**

"Being justified freely by his grace," the apostle Paul says, "through the redemption that is in Christ Jesus: whom God hath set forth to be a propitiation through faith in his blood, to declare his righteousness for the remission of sins that are past, through the forbearance of God; to declare, I say, at this time his righteousness: that he might be just, and the justifier of him which believeth in Jesus."

Here the truth is laid out in plain lines. This mercy and goodness is wholly undeserved. The grace of Christ is freely to justify the sinner without merit or claim on his part. Justification is a full, complete pardon of sin. The moment a sinner accepts Christ by faith, that moment he is pardoned. The righteousness of Christ is imputed to him, and he is not more to doubt God's forgiving grace.

There is nothing in faith that makes it our saviour. Faith cannot remove our guilt. Christ is the power of God unto salvation to all them that believe. The justification comes through the merits of Jesus Christ. He has paid the price for the sinner's redemption. Yet it is only through faith in His blood that Jesus can justify the believer.

The sinner cannot depend upon his own good works as a means of justification. He must come to the point where he will renounce all his sin, and embrace one degree of light after another, as it shines upon his pathway. He simply grasps by faith the free and ample provision made in the blood of Christ. He believes the promises of God which through Christ are made unto him sanctification and righteousness and redemption.

And if he follows Jesus, he will walk humbly in the light, rejoicing in the light, and diffusing that light to others. Being justified by faith, he carries cheerfulness with him in his obedience in all his life. Peace with God is the result of what Christ is to him. The souls who are in subordination to God, who honor Him, and are doers of His Word, will receive divine enlightenment. In the precious Word of God, there is purity and loftiness as well as beauty that, unless assisted by God, the highest powers of man cannot attain to. . . .

We are none of us excusable, under any form of trial, for letting our hold upon God become loosened. Although the compassion of man may fail, still God loves and pities, and reaches out His helping hand. God's everlasting arms encircle the soul that turns to Him for aid. . . . God loves to have His children ask Him, and trust Him to do for them those things which they cannot do for themselves.

SANCTIFIED BY FAITH AND OBEDIENCE

Herein is my Father glorified, that ye bear much fruit; so shall ye be my disciples. **John 15:8.**

Many shrink from such a life as our Saviour lived. They feel that it requires too great a sacrifice to imitate the Pattern, to bring forth fruit in good works, and then patiently endure the pruning of God that they may bring forth more fruit. But when the Christian regards himself as only a humble instrument in the hands of Christ, and endeavors to faithfully perform every duty, relying upon the help which God has promised, then he will wear the yoke of Christ and find it easy; then he will bear burdens for Christ, and pronounce them light. He can look up with courage and with confidence, and say, "I know whom I have believed, and am persuaded that he is able to keep that which I have committed unto him" (2 Tim. 1:12).

If we meet obstacles in our path, and faithfully overcome them; if we encounter opposition and reproach, and in Christ's name gain the victory; if we bear responsibilities and discharge our duties in the spirit of our Master—then, indeed, we gain a precious knowledge of His faithfulness and power. We no longer depend upon the experience of others, for we have the witness in ourselves. Like the Samaritans of old, we can say, "We have heard him ourselves, and know that this is indeed the Christ, the Saviour of the world" (John 4:42).

The more we contemplate the character of Christ, and the more we experience of His saving power, the more keenly shall we realize our own weakness and imperfection, and the more earnestly shall we look to Him as our strength and our Redeemer. . . . By faith in Christ and obedience to the law of God we may be sanctified, and thus obtain a fitness for the society of holy angels and the white-robed redeemed ones in the kingdom of glory.

It is not only the privilege but the duty of every Christian to maintain a close union with Christ and to have a rich experience in the things of God. Then his life will be fruitful in good works. . . .

When we read the lives of men who have been eminent for their piety we often regard their experiences and attainments as far beyond our reach. But this is not the case. Christ died for all; and we are assured in His Word that He is more willing to give His Holy Spirit to them that ask than are earthly parents to give good gifts to their children.

The prophets and apostles did not perfect Christian character by a miracle. They used the means which God had placed within their reach; and all who will put forth the same effort will secure the same results.

A FAITH THAT WORKS

Trust in the Lord with all thine heart; and lean not unto thine own understanding. **Prov. 3:5.**

When we speak of faith, there is a distinction that should be borne in mind. There is a kind of belief that is wholly distinct from faith. The existence and power of God, the truth of His Word, are facts that even Satan and his hosts cannot at heart deny. The Bible says that "the devils also believe, and tremble" (James 2:19); but this is not faith. Where there is not only a belief in God's Word, but a submission of the will of Him; where the heart is yielded to Him, the affections fixed upon Him, there is faith—faith that works by love and purifies the soul.

Through this faith the heart is renewed in the image of God. And the heart that in its unrenewed state is not subject to the law of God, neither indeed can be, now delights in its holy precepts, exclaiming with the psalmist, "O how love I thy law! it is my meditation all the day" (Ps. 119:97). And the righteousness of the law is fulfilled in us, "who walk not after the flesh, but after the Spirit" (Rom. 8:1).

There are those who have known the pardoning love of Christ and who really desire to be children of God, yet they realize that their character is imperfect, their life faulty, and they are ready to doubt whether their hearts have been renewed by the Holy Spirit. To such I would say, Do not draw back in despair. We shall often have to bow down and weep at the feet of Jesus because of our shortcomings and mistakes, but we are not to be discouraged. Even if we are overcome by the enemy, we are not cast off, not forsaken and rejected of God. No; Christ is at the right hand of God, who also maketh intercession for us. Said the beloved John, "These things write I unto you, that ye sin not. And if any man sin, we have an advocate with the Father, Jesus Christ the righteous" (1 John 2:1).

And do not forget the words of Christ, "the Father himself loveth you" (1 John 16:27). He desires to restore you to Himself, to see His own purity and holiness reflected in you. And if you will but yield yourself to Him, He that hath begun a good work in you will carry it forward to the day of Jesus Christ. Pray more fervently; believe more fully. . . .

The less we see to esteem in ourselves, the more we shall see to esteem in the infinite purity and loveliness of our Saviour. A view of our sinfulness drives us to Him who can pardon; and when the soul, realizing its helplessness, reaches out after Christ, He will reveal Himself in power. The more our sense of need drives us to Him and to the Word of God, the more exalted views we shall have of His character, and the more fully we shall reflect His image.

TRUE RELIGION PROMOTES HEALTH

[Wisdom's] ways are ways of pleasantness, and all her paths are peace. Prov. 3:17.

This world is not all sorrow and misery. "God is love" is written upon every opening bud, upon the petals of every flower, and upon every spire of grass. Though the curse of sin has caused the earth to bring forth thorns and thistles, there are flowers upon the thistles and the thorns are hidden by roses. All things in nature testify to the tender, fatherly care of our God and to His desire to make His children happy. His prohibitions and injunctions are not intended merely to display His authority, but in all that He does He has the well-being of His children in view. He does not require them to give up anything that it would be for their best interest to retain.

The opinion which prevails in some classes of society, that religion is not conducive to health or to happiness in this life, is one of the most mischievous of errors. The Scripture says: "The fear of the Lord tendeth to life: and he that hath it shall abide satisfied" (Prov. 19:23). "What man is he that desireth life, and loveth many days, that he may see good? Keep thy tongue from evil, and thy lips from speaking guile. Depart from evil, and do good; seek peace, and pursue it" (Ps. 34:12-14). The words of wisdom "are life unto those that find them, and health to all their flesh" (Prov. 4:22).

True religion brings man into harmony with the laws of God, physical, mental, and moral. It teaches self-control, serenity, temperance. Religion ennobles the mind, refines the taste, and sanctifies the judgment. It makes the soul a partaker of the purity of heaven. Faith in God's love and overruling providence lightens the burdens of anxiety and care. It fills the heart with joy and contentment in the highest or the lowliest lot. Religion tends directly to promote health, to lengthen life, and to heighten our enjoyment of all its blessings. It opens to the soul a never-failing fountain of happiness. Would that all who have not chosen Christ might realize that He has something vastly better to offer them than they are seeking for themselves. . . .

There is an intimate relation between the mind and the body, and in order to reach a high standard of moral and intellectual attainment the laws that control our physical being must be heeded. To secure a strong, well-balanced character, both the mental and the physical powers must be exercised and developed. What study can be more important . . . than that which treats of this wonderful organism that God has committed to us, and of the laws by which it may be preserved in health?

ENLIGHTENED TO FULL RADIANCE

If we follow on to know the Lord: his going forth is prepared as the morning. **Hosea 6:3.**

We are living amid the perils of the last days, and we are to cleanse ourselves from all defilement, and put on the robe of Christ's righteousness. The work of God is to be steadily carried forward. We are to bring ourselves, body, soul, and spirit, into subjection to Christ. Unless we do this, the health of both body and soul will be endangered.

God desires His workers to gain daily an understanding of how to reason logically from cause to effect, arriving at wise, safe conclusions. He desires them to add to the strength of the memory. We cannot afford to make mistakes. As little children we are to sit at the feet of Christ, learning of Him how to work successfully. We are to ask God for sound judgment, and for light to impart to others. There is need of knowledge that is the fruit of experience. We should not allow a day to pass without gaining an increase of knowledge in temporal and spiritual things. We are to plant no stakes that we are not willing to take up and plant farther on, nearer the heights we hope to ascend.

The highest education is to be found in training the mind to advance day to day. The close of each day should find us a day's march nearer the overcomer's reward. Day by day our understanding is to ripen. Day by day we are to work out conclusions that will bring a rich reward in this life, and in the life to come. Looking daily to Jesus, instead of to what we ourselves have done, we shall make decided advancement in temporal as well as spiritual knowledge.

The end of all things is at hand. What we have done must not be allowed to place the period to our work. The Captain of our salvation says,

"Advance. The night cometh, in which no man can work." Constantly we are to increase in usefulness. Our lives are always to be under the power of Christ. Our lamps are to be kept burning brightly.

Prayer is a heaven-ordained means of success. Appeals, petitions, entreaties, between man and man, move men, and act as a part in controlling the affairs of nations. But prayer moves heaven. That power alone that comes in answer to prayer will make men wise in the wisdom of heaven, and enable them to work in the unity of the Spirit, joined together by the bonds of peace. Prayer, faith, confidence in God, bring a divine power that sets human calculations at their real worth—nothingness. . . .

He who places himself where God can enlighten him advances, as it were, from the partial obscurity of dawn to the full radiance of noonday.

THE TEMPLE OF GOD

He died for all, that they which live should not henceforth live unto themselves, but unto him which died for them, and rose again. **2 Cor. 5:15.**

Man is God's workmanship, His masterpiece, created for a high and holy purpose; and on every part of the human tabernacle God desires to write His law. Every nerve and muscle, every mental and physical endowment, is to be kept pure.

God designs that the body shall be a temple for His Spirit. How solemn then is the responsibility resting on every soul. If we defile our bodies, we are doing harm not only to ourselves, but to many others. . . .

Christ died that the moral image of God might be restored in humanity, that men and women might be partakers of the divine nature, having escaped the corruption that is in the world through lust. We are to use no power of our being for selfish gratification; for all our powers belong to Him, and are to be used to His glory. . . .

The human house, God's building, requires close, watchful guardianship. With David we can exclaim, "I am fearfully and wonderfully made." God's workmanship is to be preserved, that the heavenly universe and the apostate race may see that men and women are temples of the living God.

The perfection of character which God requires is the fitting up of the whole being as a temple for the indwelling of the Holy Spirit. The Lord requires the service of the entire being. He desires men and women to become all that He has made it possible for them to be. It is not enough for certain parts of the human machinery to be used. All parts must be brought into action, or the service is deficient. . . .

The physical life is to be carefully educated, cultivated, and developed, that through men and women the divine nature may be revealed in its fullness. God expects men to use the intellect He has given them. He expects them to use every reasoning power for Him. They are to give the conscience the place of supremacy that has been assigned to it. The mental and physical powers, with the affections, are to be so cultivated that they can reach the highest efficiency. Thus Christ is represented to the world. . . .

Is God pleased to see any of the organs or faculties He has given man neglected, misused, or deprived of the health and efficiency it is possible for them to have? Then cultivate the gift of faith. Be brave, and overcome every practice which mars the soul temple. We are wholly dependent on God, and our faith is strengthened by believing, though we cannot see God's purpose in His dealing with us, or the consequence of this dealing. Faith points forward and upward to things to come, laying hold of the only power that can make us complete in Him.

AN ARGUMENT
INFIDELS CANNOT RESIST

While ye have light, believe in the light, that ye may be the children of light. **John 12:36.**

A well-ordered Christian household is an argument that the infidel cannot resist. He finds no place for his cavils [trivial faultfinding]. And the children of such a household are prepared to meet the sophistries of infidelity. They have accepted the Bible as the basis of their faith, and they have a firm foundation that cannot be swept away by the incoming tide of skepticism.

Said Christ, "Ye are the light of the world." He has committed talents to our keeping. What are we doing with His entrusted gifts? Are we letting our lights shine by using them for His glory and the benefit of our fellow men, or are we using them to advance our own selfish interests? Many are using them selfishly. They do not seem to realize that we are all judgment-bound, and must soon give an account for the use we have made of our God-given opportunities to do good. But what excuse will they give in that great day for not using in the cause of God their skill, their education, their tact, and their perseverance and zeal?

We need divine help if we would keep our lights burning. But Jesus died to provide that aid. He extends the invitation: "Let him take hold of my strength, that he may make peace with me; and he shall make peace with me." Cling to the arm of Infinite Power; then you will find Him precious to your soul, and all heaven will be at your command. "If we walk in the light, as he is in the light," we shall have the companionship of holy angels. To "Joshua" it was said, "Thus saith the Lord of hosts: If thou wilt walk in my ways, and if thou wilt keep my charge, . . . I will give thee places to walk among these that stand by." And who are "these that stand by"? They are the angels of God. Joshua must have a living, confiding trust in God every day; and then angels would walk with him, and the power of God would rest upon him in all his labors.

Then, Christian friends, fathers and mothers, let your light grow dim—no, never! Let your heart grow faint, or your hands weary—no, never! And by and by the portals of the celestial city will be opened to you; and you may present yourselves and your children before the throne, saying, "Here am I, and the children whom Thou hast given me." And what a reward for faithfulness that will be, to see your children crowned with immortal life in the beautiful city of God!

Reflecting Christ   November 14

FAMILY WORSHIP
NOT TO BE NEGLECTED

Trust . . . in the living God, who giveth us richly all things to enjoy. **1 Tim. 6:17.**

We should be much happier and more useful, if our homelife and social intercourse were governed by the principles of the Christian religion, and illustrated the meekness and simplicity of Christ. . . . Let visitors see that we try to make all around us happy by our cheerfulness, sympathy, and love.

While we endeavor to secure the comfort and happiness of our guests, let us not overlook our obligation to God. The hour of prayer should not be neglected for any consideration. . . . At an early hour of the evening, when you can pray unhurriedly and understandingly, present your supplication, and raise your voices in happy, grateful praise. Let all who visit Christians see that the hour of prayer is the most sacred, the most precious, and the happiest hour of the day. Such an example will not be without effect.

These seasons of devotion exert a refining, elevating influence upon all who participate in them. Right thoughts and new and better desires will be wakened in the hearts of the most careless. The hour of prayer brings a peace and rest grateful to the weary spirit; for the very atmosphere of a Christian home is that of peace and restfulness.

In every act the Christian should seek to represent his Master, to make His service appear attractive. . . .

Nine tenths of the trials and perplexities that so many worry over are either imaginary, or brought upon themselves by their own wrong course. They should cease to talk of these trials, and [cease] to magnify them. The Christian may commit every worriment, every disturbing thing to God. Nothing is too small for our compassionate Saviour to notice; nothing is too great for Him to carry.

Then let us set our hearts and homes in order; let us teach our children that the fear of the Lord is the beginning of wisdom; and let us, by a cheerful, happy, well-ordered life, express our gratitude and love to Him "who giveth us richly all things to enjoy." But above all things, let us fix our thoughts and the affections of our hearts on the dear Saviour who suffered for guilty man, and thus opened heaven for us.

Love to Jesus cannot be hidden, but will make itself seen and felt. It exerts a wondrous power. It makes the timid bold, the slothful diligent, the ignorant wise. It makes the stammering tongue eloquent, and rouses the dormant intellect into new life and vigor. It makes the desponding hopeful, the gloomy joyous. Love to Christ will lead its possessor to accept responsibilities and cares for His sake, and to bear them in His strength.

FAMILIES TO REFLECT
THE GOODNESS OF GOD

As the father has compassion on his children, so the Lord has compassion on those that fear him. **Ps. 103:13, NIV.**

Bring the sunshine of heaven into your conversation. By speaking words that encourage and cheer, you will reveal that the sunshine of Christ's righteousness dwells in your soul. Children need pleasant words. It is essential to their happiness to feel approval resting upon them. Strive to overcome harshness of expression, and cultivate soft tones. Catch the beauty contained in the lessons of God's Word, and cherish this as essential to the happiness and success of your homelife. In a happy environment the children will develop dispositions that are sweet and sunshiny.

True beauty of character is not something that shines out only on special occasions; the grace of Christ dwelling in the soul is revealed under all circumstances. He who cherishes this grace as an abiding presence in the life will reveal beauty in character under trying as well as under easy circumstances. In the home, in the world, in the church, we are to live the life of Christ. There are souls all around in need of conversion. When the law of God is written upon the heart, and is witnessed to in a holy character, those who know not the power of the grace of Christ will be led to desire it, and will be converted.

A solemn review is now taking place in the courts above. The thought of the decisions now being made in heaven should urge parents to diligence in training their children in the fear and love of God. Not by severe words and punishment for wrongdoing will the most be accomplished, but by watchfulness and prayer, lest they be taken by the snares of the enemy. . . .

Every family that has a knowledge of the truth for this time, is to make it known to others. The Lord's people are to get ready for the doing of a special work. The children as well as the older members of the family are to act their part in seeking to save those who are perishing. From His youth Christ was, to all with whom He associated, an influence that drew them toward higher things. So the youth today may exert a power for good that will draw souls to God.

Parents need to appreciate more fully the responsibility and honor that God has placed upon them, in making them, to the child, the representative of Himself. The character revealed in the contact of daily life will interpret to the child, for good or for evil, those words of God:

"Like as a father pitieth his children, so the Lord pitieth them that fear him." "As one whom his mother comforteth, so will I comfort you."

BE ONE, AS CHRIST
AND THE FATHER ARE ONE

Now I am no more in the world, but these are in the world, and I come to thee. Holy Father, keep through thine own name those whom thou hast given me, that they may be one, as we are. **John 17:11.**

Where shall we find the purity, goodness, and holiness where we shall be secure? Where is the fold where no wolves will enter? I tell you . . . the Lord has an organized body through whom He will work. There may be more than a score of Judases among them; there may be a rash Peter who will under circumstances of trial deny his Lord; there may be persons represented by John whom Jesus loved, but he may have a zeal that would destroy men's lives by calling down fire from heaven upon them to revenge an insult to Christ and to the truth. But the great Teacher seeks to give lessons of instruction to correct these existing evils. He is doing the same today with His church. He is pointing out their dangers. He is presenting before them the Laodicean message.

He shows them that all selfishness, all pride, all self-exaltation, all unbelief and prejudice, which lead to resistance of the truth and turn away from the true light, are dangerous, and unless repented of, those who cherish these things will be left in darkness as was the Jewish nation. Let every soul now seek to answer the prayer of Christ. Let every soul echo that prayer in mind, in petitions, in exhortations, that they all may be one even as Christ is one with the Father, and work to this end. In the place of turning the weapons of warfare within our own ranks, let them be turned against the enemies of God and the truth. Echo the prayer of Christ with your whole heart: "Holy Father, keep through thine own name those whom thou hast given me, that they may be one, as we are. I pray not that thou shouldest take them out of the world, but that thou shouldest keep them from the evil" (John 17:11-15). . . .

The door of the heart must be opened to the Holy Spirit, for this is the sanctifier, and the truth is the medium. There must be an acceptance of the truth as it is in Jesus. This is the only genuine sanctification: "Thy word is truth." Oh, read the prayer of Christ for unity, "Keep through thine own name those whom thou hast given me, that they may be one as we are." The prayer of Christ is not only for those who are now His disciples, but for all those who shall believe on Christ through the words of His disciples, even to the end of the world. . . .

The Lord has had a church from that day, through all the changing scenes of time to the present period. . . . The Bible sets before us a model church. They are to be in unity with each other, and with God. When believers are united in Christ the living vine, the result is that they are one with Christ, full of sympathy and tenderness and love.

THE ROUTE TO GREATER
SPIRITUAL LIFE IN THE CHURCH

Marvel not that I said unto thee, Ye must be born again. **John 3:7.**

The question is often asked, Why is there not more power in the church? why not more vital godliness? The reason is, the requirements of God's Word are not complied with in verity and in truth; God is not loved supremely, and our neighbor as ourselves. This covers the entire ground. Upon these two commandments hang all the law and the prophets. Let these two requirements of God be obeyed explicitly, and there would be no discord in the church, no inharmonious notes in the family. With many the work is too superficial. Outward forms take the place of the inner work of grace. . . . The theory of the truth has converted the head, but the soul temple has not been cleansed from its idols. . . .

True conviction of sin, real heart sorrow because of wickedness, death to self, the daily overcoming of defects of character, and the new birth—these, represented as old things, Paul says had passed away, and all things had become new. Such a work many know nothing of. They grafted the truth into their natural hearts, and then went on as before, manifesting the same unhappy traits of character. What is now needed is the plain testimony borne in love from lips touched with living fire.

Church members do not show that living connection with God that they must have in order to win souls from darkness to light. Make the tree good, and good fruit will be the result. The work of the Spirit of God upon the heart is essential to godliness. It must be received into the hearts of those who accept the truth, and create in them clean hearts, before one of them can keep His commandments and be doers of the Word. "Marvel not," said the great Teacher unto the astonished Nicodemus, "Marvel not that I said unto thee, Ye must be born again."

The Bible is not studied as much as it should be; it is not made the rule of life. Were its precepts conscientiously followed, and made the basis of character, there would be steadfastness of purpose that no business speculations or worldly pursuits could seriously influence. A character thus formed, and supported by the Word of God, will abide the day of trial, of difficulties, and dangers. The conscience must be enlightened, and the life sanctified by the love of the truth received into the heart, before the influence will be saving upon the world.

What is needed is men of action for the time, prompt, determined, firm as a rock to principle, and prepared to meet any emergency. Why we are so weak, why there are so many irresponsible men among us, is because they do not connect with God; they have not an indwelling Saviour, and do not feel the love of Christ ever fresh and new. . . . No earthly relationship is as strong as this love. Nothing can compare with it.

REFLECTING LIGHT
FROM THE SUN OF RIGHTEOUSNESS

And we are his witnesses of these things; and so is also the Holy Ghost, whom God hath given to them that obey him. **Acts 5:32.**

God wants every member of the church to stand faithfully at his post of duty, to realize his responsibility, and create a heavenly atmosphere about his soul by continually gathering the bright rays of the Sun of Righteousness to shed upon the pathway of those about him. . . .

We are to be representatives of Christ, as Christ was a representative of the Father. We want to be able to attract souls to Jesus, to point them to the Lamb of Calvary, who taketh away the sin of the world. Christ does not clothe sin with His righteousness, but He removes the sin, and in its place He imputes His own righteousness. When your sin is cleansed, the righteousness of Christ goes before you, and the glory of the Lord is your rearward. Your influence will then be decidedly on the side of Christ; for instead of making self a center, you will make Christ a center, and will feel that you are a guardian of sacred trusts.

When you remember that Christ has paid the price of His own blood for your redemption and for the redemption of others, you will be moved to catch the bright rays of His righteousness, that you may shed them upon the pathway of those around you. You are not to look to the future, thinking that at some distant day you are to be made holy; it is now that you are to be sanctified through the truth. . . . Jesus says, "But ye shall receive power, after that the Holy Ghost is come upon you: and ye shall be witnesses unto me . . . unto the uttermost part of the earth" (Acts 1:8). We are to receive the Holy Ghost. . . . The Holy Spirit is the Comforter that Christ promised to His disciples to bring all things to their remembrance whatsoever He had said unto them.

Then let us cease to look to ourselves, but look to Him from whom all virtue comes. No one can make himself better, but we are to come to Jesus as we are, earnestly desiring to be cleansed from every spot and stain of sin, and receive the gift of the Holy Spirit. . . . By living faith we must lay hold of His promise, for He has said, "Though your sins be as scarlet, they shall be as white as snow; though they be red like crimson, they shall be as wool."

We are to be witnesses for Christ, reflecting upon others the light which the Lord permits to shine upon us. We are to be as faithful soldiers marching under the bloodstained banner of Prince Emmanuel. . . . The Captain of our salvation knows the plan of the battle, and we shall come off more than conquerors through Him.

PRAISE TO GOD
HAS IRRESISTIBLE POWER

They that feared the Lord spake often one to another: and the Lord hearkened, and heard it, and a book of remembrance was written before him for them that feared the Lord, and that thought upon his name. **Mal. 3:16.**

To the Christian is granted the joy of gathering rays of eternal light from the throne of glory, and of reflecting these rays not only on his own path, but on the paths of those with whom he associates. By speaking words of hope and encouragement, of grateful praise and kindly cheer, he may strive to make those around him better, to elevate them, to point them to heaven and glory, and to lead them to seek, above all earthly things, the eternal substance, the immortal inheritance, the riches that are imperishable.

302

"Rejoice in the Lord alway," says the apostle, "and again I say, Rejoice." Wherever we go, we should carry an atmosphere of Christian hopefulness and cheer; then those who are out of Christ will see attractiveness in the religion we profess; unbelievers will see the consistency of our faith. We need to have more distinct glimpses of heaven, the land where all is brightness and joy. We need to know more of the fullness of the blessed hope. If we are constantly "rejoicing in hope," we shall be able to speak words of encouragement to those whom we meet. . . .

Not alone in daily association with believers and unbelievers are we to glorify God by speaking often one to another in words of gratitude and rejoicing. As Christians, we are exhorted not to forsake the assembling of ourselves together, for our own refreshing, and to impart the consolation we have received. In these meetings, held from week to week, we should dwell upon God's goodness and manifold mercies, upon His power to save from sin. In features, in temper, in words, in character, we are to witness that the service of God is good. Thus we proclaim that "the law of the Lord is perfect, converting the soul."

Our prayer and social meetings should be seasons of special help and encouragement. . . . This can best be done by having a fresh experience daily in the things of God, and by not hesitating to speak of His love in the assemblies of His people. . . .

If we thought and talked more of Jesus, and less of ourselves, we should have much more of His presence. If we abide in Him, we shall be so filled with peace, faith, and courage, and shall have so victorious an experience to relate when we come to meeting, that others will be refreshed by our clear, strong testimony for God. These precious acknowledgments to the praise of the glory of His grace, when supported by a Christlike life, have an irresistible power, which works for the salvation of souls.

JESUS WAS A FRIEND
TO EVERY HUMAN BEING

Then said he, Lo, I come to do thy will, O God. **Heb. 10:9.**

Christ's dignity as a divine teacher was of an order higher than the dignity of priests and rulers. It was distinct from all worldly pomp; for it was divine. He dispensed with all worldly display, and showed that He regarded the gradations of society, fixed by opulence and rank, as of no value. He had . . . stepped down from His high command to bring to human beings power to become the sons of God; and earthly rank was not of the least value with Him. He could have brought with Him ten thousand angels if they would have helped Him in His work of redeeming the race.

Christ passed by the homes of the wealthy, the courts of royalty, the renowned seats of learning, and made His home in obscure and despised Nazareth. His life, from its beginning to its close, was a life of lowliness and humility. Poverty was made sacred by His life of poverty. He would not put on a dignity of attitude that would debar men and women, however lowly, from coming into His presence and listening to His teaching. . . .

No teacher ever placed such a signal honor upon man as did our Lord Jesus Christ. He was known as the friend of publicans and sinners. He mingled with all classes, and sowed the world with truth. In the marketplace and the synagogue He proclaimed His message. He relieved every species of suffering, both physical and spiritual. Beside all waters He sowed the seeds of truth. His one desire was that all might have spiritual and physical soundness. He was the friend of every human being. Was He not pledged to bring life and light to all who would receive Him? Was He not pledged to give them power to become the sons of God? He gave Himself wholly and entirely to the work of soul-saving. . . .

As He "went about doing good," every day's experience was an outpouring of His life. In one way only could such a life be sustained. Jesus lived in dependence upon God and communion with Him. To the secret place of the Most High, under the shadow of the Almighty, men now and then repair; they abide for a season, and the result is manifest in noble deeds; then their faith fails, the communion is interrupted, and the lifework marred. But the life of Jesus was a life of constant trust, sustained by continual communion; and His service for heaven and earth was without failure or faltering. As a man He supplicated the throne of God, until His humanity was charged with a heavenly current that connected humanity with divinity. Receiving life from God, He imparted life to men.

ENCOURAGE A SPIRIT
OF KINDLINESS

To speak evil of no one, to avoid quarreling, to be gentle, and to show perfect courtesy toward all men. **Titus 3:2, RSV.**

How many useful and honored workers in God's cause have received a training amid the humble duties of the most lowly positions in life! Moses was the prospective ruler of Egypt, but God could not take him from the king's court to do the work appointed him. Only when he had been for forty years a faithful shepherd was he sent to be the deliverer of his people. Gideon was taken from the threshing-floor to be the instrument in the hands of God for delivering the armies of Israel. Elisha was called to leave the plow and do the bidding of God. Amos was a husbandman, a tiller of the soil, when God gave him a message to proclaim.

All who become coworkers with Christ will have a great deal of hard, uncongenial labor to perform, and their lessons of instruction should be wisely chosen, and adapted to their peculiarities of character, and the work which they are to pursue.

The Lord has presented to me, in many ways and at various times, how carefully we should deal with the young—that it requires the finest discrimination to deal with minds. Everyone who has to do with the education and training of youth needs to live very close to the great Teacher, to catch His spirit and manner of work. Lessons are to be given which will affect their character and lifework.

They should be taught that the gospel of Christ tolerates no spirit of caste, that it gives no place to unkind judgment of others, which tends directly to self-exaltation. The religion of Jesus never degrades the receiver, nor makes him coarse and rough; nor does it make him unkind in thought and feeling toward those for whom Christ died. . . .

Some are in danger of making the externals all-important, of overestimating the value of mere conventionalities. . . .

Anything that would encourage ungenerous criticism, a disposition to notice and expose every defect or error, is wrong. It fosters distrust and suspicion, which are contrary to the character of Christ, and detrimental to the mind thus exercised. Those who are engaged in this work gradually depart from the true spirit of Christianity.

The most essential, enduring education is that which will develop the nobler qualities, which will encourage a spirit of universal kindliness, leading the youth to think no evil of anyone, lest they misjudge motives and misinterpret words and actions. The time devoted to this kind of instruction will yield fruit to everlasting life.

Reflecting Christ   November 22

THE ETERNAL REWARD
OF REACHING OUT

When thou makest a feast, call the poor, the maimed, the lame, the blind: and thou shalt be blessed; for they cannot recompense thee: for thou shalt be recompensed at the resurrection of the just. **Luke 14:13, 14.**

It is the reward of Christ's workers to enter into His joy. That joy, to which Christ Himself looks forward with eager desire, is presented in His request to His Father, "I will that they also, whom thou hast given me, be with me where I am."

The angels were waiting to welcome Jesus, as He ascended after His resurrection. The heavenly host longed to greet again their loved Commander, returned to them from the prison house of death. Eagerly they pressed about Him as He entered the gates of heaven. But He waved them back. His heart was with the lonely, sorrowing band of disciples whom He had left upon Olivet. It is still with His struggling children on earth, who have the battle with the destroyer yet to wage. "Father," He says, "I will that they also, whom thou hast given me, be with me where I am."

Christ's redeemed ones are His jewels, His precious and peculiar treasure. "They shall be as the stones of a crown"—"the riches of the glory of his inheritance in the saints." In them "he shall see the travail of his soul, and shall be satisfied."

And will not His workers rejoice when they, too, behold the fruit of their labors? . . .

Every impulse of the Holy Spirit leading men to goodness and to God is noted in the books of heaven, and in the day of God everyone who has given himself as an instrument for the Holy Spirit's working will be permitted to behold what his life has wrought.

Wonderful will be the revealing as the lines of holy influence, with their precious results, are brought to view. What will be the gratitude of souls that will meet us in the heavenly courts, as they understand the sympathetic, loving interest which has been taken in their salvation! All praise, honor, and glory will be given to God and to the Lamb for our redemption; but it will not detract from the glory of God to express gratitude to the instrumentality He has employed in the salvation of souls ready to perish.

The redeemed will meet and recognize those whose attention they have directed to the uplifted Saviour. What blessed converse they have with these souls! "I was a sinner," it will be said, . . . "and you came to me, and drew my attention to the precious Saviour as my only hope. And I believed in Him." . . . What rejoicing there will be as these redeemed ones meet and greet those who have had a burden in their behalf!

STRICT INTEGRITY
TO MARK THE CHRISTIAN

Thou shalt have a perfect and just weight, a perfect and just measure shalt thou have: that thy days may be lengthened in the land which the Lord thy God giveth thee. **Deut. 25:15.**

In all the details of life, Christians are to follow the principles of strict integrity. These are not the principles that govern the world; for there Satan is master, and his principles of deception and oppression bear sway. But

Christians serve under a different Master, and their actions must be wrought in God. They must put aside all desire for selfish gain.

To some, deviation from perfect fairness in business deal[s] may look like a small thing, but our Saviour does not thus regard it. His words on this point are plain and explicit: "He that is faithful in that which is least is faithful also in much; and he that is unjust in the least is unjust also in much." A man who will overreach in a small matter will overreach in a large matter if the temptation comes to him.

Christ's followers are obliged to be more or less connected with the world in business matters. In His prayer for them the Saviour says, "I pray not that thou shouldest take them out of the world, but that thou shouldest keep them from the evil." Christians are to buy and sell with the realization that the eye of God is upon them. Never are they to use false balances or deceitful weights. . . .

In every action of life the true Christian is just what he desires those around him to think he is. He is guided by truth and uprightness. He does not scheme; therefore he has nothing to gloss over. He may be criticized, he may be tested; but through all, his unbending integrity shines out like pure gold. He is a friend and benefactor to all connected with him; and his fellow men place confidence in him; for he is trustworthy.

Does he employ laborers to gather in his harvest? He does not keep back their hard-earned money. Has he means for which he has no immediate use? He relieves the necessities of his less fortunate brother. He does not seek to enlarge his possessions by taking advantage of the untoward circumstances of his neighbor. He accepts only a fair price for that which he sells. If there are defects in the articles sold, he frankly tells the buyer, even though by so doing he may seem to work against his own pecuniary interests.

A man may not have a pleasant exterior; but if he has a reputation for straightforward, honest dealing, he is respected. . . . A man who steadfastly adheres to the truth wins the confidence of all. Not only do Christians trust him; worldings are constrained to acknowledge the worth of his character.

WE ARE TO REFLECT CHRIST'S LOVE

Then said Jesus to them again, Peace be unto you: as my Father hath sent me, even so send I you. **John 20:21.**

We should earnestly seek to know and appreciate the truth, that we may present it to others as it is in Jesus. We need to have a correct estimate of the value of our own souls; then we would not be as reckless in regard to our course of action as at present. We would seek most earnestly to know God's way; we would work an opposite direction from selfishness, and our constant prayer would be that we might have the mind of Christ, that we might be molded and fashioned after His likeness. It is in looking to Jesus and beholding His loveliness, having our eyes steadfastly fixed upon Him, that we become changed into His image. He will give grace to all that keep His way, and do His will, and walk in truth. . . .

I beseech you whose names are registered on the church book as worthy members, to be indeed worthy, through the virtue of Christ. Mercy and truth and the love of God are promised to the humble and contrite soul. . . .

All heaven is filled with amazement, that when this love, so broad, so deep, so rich and full, is presented to men who have known the grace of our Lord Jesus Christ, they are so indifferent, so cold and unmoved. . . .

The infinite treasures of truth have been accumulating from age to age. No representation could adequately impress us with the extent, the richness, of these vast resources. They are awaiting the demand of those who appreciate them. These gems of truth are to be gathered up by God's remnant people, to be given by them to the world; but self-confidence and obduracy of soul refuse the blessed treasure. "God so loved the world, that he gave his only begotten Son, that whosoever believeth in him should not perish, but have everlasting life." Such love cannot be measured, neither can it be expressed. John calls upon the world to behold "what manner of love the Father hath bestowed upon us, that we should be called the sons of God." It is a love that passeth knowledge.

In the fullness of the sacrifice, nothing was withheld. Jesus gave Himself. God designs that His people shall love one another as Christ loved us. They are to educate and train the soul for this love. They are to reflect this love in their own character, to reflect it to the world. Each should look upon this as his work. . . . Christ's fullness is to be presented to the world by those who have become partakers of His grace. They are to do that for Christ which Christ did for the Father—represent His character.

CHARACTER IS POWER

We have peace with God through our Lord Jesus Christ: by whom also we have access by faith into this grace wherein we stand, and rejoice in hope of the glory of God. Rom. 5:1, 2.

Christ has given us no assurance that to attain perfection of character is an easy matter. A noble, all-round character is not inherited. It does not come to us by accident. A noble character is earned by individual effort through the merits and grace of Christ. God gives the talents, the powers of the mind; we form the character. It is formed by hard, stern battles with self. Conflict after conflict must be waged against hereditary tendencies. We shall have to criticize ourselves closely, and allow not one unfavorable trait to remain uncorrected. . . .

A character formed according to the divine likeness is the only treasure that we can take from this world to the next. Those who are under the instruction of Christ in this world will take every divine attainment with them to the heavenly mansions. . . .

The heavenly intelligences will work with the human agent who seeks with determined faith that perfection of character which will reach out to perfection in action. To everyone engaged in this work Christ says, I am at your right hand to help you.

As the will of man cooperates with the will of God, it becomes omnipotent. Whatever is to be done at His command may be accomplished in His strength. All His biddings are enablings.

Character is power. The silent witness of a true, unselfish, godly life carries an almost irresistible influence. By revealing in our own life the character of Christ we cooperate with Him in the work of saving souls. It is only by revealing in our life His character that we can cooperate with Him. And the wider the sphere of our influence, the more good we may do. When those who profess to serve God follow Christ's example, practicing the principles of the law in their daily life; when every act bears witness that they love God supremely and their neighbor as themselves, then will the church have power to move the world. . . .

We know not what results a day, an hour, or a moment may determine, and never should we begin the day without committing our ways to our heavenly Father. . . . When unconsciously we are in danger of exerting a wrong influence, the angels will be by our side, prompting us to a better course, choosing our words for us, and influencing our actions. Thus our influence may be a silent, unconscious, but mighty power in drawing others to Christ and the heavenly world.

JESUS SHOWED US HOW TO LIVE

I received mercy for this reason, that in me, . . . Jesus Christ might display his perfect patience for an example to those who were to believe in him for eternal life. 1 Tim. 1:16, RSV.

He [Jesus] was a teacher, such an educator as the world never saw or heard before. He spake as one having authority, and yet He invites the confidence of all. "Come unto me, all ye that labour and are heavy laden, and I will give you rest. Take my yoke upon you, and learn of me; for I am meek and lowly in heart: and ye shall find rest unto your souls. For my yoke is easy, and my burden is light" (Matt. 11:28-30).

The only-begotten Son of the infinite God has, by His words, His practical example, left us a plain pattern which we are to copy. By His words He has educated us to obey God, and by His own practice He has showed us how we can obey God. This is the very work He wants every man to do, to obey God intelligently, by precept and example teach others what they must do in order to be obedient children of God.

Jesus has helped the whole world to an intelligent knowledge of His divine mission and work. He came to represent the character of the Father to our world, and as we study the life, the words, and works of Jesus Christ, we are helped in every way in the education of obedience to God; and as we copy the example He has given us, we are living epistles known and read of all men. We are the living human agencies to represent in character Jesus Christ to the world.

Not only did Christ give explicit rules showing how we may become obedient children, but He showed us in His own life and character just how to do those things which are right and acceptable with God, so there is no excuse why we should not do those things which are pleasing in His sight. . . .

The great Teacher came to our world to stand at the head of humanity, to thus elevate and sanctify humanity by His holy obedience to all of God's requirements, showing it is possible to obey all the commandments of God. He has demonstrated that a lifelong obedience is possible. Thus He gives chosen, representative men to the world, as the Father gave the Son, to exemplify in their life the life of Jesus Christ.

In Him was found the perfect ideal. To reveal this ideal as the only true standard for attainment; to show what every human being might become; what, through the indwelling of humanity by divinity, all who received Him would become—for this, Christ came to the world. He came to show how men are to be trained as befits the sons of God; how on earth they are to practice the principles and to live the life of heaven.

THE VALUE OF PAIN

For I reckon that the sufferings of this present time are not worthy to be compared with the glory which shall be revealed in us. **Rom. 8:18.**

In the experience of the apostle John under persecution, there is a lesson of wonderful strength and comfort for the Christian. God does not prevent the plottings of wicked men, but He causes their devices to work for good to those who in trial and conflict maintain their faith and loyalty. Often the gospel laborer carries on his work amid storms of persecution, bitter opposition, and unjust reproach. At such times let him remember that the experience to be gained in the furnace of trial and affliction is worth all the pain it costs. Thus God brings His children near to Him, that He may show them their weakness and His strength. He teaches them to lean on Him. Thus He prepares them to meet emergencies, to fill positions of trust, and to accomplish the great purpose for which their powers were given them.

In all ages God's appointed witnesses have exposed themselves to reproach and persecution for the truth's sake. Joseph was maligned and persecuted because he preserved his virtue and integrity. David, the chosen messenger of God, was hunted like a beast of prey by his enemies. Daniel was cast into a den of lions because he was true to his allegiance to heaven. Job was deprived of his worldly possessions, and so afflicted in body that he was abhorred by his relatives and friends; yet he maintained his integrity.

Jeremiah could not be deterred from speaking the words that God had given him to speak; and his testimony so enraged the king and princes that he was cast into a loathsome pit. Stephen was stoned because he preached Christ and Him crucified. Paul was imprisoned, beaten with rods, stoned, and finally put to death because he was a faithful messenger for God to the Gentiles. And John was banished to the Isle of Patmos "for the word of God, and for the testimony of Jesus Christ."

These examples of human steadfastness bear witness to the faithfulness of God's promises—of His abiding presence and sustaining grace. They testify to the power of faith to withstand the powers of the world. . . .

They bore witness to the power of One mightier than Satan. . . . Through trial and persecution the glory—the character—of God is revealed in His chosen ones. The believers in Christ, hated and persecuted by the world, are educated and disciplined in the school of Christ. On earth they walk in narrow paths; they are purified in the furnace of affliction.

Reflecting Christ   November 28

THOSE WHO RETURN
TO THE OLD PATHS

And the ransomed of the Lord shall return, and come to Zion with songs and everlasting joy upon their heads: they shall obtain joy and gladness, and sorrow and sighing shall flee away. **Isa. 35:10.**

The world is full of men and women who manifest no sense of obligation to God for their entrusted gifts. They do not realize that God has entrusted them with talents, not for self-glorification, but for His own name's glory. They are eager for distinction. . . .

There are men whom God has qualified with more than ordinary ability. They are deep thinkers, energetic, and thorough. But many of them are bent upon the attainment of their own selfish ends, without regard to the honor and glory of God. Some of these have seen the light of truth, but because they honored themselves, and did not make God first and last and best in everything, they have wandered away from Bible truth into skepticism and infidelity. When these are arrested by the chastisements of God, and through affliction are led to inquire for the old paths, the mist of skepticism is swept from their minds. Some of them repent, return to the old love, and set their feet in the way cast up for the ransomed of the Lord to walk in. No longer are they actuated by the love of money or by selfish ambition. The Spirit of God working upon the heart is valued by them more highly than gold or the praise of men. When this amazing change is wrought, the thoughts are directed by the Spirit of God into new channels, the character is transformed, and the aspirations of the soul reach out toward heavenly things.

True religion has power today. It enables men to overcome the stubborn influence of pride, selfishness, and unbelief, and in the simplicity of true godliness to reveal a living connection with heaven. The grace which Christ imparts makes it possible for men to rise superior to all the infatuating temptations of Satan. It will lead them to the cross of Jesus as active, devoted, loyal workers for the advancement of the truth of heaven.

Fidelity to God has marked the heroes of faith from age to age. As they have been brought conspicuously before the world their light has shone forth. Their obedience to the command of Christ, "Go forward," has led others to glorify God.

There are today moral heroes, men and women who are living noble lives of self-denial. They have no ambition for worldly fame. Their will is subordinate to the will of God. The love of God inspires their ministry. To do good and to save souls is their highest aim.

These have gained genuine knowledge, even the knowledge set forth by Christ in the words, "This is life eternal, that they might know thee the only true God, and Jesus Christ, whom thou hast sent" (John 17:3).

GOD HAS A TENDER CARE
FOR HIS PEOPLE

The eyes of the Lord are upon the righteous, and his ears are open unto their cry. **Ps. 34:15.**

You must not sink down discouraged. The fainthearted will be made strong; the desponding will be made to hope. God has a tender care for His people. His ear is open unto their cry. I have no fears for God's cause. He will take care of His own cause. Our duty is to fill our lot and place, live . . . humble at the foot of the cross, and live faithful, holy lives before Him. While we do this we shall not be ashamed, but our souls will confide in God with holy boldness.

God has released us from burdens; He has set us free. . . . Our enemies may triumph. They may speak lying words, and their slandering tongue frame slander, deceit, guile; yet will we not be moved. We know in whom we believe. We have not run in vain, neither labored in vain. Jesus knows us. . . . A reckoning day is coming and all will be judged according to the deeds that are done in the body. . . .

It is true the world is dark. Opposition may wax strong. The trifler and scorner may grow bolder and harder in their iniquity. Yet, for all this, we will not be moved. We have not run as uncertain. No, no. My heart is fixed, trusting in God. We have a whole Saviour. We can rejoice in His rich fullness. I long to be more devoted to God, more consecrated to Him. This world is too dark for me. Jesus said He would go away and prepare mansions for us, that where He is we may be also. Praise God for this. My heart leaps with joy at the cheering prospect.

Religion is made to dwell too much in an iron case. Pure religion and undefiled leads us to a childlike simplicity. We want to pray and talk with humility, having a single eye to the glory of God. There has been too much of a form of godliness without the power. The outpouring of the Spirit of God will lead to a grateful acknowledgment of the same; and while we feel and realize the wondrous love of God, we shall not hold our peace, we shall sacrifice to God with the voice of thanksgiving and make melody to Him with our hearts and voices. Let us plant our feet upon the Rock of Ages and then we will have abiding support and consolation. Our soul will repose in God with unshaken confidence.

Why do we so seldom visit the fountain when it is full and free? Our souls often need to drink at the fountain in order to be refreshed and flourish in the Lord. Salvation we must have. Without vital godliness our religion is vain. A form will be of no advantage to us. We must have the deep workings of the Spirit of God.

313

CHRISTIANS TO REFLECT
THE LIGHT OF HEAVEN

A city that is set on an hill cannot be hid. Neither do men light a candle, and put it under a bushel, but on a candlestick; and it giveth light unto all that are in the house. **Matt. 5:14, 15.**

"Ye are the light of the world," said Christ to His disciples. As the sun goes forth in the heavens, dispelling the shades of night, and filling the world with brightness, so must the followers of Jesus let their light shine to dispel the moral darkness of a world lying in sin. But they have no light of themselves; it is the light of Heaven which they are to reflect to the world.

"A city that is set on a hill cannot be hid." Our thoughts and purposes are the secret springs of action, and hence determine the character. The purpose formed in the heart need not be expressed in word or deed in order to make it sin, and bring the soul into condemnation. Every thought, feeling, and inclination, though unseen by men, is discerned by the eye of God. But it is only when the evil that has taken root in the heart reaches its fruition in the unlawful word or deed that man can judge the character of his fellowman.

The Christian is Christ's representative. He is to show to the world the transforming power of divine grace. He is a living epistle of the truth of God, known and read of all men. The rule given by Christ by which to determine who are His true followers is, "By their fruits ye shall know them." . . .

The Christian's godly life and holy conversation are a daily testimony against sin and sinners. But he must present Christ, not self. Christ is the great remedy for sin. Our compassionate Redeemer has provided for us the help we need. He is waiting to impute His righteousness to the sincere penitent, and to kindle in his heart such divine love as only our gracious Redeemer can inspire. Then let us who profess to be His witnesses on earth, His ambassadors from the court of heaven, glorify Him whom we represent, by being faithful to our trust as light bearers to the world.

Everyone who at last secures eternal life will hear manifest zeal and devotion in the service of God. He will not desert the post of duty at the approach of trial, hardship, or reproach. He will be a diligent student of the Scriptures, and will follow the light as it shines upon his pathway. When some plain, scriptural requirement is presented he will not stop to inquire, What will my friends say, if I take my position with the people of God? Knowing his duty, he will do it heartily and fearlessly.

Of such truehearted followers Jesus declares that He is not ashamed to call them brethren. The God of truth will be on their side, and will never forsake them. All apparent losses for Christ's sake will count to them as infinite gain.

THE KEYNOTE OF SCRIPTURE

I know that my redeemer liveth, and that he shall stand at the latter day upon the earth. **Job. 19:25.**

One of the most solemn and yet most glorious truths revealed in the Bible is that of Christ's second coming, to complete the great work of redemption. To God's pilgrim people, so long left to sojourn in "the region and shadow of death," a precious, joy-inspiring hope is given in the promise of His appearing, who is "the resurrection and the life," to "bring home again His banished." The doctrine of the second advent is the very key-note of the Sacred Scriptures. From the day when the first pair turned their sorrowing steps from Eden, the children of faith have waited the coming of the Promised One to break the destroyer's power and bring them again to the lost Paradise. . . . Enoch, only the seventh in descent from them that dwelt in Eden, he who for three centuries on earth walked with his God, was permitted to behold from afar the coming of the Deliverer. "Behold," he declared, "the Lord cometh with ten thousands of his saints, to execute judgment upon all." The patriarch Job in the night of his affliction exclaimed with unshaken trust: "I know that my redeemer liveth, and that he shall stand at the latter day upon the earth: . . . in my flesh shall I see God: whom I shall see for myself, and mine eyes shall behold, and not another."

May the God of all grace so enlighten your understanding that you may discern eternal things, that by the light of truth your own errors, which are many, may be discovered to you just as they are, that you may make the necessary effort to put them away, and in the place of this evil, bitter fruit may bring forth fruit which is precious unto eternal life.

Humble your poor, proud, self-righteous heart before God; get low, very low, all broken in your sinfulness at His feet. Devote yourself to the work of preparation. Rest not until you can truly say: My Redeemer liveth, and, because He lives, I shall live also.

If you lose heaven, you lose everything; if you gain heaven, you gain everything. Do not make a mistake in this matter, I implore you. Eternal interests are here involved.

HE SHALL REIGN FOREVER

The seventh angel sounded; and there were great voices in heaven, saying, The kingdoms of this world are become the kingdoms of our Lord, and of his Christ; and he shall reign for ever and ever. **Rev. 11:15.**

The coming of Christ to usher in the reign of righteousness has inspired the most sublime . . . utterances of the sacred writers. . . . The psalmist sang of the power and majesty of Israel's King: . . . "Let the heavens rejoice, and let the earth be glad . . . before the Lord: for he cometh, for he cometh to judge the earth: he shall judge the world with righteousness, and the people with his truth." Psalm 96:11-13.

Said the prophet Isaiah: . . . "He will swallow up death in victory; and the Lord God will wipe away tears from off all faces; and the rebuke of his people shall he take away from off all the earth; for the Lord hath spoken it. . . ." Isaiah 25:8. . . .

When the Saviour was about to be separated from His disciples, He comforted them in their sorrow with the assurance that He would come again: "Let not your heart be troubled. . . . In my Father's house are many mansions. . . . I go to prepare a place for you. And if I go and prepare a place for you, I will come again, and receive you unto myself." John 14:1-3. . . .

The angels who lingered upon Olivet after Christ's ascension repeated to the disciples the promise of His return: "This *same* Jesus, which is taken up from you into heaven, shall *so* come in like manner as ye have seen him go into heaven." Acts 1:11. And the apostle Paul, speaking by the Spirit of Inspiration, testified: "The Lord *himself* shall descend from heaven with a shout, with the voice of the archangel, and with the trump of God." 1 Thessalonians 4:16. Says the prophet of Patmos: "Behold, he cometh with clouds; and every eye shall see him." Revelation 1:7.

About His coming cluster the glories of that "restitution of all things, which God hath spoken by the mouth of all his holy prophets since the world began." Acts 3:21. Then the long-continued rule of evil shall be broken; "the kingdoms of this world" will become "the kingdoms of our Lord, and of his Christ; and he shall reign for ever and ever." Revelation 11:15.

UPLIFT JESUS AS THE CENTER

I am the root and the offspring of David, and the bright and morning star. **Rev. 22:16.**

The perils of the last days are upon us, and in our work we are to warn the people of the danger they are in. Let not the solemn scenes which prophecy has revealed be left untouched. If our people were half awake, if they realized the nearness of the events portrayed in the Revelation, a reformation would be wrought in our churches, and many more would believe the message. We have no time to lose. . . . Advance new principles, and crowd in the clear-cut truth. It will be as a sword cutting both ways. But be not too ready to take a controversial attitude. There will be times when we must stand still and see the salvation of God. Let Daniel speak, let the Revelation speak, and tell what is truth. But whatever phase of the subject is presented, uplift Jesus as the center of all hope, "the root and the offspring of David, and the bright and morning star."

We do not go deep enough in our search for truth. Every soul who believes present truth will be brought where he will be required to give a reason of the hope that is in him. The people of God will be called upon to stand before kings, princes, rulers, and great men of the earth, and they must know that they do know what is truth. They must be converted men and women. God can teach you more in one moment by His Holy Spirit than you could learn from the great men of the earth. The universe is looking upon the controversy that is going on upon the earth. At an infinite cost, God has provided for every man an opportunity to know that which will make him wise unto salvation. How eagerly do angels look to see who will avail himself of this opportunity! When a message is presented to God's people, they should not rise up in opposition to it; they should go to the Bible, comparing it with the law and the testimony, and if it does not bear this test, it is not true. God wants our minds to expand. He desires to put His grace upon us. We may have a feast of good things every day, for God can open the whole treasure of heaven to us.

GOD'S JUDGMENTS IN THE LAND

Men's hearts failing them for fear, and for looking after those things which are coming on the earth. **Luke 21:26.**

O that God's people had a sense of the impending destruction of thousands of cities, now almost given to idolatry! . . .

Not long ago a very impressive scene passed before me. I saw an immense ball of fire falling among some beautiful mansions, causing their instant destruction. I heard someone say, "We knew that the judgments of God were coming upon the earth, but we did not know that they would come so soon." Others said, "You knew? Why then did you not tell us? We did not know." On every side I heard such words spoken. . . .

Soon grievous troubles will arise among the nations—trouble that will not cease until Jesus comes. As never before we need to press together, serving Him who has prepared His throne in the heavens and whose kingdom ruleth over all. God has not forsaken His people, and our strength lies in not forsaking Him.

The judgments of God are in the land. The wars and rumors of wars, the destruction by fire and flood, say clearly that the time of trouble, which is to increase until the end, is very near at hand. We have no time to lose. The world is stirred with the spirit of war. The prophecies of the eleventh of Daniel have almost reached their final fulfillment. . . .

Last Friday morning, just before I awoke, a very impressive scene was presented before me. I seemed to awake from sleep but was not in my home. From the windows I could behold a terrible conflagration. Great balls of fire were falling upon houses, and from these balls fiery arrows were flying in every direction. It was impossible to check the fires that were kindled, and many places were being destroyed. The terror of the people was indescribable.

Strictly will the cities of the nations be dealt with, and yet they will not be visited in the extreme of God's indignation, because some souls will yet break away from the delusions of the enemy, and will repent and be converted, while the mass will be treasuring up wrath against the day of wrath.

A HIGH STANDARD

And ye shall be holy unto me: for I the Lord am holy, and have severed you from other people, that ye should be mine. **Lev. 20:26.**

I also saw many do not realize what they must be in order to live in the sight of the Lord without a high priest in the sanctuary through the time of trouble. Those who receive the seal of the living God and are protected in the time of trouble must reflect the image of Jesus fully.

I saw that many were neglecting the preparation so needful and were looking to the time of "refreshing" and the "latter rain" to fit them to stand in the day of the Lord and to live in His sight. Oh, how many I saw in the time of trouble without a shelter! They had neglected the needful preparation; therefore they could not receive the refreshing that all must have to fit them to live in the sight of a holy God. Those who . . . fail to purify their souls in obeying the whole truth . . . will come up to the time of the falling of the plagues, and then see that they needed to be hewed and squared for the building. But there will be . . . no Mediator to plead their cause before the Father. Before this time the awfully solemn declaration has gone forth, "He that is unjust, let him be unjust still: and he which is filthy, let him be filthy still: and he that is righteous, let him be righteous still: and he that is holy, let him be holy still."

I saw that none could share the "refreshing" unless they obtain the victory over every besetment, over pride, selfishness, love of the world, and over every wrong word and action. We should, therefore, be drawing nearer and nearer to the Lord and be earnestly seeking that preparation necessary to enable us to stand in the battle in the day of the Lord. Let all remember that God is holy and that none but holy beings can ever dwell in His presence.

We are today to watch that we offend not in word or deed. . . . We must today seek God and be determined that we will not rest satisfied without His presence. We should watch and work and pray as though this were the last day that would be granted us. How intensely earnest, then, would be our life. How closely would we follow Jesus in all our words and deeds.

SPIRITUAL GIANT OR DWARF?

Having therefore these promises, dearly beloved, let us cleanse ourselves from all filthiness of the flesh and spirit, perfecting holiness in the fear of God. 2 Cor. 7:11.

The Lord reproves and corrects the people who profess to keep His law. He points out their sins and lays open their iniquity because He wishes to separate all sin and wickedness from them, that they may perfect holiness in His fear and be prepared to die in the Lord or to be translated to heaven. . . .

God will accept nothing but purity and holiness; one spot, one wrinkle, one defect in the character, will forever debar them from heaven, with all its glories and treasures.

Most professed Christians have no sense of the spiritual strength they might obtain were they as ambitious, zealous, and persevering to gain a knowledge of divine things as they are to obtain the paltry, perishable things of this life. The masses professing to be Christians have been satisfied to be spiritual dwarfs. They have no disposition to make it their object to seek first the kingdom of God and His righteousness; hence godliness is a hidden mystery to them, they cannot understand it. They know not Christ by experimental knowledge.

Ample provisions have been made for all who sincerely, earnestly, and thoughtfully set about the work of perfecting holiness in the fear of God. Strength, grace, and glory have been provided through Christ, to be brought by ministering angels to the heirs of salvation. None are so low, so corrupt and vile, that they cannot find in Jesus, who died for them, strength, purity, and righteousness, if they will put away their sins, cease their course of iniquity, and turn with full purpose of heart to the living God. He is waiting to strip them of their garments, stained and polluted by sin, and to put upon them the white, bright robes of righteousness; and He bids them live and not die. In Him they may flourish. Their branches will not wither nor be fruitless. If they abide in Him, they can draw sap and nourishment from Him, be imbued with His Spirit, walk even as He walked, overcome as He overcame, and be exalted to His own right hand.

December 7

A CRISIS AHEAD

Alas for the day! for the day of the Lord is at hand, and as a destruction from the Almighty shall it come. **Joel 1:15.**

The prophecies which the great I AM has given in His word, uniting link after link in the chain of events, from eternity in the past to eternity in the future, tell us where we are today in the procession of the ages, and what may be expected in the time to come. All that prophecy has foretold as coming to pass, until the present time, has been traced on the pages of history, and we may be assured that all which is yet to come will be fulfilled in its order.

Today the signs of the times declare that we are standing on the threshold of great and solemn events. Everything in our world is in agitation. Before our eyes is fulfilling the Saviour's prophecy of the events to precede His coming: "Ye shall hear of wars and rumors of wars. . . . Nation shall rise against nation, and kingdom against kingdom: and there shall be famines, and pestilences, and earthquakes, in divers places."

The present is a time of overwhelming interest to all living. Rulers and statesmen, men who occupy positions of trust and authority, thinking men and women of all classes, have their attention fixed upon the events taking place about us. They are watching the relations that exist among the nations. They observe the intensity that is taking possession of every earthly element, and they recognize that something great and decisive is

320

about to take place—that the world is on the verge of a stupendous crisis.

The Bible, and the Bible only, gives a correct view of these things. Here are revealed the great final scenes in the history of our world, . . . the sound of their approach causing the earth to tremble and men's hearts to fail them for fear.

Today men and nations are being tested by the plummet in the hand of Him who makes no mistake. All are by their own choice deciding their destiny, and God is overruling all for the accomplishment of His purposes.

Christians should be preparing for what is soon to break upon the world as an overwhelming surprise, and this preparation they should make by diligently studying the word of God and striving to conform their lives to its precepts.

Maranatha   December 8

TEACHING FROM HOUSE TO HOUSE

I kept back nothing that was profitable unto you, but have shewed you, and have taught you publickly, and from house to house. **Acts 20:20.**

Among the members of our churches there should be more house-to-house labor in giving Bible readings and distributing literature. . . . As we sow beside all waters we shall realize that "he which soweth bountifully shall reap also bountifully."

Christ's example must be followed by those who claim to be His children. Relieve the physical necessities of your fellow men, and their gratitude will break down the barriers and enable you to reach their hearts. . . . Women as well as men can engage in the work. . . . They can do in families a work that men cannot do, a work that reaches the inner life. They can come close to the hearts of those whom men cannot reach. Their work is needed. Discreet and humble women can do a good work in explaining the truth to the people in their homes. The word of God thus explained will do its leavening work, and . . . whole families will be converted. . . .

In the home circle, at your neighbor's fireside, at the bedside of the sick, in a quiet way you may read the Scriptures and speak a word for Jesus and the truth. Precious seed may thus be sown that will spring up and bring forth fruit. . . .

There is missionary work to be done in many unpromising places. The missionary spirit needs to take hold of our souls, inspiring us to reach classes for whom we had not planned to labor and in ways and places that we had no idea of working. The Lord has His plan for the sowing of the gospel seed. In sowing according to His will, we shall so multiply the seed that His word may reach thousands who have never heard the truth.

Thousands upon thousands, and ten thousand times ten thousand angels are waiting to co-operate with members of our churches in communicating the light that God has generously given, that a people may be prepared for the coming of Christ.

Our sisters, the youth, the middle-aged, and those of advanced years, may act a part in the closing work for this time; and in doing this as they have opportunity, they will obtain an experience of the highest value to themselves. In forgetfulness of self, they will grow in grace.

December 9   Maranatha

A CHARACTER
THE WORLD WILL RECOGNIZE

That ye may be blameless and harmless, the sons of God, without rebuke, in the midst of a crooked and perverse nation, among whom ye shine as lights in the world. **Phil. 2:15.**

It is God's purpose to manifest through His people the principles of His kingdom. That in life and character they may reveal these principles, He desires to separate them from the customs, habits, and practices of the world. . . . By beholding the goodness, the mercy, the justice, and the love of God revealed in His church, the world is to have a representation of His character. And when the law of God is thus exemplified in the life, even the world will recognize the superiority of those who love and fear and serve God above every other people in the world.

Seventh-day Adventists, above all people, should be patterns of piety, holy in heart and in conversation. To them have been entrusted the most solemn truths ever committed to mortals. Every endowment of grace and power and efficiency has been liberally provided. They look for the near return of Christ in the clouds of heaven. For them to give to the world the impression that their faith is not a dominating power in their lives is greatly to dishonor God.

Because of the increasing power of Satan's temptations, the times in which we live are full of peril for the children of God, and we need to learn constantly of the Great Teacher, that we may take every step in surety and righteousness. Wonderful scenes are opening before us; and at this time a living testimony is to be borne in the lives of God's professed people, so that the world may see that in this age, when evil reigns on every side, there is yet a people who are laying aside their will and are seeking to do God's will—a people in whose hearts and lives God's law is written. . . .

Their thoughts are to be pure, their words noble and uplifting. The religion of Christ is to be interwoven with all that they do and say. They are to be a sanctified, purified, holy people, communicating light to all with whom they come in contact. It is His purpose that by exemplifying the truth in their lives, they shall be a praise in the earth. The grace of Christ is sufficient to bring this about.

PROVE ALL THINGS

Beware of false prophets, which come to you in sheep's clothing, but inwardly they are ravening wolves. Matt. 7:15.

In the work in which my husband and I were called by the providence of God to act a part, even from its very beginning in 1843 and 1844, we have had the Lord to devise and plan for us, and He has worked out His plans through His living agents. False paths have been so often pointed out to us, and the true and safe paths so clearly defined in all the enterprises connected with the work given us to do, that I can say of a truth I am not ignorant of Satan's devices, nor of the ways and works of God. We have had to tax every power of mind, relying upon wisdom from God to guide us in our investigations, as we have had to review the different theories brought to our attention, weighing their merits and defects in the light shining from the Word of God and the things God has revealed to me through His Word and the testimonies, in order that we might not be deceived nor deceive others. We surrendered our will and way to God, and most earnestly supplicated His aid; and we never sought in vain. Many years of painful experience in connection with the work of God have made me acquainted with all kinds of false movements. Many times I have been sent to different places with the message, "I have a work for you to do in that place; I will be with you." When the occasion came, the Lord gave me a message for those who were having false dreams and visions, and in the strength of Christ I bore my testimony at the Lord's bidding. . . .

During the past forty-five years, I have had to meet persons claiming to have from God messages of reproof to others. This phase of religious fanaticism has sprung up again and again since 1844. Satan has worked in many ways to establish error. Some things spoken in these visions came to pass; but many things—in regard to the time of Christ's coming, the end of probation, and the events to take place—proved utterly false. . . .

"Take heed therefore how ye hear" (Luke 8:18), is an admonition of Christ. . . . Examine closely, "prove all things" (1 Thess. 5:21). . . . This is the counsel of God; shall we heed it?

323

MOVING INTO LINE

The humble shall see this, and be glad: and your heart shall live that seek God. **Ps. 69:32.**

It is your privilege to be glad in the Lord, and to rejoice in the knowledge of His sustaining grace. Let His love take possession of mind and heart. Guard against becoming overwearied, careworn, depressed. Bear an uplifting testimony. Turn your eyes away from that which is dark and discouraging, and behold Jesus, our great Leader, under whose watchful supervision the cause of present truth, to which we are giving our lives and our all, is destined to triumph gloriously. . . .

Oh, let it be seen . . . That Jesus is abiding in the heart, sustaining, strengthening, comforting. It is your privilege to be endowed, from day to day, with a rich measure of His Holy Spirit, and to have broadened views of the importance and scope of the message we are proclaiming to the world. The Lord is willing to reveal to you wondrous things out of His law. Wait before Him with humility of heart. Pray most earnestly for an understanding of the times in which we live, for a fuller conception of His purpose, and for increased efficiency in soulsaving. . . .

It will be well for us to consider what is soon to come upon the earth. This is no time for trifling or self-seeking. If the times in which we are living fail to impress our minds seriously, what can reach us? . . .

Men of clear understanding are needed now. God calls upon those who are willing to be controlled by the Holy Spirit to lead out in a work of thorough reformation. I see a crisis before us, and the Lord calls for His laborers to come into line. Every soul should now stand in a position of deeper, truer consecration to God than during the years that have passed. . . .

I have been deeply impressed by scenes that have recently passed before me in the night season. There seemed to be a great movement—a work of revival—going forward in many places. Our people were moving into line, responding to God's call. . . . Shall we not heed His voice? Shall we not trim our lamps, and act like men who look for their Lord to come? The time is one that calls for light bearing, for action.

PREPARATION FOR
WHAT LIES AHEAD

Seek ye the Lord, all ye meek of the earth, which have wrought his judgment; seek righteousness, seek meekness: it may be ye shall be hid in the day of the Lord's anger. **Zeph. 2:3.**

Transgression has almost reached its limit. Confusion fills the world, and a great terror is soon to come upon human beings. The end is very near. God's people should be preparing for what is to break upon the world as an overwhelming surprise.

The "time of trouble, such as never was," is soon to open upon us; and we shall need an experience which we do not now possess and which many are too indolent to obtain. It is often the case that trouble is greater in anticipation than in reality; but this is not true of the crisis before us. The most vivid presentation cannot reach the magnitude of the ordeal. In that time of trial, every soul must stand for himself before God. "Though Noah, Daniel, and Job" were in the land, "as I live, saith the Lord God, they shall deliver neither son nor daughter; they shall but deliver their own souls by their righteousness." Ezekiel 14:20.

The last great conflict between truth and error is but the final struggle of the long-standing controversy concerning the law of God. Upon this battle we are now entering—a battle between the laws of men and the precepts of Jehovah, between the religion of the Bible and the religion of fable and tradition.

We should study the great waymarks that point out the times in which we are living. . . . We should now pray most earnestly that we may be prepared for the struggles of the great day of God's preparation.

Those who place themselves under God's control, to be led and guided by Him, will catch the steady tread of the events ordained by Him to take place. Inspired with the Spirit of Him who gave His life for the life of the world, they will no longer stand still in impotency, pointing to what they cannot do. Putting on the armor of heaven, they will go forth to the warfare, willing to do and dare for God, knowing that His omnipotence will supply their need.

RELIEF OF
PHYSICAL SUFFERING

And as ye go, preach, saying, The kingdom of heaven is at hand.
Heal the sick, cleanse the lepers, raise the dead, cast out devils: freely ye
have received, freely give. **Matt. 10:7, 8.**

Perilous times are before us. The whole world will be involved in
perplexity and distress, disease of every kind will be upon the human
family, and such ignorance as now prevails concerning the laws of health
would result in great suffering and the loss of many lives that might be
saved. . . .

As religious aggression subverts the liberties of our nation, those who
would stand for freedom of conscience will be placed in unfavorable
positions. For their own sake, they should, while they have opportunity,
become intelligent in regard to disease, its causes, prevention, and cure.
And those who do this will find a field of labor anywhere. There will be
suffering ones, plenty of them, who will need help, not only among those
of our own faith, but largely among those who know not the truth.

The medical work done in connection with the giving of the third
angel's message, is to accomplish wonderful results. It is to be a
sanctifying, unifying work, corresponding to the work which the great
Head of the church sent forth the first disciples to do.

Calling these disciples together, Christ gave them their commission:
. . . "And as ye go, preach, saying, The kingdom of heaven is at hand.
Heal the sick, cleanse the lepers, raise the dead, cast out devils: freely ye
have received, freely give." "Behold, I send you forth as sheep in the
midst of wolves: be ye therefore wise as serpents, and harmless as doves."
Matthew 10:7, 8, 16.

It is well for us to read this chapter and let its instruction prepare us for
our labors. The early disciples were going forth on Christ's errands, under
His commission. His Spirit was to prepare the way before them. They were
to feel that with such a message to give, such blessings to impart, they
should receive a welcome in the homes of the people.

God reaches hearts through the relief of physical suffering. A seed of
truth is dropped into the mind, and is watered by God. Much patience may
be required before this seed shows signs of life, but at last it springs up,
and bears fruit unto eternal life.

How slow men are to understand God's preparation for the day of His
power!

THE CORRUPTION
OF TRUTH

Then if any man shall say unto you, Lo, here is Christ, or there;
believe it not. **Matt. 24:23.**

Before the last developments of the work of apostasy there will be a
confusion of faith. There will not be clear and definite ideas concerning the
mystery of God. One truth after another will be corrupted.

After the truth has been proclaimed as a witness to all nations, every
conceivable power of evil will be set in operation, and minds will be
confused by many voices crying, "Lo, here is Christ; lo, He is there. This
is the truth, I have the message from God, He has sent me with great
light." Then there will be a removing of the landmarks, and an attempt to
tear down the pillars of our faith. A more decided effort will be made to
exalt the false sabbath, and to cast contempt upon God Himself by
supplanting the day He has blessed and sanctified. This false sabbath is to
be enforced by an oppressive law.

In the future, deception of every kind is to arise, and we want solid
ground for our feet. We want solid pillars for the building. Not one pin is
to be removed from that which the Lord has established. The enemy will
bring in false theories, such as the doctrine that there is no sanctuary. This
is one of the points on which there will be a departing from the faith.

There will be false dreams and false visions, which have some truth,
but lead away from the original faith. The Lord has given men a rule by
which to detect them: "To the law and to the testimony: if they speak not
according to this word, it is because there is no light in them" (Isa. 8:20).

As we near the end of time, falsehood will be so mingled with truth,
that only those who have the guidance of the Holy Spirit will be able to
distinguish truth from error. We need to make every effort to keep the way
of the Lord. We must in no case turn from His guidance to put our trust in
man. The Lord's angels are appointed to keep strict watch over those who
put their faith in the Lord, and these angels are to be our special help in
every time of need. Every day we are to come to the Lord with full
assurance of faith, and to look to Him for wisdom. . . . Those who are
guided by the Word of the Lord will discern with certainty between
falsehood and truth, between sin and righteousness.

THE SHAKING TIME

And because iniquity shall abound, the love of many shall wax cold.
Matt. 24:12.

Just as soon as the people of God are sealed in their foreheads—it is not any seal or mark that can be seen, but a settling into the truth, both intellectually and spiritually, so they cannot be moved—just as soon as God's people are sealed and prepared for the shaking, it will come. Indeed, it has begun already; the judgments of God are now upon the land, to give us warning, that we may know what is coming.

The days are fast approaching when there will be great perplexity and confusion. Satan, clothed in angel robes, will deceive, if possible, the very elect. There will be gods many and lords many. Every wind of doctrine will be blowing. . . .

The mark of the beast will be urged upon us. Those who have step by step yielded to worldly demands and conformed to worldly customs will not find it a hard matter to yield to the powers that be, rather than subject themselves to derision, insult, threatened imprisonment, and death. The contest is between the commandments of God and the commandments of men. In this time the gold will be separated from the dross in the church. True godliness will be clearly distinguished from the appearance and tinsel of it. Many a star that we have admired for its brilliancy will then go out in darkness. Chaff like a cloud will be borne away on the wind, even from places where we see only floors of rich wheat. All who assume the ornaments of the sanctuary, but are not clothed with Christ's righteousness, will appear in the shame of their own nakedness.

But there are men who will receive the truth, and these will take the places made vacant by those who become offended and leave the truth. . . .

Men of true Christian principle will take their place, and will become faithful, trustworthy householders, to advocate the word of God in its true bearings, and in its simplicity. The Lord will work so that the disaffected ones will be separated from the true and loyal ones. . . . The ranks will not be diminished. Those who are firm and true will close up the vacancies that are made by those who become offended and apostatize.

THE SEALING
AND THE LATTER RAIN

Nevertheless the foundations of God standeth sure, having this seal,
The Lord knoweth them that are his. And, Let every one that nameth the
name of Christ depart from iniquity. **2 Tim. 2:19.**

Before the work is closed up and the sealing of God's people is finished, we shall receive the outpouring of the Spirit of God. Angels from heaven will be in our midst.

Our heavenly Father claims not at our hands that which we cannot perform. He desires His people to labor earnestly to carry out His purpose for them. They are to pray for power, expect power, and receive power, that they may grow up into the full stature of men and women in Christ Jesus.

Not all members of the church are cultivating personal piety; therefore they do not understand their personal responsibility. They do not realize that it is their privilege and duty to reach the high standard of Christian perfection. . . . Are we looking forward to the latter rain, confidently hoping for a better day, when the church shall be endued with power from on high and thus fitted for work? The latter rain will never refresh and invigorate the indolent, who do not use the powers God has given them.

We are in great need of the pure, life-giving atmosphere that nurtures and invigorates the spiritual life. We need greater earnestness. The solemn message given us to give to the world is to be proclaimed with greater fervency, even with an intensity that will impress unbelievers, leading them to see that the Most High is working with us, that He is the source of our efficiency and strength. . . .

Are you using all your powers in an effort to bring the lost sheep back to the fold? There are thousands upon thousands in ignorance who might be warned. Pray as you have never prayed before for the power of Christ. Pray for the inspiration of His Spirit, that you may be filled with a desire to save those who are perishing. Let the prayer ascend to heaven, "God be merciful unto us, and bless us; and cause his face to shine upon us; that thy way may be known upon earth, thy saving health among all nations" (Ps. 67:1, 2).

"IN THESE HOURS OF PROBATION"

I have heard thee in a time accepted, and in the day of salvation have I succoured thee: behold, now is the accepted time; behold, now is the day of salvation. 2 Cor. 6:2.

We believe without a doubt that Christ is soon coming. This is not a fable to us; it is a reality. We have no doubt, neither have we had a doubt for years, that the doctrines we hold today are present truth, and that we are nearing the judgment. We are preparing to meet Him who, escorted by a retinue of holy angels, is to appear in the clouds of heaven to give the faithful and the just the finishing touch of immortality. When He comes He is not to cleanse us of our sins, to remove from us the defects in our characters, or to cure us of the infirmities of our tempers and dispositions. If wrought for us at all, this work will all be accomplished before that time. When the Lord comes, those who are holy will be holy still. Those who have preserved their bodies and spirits in holiness, in sanctification and honor, will then receive the finishing touch of immortality. But those who are unjust, unsanctified, and filthy will remain so forever. No work will then be done for them to remove their defects and give them holy characters. The Refiner does not then sit to pursue His refining process and remove their sins and their corruption. This is all to be done in these hours of probation. It is *now* that this work is to be accomplished for us.

We embrace the truth of God with our different faculties, and as we come under the influence of that truth, it will accomplish the work for us which is necessary to give us a moral fitness for the kingdom of glory and for the society of the heavenly angels. We are now in God's workshop. Many of us are tough stones from the quarry. But as we lay hold upon the truth of God, its influence affects us. It elevates us and removes from us every imperfection and sin, of whatever nature. Thus we are prepared to see the King in His beauty and finally to unite with the pure and heavenly angels in the kingdom of glory. It is here that this work is to be accomplished for us, here that our bodies and spirits are to be fitted for immortality.

HIGH SPIRITUAL STATE ATTAINABLE

Now unto him that is able to keep you from falling, and to present you faultless before the presence of his glory with exceeding joy. **Jude 24.**

Christ was obedient to every requirement of the law. . . .

By His perfect obedience He has made it possible for every human being to obey God's commandments. When we submit ourselves to Christ, the heart is united with His heart, the will is merged in His will, the mind becomes one with His mind, the thoughts are brought into captivity to Him; we live His life. This is what it means to be clothed with the garment of His righteousness. Then as the Lord looks upon us He sees, not the fig-leaf garment, not the nakedness and deformity of sin, but His own robe of righteousness, which is perfect obedience to the law of Jehovah.

Through the plan of redemption, God has provided means for subduing every sinful trait, and resisting every temptation, however strong.

The strongest temptation is no excuse for sin. However great the pressure brought to bear upon the soul, transgression is our own act. It is not in the power of earth or hell to compel any one to sin. The will must consent, the heart must yield, or passion cannot overbear reason, nor iniquity triumph over righteousness.

If you will stand under the bloodstained banner of Prince Emmanuel, faithfully doing His service, you need never yield to temptation; for One stands by your side who is able to keep you from falling.

We need not retain one sinful propensity. . . . [Eph. 2:1-6 quoted.] . . .

As we partake of the divine nature, hereditary and cultivated tendencies to wrong are cut away from the character, and we are made a living power for good. Every learning of the divine Teacher, daily partaking of His nature, we cooperate with God in overcoming Satan's temptations. God works, and man works, that man may be one with Christ as Christ is one with God. Then we sit together with Christ in heavenly places. The mind rests with peace and assurance in Jesus.

WHO RECEIVE THE SEAL?

And in their mouth was found no guile: for they are without fault before the throne of God. **Rev. 14:5.**

Only those who receive the seal of the living God will have the passport through the gates of the Holy City. . . .

The seal of the living God will be placed upon those only who bear a likeness to Christ in character.

As wax takes the impression of the seal, so the soul is to take the impression of the Spirit of God and retain the image of Christ.

Many will not receive the seal of God because they do not keep His commandments or bear the fruits of righeousness.

The great mass of professing Christians will meet with bitter disappointment in the day of God. They have not upon their foreheads the seal of the living God. Lukewarm and halfhearted, they dishonor God far more than the avowed unbeliever. They grope in darkness, when they might be walking in the noonday light of the Word, under the guidance of One who never errs. . . .

Those whom the Lamb shall lead by the fountains of living waters, and from whose eyes He shall wipe away all tears, will be those now receiving the knowledge and understanding revealed in the Bible, the Word of God. . . .

We are to copy no human being. There is no human being wise enough to be our criterion. We are to look to the man Christ Jesus, who is complete in the perfection of righteousness and holiness. He is the author and finisher of our faith. He is the pattern man. His experience is the measure of the experience that we are to gain. His character is our model. Let us, then, take our minds off the perplexities and the difficulties of this life, and fix them on Him, that by beholding we may be changed into His likeness. We may behold Christ to good purpose. We may safely look to Him; for He is all-wise. As we look to Him and think of Him, He will be formed within, the hope of glory.

Let us strive with all the power that God has given us to be among the hundred and forty-four thousand.

December 20   Maranatha

A TIME OF TROUBLE SUCH AS NEVER WAS

And at that time shall Michael stand up, the great prince which standeth for the children of thy people: and there shall be a time of trouble, such as never was since there was a nation even to that same time: and at that time thy people shall be delivered, every one that shall be found written in the book. Dan. 12:1.

When the third angel's message closes, mercy no longer pleads for the guilty inhabitants of the earth. The people of God have accomplished their work. They have received "the latter rain," "the . . . refreshing . . . from the presence of the Lord,'' and they are prepared for the trying hour before them. Angels are hastening to and fro in heaven. An angel returning from the earth announces that his work is done; the final test has been brought upon the world, and all who have proved themselves loyal to the divine precepts have received ''the seal of the living God.'' Then Jesus ceases His intercession in the sanctuary above. He lifts His hands and with a loud voice says, ''It is done.'' . . .

When He leaves the sanctuary, darkness covers the inhabitants of the earth. In that fearful time the righteous must live in the sight of a holy God without an intercessor. The restraint which has been upon the wicked is removed, and Satan has entire control of the finally impenitent. God's long-suffering has ended. The world has rejected His mercy, despised His love, and trampled upon His law. The wicked have passed the boundary of their probation; the Spirit of God, persistently resisted, has been at last withdrawn. Unsheltered by divine grace, they have no protection from the wicked one. Satan will then plunge the inhabitants of the earth into one great, final trouble. As the angels of God cease to hold in check the fierce winds of human passion, all the elements of strife will be let loose. The whole world will be involved in ruin more terrible than that which came upon Jerusalem of old.

Those only who have clean hands and pure hearts will stand in that trying time. . . . Now is the time, while the four angels are holding the four winds, to make our calling and election sure.

ANGELIC PROTECTION
IN THE TIME OF TROUBLE

Come, my people, enter thou into thy chambers, and shut thy doors about thee: hide thyself as it were for a little moment, until the indignation be overpast. **Isa. 26:20.**

In the day of fierce trial He [Christ] will say, ''Come, my people, enter thou into thy chambers, and shut thy doors about thee: hide thyself as it were for a little moment, until the indignation be overpast.'' What are the chambers in which they are to hide? They are the protection of Christ and holy angels. The people of God are not at this time all in one place. They are in different companies, and in all parts of the earth.

I saw the saints leaving the cities and villages, and associating together in companies, and living in the most solitary places. Angels provided them food and water, while the wicked were suffering from hunger and thirst.

During the night a very impressive scene passed before me. There seemed to be great confusion and the conflict of armies. A messenger from the Lord stood before me, and said, "Call your household. I will lead you; follow me." He led me down a dark passage, through a forest, then through the clefts of mountains, and said, "Here you are safe." There were others who had been led to this retreat. The heavenly messenger said, "The time of trouble has come as a thief in the night, as the Lord warned you it would come."

In the time of trouble just before the coming of Christ, the righteous will be preserved through the ministration of heavenly angels; but there will be no security for the transgressor of God's law. Angels cannot then protect those who are disregarding one of the divine precepts.

In the closing period of Earth's history the Lord will work mightily in behalf of those who stand steadfastly for the right. . . . In the midst of the time of trouble—trouble such as has not been since there was a nation—His chosen ones will stand unmoved. Satan with all the hosts of evil cannot destroy the weakest of God's saints. Angels that excel in strength will protect them, and in their behalf Jehovah will reveal Himself as a "God of gods," able to save to the uttermost those who have put their trust in Him.

GOD'S PEOPLE DELIVERED

Thus saith the Lord, Even the captives of the mighty shall be taken away, and the prey of the terrible shall be delivered: for I will contend with him that contendeth with thee, and I will save thy children. **Isa. 49:25.**

When the protection of human laws shall be withdrawn from those who honor the law of God, there will be, in different lands, a simultaneous movement for their destruction. As the time appointed in the decree draws near, the people will conspire to root out the hated sect. It will be determined to strike in one night a decisive blow, which shall utterly silence the voice of dissent and reproof.

The people of God—some in prison cells, some hidden in solitary retreats in the forests and the mountains—still plead for divine protection, while in every quarter companies of armed men, urged on by hosts of evil angels, are preparing for the work of death. It is now, in the hour of utmost extremity, that the God of Israel will interpose for the deliverance of His chosen. . . .

With shouts of triumph, jeering, and imprecation, throngs of evil men are about to rush upon their prey, when, lo, a dense blackness, deeper than the darkness of the night, falls upon the earth. Then a rainbow, shining with the glory from the throne of God, spans the heavens and seems to encircle each praying company. The angry multitudes are suddenly arrested. Their mocking cries die away. The objects of their murderous rage are forgotten. With fearful forebodings they gaze upon the symbol of God's covenant and long to be shielded from its overpowering brightness.

By the people of God a voice, clear and melodious, is heard saying, "Look up," and lifting their eyes to the heavens, they behold the bow of promise. The black, angry clouds that covered the firmament are parted, and like Stephen they look up steadfastly into heaven and see the glory of God and the Son of man seated upon His throne.

While all the world is plunged in darkness, there will be light in every dwelling of the saints. They will catch the first light of His second appearing.

THE DAY AND HOUR
OF CHRIST'S COMING ANNOUNCED

But of that day and hour knoweth no man, no, not the angels of heaven, but my Father only. **Matt. 24:36.**

The voice of God is heard from heaven, declaring the day and hour of Jesus' coming, and delivering the everlasting covenant to His people. Like peals of loudest thunder His words roll through the earth.

He spoke one sentence, and then paused, while the words were rolling through the earth. The Israel of God stood with their eyes fixed upward, listening to the words as they came from the mouth of Jehovah and rolled through the earth like peals of loudest thunder. It was awfully solemn. At the end of every sentence the saints shouted, "Glory! Hallelujah!"

The living saints, 144,000 in number, knew and understood the voice, while the wicked thought it was thunder and an earthquake.

The Israel of God stand listening, with their eyes fixed upward. Their countenances are lighted up with His glory, and shine as did the face of Moses when he came down from Sinai. The wicked cannot look upon them. And when the blessing is pronounced on those who have honored God by keeping His Sabbath holy, there is a mighty shout of victory.

Then commenced the jubilee, when the land should rest.

A glorious light shone upon them [the saints]. How beautiful they then looked! All marks of care and weariness were gone, and health and beauty were seen in every countenance. Their enemies, the heathen around them, fell like dead men; they could not endure the light that shone upon the delivered, holy ones. This light and glory remained upon them, until Jesus was seen in the clouds of heaven.

And I saw a flaming cloud come where Jesus stood. Then Jesus . . .

took His place on the cloud which carried Him to the East, where it first appeared to the saints on earth—a small black cloud which was the sign of the Son of man. While the cloud was passing from the Holiest to the East, which took a number of days, the synagogue of Satan worshipped at the saint's feet.

THE GENERAL RESURRECTION OF THE RIGHTEOUS

Awake and sing, ye that dwell in dust: for thy dew is as the dew of herbs, and the earth shall cast out the dead. Isa. 26:19.

The King of kings descends upon the cloud, wrapped in flaming fire. The heavens are rolled together as a scroll, the earth trembles before Him, and every mountain and island is moved out of its place. . . .

Amid the reeling of the earth, the flash of lightning, and the roar of thunder, the voice of the Son of God calls forth the sleeping saints. He looks upon the graves of the righteous, then, raising His hands to heaven, He cries: "Awake, awake, awake, ye that sleep in the dust, and arise!" Throughout the length and breadth of the earth the dead shall hear that voice, and they that hear shall live. And the whole earth shall ring with the tread of the exceeding great army of every nation, kindred, tongue, and people. From the prison house of death they come, clothed with immortal glory, crying: "O death, where is thy sting? O grave, where is thy victory?" 1 Corinthians 15:55. And the living righteous and the risen saints unite their voices in a long, glad shout of victory.

All come forth from their graves the same in stature as when they entered the tomb. . . . But all arise with the freshness and vigor of eternal youth. . . . The mortal, corruptible form, devoid of comeliness, once polluted with sin, becomes perfect, beautiful, and immortal. All blemishes and deformities are left in the grave. . . .

The living righteous are changed "in a moment, in the twinkling of an eye." At the voice of God they were glorified; now they are made immortal and with the risen saints are caught up to meet their Lord in the air. Angels "gather together his elect from the four winds, from one end of heaven to the other."

As the little infants come forth immortal from their dusty beds, they immediately wing their way to their mothers' arms.

Friends long separated by death are united, nevermore to part, and with songs of gladness ascend together to the City of God.

336

WE SHALL RECOGNIZE
EACH OTHER

Then shall I know even as also I am known. **1 Cor. 13:12.**

We shall know our friends, even as the disciples knew Jesus. They may have been deformed, diseased, or disfigured, in this mortal life, and they rise in perfect health and symmetry; yet in the glorified body their identity will be perfectly preserved. . . . In the face radiant with the light shining from the face of Jesus, we shall recognize the lineaments of those we love.

The redeemed will meet and recognize those whose attention they have directed to the uplifted Saviour. What blessed converse they have with these souls! "I was a sinner," it will be said, "without God and without hope in the world, and you came to me and drew my attention to the precious Saviour as my only hope. . . ." Others will say, "I was a heathen in heathen lands. You left your friends and comfortable home and came to teach me how to find Jesus and believe in Him as the only true God. I demolished my idols and worshiped God, and now I see Him face to face. I am saved, eternally saved, ever to behold Him whom I love. . . ."

Others will express their gratitude to those who fed the hungry and clothed the naked. "When despair bound my soul in unbelief, the Lord sent you to me," they say, "to speak words of hope and comfort. You brought me food for my physical necessities, and you opened to me the Word of God, awakening me to my spiritual needs. You treated me as a brother. You sympathized with me in my sorrows, and restored my bruised and wounded soul, so that I could grasp the hand of Christ that was reached out to save me. In my ignorance you taught me patiently that I had a Father in heaven who cared for me. You read to me the precious promises of God's Word. You inspired in me the faith that He would save me. My heart was softened, subdued, broken, as I contemplated the sacrifice which Christ had made for me. . . . I am here, saved, eternally saved, ever to live in His presence and to praise Him who gave His life for me."

What rejoicing there will be as these redeemed ones meet and greet those who have had a burden in their behalf! And those who have lived, not to please themselves, but to be a blessing to the unfortunate who have so few blessings—how their hearts will thrill with satisfaction!

FAMILIES WILL BE REUNITED

Thus saith the Lord; Refrain thy voice from weeping, and thine eyes from tears: for thy work shall be rewarded, saith the Lord; and they shall come again from the land of the enemy. And there is hope in thine end, saith the Lord, that thy children shall come again to their own border. **Jer. 31:16, 17.**

Christ is coming with clouds and with great glory. A multitude of shining angels will attend Him. He will come to raise the dead, and to change the living saints from glory to glory. He will come to honor those who have loved Him, and kept His commandments, and to take them to Himself. He has not forgotten them nor His promise. There will be a relinking of the family chain.

The day of God will reveal how much the world owes to godly mothers. . . .

When the judgment shall sit, and the books shall be opened; when the "well done" of the great Judge is pronounced, and the crown of immortal glory is placed upon the brow of the victor, many will raise their crowns in sight of the assembled universe, and pointing to their mother say: "She made me all I am through the grace of God. Her instruction, her prayers, have been blessed to my eternal salvation."

With joy unutterable, parents see the crown, the robe, the harp, given to their children. The days of hope and fear are ended. The seed sown with tears and prayers may have seemed to be sown in vain, but their harvest is reaped with joy at last. Their children have been redeemed.

Oh, wonderful redemption! long talked of, long hoped for, contemplated with eager anticipation, but never fully understood.

To His faithful followers Christ has been a daily companion and familiar friend. They have lived in close contact, in constant communion with God. Upon them the glory of the Lord has risen. In them the light of the knowledge of the glory of God in the face of Jesus Christ has been reflected. Now they rejoice in the undimmed rays of the brightness and glory of the King in His majesty. They are prepared for the communion of heaven; for they have heaven in their hearts.

December 27

WELCOME TO THE CITY OF GOD

His lord said unto him, Well done, good and faithful servant; thou hast been faithful over a few things, I will make thee ruler over many things: enter thou into the joy of thy lord. **Matt. 25:23.**

With unutterable love, Jesus welcomes His faithful ones to the joy of their Lord. The Saviour's joy is in seeing, in the kingdom of glory, the souls that have been saved by His agony and humiliation. And the redeemed will be sharers in His joy, as they behold, among the blessed, those who have been won to Christ through their prayers, their labors, and their loving sacrifice. As they gather about the great white throne, gladness unspeakable will fill their hearts, when they behold those whom they have won for Christ, and see that one has gained others, and these still others, all brought into the haven of rest, there to lay their crowns at Jesus' feet and praise Him through the endless cycles of eternity.

As the ransomed ones are welcomed to the City of God, there rings out upon the air an exultant cry of adoration. The two Adams are about to meet. The Son of God is standing with outstretched arms to receive the father of our race—the being whom He created, who sinned against his Maker, and for whose sin the marks of the crucifixion are borne upon the Saviour's form. As Adam discerns the prints of the cruel nails, he does not fall upon the bosom of his Lord, but in humiliation casts himself at His feet, crying: "Worthy, worthy is the Lamb that was slain!" Tenderly the Saviour lifts him up and bids him look once more upon the Eden home from which he has so long been exiled.

After his expulsion from Eden, Adam's life on earth was filled with sorrow. Every dying leaf, every victim of sacrifice, every blight upon the fair face of nature, every stain upon man's purity, was a fresh reminder of his sin. . . . With patient humility he bore, for nearly a thousand years, the penalty of transgression. Faithfully did he repent of his sin and trust in the merits of the promised Saviour, and he died in the hope of a resurrection. The Son of God redeemed man's failure and fall; and now, through the work of the atonement, Adam is reinstated in his first dominion.

Maranatha December 28

THINK ON HEAVENLY THINGS

These are they which came out of great tribulation, and have washed their robes, and made them white in the blood of the Lamb. **Rev. 7:14.**

John, while in vision, saw a company clothed in white robes. . . . They were seen in the temple of God. This will be the result for all who will lay hold of the merits of Christ and wash their robes in His blood. Every provision has been made so that we can sit with Christ upon His throne, but the condition is that we be in harmony with the law of God. . . .

We cannot afford to lose heaven. We ought to have our conversation on heavenly things. There there is no death nor pain. Why are we so reluctant to talk of these things? Why do we dwell upon earthly things? The apostle exhorts us to have our conversation in heaven. "For our conversation is in heaven: from whence also we look for the Saviour, the Lord Jesus Christ" (Phil. 3:20). . . . Christ will soon return to gather those who are prepared, and take them to this glorious place. "So Christ was once offered to bear the sins of many; and unto them that look for him shall he appear the second time without sin unto salvation" (Heb. 9:28).

Do we love to think of this event or do we want to put it off? . . . The more we talk of Jesus, the more we shall reflect His divine image. By beholding we become transformed. We need to bring Christ into our religious experience. When you assemble together, let the conversation be on Christ and His salvation. . . . The more we talk of Jesus the more of His matchless charms we shall behold.

Those who take no pleasure in thinking and talking of God in this life, will not enjoy the life that is to come, where God is ever present, dwelling among His people. But those who love to think of God will be in their element, breathing in the atmosphere of heaven. Those who on earth love the thought of heaven will be happy in its holy associations and pleasures. . . . "And there shall be no more curse: but the throne of God and of the Lamb shall be in it; and his servants shall serve him: and they shall see his face: and his name shall be in their foreheads" (Rev. 22:3, 4).

ONLY ONE REMINDER OF SIN

Behold, the righteous shall be recompensed in the earth: much more the wicked and the sinner. **Prov. 11:31.**

The wicked receive their recompense in the earth. Proverbs 11:31. They "shall be stubble: and the day that cometh shall burn them up, saith the Lord of hosts." Malachi 4:1. Some are destroyed as in a moment, while others suffer many days. All are punished "according to their deeds." The sins of the righteous having been transferred to Satan, he is made to suffer not only for his own rebellion, but for all the sins which he has caused God's people to commit. His punishment is to be far greater than that of those whom he has deceived. After all have perished who fell by his deceptions, he is still to live and suffer on. In the cleansing flames the wicked are at last destroyed, root and branch—Satan the root, his followers the branches.

Satan and all who have joined him in rebellion will be cut off. . . . Then "the wicked shall not be: yea, thou shalt diligently consider his place, and it shall not be"; "they shall be as though they had not been." Ps. 37:10; Obadiah 16.

The justice of God is satisfied, and the saints and all the angelic host say with a loud voice, Amen.

While the earth is wrapped in the fire of God's vengeance, the righteous abide safely in the Holy City. Upon those that had part in the first resurrection, the second death has no power (Rev. 20:6). While God is to the wicked a consuming fire, He is to His people both a sun and a shield (Ps. 84:11).

The fire that consumes the wicked purifies the earth. Every trace of the curse is swept away. No eternally burning hell will keep before the ransomed the fearful consequences of sin.

One reminder alone remains: our Redeemer will ever bear the marks of His crucifixion. . . .

All that was lost by sin has been restored. . . . God's original purpose in the creation of the earth is fulfilled as it is made the eternal abode of the redeemed. "The righteous shall inherit the land, and dwell therein for ever." Psalm 37:29.

THE IMMORTAL INHERITANCE

Giving thanks to the Father, who has qualified us to share in the inheritance of the saints in light. **Col. 1:12, RSV.**

The ransom has been paid, and it is possible for all to come to God, and through a life of obedience to attain unto everlasting life. Then how sad it is that men turn from the immortal inheritance, and live for the gratification of pride, for selfishness and display, and . . . lose the blessing which they might have both in this life and in the life to come. They might enter into the palaces of heaven, and associate on terms of freedom and equality with Christ and heavenly angels, and with the princes of God; and yet, incredible as it may seem, they turn from heavenly attractions.

The Creator of all worlds proposes to love those who believe in His only-begotten Son as their personal Saviour, even as He loves His Son. Even here and now His gracious favor is bestowed upon us to this marvelous extent. He has given to men the gift of the Light and Majesty of heaven, and with Him He has bestowed all the treasures of heaven. Much as He has promised us for the life to come, He also bestows princely gifts upon us in this life, and as subjects of His grace, He would have us enjoy everything that will ennoble, expand, and elevate our characters. It is His design to fit us for the heavenly courts above.

But Satan is contending for the souls of men. . . . He would not have them catch a glimpse of the future honor, the eternal glories, laid up for those who shall be inhabitants of heaven, or have a taste of the experience that gives a foretaste of the happiness of heaven. . . .

Those who accept Christ as their Saviour have the promise of the life that now is, and that which is to come. . . . The lowliest disciple of Christ may become an inhabitant of heaven, an heir of God to an inheritance incorruptible, and that fadeth not away. O that every one might make choice of the heavenly gift, become an heir of God to that inheritance whose title is secure from any destroyer, world without end! O, choose not the world, but choose the better inheritance! Press, urge your way toward the mark for the prize of your high calling in Christ Jesus.

OUR SAVIOUR'S HIGHEST HONOR

And one shall say unto him, What are these wounds in thine hands? Then he shall answer, Those with which I was wounded in the house of my friends. **Zech. 13:6.**

"I saw a new heaven and a new earth: for the first heaven and the first earth were passed away." Revelation 21:1. The fire that consumes the wicked purifies the earth. Every trace of the curse is swept away. . . .

One reminder alone remains: Our Redeemer will ever bear the marks of His crucifixion. Upon His wounded head, upon His side, His hands and feet, are the only traces of the cruel work that sin has wrought. Says the prophet, beholding Christ in His glory: "He had bright beams coming out of his side: and there was the hiding of his power." Habakkuk 3:4, margin. That pierced side whence flowed the crimson stream that reconciled man to God—there is the Saviour's glory, there "the hiding of his power." . . . And the tokens of His humiliation are His highest honor; through the eternal ages the wounds of Calvary will show forth His praise and declare His power.

The cross of Christ will be the science and the song of the redeemed through all eternity. In Christ glorified they will behold Christ crucified. Never will it be forgotten that He whose power created and upheld the unnumbered worlds through the vast realms of space, the Beloved of God, the Majesty of heaven, He whom cherub and shining saraph delighted to adore—humbled Himself to uplift fallen man; that He bore the guilt and shame of sin, and the hiding of His Father's face, till the woes of a lost world broke His heart and crushed out His life on Calvary's cross. That the Maker of all worlds, the Arbiter of all destinies, should lay aside His glory and humiliate Himself from love to man will ever excite the wonder and adoration of the universe. As the nations of the saved look upon their Redeemer and behold the eternal glory of the Father shining in His countenance; as they behold His throne, which is from everlasting to

342

everlasting, and know that His kingdom is to have no end, they break forth in rapturous song: "Worthy, worthy is the Lamb that was slain, and hath redeemed us to God by His own most precious blood!"

SCRIPTURE INDEX

344

345

SOURCE INDEX

Inspiring Reading
for Growing Christians

Paint the World With Love, by Jeannette Johnson. An inspiring collection of stories about unsung heroes—ordinary Adventists from all over North America—doing extraordinary things to change their corner of the world and spread the love of Jesus. Hardcover, US$9.95, Cdn$12.45.

Inspiration, by Alden Thompson. The author explains how a perfect God used imperfect human writers to meet the unique spiritual needs of ancient humanity, and how to find the essential messages in the Bible that reveal God's character for all time. He addresses such questions as: Did every fact and idea in the Bible come straight from God? What about apparent inconsistencies in Scripture? How much freedom do we have to interpret the Bible? Hardcover, 332 pages. US$15.95, Cdn$19.95.

Heaven, by David B. Smith. David Smith turns our focus from this troubled world to a place where pain, sickness, and death shatter into obsolescence; to a life without hate, disease, goodbyes, or limitations; and to the endless possibilities of fascinating things to do and see. Best of all, he gives us a foretaste of what it will be like to live in the presence of Jesus—forever! Paperback, 96 pages. Call your ABC for price.

God's Minutes, by C. L. Paddock. One of the best-loved story tellers in the SDA Church, C. L. Paddock had the ability to write stories just as compellingly as he narrated them. This newly designed edition contains stories suitable for devotional reading, for storytelling, and for worship settings. Hardcover, 320 pages. US$14.95, Cdn$18.70.

In Pastures Green, by Bev Condy. In 1975 the author left the rush of city life and took up farming in the Sierra Nevada foothills. Her stubborn, silly sheep, along with horses, cats, geese, goats, a stray dog, and friendly neighbors, gave her insights into human nature and God's love. Paperback, 96 pages. US$6.95, Cdn$8.70.

A Garden of Promises, compiled by Leslie Caza. A beautiful pocket-size book filled with promises that bring you comfort and joy in times of need. Taken from the Bible and the Spirit of Prophecy, the promises are arranged by topic. Paperback, 64 pages. US$4.95, Cdn$6.20.
